SWEET GREEKS

HEARTLAND FOODWAYS

The Heartland Foodways series seeks to encourage and publish book-length works that define and celebrate midwestern food traditions and practices. The series is open to foods from seed to plate and to foodways that have found a home in the Midwest.

A list of books in the series appears at the end of this book.

SWEET GREEKS

FIRST-GENERATION IMMIGRANT CONFECTIONERS IN THE HEARTLAND

ANN FLESOR BECK

UNIVERSITY OF ILLINOIS PRESS
Urbana, Chicago, and Springfield

Publication of this book was supported in part
by the Friends of the University of Illinois Press.

1 2 3 4 5 C P 5 4 3 2 1
♾ This book is printed on acid-free paper.

Library of Congress Cataloging-in-Publication Data
Names: Beck, Ann Flesor, 1954– author.
Title: Sweet Greeks: first-generation immigrant confectioners in the heartland / Ann Flesor Beck.
Description: Urbana: University of Illinois Press, [2020] | Series: Heartland foodways | Includes bibliographical references and index. |
Identifiers: LCCN 2020017332 (print) | LCCN 2020017333 (ebook) | ISBN 9780252043406 (cloth : alk. paper) | ISBN 9780252085314 (paperback : alk. paper) | ISBN 9780252052286 (ebook)
Subjects: LCSH: Candy industry—Illinois—History. | Confectioners—Illinois—History. | Greeks—Illinois—History. | Immigrants—Illinois—History. | Greece—Emigration and immigration—History.
Classification: LCC HD9330.C653 U5233 2020 (print) | LCC HD9330.C653 (ebook) | DDC 338.4/766415308989307730—dc23
LC record available at https://lccn.loc.gov/2020017332
LC ebook record available at https://lccn.loc.gov/2020017333

To my grandfather
Constantine "Gus" Flesor

CONTENTS

ACKNOWLEDGMENTS

This book would not have emerged without the innovative spark from Bruce Kraig, series editor at the University of Illinois Press. His enduring encouragement has been inspirational. Thanks also go to James Engelhardt, Marika Christofides, and Alison Syring Bassford at the press for their editorial guidance, and to my copy editor, Julie Bush, for her meticulous reading of the text. A special nod goes to Steve Frangos, also an independent scholar, for his validation of this work and his own contributions to the growing archival collections.

To the National Hellenic Museum, I give appreciation not only for its inclusion of Greek confectioners in its archives as part of the Chicago story but also for its national focus on the first-generation pioneers. The Chicago Historical Society also has amazing archives and can be a great resource for those researching early urban records.

The librarians and historical association staff in each small town and urban center in central Illinois have been instrumental in assisting me with finding the obscure resources of Greek confectioners. They are the unsung heroes in every town. The staff at the Abraham Lincoln Presidential Library and the Lincoln Library in Springfield not only assisted with records but also led me to second- and third-generation Greeks in the area for more personal accounts of their ancestors.

I am grateful to those second-generation Greeks still with us who shared their stories so they will not be forgotten. The third-generation

Greeks appreciate the passion and sacrifices made to forge new beginnings in America.

Although numerous keen eyes and sharp minds have read the text many times over, I alone take responsibility for any errors that appear. I should note, however, that for a historian of early Greek immigrant history, there are a number of areas where one's research can become terribly befuddled. The main problem areas I encountered were these: (1) The spelling of Greek family names, which were often purposely changed or inaccurately transliterated or transcribed. Where variations occurred, I added them in parentheses or in a note (or even marked the discrepancy with a *sic*). (2) The Greek town of origin. Many of these towns were very small, and their spelling was, again, often inaccurately transliterated (as on draft registration cards). Plus, names of towns have changed over the 100-plus years covered in this book. I generally provide the spelling as it was where I found it—on a draft card, in an obituary, or among naturalization papers, for example—even if I was unable to locate a town by that name on a map. (3) Accurate dates for nearly anything—birth, death, marriage, or date of arrival in America. There are entries on the website Find A Grave where the image of the gravestone clearly shows one birth date while the accompanying obituary has another. I have usually gone with the gravestone unless I have convincing evidence to the contrary and comment on obvious discrepancies in a note. (4) Newspapers files that no longer exist. Newspapers have been one of my most valuable sources, but for many of the small towns, the local newspaper files are no longer available. Even in Tuscola, the "hometown" of this book, the newspapers before about 1940 disappeared sometime between 2011, when I first began my research, and the last two or three years (after the paper was sold). And particular to this study, (5) the styling of "Candy Kitchen" or "Kandy Kitchen." There is no *c* in the Greek language, only a *k* (kappa), so the natural spelling for the immigrant was "Kandy." I have tried to use the spelling that the Greek confectioner used, but my own grandfather used both spellings almost interchangeably. Even following their mid-1920s experiences with the KKK, one still finds Greek "Kandy Kitchens."

This book would not have been written without the support of my sister, Devon Flesor Story. She has been my business and confectionery partner for over fifteen years. It takes a lot of commitment and talent to do what she does. Thanks also go to my brother, Scott Flesor, for his assistance on vacation and reminding us why we do what we do. My coworkers at Flesor's Candy Kitchen are the best and have also supported this endeavor.

Special thanks go to James Anderson and David Dennard for their decades of encouragement. As historians of the highest caliber, they have set a high bar for all of us, and rightly so.

There is not enough space for the gratitude and respect I have for my partner and husband, Roger B. Beck. He encouraged me from the beginning of the project and has been a keen editorial eye and my genuine soul mate.

INTRODUCTION

It's a good story.
—Paul Flesor, second-generation Greek American

When I was a young woman in the 1970s, *Saturday Night Live* was the popular television show to watch. One of the sketches featured John Belushi as the owner of a "Greek diner," where he spoke broken English and served burgers with a certain brand of soda—no exceptions. While I thought it was humorous, it was also a bit embarrassing to me as a product of a Greek American family in that business. I grew up in a confectionery and small restaurant, and there, on national television, was the stereotyped immigrant family working hard, but clearly comedic. Even before the advent of television, 1930s radio featured the popular Greek chef Nick Parkyakarkus in another depiction of a Greek diner that had become so much a part of America's fabric in such a short time. Textbooks cited math problems featuring Greek confectioners who were established on the corners of downtowns in most small towns in America, and certainly in the Midwest, where I grew up. How did this immigrant group become such a part of mainstream American food culture in such a relatively short time? How did confectioneries, diners, and restaurants become their business niche? What is that story?

After I grew older and left my small town to pursue other career paths, eventually I returned to my hometown and our family confectionery business. As time passed, customers began relating their stories about Greek confectioners in their own hometowns or neighborhoods in larger urban centers. The second-generation Greeks themselves ventured into my world. I then decided to explore the experiences of first-generation Greek confectioners and some restaurateurs in central Illinois, and the result is this honorific to my grandfather and the thousands of Greeks who left their homeland and came to America to establish businesses and lives so unlike the ones they had in the mountains of the Peloponnese.

Greeks did not immigrate to America in massive numbers until the late 1800s and early 1900s. Multiple factors provided the impetus for leaving their country and heading to the United States. My grandfather Gus Flesor was one of the primarily male migrants who left his small village and came to America to escape poverty and create a new life. It is his journey and that of the entrepreneurs who created a food business in urban centers and small towns that we shall explore—a journey that was replicated thousands of times. How my grandfather decided to leave his homeland, navigate a strange environment, learn a new language, and develop a trade so disparate from his small farm upbringing is a testament to adaptability and accommodation. It is an American immigrant story.

Constantine "Gus" Flesor was born in 1879 in Pigadakia, a small village in the Peloponnesian hills, about twenty to twenty-five miles south of Tripoli, just to the east off the E961 highway that runs between Tripoli and Sparta. (See map 1 in chapter 1.) In early 1901, while still a young man, he immigrated to America. My uncle George later related that Gus, his father, grew up on a farm and was given $100 for his passage to America. At the time of his migration, he left behind two brothers and a sister. He claimed to have sailed first to Marseilles, France, and then on to Ellis Island with 2,500 other immigrants.[1] When I was young, my grandfather told me that his family was very poor and there was not enough income to support everyone; in addition, there was always the concern of conscription into the Greek army. Both of these reasons served as catalysts for many males in his village to immigrate.

Later in 1901 he made his way to Chicago, and from there he took the railroad south to central Illinois and Champaign-Urbana, a university center where his relative Pete Vriner and Pete's partner, George Vaky, two early Greek immigrants to central Illinois, had established a confectionery.[2] Vriner and Vaky had also opened a small candy shop south of Champaign, in Tuscola, Illinois, in 1901, so my grandfather took the train south to Tuscola to live and work there as an apprentice confectioner. He soon learned enough to know that he wanted to stay in the business and become the owner. After apprenticing for a short time, he left to go west and work on the railroads to earn enough money to buy the business and settle in a small town in the cornfields of Illinois. There were keen challenges in establishing a business, bringing family members to America, learning English, and withstanding overt discrimination. It took perseverance and decades of hard work to make it in America. Yet, my grandfather was successful.

Let me share a bit of history about Tuscola. Located in east-central Illinois, it has a population of approximately 4,500 people, a figure that has not changed much over the last several decades. Founded in the mid-1800s, it was a typical midwestern town, settled by German, Irish, and English settlers.

In 1957, one of Tuscola's newspapers celebrated its "first 100 years" by posing the question, "Why Tuscola?"[3] In answering that query, the writer suggested that as American territory expanded westward, Douglas County, Illinois, had been initially passed by because the "treeless prairie and marsh land was thought not fit for man or beast."[4] It was the railroad that put the town on the map.[5] The centennial celebration included the names and occupations of early settlers, mostly with English surnames; told the "struggle" by Irish settlers in 1875 to establish the Catholic Church in the town; and gave the overall general sense that Tuscola's founding had been a good and righteous effort without turmoil or discord. Businesses developed and flourished, the railroads served the agricultural and industrial growth of the county, and the population grew accordingly. In 1859 Tuscola became the county seat for Douglas County.[6] Most of the original settlers were of northern European stock. It was not until the mass migration of southeastern Europeans and African Americans heading north for opportunity that the composition of the population in most central Illinois small towns changed.

In his 1951 study of immigrants, Oscar Handlin observed that "immigrants *were* American history."[7] Yet, Tuscola's newer immigrant population, some of the millions who left their families and traveled across the globe to new homes in large cities or small rural communities, received only passing notice in the centennial celebration materials. There was one quick mention of my Greek grandfather, Gus Flesor, observing that he had the longest continuous operation of a business by one man in any business in Tuscola.[8] The newspaper also noted, "Mr. Flesor was born near Tripoli, Greece . . . and came to America in 1901. He began work in a confectionery in the same building where the business is now located the same year. In 1904 he bought the business and has operated it ever since." "The Candy Kitchen," the reporter observed, "is a prominent landmark in the community."[9] The reporter made no mention of the overt resistance to my grandfather's business establishment by the Ku Klux Klan in the 1920s. He also failed to relate that my grandfather's family and the families of his two brothers were the only southern European immigrants to settle in Tuscola in the early twentieth century. Nor was there any mention of the African American families who lived in town or of the locals' resistance to the Irish Catholics. Tuscola's minority immigrants were not recognized when trying to answer the question of "Why Tuscola?" for the centennial celebration, nor was ethnic conflict recognized as part of Tuscola's history.

My sister, Devon, and I are the third generation of Greek Americans who currently own and operate Flesor's Candy Kitchen in Tuscola. My grandfather's business was open until the late 1970s when my father, Paul, who had taken over the business in the mid-1960s, retired. Gus's three grandchildren through Paul—Ann, Scott, and Devon—grew up in the store, but we all left town after high school to attend college and forge our own lives in very different third-generation Greek American ways.

In 2003, my sister and I had returned to central Illinois. Driving down Main Street in Tuscola one afternoon, I noted a "For Sale" sign in the window of my grandfather's store. The building had been vacant for almost thirty years. I thought, "What if we revived the business and reopened the family confectionery and soda fountain?" I approached my sister cautiously with the idea, and she immediately responded so positively that we set the project in motion. Eighteen months later, in the autumn of 2004, Flesor's was reborn. As the years have passed, many customers have shared their own family stories about their Greek grandparents, aunts, uncles, and other relatives in the small towns of east-central Illinois. Other customers recall the downtown Greek confectioneries of their childhood—ones in Arcola, Mattoon, Villa Grove, and other towns up and down the railroad lines or main roads across Illinois. They share stories of the one Greek immigrant family who established a home in a strange place and became a piece of the community fabric. While larger Greek immigrant communities developed in central Illinois cities such as Champaign-Urbana, Decatur, Danville, and Springfield, the lonely settler stories in the small outlying towns began to coalesce into a narrative of the "downstate" communities. This story is one that was replicated in multiple small towns and cities in the Midwest.

A foundation in immigration history is integral to the process of researching Greek immigration to America. Marcus Lee Hansen contended that the "source material from which the history of immigration can be drawn is infinite."[10] He suggested that the methodology employed for one's study should be comprehensive. It should be a holistic approach, integrating many different disciplines, and be broad enough to include immigration statistics, as well as such varied source materials as personal accounts, church records, occupational trends, oral interviews, and newspaper articles.

For this study, we shall examine the foundations of Greek history and the impetus for mass migration to America. Immigration to America from 1880 to 1930 was socially, politically, and culturally challenging. Then we shall explore the midwestern binary Greek urban settlements of Chicago and St. Louis before moving out into the small cities and towns in central Illinois. While most studies of Greek immigrants have focused on their lives in urban areas, which is where the majority of Greeks settled, this is one of the few studies that explores the settlement of Greeks, often a single man or a family, in rural America.[11] In the process of exploring Greek immigration to small towns, I emphasize chain migration, immigrant networking, resistance by local citizens to these newly arrived southeastern Europeans, education and acculturation, "niche" businesses (such as confectioneries and restaurants), entrepreneurship, and the success or willingness of succeeding generations to maintain the businesses founded by the first generation of Greek immigrants.

This is also a very personal story, particularly of my grandfather Flesor's journey to America, his life, and his legacy. It is a rich story, a micro-history of Greek immigration from his tiny village in Greece to Ellis Island, to Chicago, to east-central Illinois, to the west to work on the railroads, and back to Tuscola. In addressing the place of micro-histories in current scholarship, Pierre Force has observed, "One might be tempted to dismiss this kind of work as pandering to the popular obsession with genealogy and to argue that studying the history of one family will never yield any generalizable results." He contends, however, that these types of studies tell us much about the complexity of specific cultures and their survival.[12] Moreover, Earl Lewis adds that memories are "defined from the inside out" and cites David Thelen's observation that the "struggle for possession and interpretation of memory is rooted in the conflict and interplay among social, political, and cultural interests and values in the present."[13] Richard White's *Remembering Ahanagran: A History of Stories* melds history and memory while recounting the story of his mother's life in Ireland and her immigration to the United States. He says, "Most of us live with our family stories, but generally we don't think about them very often. I think about them constantly."[14] White acknowledges that he once believed the memories of his mother to be history, but as a historian, he now feels that history is the "energy of memory." We can utilize memory as the guide to history.[15] The purpose and intention of collecting stories and weaving them into history is to define "what America is and means and who gets to define it."[16]

One critical aspect of melding history and memory is the importance of place. Ned Kaufman pinpoints the value of place subsumed within its story and storyscape, connecting people and places and revealing the social value and sense of place.[17] He asks us to consider that place supports the perpetuation of socially useful narratives, and when put together, multiple places become part of the cultural heritage.[18] The story of central Illinois Greek pioneers is one small facet of America's history, and the focus on Greek confectioneries is central to the discourse as well. Individual experiences make the narrative come alive.

Austin Lunch: Greek-American Recollections is a rich and vibrant collection of family and friends' stories related by Constance Constant, who recalls the history of her own Greek family's immigrant experience and their family restaurant in Chicago, Austin Lunch. Her hope was to preserve "a flicker of time, of place, and of some of the good people who lived . . . so the stories would not be completely extinguished."[19] It is an excellent example of immigration to an urban setting with the interplay of social and cultural history as well as the intense descriptive of "place." Constant's mother escaped extreme poverty in the Peloponnese region of Greece and came in the 1920s on one of the last immigrant ships to dock in New York Harbor. In remembering that experience, her mother believed that "most immigrants didn't feel worthy enough to be welcomed into America. . . . Quietly matriculating through Ellis Island, they put all of their efforts into blending with the new culture, trying not to stand out, preferring even to be invisible to avoid disdain by ordinary Americans and harassment by vicious men wearing white sheets."[20] Constant also included her mother's recollections of how the family patriarch began his life in America at the turn of the century as a shoeshine boy. After World War I, he left that job and went to work for free in a Greek-owned restaurant to learn the trade. Eventually he pooled his meager resources with his brother and a close friend to open the Austin Lunch, named for the street corner where Austin intersects with Clark.[21] The author recalls, "Our childhood years were very different from those of our parents, who were raised in the sunny, fresh air of rural Greek villages. Nick [her brother] and I grew up in the Austin Lunch. We looked within its dark walls and tobacco-scented and smoke-filled air for parenting, comfort, and sustenance."[22] Despite some financial hardships during the Depression, the Austin Lunch survived. It was always referred to as "the store," as were most of the retail businesses by the Greeks. "The word was pronounced with reverence when applied to one's own enterprise."[23]

My family always referred to Grandfather's business as "the store" as well, and we still do today. While not always a term of reverence (especially after a long day and perhaps night of making candy), the moniker is the symbol of the visceral smells of chocolate, popcorn, sweet syrup, and tobacco and of remembrances of family members coming and going. I believe most of the first-generation Greeks took great pride in their stores. These buildings, those sacred places to the first-generation Greeks, generally became icons of success not only for the immigrants but also for many of the small towns in which they were located. Usually situated on the Main Streets of all the towns documented in this study, the Greek confectioneries and soda fountains were often anchor businesses in once-thriving small-town American downtowns.

As mentioned at the beginning of this chapter, Greeks had rapidly become part of the American lexicon. A problem in a 1909 mathematics text, for example, read, "A Greek confectioner bought 12 bushels of chestnuts at $2.50 per bushel and retailed them at 5¢ per pint. Find his gain."[24] Similarly, a 1918 Minnesota Course of Study guide noted that "sixth-grade pupils . . . enjoy learning bits of foreign languages. If encouraged, they will gather from public speakers, from visitors or helpers in the home, from the German shoemaker, from the Greek confectioner, the Italian fruit vendor, or the Chinese laundryman, bits of foreign speech that will vitalize all language's study."[25] Steve Frangos contends that "few Greeks today realize that from the early 1870's until just after World War II, their compatriots held a commanding presence in the American confectionary industry, dishing up tons of sinfully sweet treats from behind the counters of their candy stores and ice cream parlors."[26] Indeed, the 1940 WPA guide to New York state observed that "the Greeks are famous for their 'candy kitchens,' an institution which no sizable town is without."[27]

In a 1938 essay, Marcus Lee Hansen first presented a hypothesis he called "the principle of third generation interest," which stated, "What the son wishes to forget the grandson wishes to remember." This became known as Hansen's Law. It predicts that some degree of ethnicity is preserved among immigrants, weakens in their offspring, but receives renewed interest among their grandchildren.[28]

It is a good story that gives us a slice of food history and reveals how an immigrant group, within a very short span of time, brought their social and historical culture, food mores, and exceptional identity to America. Adapting to the accelerating change in industrial America, Greek farmer immigrants became confectioners and restaurateurs in urban centers and small towns. Let us begin with some historical, geographical, and cultural foundations.

CHAPTER 1

FOUNDATIONS

We were so poor.
—Gus Flesor, first-generation Greek immigrant

From the 1880s through the 1930s, hundreds of thousands of Greeks immigrated to America. Each had his or her own personal reasons for leaving, but there were also larger factors at work in their homeland that led to their departures. In this chapter we discuss some of these, beginning with the geography of Greece, which has so significantly shaped the country's past and the daily lives of its peoples. We will then turn to Greece's long and turbulent history, omnipresent Orthodox religion, constantly shifting politics, and ubiquitous economic crises. Defining what it means to be Greek is a theme that runs throughout.

Greece's geography is central to this immigration story. Some 80 percent of Greece is mountainous. Indeed, historian Stephanie Lynn Budin has observed, "The best three words to describe the Greek mainland are *rocky*, *hilly*, and *mountainous*."[1] This terrain has significantly influenced Greek history and its people. Budin continues, "It caused many individual city-states to be cut off from their neighbors, and the city-states consequently evolved with a strong sense of regionalism and political independence from one another. This also forced Greeks to travel a great deal by sea, which led very early on to long-distance trade and naval prowess."[2] Greek traders and settlers established Greek communities all along the coasts and on the Mediterranean islands. Trade among the Greek mainland and island communities proliferated, and ports and more urban centers, like Athens and Patras, enabled Greek fishermen and farmers to sell their goods and produce externally to other countries.

Greece's mountains are steep and abrupt. Due to this rugged topography, only 19 percent of the land is arable, and only 8 percent is viable for permanent crop use. The Greek countryside generally does not allow for cattle to graze, but the "scrubby, dry, rocky surface of the land . . . is ideal for sheep and goats."[3] There are few large trees.[4] Olive trees and grapevines are what grow best. Moreover, Greece has a Mediterranean climate, with hot, dry summers and mild, damp winters. Rainfall varies between heavy storms and long droughts, making farming precarious.[5] "When the Greeks began to travel and settle in other parts of the Mediterranean, they found almost everywhere outside Greece [land] more fertile and easier to work," notes historian Charles Freeman.[6]

The majority of Greek immigrants in this story were, like my grandfather, from a region known as the Peloponnese.[7] The Peloponnese makes up about 12 percent of Greece's total landmass. Olympia, home of the ancient Olympic Games, is located on the northwestern coast. Mycenae, Corinth, and Argos all are on the eastern side of the Peloponnese.[8] The heart of this region is from Tripoli (in the region of Arcadia) in the north to Sparta (in the region of Laconia) in the south. The geography, climate, and culture of the Peloponnese is a textbook example of all the conditions described above—mountainous, unpredictable rainfall patterns, poor soil, and strong regional divisions and politics.

Such conditions limited the peasant diet to local and seasonal produce, such as leafy greens foraged from the hills and vegetables cultivated in small fields or gardens. The daily fare consisted of grains that became the staple of breads, olives for consumption and oil production, and beans and legumes that complemented some local cheeses, yogurt, and the occasional meats. Farmers could own a small herd of goats, a lamb, or a pig.[9] Today we consider this food indicative of creativity and healthfulness as depicted in the "Mediterranean diet." Typical recipes featured vegetable stews comprised of green beans, zucchini, artichokes, and greens cooked in olive oil with onions and garlic; tomatoes or grape leaves stuffed with rice or ground meat; and legumes such as beans, lentils, and chickpeas that were made into soups or pies and spiced with dried oregano or fresh celery, dill, and wild fennel.[10]

MAP 1. Greece. (Courtesy Bill Nelson.)

Sweets were an integral part of the Greek diet reaching back into ancient times and transcending the centuries. As an example, dried figs were a dessert staple, harking back to the Mycenaean era (thirteenth century BC). They were served sandwiched with walnuts and sesame seeds. Ancient banquets ended with flat wheat or barley cakes with honey. Almonds with honey were always popular. Today, in modern Greece, many sweets are still made with these ingredients.[11]

Some of the earliest Greek literature expresses an appreciation of food. The Homeric epics, the *Iliad* and the *Odyssey*, written before 700 BC, are filled with descriptions of feasts and shared meals of roast meat and red wine. A poet from Sparta, Alcman, (late seventh century BC), wrote verses praising five wines of the southern Peloponnese and a hot bean soup. Hippocrates (c. 460–c. 370 BC) developed dietary theories and promoted certain foodstuffs that contributed to human health. Texts from around 350 BC, by which time olives, olive oil, and wine had already been in production for over a thousand years, contain detailed discussions of the costs, preparation, and consumption of certain foods. By this time as well, each city or village had begun to develop its own food and wine specialties.[12]

Throughout the 1600s and up until the mid-1800s, European travelers took time to write about their personal experiences eating Greek food. In 1676, English adventurer and author Francis Vernon traveled through the Peloponnese and saw forests filled with game. In the early 1880s, British researcher W. M. Leake reported sightings of deer and wild hogs and bushes of gooseberries and strawberries.[13] Some travelers also noted how trade was an integral driver of food production. Olive oil, honey, butter, cheese, raisins, currants, figs, wine, grain, nuts, and berries found their way from the region to markets in England and Italy.[14] But the local environment and overseas markets were not the only determinants of Greek cuisine; it was also influenced throughout the centuries by those who conquered the country, such as the Arabs, Turks, French, and English.[15] It was this culinary tradition Greeks brought with them to America, where they then began to create new food and confectionery delights. However, it was the stark departure from these food origins that made the evolution into the confectionery and food trades in America so striking.

Greece's geography could certainly make life hard, and many of the immigrants came from very poor and humble beginnings. "It is within this setting of mountain and sea with all the challenges they brought both to seafarers and to farmers that a Greek identity was cradled," Freeman stated.[16] Despite it being a "land of poverty, restlessness, [and] unstable rule,"[17] the first generation of Greek immigrants arrived in the United States feeling "passionately about the land of their birth,"[18] and particularly about its rich heritage, going back to the glorious age of ancient and classical Greece. To understand this passion, we must recount briefly the greatest peoples and achievements in Greece's distant past, before discussing recent times in more detail.

Greek immigrants called themselves "Hellenes," coming from "Hellas," which harks back to 3000 BC and the Bronze Age period scholars call the Helladic.[19] The Helladic period saw the rise of one of Europe's first civilizations and was "the archetype for the cultural, intellectual, and spiritual development of later civilizations."[20] But Greek history as remembered in school textbooks and in popular conceptions of "Greece" begins with the Minoan civilization around 1700 BC on the island of Crete. For about 250 years the Minoans dominated the Aegean world, carrying on long-distance trade with Europe, Egypt, and the Near East,[21] developing one of the earliest written languages.[22] Sometime after 1400 BC, the Mycenaeans, a new civilization that evolved in the Peloponnese, overran the Minoan capital of Knossos. Over the next three hundred years, the Mycenaeans set up great trading networks across the Mediterranean and Aegean Seas.[23] This was the time of the Trojan War (c. 1260–1240 BC) and the beginning of the Homeric age (c. 1200–750 BC), with its story telling, myth making, and hero worshipping.[24]

The Mycenaean civilization began to decline around 1100 BC, and there followed a period of about three hundred years known as the Greek Dark Ages, about which we know little. After around 800 BC, however, there was an explosion of change and invention. Cities, such as Athens and Sparta, were evolving into city-states, or poleis.[25] In 776 BC, the first Olympic Games were held, and these, along with other Panhellenic festivals at religious centers such as Delphi and Olympia, brought Greeks together as a collective culture.[26] Freeman notes that perhaps "the earliest evidence that the Greeks recognized themselves as a distinctive culture came from an inscription at Olympia dating from 600 BC which spoke of the judges of the games as *hellanodikai* ('Greek judges')." These games drew all the city-states and peoples together, and only "Greeks" could participate.[27]

By 490 BC, Athens had become a military power and turned back a Persian invasion at the battle of Marathon in that year, followed by a great naval victory at Salamis in 480 BC.[28] In the mid-400s, Greece entered a "Golden Age," famous for producing writers and artists like Sophocles, Euripides, and Aristophanes; the first historians, Herodotus and Thucydides; the prominent statesman and general Pericles; the father of medicine, Hippocrates; and mathematicians Pythagoras, Euclid, and

Archimedes. Sculptors and architects left the world masterpieces in stone that still survive today.[29] The Golden Age ended with the Peloponnesian Wars (431–404 BC), pitting Sparta and its allied city-states against Athens and its allies. The wars had a devasting effect on all sides, impoverishing the land and weakening the cities. Three of the most renowned philosophers in world history, Socrates, Plato, and Aristotle,[30] tried to make sense of the times, and of life, in the succeeding decades. Order was restored in the 330s when Philip II of Macedon, followed by his more famous son, Alexander the Great, conquered and united Greece and then spread Greek influence and culture, and the Greek language, to Turkey, North Africa, Egypt, Syria, Mesopotamia, Persia, and India.[31]

After Alexander's death in 323 BC the Hellenistic Period began (323–30 BC), during which time Greek culture and language continued to impact much of the eastern Mediterranean world. This was particularly true in Ptolemaic Egypt, where Greek was the official language until the death of Queen Cleopatra, the last of the Ptolemaic rulers, in 30 BC following the Roman conquest of her land.[32] Under Roman rule until the fourth century, Greece enjoyed a period of peace and prosperity, and Greek culture flourished. In AD 385 Emperor Diocletian divided the Roman Empire between the western Latin-speaking half and the eastern Greek-speaking half. He called the eastern half Byzantium, after an ancient Greek colony that was located on a site where, in AD 330, Emperor Constantine established a new capital that he called Constantinople. Because of its beauty and similarity to the Roman capital, Constantinople was often referred to as the "New Rome."[33]

In AD 391, Roman emperor Theodosius I made Christianity the official state religion, and a patriarchate was established in Constantinople with ecclesiastical jurisdiction over the eastern, Greek portion of the empire. The Greek church, however, was not as formidable in its stately power as the Latin church with its pope, and it had to subordinate its interests to those of the state. Theological and political differences resulted in a great schism between the Greek and Latin churches in 1054, when the Greek patriarch refused to recognize the Latin pope's claim to supreme power and authority. The Greek church claimed it possessed the true faith, for its members practiced the tenets of Christian orthodoxy as taught by the original apostles.[34] As we shall see, the Orthodox Church held the Greek communities together through the following centuries of foreign invasion and rule, especially under the Muslim Ottoman Turks. After immigrants arrived in America, it was the church that continued to give them that sense of belonging and community in what was a strange, and sometimes even hostile, environment. The deep passion for the church felt by the first generation of Greek immigrants and their children became part of their heritage.

During the course of its long history, Byzantium, and particularly the Greek mainland and surrounding islands, were overrun by Persians, Arabs, Turks, and Slavs. This resulted, as Helen Papanikolas has noted, in a "varied and deeply rooted . . . Greek heritage. . . . Each tribe, each army left some of their blood to mix with the Greeks on the stony land and some of it in children's veins. The invaders left words that were incorporated into the Greek language, but they themselves were taken in and assimilated."[35] By the early second millennium, western European conquerors and merchants had also become intrigued and attracted to the Byzantine Empire, both by its wealth and by its weakness. Constantinople was sacked in 1204 by the armies of the Fourth Crusade, and some of the Aegean Islands fell to French crusaders.[36] The French also separated some of the conquered Greek territory into feudal states, creating a "New France" and making the infusion of Western institutions into Greek society inevitable.[37] But the Byzantine Empire remained generally intact for nearly twelve centuries, until the capture of Constantinople by the Ottoman Turks in 1453.

During the centuries of Ottoman rule, from 1453 to 1821, Turkish rulers generally treated Greeks on the mainland and the islands as inferior, marking the origin of the hatred between Greeks and Turks and the recurring conflicts between the two peoples. Christianity was subsumed under Islam.

Despite the tumultuous four centuries of Ottoman rule, it was the Greek Orthodox religion that codified the criterion for defining Greek identity. "To be an Orthodox Christian was to be a Greek, just as a Greek who converted to Islam thereby became a Turk," observe historians Rinn S. Shinn and Eugene K. Keefe.[38] Under the Ottoman Turks, each religious community was regarded as autonomous, which allowed the Greek Orthodox Church to wield power, despite the downgraded status of Christianity. The patriarch of Constantinople was the church's spiritual head and was also responsible for the civil administration of the populace, thereby giving him tremendous power as the political head of the Greek community.[39] This arrangement allowed the Greeks to survive as a people during centuries under foreign rule.[40]

In the course of the eighteenth century, as corruption within the Turkish ruling class grew and the ideological and economic foundations of the empire began to erode,[41] a nascent Greek nationalist movement began to emerge in the "entrepreneurial, widely dispersed and prosperous mercantile class, whose activities were as much based outside as within the Ottoman domains."[42] This Greek mercantile class expanded their trade into Asia Minor, central Europe, and the Black Sea. They "dominated commerce in the Aegean, and their profits, much of what was returned to the mainland, helped to provide funds for education and cultural development in Greece."[43] Richard Clogg points out how it was these merchants who were responsible for supporting the intellectual revival that led to a national consciousness, an awareness that being Greek meant more than simply being an Orthodox Christian. They endowed schools and libraries and promoted a secular literature for a specifically Greek audience. Perhaps most importantly, they enabled young Greeks to study in western European universities, where "they came into contact not only with the heady ideas of the Enlightenment, of the French Revolution and of romantic nationalism, but they were made aware of the extraordinary hold which the language and civilization of ancient Greece had over the minds of their educated European contemporaries."[44] Thus, not only did Greek commerce and culture and the church survive and spread under Ottoman rule, but Greek nationalist sentiments also developed, which led to the formation of a Greek independence movement during the first two decades of the 1800s.

In the spring of 1821, a full-scale rebellion against Ottoman rule began in the mountainous Peloponnese, where there had always been strong and violent opposition to the Muslim Ottomans, touching off the Greek War of Independence. The Greek Revolution, as it was also known, was not simply a political event but also a time when Greeks expressed and reaffirmed their Hellenism, or Greekness, and underscored the importance of Greece to European civilization. Although small farmers, shepherds, and peasants fomented the revolution in the Peloponnese area, it was Greek intellectuals who became the national voice of Greece and sought acceptance in the West "by tracing a direct relationship between their own modern nation and European culture, taking advantage of the prominent position Hellenism enjoyed in the West."[45] They promoted Greece's uniqueness in world history.

For the creation of a national identity, a sense of collective destiny needed to be developed with a national story. Thus, a link between classical, ancient Greece and the present offered a unified Greek voice to the world. Greek intellectuals fashioned a national story that ran like this: "Oppressed, humiliated, denied enlightenment, Greeks should rebel against the Turks; they should realize that, rather than the toiling peasants of a decaying Oriental empire, they were the descendants of ancient Hellas, the spring of Europe and modern Enlightenment."[46] A cultural, linguistic, historical, geographic, and ethnic integrity became the narrative and was transformed into Greek nationalism.[47]

This narrative also spread throughout the West, garnering in Europe and in the United States great popular sympathy for the Greek cause during the Greek War of Independence in 1821. The classical Greek heritage embedded by then in Western culture inspired such notable figures as Lord Byron and the physician Samuel Howe to travel to Greece and join the revolutionaries.[48] The London Philhellenic Committee loaned approximately £3 million in 1824 and 1825 to the cause. Scholars in Scotland, artists in France, poets, and other writers and politicians throughout Europe and the United States galvanized great public sympathy for the Greeks, and Philhellenism became romanticized as young intellectuals related modern events in Greece to those of Greece's ancient past.[49] The words of Percy Bysshe Shelley, who had never been to Greece, represent the naïveté and false assumptions that many of these young romantics held: "We are all Greeks. Our laws, our literature, our religion, our arts have their roots in Greece. But for Greece, we might still have been savages and idolaters."[50]

Official United States policy toward the war remained one of cautious support because of the significant commercial interest in the Middle East and the sense that America should maintain a neutral stance with regard to the Ottoman government. US government reticence, however, was in sharp contrast to the "Greek fever" popularized by the public press in the 1820s. Newspaper articles recorded key battles and recounted stories of Greek personalities. Some Americans raised funds for the Greek armies. From a religious perspective, many Americans viewed the Greek War of Independence as a Christian struggle against Islam and tyranny. The US government did not interfere with these private efforts, which eventually ebbed as the war ended.[51]

Although the war for Greek independence against the Ottoman Turks continued until 1832, a Greek National Assembly was formed in 1827 and elected Ioannis Kapodistrias (John Capodistrias, 1776–1831) as head of state, with the Greek title of governor (*kyvemetes*). A native of the Greek island of Corfu, Kapodistrias trained as a medical doctor and then became a diplomat, serving for some years as a foreign minister for the Russian tsar Alexander I. He was one of the most admired and illustrious European diplomats, and certainly Greece's most famous politician. His biographer calls him "the first international civil servant."[52]

After negotiating a peace treaty with the European powers and the Ottoman Empire in 1830, Kapodistrias attempted a program of reform and modernization. He reestablished a standing militia, introduced medical protocol to stem epidemics, created the first modern Greek currency, organized local civil administration, and introduced potato cultivation. He is now considered the founder of Greek independence and the father of the modern Greek state.[53] Despite his many positive accomplishments, however, Kapodistrias was not supported by many of the traditional clans that had wielded economic and political power before and during the war. On his way to church on October 9, 1931, an assassin struck him down. Kapodistrias's younger brother Augustinos succeeded him as governor, but his rule lasted only six months while Greece fell into chaos.[54]

At the London Conference of May 1832, the Great Powers (France, Britain, and Russia), without Greek input, met to create a stable government in Greece and established the Kingdom of Greece as a free and independent Greek state. The Greek crown was bestowed upon Otto, the younger son of the king of Bavaria. Otto was a minor at this juncture, so Bavarian regents governed the country until 1835. The Great Powers also moved to put an end to the Greek War of Independence with the Ottoman Turks. On July 21, 1832, the Great Powers and the Ottoman Empire concluded the Treaty of Constantinople, which set the boundaries for the new kingdom of Greece.[55]

The new kingdom had been ravaged by years of war and the country was in chaos, in some places depopulated and in others crowded with refugees. Peasants still practiced primitive forms of agriculture to produce crops on what were often marginal soils at best. During the war the Greek government took possession of nearly nine million acres of land that had been taken from, or was occupied after being abandoned by, its former Muslim Ottoman owners. The Bavarian regents designed a scheme to nationalize the lands.[56] These would then be distributed to uprooted peasants, itinerant workers, indigent veterans, refugees, and others for their own well-being and to establish a tradition of private ownership of land.[57] Every Greek family received a credit of 2,000 drachmas with which they could purchase at auction a twelve-acre farm. For various reasons, not the least of which was the complex application process required of the peasants, the plan was doomed from the outset and was a complete failure.

Meanwhile, agricultural production for cash markets continued to be nearly nonexistent, because Greek farmers had almost no access to them.[58] William McGrew, in his extensive study of land tenure in nineteenth-century Greece, estimates that in the 1850s there were fewer than 100 total miles of roads in the country, and most of these were approaches to the major towns; by 1862 there were still only 150 miles of roads.[59] Alice Scourby figured that in the 1870s, 82 percent of the Greek population lived in rural villages, on land two-thirds of which was mountainous.[60] The principal agricultural products were currants, wheat, olives, figs, corn, hashish, tobacco, and vegetables. Villages were typically self-sustaining and produced little surplus. Most of the railroads were privately owned, and the cost of moving products to urban areas for consumption or export ate up most, if not all, of the profits.[61]

McGrew describes a typical village, Karpofora in Messenia, in the southwestern Peloponnese, "which in the nineteenth century had no road wide enough for a cart to pass. Though situated close to a fertile plain and only a few miles from the sea, its fundamentally family-subsistence economy had very weak links to the cash market until about 1880. Produce could not be moved from Greek villages across mountains, rivers, and marshes. Only large expenditures of capital could hasten the otherwise slow process of economic growth, but capital was the resource in shortest supply."[62]

The Bavarian regents also turned their attention to developing the new nation's cultural institutions. Although their actions were unpopular, they did put in place modern systems of education, justice, military, and administration. The regents established a centralized bureaucracy that replaced the local and autonomous control of the landowners and priests. The Orthodox Church was declared independent yet subordinate to the state. King Otto was a Roman Catholic but now official head of the Orthodox Church. Athens was restored as the country's capital in 1834,[63] although it was not much more than a "dusty village." The intent was for Athens to be the symbol of the classical period of Greece's history merging into the modern times.[64] None of this satisfied the Greek nationalists, however, who resented foreign rule, no matter how beneficial.

Greek nationalists led a revolt in 1843 and forced Otto to draft a constitution granting universal male suffrage. Otto also convened a Greek National Assembly. One important member of the National Assembly was Ioannis Kolettis (1773–1847). A charismatic politician, Kolettis was elected prime minister in 1844. There was constant tension between Otto and Kolettis, however, which resulted in a confusing struggle over power and patronage. During debates between the two in 1844, Kolettis referred to the *Megali Idéa* (Greek for the "Big Idea")—the nationalist goal of Greek unification of all the lands and islands of the former Byzantine Empire, with Constantinople as the capital. It was nationalism without boundaries. As one early nationalist, Benjamin of Lesvos, declared, "Nature has set limits to the aspirations of other men, but not to those of the Greeks. The Greeks were not in the past and are not now subject to the laws of nature."[65] At the time, only about a third of all Greeks of the old Ottoman Empire resided within the boundaries of the new Greek state; the rest lived under Turkish rule. The "Big Idea" dominated Greek politics for the remainder of the nineteenth century and into the early twentieth century.[66]

In 1863 Greek nationalists forced King Otto from power and asked Britain, Russia, and France to find a replacement for him. They chose a young Danish prince, William George (1845–1913) of the House of Glücksburg, and the National Assembly elected him King George I of the Hellenes. George had married a Russian grand duchess, and his two sisters, Alexandra and Dagmar, were the wives of the British king Edward VII and the tsar Alexander III of Russia, respectively. His wife was Russian Orthodox, and to further demonstrate his allegiance to the church, he allowed his sons to be raised in the Greek Orthodox faith.[67] George I ruled as king until his death in 1913. He founded a dynasty, the House of Glücksburg, which lasted until 1973, when the Greek military junta in power abolished it.[68]

George proved a popular and influential king and supported constitutionalism, but his reign also had its challenges; for example, there were five different governments between 1867 and 1870.[69] And daily life changed very little for the majority of the Greek population during George's reign. Approximately 75 percent still lived in small villages and were small-scale farmers, many in abject poverty without amenities such as running water or supportive infrastructure such as adequate transportation services. There was no notable middle class, and the small wealthy class of merchants, ship owners, and civil servants contrasted starkly with the large peasant class.[70] George did engage in an effort to systematize public education, and the University of Athens, founded in 1837, assisted in the development of a more educated middle-class elite of liberal arts experts and engineers.[71]

When King George I took the throne, the population of Greece was approximately 750,000. The new state comprised central Greece, the Peloponnese, and the Aegean Islands of the Cyclades. Macedonia and Thessaly remained part of the Ottoman Empire. The British held the Ionian Islands, which they ceded to Greece in 1864. This added approximately 1,800 square miles to Greece's landmass and increased its population by 236,000.[72] In 1881 Greece annexed Thessaly.[73]

In the 1880s the Greek economy continued to decline as imports, especially manufactured products and food grains, measured far in excess of exports. Approximately 75 percent of adult males were engaged in agriculture, fishing, or forestry in 1870, and that number fell only to 62 percent by 1907. Agricultural development made limited progress during the nineteenth century, as primitive farming methods and marginal lands continued to hinder greater crop production. William Moffett, US consul in Athens, reported in 1888 that "it is common to find the wooden plow and the rude mattock [hand tool for digging and chopping], which were in use 2,000 years ago. Fields are plowed up or scratched over, and crops replanted . . . until the exhausted soil will bear no more. Fertilizers are not used to any appreciable extent." The agricultural "methods in use can be readily learned by a study of the practices of the ancient Egyptians. Greece has olives and grapes in abundance, and of quality not excelled; but Greek olive oil and Greek wine will not bear transportation."[74]

Currants and olives became the main export crops. This near total dependency on these two crops, and particularly currants, proved disastrous. The majority of currants came from the Peloponnese and some of the Greek islands and provided "practically the whole currant supply of the world." Sociologist Henry Pratt Fairchild wrote disapprovingly that "the dependence of the whole Greek people on the currant crop is almost pathetic."[75] In the mid-1800s France's entire grape production was struck by a severe blight caused by the phylloxera aphid. These tiny pests destroyed perhaps two-thirds of France's vineyards.[76] This forced France to purchase Greek currants to replace the grape for French wine making. Between 60,000 and 70,000 tons, or approximately half of Greece's total currant production, were shipped to France in the last decades of the nineteenth century.[77] Fairchild pronounced disparagingly that greed then seized the Greek farmers, many of whom, "allured by the promise of large and speedy profits in currant raising, . . . cut down their fine old olive orchards and planted the ground with vines."[78]

The French meanwhile were working feverishly to find a solution to the blight. They found their answer in the grafting of resistant American rootstocks, which were not susceptible to the phylloxera aphid, to branches of French vines. By the early 1900s French vineyards had been replanted and replenished (the "Reconstitution," as it was called).[79] To force a return to French currants, France (and Russia also) enacted tariffs legislating Greek currants out of its market. This was an unmitigated economic disaster for the Greeks.[80] And thus, as Fairchild points out, for the Greek people from time immemorial "the traditional method of relief . . . from the burdens of their existence . . . is emigration."[81] The exodus was greatest from the Peloponnese, the region where many Greek immigrants to central Illinois originated. Ironically, the main point of embarkation for immigrants to America was the port of Patras on the northwest coast, which was also the main shipping port for the currant crops.[82]

Greece's massive financial problems added to the country's woes. Greece had taken on major debts to finance its wars and conflicts, and by 1887 approximately 40 percent of the governmental budget went to servicing the national debt. To this was added the expense of expanding Greece's educational system. Between 1860 and 1900, male enrollment in primary schools increased from 44,000 to 178,000; secondary school enrollment rose from 6,000 to 240,000; and university student enrollment went from 1,100 to 3,300. For girls, significant improvement was made in primary school enrollment, growing from 8,000 to 82,000.[83] But by the early 1890s, the Greek government was over 75 million drachmas in arrears.[84] This, coupled with the momentous decline of currant prices, brought about economic collapse. By 1893, Greece was bankrupt.[85]

Greece's financial difficulties as well as political turmoil did not prevent the country from agreeing to host the Games of the I Olympiad, the first international Olympic Games of the modern era, in April 1896. Expected to cost 3,740,000 gold drachmas (about $20 million at that time), King George and government leaders managed, through private gifts, public donations, and a special set of postage stamps issued to commemorate the games, to raise enough funding to put them on. Despite the costs, the games were a success and revived Greek patriotism.[86]

This patriotism found a new focus in the following years as long-standing disagreements over territorial possessions, particularly over the "Cretan Question," between Greece and the Ottoman Turks, became more heated. Although the majority of people living on Crete were Greeks, the island remained under Ottoman rule.

In January 1897, Cretan Greeks revolted against the Turks. While putting down the rebellion, Ottoman Muslim forces carried out massacres against the Greek Christian population. With extreme Greek nationalist politicians calling for retaliation, King George moved to seize the island on February 3, 1897, sending a Greek force of about 1,800 men and Greek warships. King George's actions spurred the Great Powers to intervene, and they declared on February 25, 1897, that Crete was to come under autonomous administration but under Ottoman suzerainty. All Greek and Ottoman forces were to be removed from the island. The Turks removed their troops, but the Greeks refused and dispatched more troops. The Ottoman sultan, Abdul Hamid II, declared war. Despite Greek prime minister Theodoros Deligiannis (in office 1895–97) and King George throwing their full support behind the war and receiving the enthusiastic endorsement of masses of Greek patriots, the Turks quickly defeated the Greeks by the end of April 1897. Further rioting and conflicts between Greeks and Turks in late 1898, however, finally resulted in Great Britain, France, Italy, and Russia officially granting Crete autonomy, but under Ottoman suzerainty, as originally proposed in 1897. The autonomous Cretan state remained independent until December 1913.

There were both positive and negative outcomes of these events. Not all Greeks supported the war, so it became a significant impetus to immigration in the late 1890s, as it required forced military service.[87] For those who supported the war, however, together with those still celebrating the success of the Olympic Games, there evolved the sense of a genuinely nationalist movement that was uniquely Greek, defined by the country and not just by religious affiliation.[88]

Another positive outcome was the emergence of a Cretan politician, Eleftherios Venizelos (1864–1936), who would become "the most charismatic politician of the first half of the twentieth century."[89] British prime minister David Lloyd George called him "the greatest statesman Greece had thrown up since the days of Pericles."[90] A lawyer by training, Venizelos had joined the island's Liberal Party in 1889, and his reputation reached near mythical proportions when he led a force of about 2,000 rebels against Ottoman military positions in the revolt of January–February 1897. In 1905 he led what became known as the Theriso Revolution. In this insurrection Venizelos organized a provisional government (centered in his mother's hometown of Theriso). He initially sought complete independence from the Ottomans, with an eventual goal of forming a single political union between Crete and the kingdom of Greece. In the autumn of 1912, at the onset of the First Balkan War, the Greek government officially declared union with Crete—Crete was now part of the Greek territory. This union was internationally recognized in December 1913.[91]

Meanwhile, Venizelos's actions in Crete had moved him onto the national Greek stage, and in 1910 his Liberal Party won a majority of the seats in the Greek National Assembly. In 1911, as prime minister, Venizelos's party introduced and enacted almost fifty constitutional amendments. These related to land reform as well as social reforms, such as minimum wages for women and children and the legalization of trade unions. Taxation was addressed and a progressive tax system was installed, although it did not detract from the traditional reliance on taxing the poor. Venizelos was supported by the business class and sought to gain appeal from the working classes. He personally took charge of the army and marine ministries. All of these policies created a new positive energy for Greece as a nation.[92]

While nationalism was reignited, the reality of Greek peasant life was quite another story. The war resulted in higher taxes, and once again the disproportionate share of the burden fell upon the rural citizens. Tax revenue was spent on infrastructure, primarily in Athens, to support the building of public structures, streetcars, and power systems, in addition to ports, rather than on rural areas. In Fairfield's caustic words, "An indifferent government squandered public funds on party parasites and ignored the welfare of the peasants."[93] Scholar Theodore Saloutos agreed with Fairchild, writing that "even Cretans as late as 1912, fourteen years after they had gained their independence from the Turks, complained that they found themselves in the same depressed state they had known under Ottoman rule."[94] Politicians rarely traveled outside of Athens to inspect the rural areas and inquire about peasant needs.

Meanwhile, proponents of the "Big Idea" shifted their focus geographically to the north of Greece, and especially to the region of Macedonia, which had been a battleground between the Ottoman Empire and Bulgaria, Greece, and Serbia since 1903. These three countries together with Montenegro formed the Balkan League in 1912, in opposition to Ottoman rule, and on October 8, 1912, they attacked the Turks, touching off the First Balkan War. Although the Treaty of London (May 1913) forced Turkey to surrender nearly all of its European territory to the Balkan League, Bulgaria remained unhappy with the terms. This led to a Second Balkan War in June 1913 that pitted Bulgaria again a new alliance of Serbia, Greece, the Ottomans, and Romania. Threatened with being overrun by the allied forces, Bulgaria agreed to the Treaty of Bucharest in August 1913, ending the war. The peace agreement awarded Crete, the Aegean Islands, and Macedonia (including Thessaloniki) to Greece. This increased Greece's landowning by 70 percent and added 2 million people to its population, increasing it from 2.8 million to 4.8 million.[95]

On March 18, 1913, King George I was assassinated in Thessaloniki, and his son, Constantine, succeeded him. King Constantine was ruler in name only, however, as Venizelos held the real power as prime minister.[96] None of King George's successors was ever able to gain the public support or be as influential and powerful as George had been.

When the Great War broke out in August 1914, Greece declared its neutrality. It remained neutral until May 1917, when it entered the war on the Allied side against the Central Powers. But events on the ground were much more complex than that. Venizelos aligned himself with Britain, France, and Russia against the Central Powers at the onset of World War I in 1914, believing that they would win and also that they had the power to blockade Greece and the Greek populations in its various possessions. He is famously quoted as saying, "One cannot kick against geography."[97] King Constantine, however, who had a German wife, was the brother-in-law of Kaiser Wilhelm II and publicly supported Germany and Austria. Constantine did not push to ally Greece with Germany but argued for strict Greek neutrality. The king and prime minister were thus openly at odds, which led to a national schism between the anti-Venizelos royalist faction and the Venizelos faction. The dispute became so intense that in February 1915 Venizelos resigned but was then reelected and formed a new government. In December 1915 King Constantine forced Venizelos to resign again and dissolved the Parliament. This ongoing conflict divided Greeks politically, both at home and abroad.[98] In May 1916, pleading his neutral position, King Constantine surrendered a crucial fortress to the Central Powers, and in August pro-Venizelos troops in Thessaloniki spearheaded a coup against the government. Venizelos established a provisional government based there and formed a private army to join the Allies. By this time, the Allies had begun a blockade pressuring Constantine to turn over Athens to them.[99]

In June 1917 Britain and France used their authority as "protecting powers," which they had technically held from the early 1800s, to push for Greece to adopt a constitutional form of government and to demand King Constantine's abdication. His younger son, Alexander, who sided with the Allies, was made king.[100]

Venizelos returned to Athens in late May 1917, unified the government and the country, and officially led Greece into war against the Germans and Austrians. This action proved decisive in the eventual outcome of the war. Numbering 300,000 men, the Greek army now moved north along with an Allied force on the so-called Macedonian front. The Greek forces were the critical mass the Allies needed to defeat Bulgaria, recapture Serbia, and threaten Hungary. Rather than be invaded, Austria-Hungary surrendered in November 1918, leaving no obstacles between the Allied armies and southern Germany, where the Germans were unprepared to fight a war.[101] On November 11, 1918, the Germans signed an armistice with the Allied forces. As a reward, Venizelos was invited to the Paris peace talks as Greece's chief representative. A skilled diplomat, Venizelos emerged victorious from the talks—Greece was awarded several new territories for its war efforts.

The war did not end the conflict between the pro-royalist supporters and Venizelos supporters, however, and the feuds carried on for the next twenty years. Two philosophies were in contention: one for a modern and progressive Greek capitalist republic, and the other for a conservative constitutional monarchy.[102] Greece has remained in political turmoil throughout the twentieth and early twenty-first centuries.

Yirogos D. Kalogeras contends that Greece's rich history makes Greeks "of particular interest" as an immigrant ethnic group of study. For example, they were endowed with "a very old illustrious history," and their countries of origin in regard to immigration to the United States included not only Greece but countries and regions in eastern Europe and the former Ottoman Empire. The immigrants also spoke languages other than Greek, adding complexity to their linguistic, geographic, and political background.[103]

This complexity is perhaps best epitomized in a brief biographical essay by Charles Moskos Jr., who describes growing up in an area of Albania to parents who were "born Ottoman subjects of Greek ethnic stock." The villages surrounding the main town, Argyrocastro, "were predominantly Greek Orthodox. In the town itself, however, Albanian Muslims outnumbered Greek Christians by about three to one. Christians dominated the commerce of the city, but Muslims owned most of the real estate. Many of the Christians spoke Albanian, but they identified with their co-religionists in 'liberated Greece' across the border to the south. Such sectarian cum national demographics were the paramount social facts of my father's (b. 1898) upbringing." His father left from Patras to Corfu, and then from Italy to America, following his two older brothers and a maternal uncle who were already in Chicago. "The decision to emigrate to America was inevitable," and in December 1916, "my father—who was born under Ottoman rule, who spoke Albanian as his first tongue, who was technically Greek, who was presumably recorded as an Italian immigrant, and who was to become an American citizen—arrived at Ellis Island."[104]

Thus, "Who are the folk? . . . Who are these Hellenes and from what history were they born?"[105] The renowned Greek scholar John Myres once titled a lecture "Who Were the Greeks?" and famously answered, "The Greeks were never wholly 'one people,' but were ever in the process of becoming."[106] And for those who immigrated, the question took on ever new meaning, as now these Greek immigrants were also to become Americans.

CHAPTER 2

THE JOURNEY

1880–1930

"Farewell" I wailed, "my native land, Goodbye!"
—Demetrios A. Michalaros, *Sonnets of an Immigrant*

In his fictional account of first-generation Greeks in America, Harry Mark Petrakis recounts the story of the Cretan Greek Kostas Volakis, the only son of Marko, a goat herdsman.[1] Sponsored by his father's cousin Stathis Glavas, a restaurant owner in Chicago, Kostas comes to America in 1919. Before his journey, he marries Katerina Paterakis, "the plainest of four daughters of a teacher in a village across the mountains, a girl betrothed at twenty-one by the grace of a dowry supplied by a brother in Melbourne and another brother in Athens."[2] The dowry is used to pay for their passage to America. Arriving in Chicago, the two live in a tenement and both work twelve- to eighteen-hour days. Katerina becomes pregnant, which ends her employment, but the son dies in childbirth. A year later a daughter is born, followed by two sons and another daughter. Kostas becomes successful and learns to read and write from the local Greek priest. When his father's cousin returns to Greece, Kostas takes over the restaurant and manages to live through the Depression. The story ends with Kostas approaching sixty and reflecting upon his life. This simple, "typical" Greek immigrant tale contains elements of the thousands of true stories of the first Greek immigrants to America.

When Greek immigrants determined they would leave their homeland, establish a new life in a difficult environment so different from the life they knew, become literate in a new language, and create a business niche that would allow them and their families to survive, they literally sailed off into the great unknown. Navigating this new territory while maintaining one's identity creates the common storyline of first-generation Greek Americans.[3]

Very few Greeks immigrated to the United States before the 1850s, but we do find a few notable individual Greek settlers residing in New York, Chicago, and New Orleans midcentury. Some of these early Greek immigrants include Evangelides Apostolides Sophocles, who was a professor at Harvard in 1842; John M. Rodonaki, the Greek consul in Boston in 1850; Spyros Bazanos, a well-known restaurateur in New York City in 1857; the Reverend Agapius Honcurenko, who served as a priest in New Orleans in 1865; and Michael Anagnos, a teacher at the Perkins Institution for the Blind in Boston in 1868. It is possible to cite these individual cases because the numbers of Greeks residing in America, let alone ones making names for themselves, were so small. Even by the early 1880s, fewer than 200 Greeks were arriving annually in the United States. In 1890 there were 698 Greeks living in Chicago.[4] These figures changed dramatically over the next five decades.[5]

During the mid- and late 1880s approximately 2,000 Greeks, mostly male, arrived in America, primarily from the Sparta region. Over 15,000 Greeks from a wider geographic region came during the next decade. The largest wave of Greek immigration, however, took place during the first two decades of the twentieth century; from 1900 to 1915 almost one in four Greek males between the ages of fifteen and forty-five immigrated to America.[6] Most studies of this mass Greek immigration to America have focused on Greek settlement in large urban areas such as New York, Chicago, or Boston. Many Greek immigrants, however, also journeyed to other communities in the Midwest and western United States to work on the railroads, in the mines, or on ranches and farms. And, as my grandfather's story illustrates, hundreds left the urban centers and dispersed to small towns across the country and became independent businessmen and businesswomen.

So, what were the paths of migration from Greece to America? Thomas Gallant identifies three basic flows: (1) mostly men and a few women who had lived in Greek cities for a while or who were recently arrived from the countryside and could not survive financially, thus propelling them to America; (2) those coming directly from the countryside, comprising 16 percent of the immigrants; and (3) small groups of merchants and skilled workers. Most of this last group left from cities and "constituted the majority of those who moved as couples or as complete families."[7] Gallant concludes that most immigrants went initially to the Greek cities to find work and then departed from there for new opportunities abroad.[8]

The factors driving the overseas immigration were "for the most part the same ones that caused the shift in population from the countryside to Athens. Relative rural over-population, a scarcity of labor, and low wages made it simply impossible for households with more than one or two sons to make ends meet. They could also not ensure for the continuation of the family into the next generation by providing dowries and inheritances that could sustain new households."[9] This was particularly a problem when nearly 60 percent of Greek families had five or more children.[10] According to the 1920 Greek census, over 70 percent of the country lived in villages, and almost 52 percent of Greece's entire population resided in villages with populations of less than one thousand.[11] External events, such as the collapse of the currant market in the 1890s that wrecked the Greek economy, also made rural life much more difficult. Moreover, 63 percent of the Greek migrants to urban areas were either unskilled workers or servants. Thus, their opportunities for meaningful work were limited.[12]

Theodore Saloutos suggests that progress in developing rural infrastructure, such as the installation of an electric railway system, aided travelers in moving from the Greek interior to ports of departure such as Patras. The Corinth Canal was completed in 1893 and joined the Isthmus of Corinth with the Saronic Gulf, shortening the journey from the Adriatic and ports in Austria, France, and Italy to the Aegean Sea and its ports in Turkey, Romania, Russia, and Asia Minor. A railroad linking Piraeus and Larissa was developed, in addition to the completion of a Peloponnese railway, bringing all the sections of that part of Greece within reach of each other.[13] Adding to the new transportation opportunities was the advent of the steamship agent who traveled from village to village, extolling the great life America offered. The agent spoke to captivated audiences in coffeehouses, manufacturing the dream of new, unimaginable opportunities. Saloutos observes that "for a time the most popular, if not the sole, form of advertising in the village coffeehouse and grocery store was a picture of a transoceanic liner or some other notice regarding the United States."[14]

As the number of Greeks in America increased, so, too, did chain migration, as letters from the first immigrants reached the villages and lured brothers, cousins, and neighbors.[15] Sociologist Henry Pratt Fairchild, in his quite early history (1911) of Greek immigrants, reported that by 1908 one steamship company, the Austro-American, had forty-two sailings a year from Patras to the United States. Cargo ships, headed for New York, Philadelphia, and Boston, accounted for only seven of these, while twenty-nine were immigrant ships to New York and six were to New Orleans. "Almost every important Atlantic steamship company has an agency or connection in at least one of the Greek ports," Fairchild observed, while "many immigrants still go to America by way of Naples, or even Cherbourg, or Havre."[16]

From 1900 to 1920 approximately 370,000 Greeks—and roughly 40 percent of the male population—left their country, and 95 percent of them went to the United States.[17] This mass migration out of Greece had significant consequences for the country. The great number of young men who left resulted in a labor shortage, so some large landowners had to bring in laborers from Albania and, in one of the few positive consequences, wages in some industries rose. Most of the effects, however, were negative. Factory owners replaced male immigrants with women and children at much lower wages. The Greek military suffered because fewer men were available for military service. Land went uncultivated, and many villages appeared deserted or were populated with only older people, women, and children.[18]

We should also note, though, that significant numbers of Greek immigrants eventually returned to Greece, many of them permanently. It is impossible to cite an exact number or percentage of the Greek reverse immigrants. Different authors propose conflicting numbers. Saloutos, who wrote an entire study about repatriated Greeks, posited that approximately 40 percent, or almost 200,000 immigrants, returned. Eva Sandis contends that between 1908 and 1912, 40,718 immigrants departed back to Greece and that this trend continued. Her research shows that between 1913 and 1917, over 58,000 immigrants in America listed Greece as their primary residence.[19]

PHOTO 1. Port of Patras, Greece. Greek immigrants embark in a small boat for a steamer to America, around 1910. (Library of Congress, Prints and Photographs Division, Washington, DC.)

Saloutos argues that the first wave of returnees was due to the U.S. financial panic of 1907 and the subsequent economic recession. Greek railroad workers, of which there were thousands, were the first to leave, and those toiling in industrial unskilled jobs also experienced hardships and returned. Additionally, the Balkan Wars in 1912 and 1913 drew men back to fight. One source estimates that 57,000 Greek Americans volunteered for service in the wars, but it is difficult to know how many of these came back to America following the wars.[20] Of course, Greeks were not the only immigrants who resided in America for a while and then returned home.

Saloutos cites one newspaper in Athens estimating the weekly departure of all nationalities from America back to their homelands at 25,000.[21]

The relatively small number of Greek women in America available to marry was also an important factor in explaining why Greek men returned to Greece: to ensure marriage with one of their own. For first-generation immigrant males, this was important.[22] The dowry system in Greece was a further driving force of immigration, as "a duty-bound brother seldom married until after his sisters had obtained husbands."[23] Unable to raise dowry funds due to various economic factors, such as the lack of jobs, failed crops, a collapsed economy, and overpopulation, fathers and sons left Greece hoping to make enough money in America to be able to send some back to their families to pay for dowries, as well as to pay for wives or sisters to come over.[24] Once they had earned enough for the dowries, they might also return home, marry, and stay.

The mass migration of so many men made life harder for Greek women back home. Steve Frangos observes, "There was an entire generation of women in Greece, especially in the Peloponnese, who never married because of the massive Greek immigration to North America. Aside from the missing men, another totally unintended difficulty arose. While brothers in North America were willing to provide a handsome dowry, finding a suitable groom in the village became increasingly problematic."[25] Women looking for husbands and those unable to provide dowries "also emigrated, hoping to find suitable mates." Saloutos finds it surprising "that more women did not take advantage of the matrimonial frontier that emigration opened up." Perhaps, he surmises, "this was too venturesome an undertaking for the usually restricted women to attempt on their own, or perhaps they believed that most men would return to Greece and thus spare them the need of going to America."[26]

It was also the case that some wives remained in Greece, and the pull to return to them could be strong. Moreover, elderly parents often required the son's presence, and there was the additional need to maintain customs and traditions for the next generation. Health and climate were also contributing factors. Thus, the causes of reverse migration were varied, but for most the primary reason was simply that their original goal of going to America and earning enough money to support the needs of their families had been accomplished. Although that was not always the case, whether successful or not, they returned to Greece. As Saloutos concludes, simply "sometimes the immigrant himself preferred the Greek way of life to the American."[27]

Although much of our story is necessarily about Greek males, we would be remiss in not discussing the first generation of Greek women who came to America as well.

Greek women started coming to America in significant numbers only after the Balkan Wars of 1912–13. They came with the intention of marrying Greek males, beginning families, making money, and returning to Greece. Some of them were intentionally selected for immigration by their parents or male relatives in Greece, and often their marriage partners had already been selected, sight unseen, through a network of matchmakers who arranged marriages. Constance Callinicos, the granddaughter of one of these "brides," says that her grandmother had never been outside her village in Greece before coming to America in 1922.[28] It is not always clear how many marriages were arranged, as some Greek women, without any prospect of a dowry (such as the refugees from Turkey noted below), were anxious to leave their villages for the opportunities America offered and faked their arranged marriage or husband. "More than one woman came as the supposed wife of an immigrant already in America," observed one historian.[29]

Many Greek immigrant women became refugees bound for America in the 1920s following the forced exchange of populations between Greece and Turkey. Some of these Greek women were left with no dowries because their families' property had been confiscated by the Turks. Most had no more formal education than their new husbands in America. The ones who were educated taught Greek school or began writing about their time in the new land.[30] There also arose the suspicion that some of the Greek women (and those of other nationalities as well) coming to the mining camps in the American West were prostitutes. Female detectives working for the US government are known to have followed groups of women from Ellis Island to the West to keep track of their activities.[31]

Prospective Greek brides and grooms sometimes exchanged photos. Not surprisingly, the men often sent photos that were not really of themselves but substitutes to entice the women to make the journey to America.[32] Not only were some of the photos fake, but they also failed to fully reflect the real circumstances of life in America. Still, in a time before the widespread availability of telephones, much less the internet, this was one method whereby a prospective couple could become acquainted over great distances. Frangos notes, "The exchange of letters between various family members soon proved a forum in which prospective brides and grooms could 'meet.' In this correspondence, photographs would often 'just happen' to be included of, say, a young man standing proudly in front of his candy store, or a flattering portrait of a Greek maiden from a rural mountain village."[33]

Arranged marriages required complex legal dowry contracts, or *ta prikia* in Greek. The process began with a bride's brother in America sending money to Greece. There a monetary exchange would take place on behalf of the groom, who sometimes lived in another town or city in America, by relatives representing the groom's family. Once both sides of the families were satisfied, the Greek woman would be put on a boat bound for America and her new husband.[34] This exchange was not just a monetary quid pro quo but required elaborate legal documents drawn up at Greek consular offices in San Francisco, Chicago, New Orleans, or New York. These included testimonies from Greek priests regarding a young man's character and bank documentation ensuring information on net worth or clear titles on property.[35]

Not all Greek men married Greek women, however. One study conducted in 1921 found that of those Greeks who lived in New York City, 22 percent of marriages were with non-Greek women between 1908 and 1912. Greeks were about in the middle among all ethnic groups studied in this respect.[36] Helen Zeese Papanikolas found that Italian, Yugoslavian, and even German and Swedish women who intermarried with young Greek men in the West "learned to speak Greek, cooked Greek foods, converted to Orthodoxy, and raised their children in the Greek tradition."[37] There remained a general expectation, however, that young Greek girls born into the second generation should obtain an education at least through high school and then marry Greek boys.[38]

Papanikolas was a Greek American ethnic historian, novelist, and folklorist who drew on her considerable collection of Greek American oral traditions gathered in her native Utah and the American West.[39] She recounted the story of one Greek woman who came to Utah in 1902 with her husband and raised eight children of her own and also took in a Greek orphan boy. Papanikolas observed that it was not uncommon for many of the mining families to have over five children.[40] In addition to her household, this immigrant woman also took in boarders to augment the family income.[41] Another woman arrived in 1909, after her husband had already moved to America. This woman also bore many children and then became a midwife.[42] A third Greek woman came over with her husband and settled in 1911 in Colorado; she was the only Greek woman among Italian, Yugoslavian, and Mexican women immigrants.[43] Many of these women, as Papanikolas noted, lived with the constant fear that their husbands or sons could be killed or injured working in the mines. These fears were well-founded. On March 8, 1924, for example, there was an explosion at the Number Two mine in Castle Gate, Utah, which killed 171 men; among these were 49 Greeks, 10 of whom had been married. Over 40 Greek children became fatherless.[44]

In the 1910s an Athenian journalist named Maria Sarantopoulou Ekonomidou came to America to visit Greek immigrant communities and to report on their living conditions in her articles back to Greece.[45] Ekonomidou traveled alone for two years throughout the Midwest and West and even into Canada to document the harsh conditions experienced by Greek male and female migrants.[46] Her accounts are some of the earliest recording daily Greek American life outside of the major cities. She asserted that the exploitive conditions in which the miners were forced to work contributed to the mine owners' profits. She concluded that the labor of the Greeks and other immigrants were "the greatest factor in the industrial progress of this country."[47] Ekonomidou was the only woman with direct access to the mining camps, particularly the one in Clear Creek, Utah, populated with Cretans and Lefkadians.[48] She was supportive of and encouraging to the young men there, quite different from the mine guards who treated the workers with contempt. She noted, "The guards are not in a position to comprehend the pain of the brave Cretan who feels dishonored to work and live among people who stare at him with contempt."[49] Ekonomidou described a life without amenities or institutional support from entities such as schools, churches, or recreation facilities that might have offset the daily grind and repetitive cycle of work.[50] In one report Ekonomidou discussed a Greek female prostitute whose sole purpose was to sing the songs of the villages, dance a bit, and move along to the next camp.[51]

The lives of the first-generation Greek immigrant women were rife with the pressures of arranged marriages, illiteracy, little or no knowledge of English, and their supportive roles as mothers, wives, and daughters.[52] Although they seldom appear in immigrant accounts, these first-generation Greek women were often protagonists in the American success story, for they were equal partners with their husbands in business. Thus, the narrative needs to be reshaped to portray women more as agents of change and influence and not simply as appendages of the males.[53] Women frequently took over their husbands' businesses and managed them quite successfully, allowing these women to enjoy a life never considered possible in Greece.[54] More local or regional micro-histories are needed to reveal and document how crucial Greek immigrant women were, both in maintaining a home and family and in supporting and participating in the family business.

Steve Frangos offers one caveat, however, to this image of the Greek family setting up home and business in America. He notes that while "some scholars mark the real beginning and establishment of Greek America" with the arrival of brides, many women were not keen to leave home and travel to America, and over half of the Greek male immigrants from 1880 to 1920 never married. Therefore, he argues, "the sociological importance of these [unmarried] men cannot be stressed enough. They not only physically embodied Greek America, they also actively helped finance the very establishment of a Greek community in North America."[55]

Most Greek immigrants had a minimum of 500 francs (roughly $150 in 1900) in their possession at the time of departure, although many had far less. This money came from accumulated savings, which had been obtained from the sale of land or animals or, less often, had been borrowed from relatives or creditors.[56] Some Greeks also mortgaged their property to provide for ship passage and pocket money.[57] The immigrants believed they could repay this money soon after their arrival in America, since they expected to be earning high wages right away. Saloutos contends that new migrants "often arrived without any clear-cut objectives in mind and without special training, trusting that they would find gold in the streets or that God would provide in one way or another."[58] Interestingly, "once an immigrant reached his destination, he wrote his parents immediately; within a few more days he followed up this initial letter with a second that contained a small sum of (often borrowed) money, but made no mention of work or working conditions. Such letters, and accompanying cash, touched off a chain reaction. It persuaded others to leave for America in the hope that they, too, could obtain ready money to forward to their families."[59]

Remittances back to Greece were real enough, however. In 1905 alone, "between four and five million dollars were received by families in Greece . . . from relatives in the United States."[60] This amount was about the average sent back to Greece annually between 1903 and 1914. The immigrants' first letters, "portraying the United States as a land of promise, often contained [money for] the cost of passage" for others to follow.[61] When the immigrant sent the money back, there was great celebration.[62]

The process of getting to America was conducted in stages. The prospective immigrant was first examined by a physician at the time of application for passage. Only about 3 percent of applicants were rejected. He or she was then required to make a deposit for the ticket purchase and received in return a certificate of reservation. After reaching a port city—Patras, for example—there was another medical examination, and then the passenger was stamped for departure. At Patras immigrants were required to sign a statement declaring whether they had a criminal record and how much money they possessed. Each person then passed through a luggage inspection line.[63] Initially the Greek government kept no records of emigration, and neither males nor females needed official permission to leave the country. The Greek government encouraged migration as the remittances were critical to the economic survival of thousands of families. In 1905, however, the government lowered the age of obligatory military service from twenty-one to nineteen to catch young potential emigrants who had not yet discharged their military obligations.[64]

In 1907, the financial crisis in the United States literally stopped emigration from Greece and money remittances back to Greece. "The building of churches and homes with money sent from the United States came to a standstill," Saloutos noted. Those Greeks who opposed immigration seized upon word of the hardships experienced by Greek sons and daughters in America during this crisis to discourage others who still wanted to migrate.[65] As soon as the American economy began to recover, however, the exodus to the United States picked up again. The outbreak of the First Balkan War in 1912 also halted emigration of able-bodied males between the ages of eighteen and forty-one. But, once peace was restored, mass migration recommenced.[66]

For the most part, Ellis Island was the portal through which most Greek immigrants passed, and the first wave of men coming through moved immediately into low-level service occupations or unskilled labor. Many headed to the western United States to work on the railroads, but most of the new arrivals gravitated initially toward urban centers, such as New York, Chicago, Boston, Lowell (Massachusetts), Philadelphia, San Francisco, Savannah, and New Orleans. By 1900 at least half of the approximately 8,500 Greeks newly arrived in the United States were living in urban areas.[67]

While urban areas on the East Coast were primary destinations for many new immigrants, so, too, were cities in the West and Midwest.

Greek immigrant workers—miners, railroad workers, lumberjacks, and construction workers—in the western part of the United States numbered about 10,000 in 1910. Despite the harsh living conditions, housing was better than it was in Greece, as was the consistency of the food, not being dependent upon specific harvests and weather conditions. Indeed, as we have discussed about the Greek diet, it followed the rhythm of the seasons, and women, in particular, adapted to what grains, vegetable, fruits, and meats were available.

Many of the Greek immigrants to central Illinois, including my grandfather, worked as railroad workers in the West to earn funding for their confectionery and other business enterprises and, of course, to remit money back to Greece. This was a hard life, made no easier by false promises of jobs and good salaries. It was in the midwestern and western states that a significant force in Greek labor history in America originated between 1885 and 1925: the padrone system. "Padrones controlled immigrant workers primarily by exploiting their geographic mobility and the family networks that sustained it," noted historian Gunther Peck.[68] They "were among the first modernizers of the unskilled labor market, directly linking isolated rural hamlets around the globe."[69] Padrones were an integral part of the chain immigration system.

The railroads also exploited and often misled and abused their unskilled immigrant laborers. They employed agents to hire newly arrived immigrants in Chicago to work out west, but con men also operated freely, and sometimes the two were the same. An editorial in the Chicago newspaper *Saloniki-Greek Press* described a case of a hundred Greek laborers from Chicago paying fees to railroad company labor agents and being transported out near Omaha, Nebraska, to work. After only a couple of days they were told to stop working and leave the place. Far from Chicago, and without money or a place to sleep, the men started tearing apart the railroad line. They were arrested, but after hearing their story the judge released them and made the railroad pay their way back to Chicago. Another article reported on either a Macedonian or Bulgarian con artist defrauding fifty Greco-Macedonians of a ten-dollar fee with promises of working on a new railroad station in Chicago. Of course, the station was never built. The editorialist called on Chicago's Greek businesspeople, especially restaurant and candy store owners, to give work to the thousands of unemployed Greeks in the city.[70]

In the 1920s, large numbers of Greek males became sheep and cattle ranchers. Many first served as shepherds for American ranchers and

Scandinavian immigrants and were paid with sheep or cattle. Some of the Greeks in Idaho, Nevada, Utah, and Colorado became prosperous ranchers. These men's wives supported the industry by feeding workers and assisting with lambing and shearing. They also traveled with their husbands and the livestock to Denver, Kansas City, and Chicago to support sales and to act, if often behind the scenes, as business partners.[71] Dan Georgakas laments that the documentation about these tens of thousands of Greeks who labored west of the Mississippi—an "important epoch of Greek-American history"—is spotty and sporadic.[72]

Residents from New England and the mid-Atlantic states had been moving to the Midwest since the 1840s, when thousands of people began relocating to this less settled, more attractive (in their opinion) region of the United States that offered new opportunities. Eastern cities were becoming overcrowded, land prices had soared, and the farmland soil was becoming depleted. As we focus upon the Midwest and our local study in central Illinois, it is important to note that during the mid-1800s, land sales in Illinois benefited from the influx of tens of thousands of new settlers anxious to purchase land. By the mid-1830s, the state had seven land offices—in Chicago, Galena, Quincy, Springfield, Danville, Vandalia, and Palestine—and over three million acres of land had been purchased.[73]

In addition to the "Yankees" came an influx of Germans and Irish to Illinois. The German population numbered 38,000 by 1850 and 131,000 by 1860. Notable German settlements developed in Quincy, Alton, Peoria, Springfield, Galena, and Peru. By 1860 the Irish numbered 87,600, with a sizable concentration in Chicago.[74] The rapid growth of rail and water transportation provided quick and easy access to most sections of the state from either coast.

Foreign-born populations continued to grow in Illinois through the remainder of the century, with Germans and Irish still leading the flow of immigrants to the state. These earlier migrants were joined by settlers from Sweden, Great Britain, and Bohemia. One Illinois scholar observes, "About three-fourths of the foreign-born lived in Illinois' cities, and most of them settled in Chicago. In 1870 more than half of the city's residents were foreign-born; in 1890 first-and second-generation immigrants constituted more than three-fourths of the population."[75] It is with the next wave, the southeastern European immigrants to the Midwest in the late eighteenth and early nineteenth centuries, that we shall first meet the Greek confectioners and restaurateurs.

CHAPTER 3

ACCULTURATION AND AMERICANIZATION

The name "Greek" was hurled on Greek immigrants as a disgraceful connotation.

—Paul Koken, Theodore N. Constant, and Seraphim George Canoutas, *A History of the Greeks in the Americas, 1453–1938*

In the early twentieth century, immigrants from southeastern and eastern Europe made up over 80 percent of the total European migrant population. Resistance in the United States to these immigrants began to manifest itself in racist and prejudicial stereotyping, including accusations of inferior intelligence. Indeed, even the relatively liberal scholar and president Woodrow Wilson, in his majestic ten-volume history of the American people, revealed his belief in such stereotypes:

> Throughout the [nineteenth] century men of the sturdy stocks of the north of Europe had made up the main strain of foreign blood which was every year added to the vital working force of the country, or else men of the Latin-Gallic stocks of France and northern Italy; but now there came multitudes of men of the lowest class from the south of Italy and men of the meaner sort out of Hungary and Poland, men out of ranks where there was neither skill nor energy nor any initiative of quick intelligence;

> and they came in numbers which increased from year to year, as if the countries of the south of Europe were disburdening themselves of the more sordid and hapless elements of their population, the men whose standards of life and of work were such as American workmen had never dreamed of hitherto.[1]

Of course, as is true for most racist and bigoted stereotypes, Wilson's characterizations did not describe the majority of these southeastern and eastern European immigrants, And, like generations of immigrants before them from northern and western Europe, those in this new wave of migrants, like my grandfather, were willing to work hard and live initially in the most appalling conditions to achieve the American dream—a new life in a new land. This required quickly adapting to a world unlike many of them had ever seen or imagined and to becoming Americans.

Greek (predominantly) male immigrants found themselves stepping off a boat into an often bewildering urban American environment. Before coming to America, life in Greece for many of them had revolved around scratching a subsistence living from poor soil in a rural setting. The farm life routine was interrupted only by religious holidays and celebrations. Devotion and loyalty to the family was deeply rooted, but the Greeks were also strongly individualistic because "underlying all institutions of Greek society is a highly-developed sense of *philotimo* (individual self-esteem), [which] derives from the concept of honor, dignity and, in a more extended sense, social worth and rank."[2] Work was very important, but if done under the authority of, and for, others, it indicated a loss of freedom—hence Greek immigrants' tendency to gravitate toward entrepreneurship in America once they were able.[3]

Although school became compulsory from 1834 for all Greek children between the ages of five and twelve, the law was not strictly enforced. In 1883, a US Bureau of Education report on education in Italy and Greece highlighted a 90 to 95 percent illiteracy rate in the districts of Thebes and the Peloponnese, the home districts of many Greek immigrants to America in the years to follow.[4] Indeed, it is astounding how many of the highly successful and astute Greek businessmen and businesswomen discussed in this study had only an eighth grade education at most, and many far less. Most of the Greek immigrants in the late 1800s and early 1900s were from agrarian backgrounds,[5] and the average illiteracy rate was approximately 27 percent for the years 1900–1908. In comparison, the illiteracy rate for Germans was 4.2; for "Hebrews" (that is, Jews), 19.4;

for North Italians, 10.4; for South Italians, 49.7; and for Scandinavians, 0.4 percent. By 1920 the overall illiteracy rate for Greeks had dropped to an acceptable 3.2 percent due to stricter enforcement of the compulsory education laws.[6]

Of course, limited formal education and weak language skills were only two of many problems faced by immigrants to America at the turn of the twentieth century. The totality of attributes immigrants had to acquire to become fully integrated into their new homes is frequently described as "Americanization." Americanization had its origins with the Puritans in Massachusetts, who set out to establish a "city upon a hill," with "the best religion, the best government, and the best society yet obtained in an imperfect world."[7] It was Benjamin Franklin, however, who refashioned the Americanization ideal by encouraging the colonists to "adopt a more secular and nationalistic mission."[8] He sought to create a "happy mediocrity" by promoting a "secular and middle class society that would overcome . . . religious extremism and also . . . do away with both the rich and the poor, with the aristocracy and the 'rabble.'"[9] In the nineteenth century "Franklin came to represent the America of innovation and enterprise, of moneymaking and getting ahead. He was everything that immigrants thought America was about."[10] Gordon Wood observes that in the several decades after Franklin's death in 1790, many considered him the "first great American."[11]

Prior to the American Revolution, however, Franklin had a very limited view of whom this "American" colonist should be. Wood maintains that Franklin "was a true-blue Englishman" and envisioned an America made up only of the English and the Indians, "the lovely White and Red." Franklin issued an "angry outcry against the massive immigration of Germans into Pennsylvania" and would have excluded not only "all Germans and black people from the New World" but also Asians, Spaniards, Italians, French, Russians, and Swedes, all of whom had what he considered a "swarthy Complexion."[12]

Still, at the time of the revolution, "most persons saw the American identity in abstract, ideological terms. For obvious and personal reasons, ethnic considerations among the Anglo-American revolutionaries drew little attention. America stood as the 'asylum of liberty,' . . . where the ideals of freedom, equality, and republicanism governed. American nationality stood open to anyone who desired to adhere to these principles."[13] The nationalization policy adopted in 1790 "bespoke great confidence in the power of American principles, institutions, and environment to transform immigrants quickly into acceptable Americans without systematic coercion."[14]

It was also true, however, that up until the 1840s, systematic coercion was seldom an option. Oscar Handlin shows that until then the issue of formal education for immigrant children was "largely irrelevant." He argues that "urban schools were decidedly class institutions, even those conducted under the auspices of Catholic orders. Neither then nor later were the established old-stock townsfolk eager to bring great hordes of foreign-born youngsters into contact with their own or to pay the taxes to support expansion."[15]

In the middle of the nineteenth century, as millions of immigrants began flooding into America from countries other than Great Britain, those of the Anglo-American ruling class found their "great confidence" in a natural Americanization process increasingly tested. Schools as a "force for cohesion in a nation characterized by heterogeneity" in sectional and class differences now had to address ethnic differences as well.[16] Handlin concludes that toward midcentury this "explosive fusion of conversion and reform transformed the mission of the schools in the view of many influential Americans," making them "less important as media for the transmittal of specific bodies of knowledge or skills . . . [and more] instruments for molding the thoughts and behavior of the next generation and thereby reshaping society."[17]

The development of public schools in the mid- and late nineteenth century furthered the Americanization process, especially of the newly arrived Irish and German Roman Catholic immigrants in urban areas. After the Civil War, New England schoolteachers and missionaries also took their nationalistic mission into the South during Reconstruction. Robert Carlson contends that following the Civil War, efforts at Americanization

> narrowed more explicitly along racial lines and influenced the late nineteenth and early twentieth century effort to Americanize the newly arriving immigrants from Southern and Eastern Europe. The militant Anglo-Saxonism that had helped to reunite North and South now challenged the newcomers as a potential threat to the nation's racial purity. The lack of faith in the heritage of these people made it easy to question their loyalty when World War I and the Russian Communist revolution engendered panic in the United States. In this atmosphere, there arose an educational campaign so intensive that Americanization education came to

be associated in popular thought almost exclusively with the attempted indoctrination of Eastern and Southern European immigrants.[18]

The arrival of eastern and southern Europeans, rather than the predominantly German, Irish, and Scandinavian immigrants who came before, coincided with the Progressive Era, a period from around the 1890s through the 1920s, when those seeking social and political reform through activism (with a Protestant tinge) met opposition from those who believed the nation's burgeoning industrialization and urbanization should be allowed to develop without restraint or government interference. Progressives sought to expose the rampant corruption they believed was prevalent in business and government so as to bring an end to all-powerful political machines and bosses (as in Chicago, Boston, and New York), and they often supported woman suffrage and progressive taxation. They were optimistic that new advances in technology and science could end hunger, fight disease, raise standards of living, and control nature (see, for example, the beliefs about the *Titanic*). Progressives worked to bring modern methods and practices to all areas of society, such as in public education, medicine, public health, housing, child rearing, and the family. They believed in an engaged internationalism and globalization, rooted in American-style democracy and capitalism.[19]

Progressives also generally supported the ideal of Americanization, although immigration reform was not one of their primary goals and there were deep divides among them over the issue. One leading historian of this period, Roger Daniels, asserts that "progressivism was not only led by a relatively narrow middle-class professional elite, but . . . for all intents and purposes, [it was] a progressivism for old American stock whites only." He continues, "While some progressive leaders, such as Theodore Roosevelt, at least paid lip service to ethnic democracy, others, such as Woodrow Wilson, were openly and blatantly racist, and contemptuous of most recent immigrants." Only when Wilson was seeking ethnic votes in the 1912 and 1916 presidential elections did he publicly modify his views about immigrants—although "not about African Americans."[20]

Professional educators at the turn of the twentieth century were influenced by "two distinct, yet interrelated phenomena that impacted the social production of race in [public] schools: Americanization and transnational dialogue."[21] Teachers grappled with the tension between preserving some aspects of immigrant "heritage" and erasing them wholesale. Pressure to adopt the latter policy grew because of the "100 percent Americanism" campaign (discussed below) during and following the Great War. Thus, "Americanizing white racial minorities would define the dominant discourse on race in public schools from 1900 to 1938," which included most immigrants of European descent. According to scholar Zoë Burkholder, "American teachers applied the test of color to determine which minorities were worth Americanizing."[22]

In 1913, just prior to political leaders' promotion of "100 percent Americanism," the US commissioner of education instructed public school teachers to respect the ideals of immigrants and "strengthen the best of their Old World lives they bring with them." For the peasant immigrant, school was "understood as an ancillary, supportive communal instrument."[23] This transnational educational strategy sought to ensure that the public schools, especially for immigrant children, would not interfere with the continued language and cultural indoctrination and education of the home country.[24]

The American progressive reformer Jane Addams believed in this idea of promoting cultural differences, in helping immigrants develop a sense of community, and in helping immigrant children understand their parents and the lands and cultures from which they came.[25] Fearful of the tide of nationalism and increasing racism and intolerance that grew stronger during the Great War, Addams called in 1919 for the adoption of a less rabid form of Americanizing of the immigrant population. She thought it important that "Americans should not make a problem for themselves by placing an unfair emphasis upon differences which are inevitable in a country such as ours" and to "utilize properly the enthusiastic patriotism engendered by the war by making it more inclusive. . . . [If] we undertake a mutual task of this sort 'how our convulsive insistencies, how our antipathies and dreads of each other' would soften down; what tolerance and good humor, what willingness to live and let live, would inevitably emerge."[26] A decade later, Addams argued that "internationalism engendered in the immigrant quarters of American cities might be recognized as an effective instrument in the cause of peace." She daily witnessed such internationalism and peaceful interaction, for while her famous settlement house in Chicago, Hull House, celebrated diversity and cultural differences, it also gathered peoples of widely diverse ethnic and religious differences to work, study, and play together.[27]

Addams's more tolerant and widely inclusive approach, however, was not one favored by most policy makers. Indeed, "seen from the point of view of racial and ethnic minorities, the [Progressive] period could very well be called the 'regressive era,' a time in which things grew a little worse, a time when nativism and racism gained strength and acceptance at all levels of society."[28]

During the Great War, a "100 percent Americanism" crusade began to spread across the republic, primarily fed by an evolving hatred of Germany and Germans, and from there to dislike of anyone not considered a true American. Theodore Roosevelt and Woodrow Wilson amplified the sentiment at the national level in the presidential campaign in 1916, and "100 percent Americanism" became a rallying cry used to exclude immigrants, socialists, Jews, and others from the national community. Theodore Roosevelt, for example, railed that "there can be no fifty-fifty Americanism in this country. There is room here for only 100 percent Americanism, only for those who are Americans and nothing else."[29] The slogan "100 percent Americanism"

> became the watchword of the anti-immigrant groups that preached a blend of scientific racism, cultural conformity, and strict obedience to authority. They ranged from the American Legion, whose national convention voted in 1919 to make its basic ideal the promotion of "100 percent Americanism" and to combat "all anti-American tendencies," to the revived Ku Klux Klan, whose Imperial Wizard promised to fight "anti-Americanism" of all kinds. . . . The word "Americanism" was appropriated by the nativist right as its sole patrimony, and "anti-Americanism" linked unpopular ethnicity and progressive politics to disloyalty to the nation itself.[30]

The "100 percent Americanism" campaign intensified even more following the sedition and espionage persecutions in 1917–18, the Red Scare in 1919–20, the immigration restriction laws of 1921 and 1924, the growth of the American Legion,[31] the Ku Klux Klan resurgence, and the spread of anti-union sentiment in the mid-1920s. All these events contributed to an "anti-hyphenism" culture that seeped into the American psyche. In a campaign speech on June 14, 1916, Theodore Roosevelt questioned German Americans' patriotism, declaring, "No good American . . . can have any feeling except scorn and detestation for those professional German-Americans who seek to make the American President in effect a viceroy of the German Emperor. . . . [There should be no] adherence to the politico-racial hyphen which is the badge and sign of moral treason."[32] Roosevelt was soon questioning the patriotism of all hyphenated Americans: "The hyphen is incompatible with patriotism"; "A hyphenated American is not American at all"; "There is no such thing as a hyphenated American who is a good American. The only man who is a good American is the man who is an American and nothing else."[33] Only a couple of days after Roosevelt's June 14 speech, members of the Democratic Party, meeting in their national convention (held in St. Louis, a heavily German American city), put a plank in their campaign platform attacking "hyphenates" and promoting Americanism. President Wilson promised to make "anti-hyphenism" the principal issue in his campaign and expanded his attacks to include pro-German Irish Americans.[34]

As one of the largest immigrant communities at the time, southeastern European immigrants became the targets of the Americanization process, and Greek Americans were not, of course, unaware of the rise of the 100 percent Americanism crusade. In these years Greek newspaper editorialists routinely discussed Americanization with such titles as "Our Societies and Clubs Must Be Americanized in Order to Succeed";[35] "Our Duty, (It Is Our Duty and to Our Benefit to Be 'American' Even More Than We Are 'Greek')";[36] and "Business and Americanism."[37] Becoming Americanized was facilitated by the many factories, YMCAs/YWCAs, settlement houses, and other community organizations that established classes for English-language instruction, citizenship, and American customs, including cooking classes. Robert Carlson noted, "Adult education developed into a profession in the United States at this time largely as a result of this campaign that involved large numbers of volunteers and all levels of America's burgeoning educational establishment."[38] As an example, at Hull House, cooking classes not only enabled new immigrant families to make their food dollars stretch but also allowed single women, in particular, to learn basic food preparation for their future family households.[39]

Thus, these shifting and conflicting vagaries in American attitudes toward the millions of newly arrived immigrants presented the immigrants themselves with many challenges as they tried to settle into their new homes and adapt to a new culture. For the early Greek immigrants in Chicago, the Orthodox Church became a focal point for the neighborhood and community. It was the church that kept alive the Greek language and allowed the people to maintain something of their Greek identity, which was closely tied to the Greek Orthodox religion itself. Greek schools, attached to the churches, offered Greek-language courses but also taught new, American-born generations about Greek culture, history, and life.

Hull House, the quintessential neighborhood settlement house, and other voluntary associations also offered Greek immigrants opportunities to maintain their identities through such activities as dances, theater, and sports, but they also taught the acculturation and Americanization essentials needed to cope with the exigencies of urban, and American, life.[40] Hull House, in particular, played an integral role in Chicago Greek community life because of its location in "Greek Town," the area near Hull House along Halsted Avenue. Greeks took every opportunity to extract any and all of its services, whatever the prevailing ideologies that formed the undergirding foundation of its purpose or intentions.

Hull House exemplified one of several reform initiatives that evolved from the progressive movement of the latter part of the nineteenth century into the first two decades of the twentieth. It was grounded in the belief that if one's social environment could be improved, then positive character changes would result. Providing the appropriate guidance and services, settlement workers sought to create a new social environment for immigrants to adjust to a new way of life in a new country and, in time, become more "American."

Prior to the Great War, organizations such as the YMCA also offered Americanization classes. After the war, the YMCA offered evening classes for immigrants seeking to qualify for citizenship. Andrew Kopan contends that mostly Greek professionals attended these classes because they could afford the nominal tuition charged. For example, the editor of the *Greek Press* newspaper learned English and citizenship requirements at the YMCA.[41]

Early Greek immigrants utilized these external institutions for learning about such matters instead of organizing any instruction within their own community. However, by the late 1930s two Greek Orthodox Church parishes sponsored Americanization classes using the services of a Chicago public school teacher. These classes were necessitated by the feeling that by that time, the Greeks remaining in Chicago were probably going to stay in the country and should become naturalized. Day classes were attended more by women and evening classes by men.[42]

Proponents of the "assimilation process" believed this was a way to transform the waves of southeastern immigrants into Americans. In the

1920s, University of Chicago urban sociologist Robert E. Park developed a theory of assimilation relating to immigrants that posited a four-stage "race-relations cycle" of contact, competition, accommodation, and assimilation.[43] Park believed certain criteria, such as language, culture, and race, which tended to divide people, could be eradicated through societal forces of change.[44] This "melting pot theory" has been characterized, however, as a naive romantic notion "due to the implicit assumption that most immigrants and their descendants are anxious to shed their social and cultural heritage."[45] The theory also implied the unbiased willingness of nativist white individuals to participate in creating positive forces of change that included immigrants and minorities in the mainstream of American society.

During the Progressive Era there was always tension between the inclusion of immigrants and the creation of a melting pot and the "Anglo-Saxon and Teutonic superiority," which became manifest in immigration restriction, discriminatory labor contractual law, and racial attacks.[46] Progressive support of imperialism and capitulation to Jim Crow systems of segregation "ensured that race thinking would retain and increase its potency."[47] In essence, a racial taxonomy was formed, with blacks at the bottom, the "in-between peoples" of southeastern Europe in the middle, and white Anglo-Saxon Protestants at the top.[48] The predominantly white Anglo-Saxon Protestant settlement house movement, despite its altruistic intentions, exemplified the prevailing racist ideologies of the time.

In addition to Americanization programs offered by settlement houses, the YMCA, and other organizations, institutional systems, such as health care, also infused a more nativist approach to the environmental impacts on the new immigrants. "Native born reformers thought the best solution for the newcomers and the public health, generally, was rapid Americanization," observed Alan M. Kraut.[49]

Scholarship on the Americanization of immigrant mothers offers a unique insight into this aspect of health care. Chicago health care reformers in the early 1900s "envisioned themselves as mediators between the Old World and the New," for their movement "was as much about modernizing immigrant mothers' attitudes and beliefs toward personal hygiene, household cleanliness, and the efficacy of early intervention in keeping young children alive as it was about safeguarding the public's health."[50] Hull House activists determined that a multifaceted attack on a wide range of physical and social maladies was the answer to lowering infant mortality rates and decreasing childbirth rates, allowing women more opportunity to care for themselves and their children.[51]

Of course, the Progressives' desire to lower immigrant birth rates was not always, or simply, a humanitarian gesture. Population control also played a role, as

> birth control advocates either acquiesced to or supported the new arguments invoking birth control as a means of preventing the proliferation of the "lower classes" and as an antidote to race suicide [of native-born whites]. Race suicide could be prevented by the introduction of birth control among Black people, immigrants and the poor in general. In this way, the prosperous whites of solid Yankee stock could maintain their superior numbers within the population. Thus class-bias and racism crept into the birth control movement when it was still in its infancy. More and more, . . . within birth control circles . . . what was demanded as a "right" for the privileged came to be interpreted as a "duty" for the poor.[52]

Not surprisingly, this desire for control of immigrant birth rates while opposing any form of birth control for the old Yankee stock found its strongest support among "traditionalists and a growing number of eugenicists who were convinced that the so-called 'native-stock,' the lineage of the Protestant Yankee, was rapidly dying out because the more educated and affluent had adopted family planning practices."[53] The eugenics movement too rose in power during the anti-hyphen, "100 percent Americanism" campaigns of the 1910s and 1920s. Eugenicists were largely responsible for convincing key members of Congress and much of the American public that immigrants from southern and eastern Europe were "overbred, underachieved, and accounted for a disproportionate number of patients in insane asylums and inmates in correctional facilities. Metaphors about the bottom of the 'melting pot' falling out and horrific visions of the coming 'mongrelization' of America stirred up resentment toward new immigrants and black Americans and increased public support for immigration restriction."[54]

Persuading immigrant women to improve personal hygiene practices, promote household cleanliness, intervene early when children were sick, and practice birth control was a tough sell, however.[55] Immigrant mothers needed to be convinced of the safety and efficacy of the health care offered to them before they would relinquish their belief systems. In this regard, Kraut writes, "In the neighborhoods where they settled, on the blocks where they lived, in the hospitals and dispensaries and pharmacies of the city, immigrants made some compromises and not others, cautiously negotiating their break from Old World definitions of health and from traditional therapeutic practices. . . . Health care providers had no choice but to become actors in the immigrant's Americanization drama, constructing a paradigm or blueprint of health care to which the foreign-born were expected to conform but often did not—right away."[56] Most immigrant groups also had their own physicians and pharmacists, individuals to whom a newcomer "could turn and explain their ills in a familiar language, where cherished customs and traditions were respected and observed," and who "treated patients with drugs drawn from another, more familiar medical tradition."[57]

Customs and traditions tied to the experiences of pregnancy, birth, infant care, and feeding were deeply embedded in centuries of culture. The health care workers "complained that Eastern European mothers insisted on feeding their children pickles, cooked cabbage, and other ethnic foods which reformers themselves found repulsive, while Italian mothers allowed family members and even neighbors to lavish physical affection on babies and small children, a custom that appeared disturbingly unhygienic."[58]

For the newly arrived Europeans, "good health" was defined as the absence of any immediately life-threatening diseases. "For generations of peasants from southern and eastern Europe, the performance of arduous physical labor remained crucial to survival, and therefore they placed a high cultural value on physical mobility," observed Lynne Curry; "one was considered to be ill only at the point at which one became totally incapable of moving about."[59]

In small towns outside of urban areas, health care practices were not as progressive as in urban centers. Rates of infant mortality—the yardsticks used by Progressive Era health and child welfare advocates "to measure society's overall state of advancement"—were lower in Chicago in 1926, 66.57 per 1,000 live births, than they were in downstate Illinois, 71.51 per 1,000 live births.[60] Despite the seemingly unlimited supply of fresh air, Illinois's rural population was decreasing due to inadequate health care and the rising costs of machinery and land. The total number of farms declined over 18 percent from 1900 to 1930.[61] Farm households in downstate Illinois often had no indoor plumbing and fewer hot-air furnaces. "Fully 59 percent of the southern farm families surveyed in 1915 drank water that had been obtained from open or uncovered wells," Curry noted.[62]

In May, June, and July 1916, my grandfather Gus Flesor was affected by the unsanitary water coming from one such well. There was an outbreak of typhoid fever in those months in Tuscola, Illinois, which spread quickly throughout Douglas County, reaching a total of 110 cases. The source of the outbreak was traced to a single well "famous for the clearness, coolness and fine flavor of its waters," but it had defective walls and was located near the privy vault of a livery stable. It serviced multiple homes as well as my grandfather's confectionery "in the manufacture of soda water" and the businesses of the local druggist and the hotel owner.[63] This epidemic was instructive to Illinois health reformers because it was a clear example of the dangers of contaminated water, which might be found "in any of these communities where wells are used as the source of domestic water supply . . . and, incidentally, that coldness and clearness and fine flavor have nothing to do with the purity of drinking water."[64] Indeed, the *Illinois Medical Journal* observed that the well "was very popular on account of the 'fine quality' of the water. The 'fine flavor' of the water in this well brings to mind the many instances of 'mineral wells' which have come into high favor until it was ascertained that the mineral taste was due to just about such things as one would expect to find in a livery stable well."[65] Armed with this example of the need to upgrade living conditions, health officials could begin to formalize clean water programs. No one ever blamed my immigrant grandfather for the Tuscola typhoid outbreak. But because many such outbreaks were transmitted by human carriers through food or water, "diseased immigrants" were often accused of being the source.[66]

World War I ushered in a new wave of patriotism and nativism. More businesses required their employees to be English-speaking and have American citizenship. Schools displayed their allegiance to the United States by eliminating German as a subject and evaluated students' degree of citizenship by noting their outward behavior.[67] Americanization reached into the schools in 1919 with the National Education Association's recommendation to Congress that all young people take a yearlong course of civic, physical, and vocational training. Criticism from more liberal factions suggested that this type of education was propaganda and that such uniformity was not only impossible to achieve but also unwarranted. Conservatives critics, including one historian of Greek immigrants, Henry Pratt Fairchild, suggested that the immigrants were "mongrelizing" the Anglo-Saxon United States.[68] As regards Americanization, Fairchild wrote,

> It is very doubtful if it is possible for even the most exceptional adult immigrant, from the southeastern European races, at least, to become thoroughly assimilated in his lifetime. The barriers of race, set for the most part by Americans, can hardly be broken down. The immigrant is still an Italian, or a Slav, or a Greek, as long as he lives. . . . The mental habits . . . which are the result of long race inheritance are very deep-seated, and can hardly be altered even after a long residence in a foreign country.[69]

The popular American press supported this view.[70]

In 1921, the National Education Association created a Department of Immigration Education. Already by this juncture in American history, however, the immigration restrictionists were galvanizing their platform to end immigration by southeastern Europeans and by other European refugees seeking asylum after the Paris treaties ending the Great War split up the old European dynasties. In concert with that view, as we have noted, eugenics and the biological categorization of racial and ethnic characteristics came to the forefront as reasons to restrict further migration to America. The continued propaganda led to literacy testing for immigrants in 1917, an emergency immigration quota in 1921, and the National Origins Act in 1924.[71] All of these forces affected Greek immigrants as they attempted to move into business, follow educational pursuits, and participate in social interactions.

As these attacks evolved, the Greek Orthodox Church played an increasingly important role as an Americanizing agent. In Greece, most individuals took on a more passive role regarding church organization and hierarchy; in America, that role was reversed because the immigrants were now responsible for the development and support of church membership, structures, and the operations of a building, staff, parochial schools, and programs. The process of creating a formalized church in America itself became an exercise in Americanization. Questions of membership, language used in the Liturgy, programming, and financial challenges duplicated the everyday difficulties faced by new immigrants. "Much as the more conservative element, among both the priests and the laity, might like to block change in the traditional religious culture, the church by its very functioning contribute[d] to the Americanization of its members and thus necessitate[d] its own development according to the American pattern," observed sociologist Mary Bosworth Treudley.[72]

Other Greek organizations, such as youth and women's groups as well as the more prestigious national groups like the American Hellenic Educational Progressive Association (or AHEPA), the Greek-American Progressive Association, and the Helicon, which stressed Americanization and success measured by education, income, and philanthropic activities, lent themselves to the less formal education of Greeks. These organizations offered a safe place to navigate issues relating to acculturation and Americanization. They assisted in the process of adapting from a village life to an urban American environment, promoted interaction among the immigrants, created an overt ethnic social structure for their own community and for the external community in which the immigrants worked or resided, and served as a clearinghouse for problems arising from being newly arrived in (to them) a foreign country.[73] Those immigrants who did not have access to the Greek church or social/cultural organizations joined other voluntary associations affiliated with their businesses or their children's schools. In many of the small towns sampled for this book, men joined, for example, the Masons and the Chamber of Commerce, and their wives became active in Parent-Teacher Associations or Eastern Star.

The Greek press was another vehicle of education and information. There were at least thirty-one publications reaching the Greek immigrant population in the first two decades of the 1900s.[74] These were extremely influential in community life, carrying international news and detailed stories about affairs back in Greece. Greek-language newspapers "kept the immigrant with little or no knowledge of English in contact with happenings in the homeland, perpetuated Old World feuds and gave rise to new ones."[75] In Chicago, the English-language *Greek Star* newspaper also promoted Americanism. One article of many, for example, reported on the installation of officers in the Hellenic Post No. 343, one of the first American Legion posts in the country. It suggested that the new members, who were the "adopted sons of America, of Greek birth, as well as those born here of Greek parentage," could mutually share in the honor of victory in World War I.[76] The same newspaper ran a series of articles in the late 1920s on "Know Illinois," which provided facts and figures on the Illinois economy.[77]

A *Greek Star* editorial for November 14, 1919, provides an interesting Greek perspective on the issue of "Americanism." It noted, in reference to the "Red Scare" of the time, that "Americanism" is a "popular word today, and rightly so, as the present industrial situation demonstrates; for a slow but mighty struggle is going on to determine whether American principles or radical foreign theory shall prevail. Americanism in this sense is not directed at race, creed, or the so-called hyphenates, but at the destructive or anti-progressive forces." What was needed, therefore, was "to differentiate between the American of foreign birth who is a good citizen and the foreigner who is a detriment to his adopted country." To do that the newspaper intended to publish a series of articles—this was the first—about Greek businesses in Chicago, particularly restaurants. These articles, it was hoped, would provide the reader with "an unprejudiced view of the nationalities in the restaurant field" while setting aside the "time worn race question."[78]

As a follow-up to this editorial, the *Greek Star* sent out investigators to 1,503 Chicago restaurants (the newspaper estimated there were then 3,000 Greek restaurants in Chicago and 1,500 confectionery stores that served lunch)[79] and interviewed 217 "Greek-American" restaurant and confectionery store owners. They chose these businesses because, as the article's author observed, "a history of the Greek in the American restaurant field would be a history of the Greek people in America, for the history of Greek-Americans and the history of Greek-American restaurants are almost identical."[80]

The *Greek Star*'s investigators asked questions such as, "Does the Greek use another name than his own for his restaurant because he has reasons for hiding his identity, because he is ashamed of his name, or for some other reason?" To this question the common answer was that their Greek names were too long or impossible to pronounce or remember. They also felt it good business practice to localize their restaurants by giving them neighborhood names. To the question, "Does the Greek pay low wages, employ only Greeks, and use un-American methods?," the investigators concluded that the Greeks paid wages that were equal to those paid by other restaurants, that nearly every nationality was represented on the payrolls, and that "the environment and the working conditions of employees were, on the average, as good as those in other restaurants visited, and there was a noticeable effort on the part of the owners to educate the employees in the finer points of cleanliness and sanitation." Greek restaurants were found to be just as sanitary as other restaurants. For the question of whether "Greeks hoard their money to send it abroad, or do they spend it in America?," the newspaper interviewed several prominent bankers in Chicago. The bankers estimated that Greeks had $8,000,000 invested in Chicago alone and that they found them to be good bond customers, thrifty, and inclined to invest their funds in real estate. Like the big-city Greeks, my grandfather in the little town of Tuscola first saved his wages from working on the railroads to buy his store and then saved the nickels and dimes he made at the Candy Kitchen to buy a farm in Douglas County. To the question of whether Greeks were naturalized American citizens, the newspaper found that "of the 3000 so-called Greek restaurants in Chicago, 90 percent were operated by American citizens of Greek extraction." The writer concluded this article with the observation that "the Greek-American is a good businessman; he is industrious, and he has vision and foresight. His rise in Chicago is due solely to these faculties, which after all are the foundation of nearly every American's success, regardless of race or nationality."[81]

In St. Louis, the other portal of Greek migration to east-central Illinois and the Midwest, settlement houses were also important refuges for newly arrived immigrants, although not to the extent that Hull House was in Chicago. In 1916, a self-reporting survey of all organizations providing social service programs in St. Louis included findings detailing the status of their programs and recommendations for future needs. Of the ninety-four different charities documented, there were eighteen neighborhood centers listed, and all but two served only native and immigrant whites.[82]

The report depicted a multifaceted approach to settlement house programs at the time. For example, the Jewish Alliance did not define itself as purely a settlement and indicated that its programs drew Jewish people from all the city's neighborhoods. Activities at the center, however, were open to everyone. The director stated, "The neighborhood [where the center was located] is now largely Italian and Polish, and Negroes come in proportion."[83]

The report also reveals the fluid nature of the immigrant neighborhoods. The Jewish Alliance was situated in a Catholic neighborhood, where the moving picture entertainments in the area attracted over ten thousand attendees, mostly Italians. The Wesley House, a Methodist settlement house, was on the verge of closing its doors at the time of the survey. The director wrote that the "Jewish people are rapidly crowding out the Irish in the neighborhood. There is a large proportion of Negroes in the neighborhood, too. The Colored Branch of the Y.W.C.A. is not more than one-third of a mile away. The Church of Holy Communion with its settlement activities is a little farther away than that."[84]

Most St. Louis settlement houses were located within neighborhoods filled with European immigrants, such as Germans, Russians, Italians, Croatians, Greeks, Irish, and English, as well as poor native white Americans. Hundreds of families were served each week through multiple services. Programs offered were day nurseries, kindergartens, literary clubs, citizenship classes, sewing, cooking, stenography, and recreational activities. Relief in the form of clothing and food was also provided, and a couple of places, such as the Guardian Angel Settlement, assisted women in securing employment.[85]

A 1916 report on immigrants in St. Louis concluded that night school for immigrants was integral to their adjustment. Fifteen night schools opened during the winter term of 1914–15 for seventy-five nights. Fourteen of them offered English to immigrants. Before immigrants could move on to other life skills classes, they had to master enough English to enable them to participate in classes in mathematics, science, dressmaking, and other practical educational offerings. The schools were located throughout the city and were well attended.[86] The YMCA also offered English classes, and over six hundred men took advantage of them. Of the total night school attendees in St. Louis in 1915, there were almost four hundred Greek males and thirteen females.[87]

Many, if not most, immigrants recognized the value of education and of reading. They were also shocked to find that in America, public libraries were open to everyone and, more importantly, free, something unimaginable in most of their mother countries. Immigrants therefore enthusiastically supported public libraries in St. Louis, which held collections of books in fifty-four different languages and offered books in the specific language of the ethnic neighborhood in which the library was located. Many of the library buildings had auditoriums and clubrooms, which were popular for the various neighborhood clubs. The libraries were also places where social service agencies, such as the YMCA, could hold English classes. Of course, English-language books were promoted, and the traveling libraries often stopped at factory sites and delivered books at the lunch hour for interested readers.[88]

The St. Louis YMCA was also instrumental in reaching out to immigrants upon their initial arrival to the city and assisting them later. YMCA employees had met over nineteen thousand newcomers at the train station, and over sixteen thousand had been given direct service of some type. The YMCA secretaries kept in touch with most of the male immigrants while they remained in the city, and most were urged to take English and citizenship classes. The YMCA believed its duty was to provide these services because "the largest percentage of immigrants coming to this country . . . are from Southeastern Europe, and thousands of them settle in our city every year to make their homes with us. They are looking to the American people to give them an opportunity to make the most of their lives as residents of our community, and as citizens of this great country of ours."[89]

Away from Chicago and St. Louis, in the smaller towns and cities in Illinois, the country life movement arose as a rural response to the progressive movement and urbanization. It began in 1908 when President Theodore Roosevelt created the Commission on Country Life to investigate rural issues. The country life movement then evolved from the findings of this commission as "an attempt to improve the standard of living of rural dwellers, primarily through various educational initiatives."[90] The popularity of the country life movement grew out of a rural need to respond to the rapid urban development of the 1890s. The financial panic of 1893, which witnessed thousands of labor strikes, catapulted the unemployment rate to 25 percent in some regions. The decline in the 1890s in agricultural jobs, from employing nine-tenths of the nation's population to just one-third in 1900, was notable and alarming. Frederick Jackson Turner's declaration that the frontier was closed as of 1893, philosopher William James's criticism of the gilded age capitalists, and Thorstein Veblen's theory of the leisure class[91] set the foundation for the rural-urban bifurcation of "traditional American values and institutions."[92] Rural values were based upon more nativist ideologies. The increased urbanization and immigration in the early twentieth century created paranoia among those "who believed the strength of the nation was derived from 'native stock' in the countryside."[93] Advocates of country life became influential in the rural areas through their presence in the Boy Scouts and Girl Scouts and, most importantly, through the 4-H movement, which still exists in many small towns more than a century later.[94]

The two philosophies of progressivism and country life intermingled in the smaller cities located in central Illinois, such as Champaign-Urbana, Decatur, Danville, and Springfield. Social services, the YMCA and YWCA and other organizations, and the Greek church offered some help with Americanization, language learning, and general education. Still, there were no settlement houses and limited social service agencies, and public schools generally did not offer adult education classes.

From a general survey of the 1940 US federal census, which was the first census to have a category for "Highest Grade of School Completed," it appears that most first-generation Greek male immigrants to central Illinois were literate, meaning they could read and write some Greek and possessed an average eighth grade education or less. From the same census it appears that Greek female immigrants had an average fourth grade education at best. For these early Greek immigrants, the possibility of obtaining a formal education was no longer open to them. Thus, they had to learn on the street, on the job, and from each other. They learned about business from the few who came before them, from the suppliers traveling up and down the highways and railroad lines, and from benefactors in their small towns, who took the time to explain the exigencies of life and business in America and in the Midwest.

Given these obstacles, the Greek immigrant nonetheless scrapped and saved and worked and risked his or her way to success. In the 1940s, Helen Balk offered a historical overview of Greek economic contributions to the United States up to that time. After initially laboring in unskilled, entry-level jobs in factories, railroads, or mines or on farms, Greek immigrants took the money they had saved and invested it in small businesses. It was common for several Greeks to pool their resources and open a variety store, a confectionery, a shoe-shining business, or a flower mart. Balk noted, "Trade in fruit, candy, and flowers can be started with small capital and little experience. The turnover is almost daily. Only small funds are tied up in the business at any one time, but they can gradually be expanded until profitable proportions are reached."[95] Of particular relevance to this study, approximately 90 percent of Greeks in the United States in the 1940s were congregated in urban areas and only 7 percent resided in rural areas; less than 2 percent of these latter, however, were farmers or settled on farms.[96] True to their belief in *philotimo*, Greeks, as a whole, were economically self-sufficient and independent. To become impoverished and dependent upon public aid was inexcusable and would lose one the respect of his or her fellow countrymen. Independent entrepreneurs among first-generation Greeks were of lower-middle-class status but highly respected, as they had risen above their peasant class in Greece.[97] Initially the goal of just making seed money for later investment (and to remit to Greece) meant railroad work in the Midwest and West, shoe shining in Chicago, and peddling. These then led to more established fruit, vegetable, and confectionery shops that were taken over from the Irish and Italians. Hot dog stands morphed into restaurants.[98]

Greeks ventured into fields where they thought there was a niche not already occupied by other ethnic groups. Opportunities were identified through chain migration and networking. After becoming embedded in a business, individuals then broke away from the more established group and settled in smaller towns and cities so that, by the 1940s, "almost all small towns have at least one Greek citizen or representative. Sometimes a Greek who has established himself in a business starts a branch of that business in another city and sends a compatriot to manage it. When the manager has saved sufficient funds he may buy the business and run it for himself."[99]

Naturalization statistics are also good indicators of residential permanence and economic stability. In 1910, approximately 75,000 Greek males over the age of twenty-one were eligible for citizenship. Only 6.6 percent were naturalized, and just 6.1 percent had taken out their first applications. By 1920, approximately 176,000 were eligible for citizenship and 16.8 percent were naturalized, 117,290 were aliens at that time, and 21,451 had applied for their first papers. In 1930, of 174,526 foreign-born Greeks, 65,977 were aliens, 78,059 or 44 percent were citizens, and 25,112 had applied for citizenship.[100] First-generation Greek males were initially ambivalent about remaining in the United States, but once they were married, they found it difficult to leave. Sociologist George A. Kourvetaris observed, "First-generation Greek families were as a rule patriarchal, stable, and closely-knit."[101] Home ownership was another indicator of stability, and in Chicago, 56 percent of first-generation Greeks owned their own home.[102]

Having traveled thousands of miles by ship across the ocean and hundreds of miles across the United States by train, the typical Greek immigrant arrived in Chicago or St. Louis with a limited education, little or no English, and few job skills except perhaps in basic trades. He or she had to learn to adapt and survive in a country unlike any the migrant had ever known, a country that was becoming increasingly hostile to foreign immigrants from eastern and southern Europe.

Next we shall see how some Americans in Chicago and St. Louis tried to help Greek immigrants integrate into the American way of life and how the Greeks initially found their niche in the candy and food business.

CHAPTER 4

FINDING A NICHE IN CHICAGO AND ST. LOUIS

Chicago! Beloved harbor of my hopes.
—Demetrios A. Michalaros, "Chicago,"
Sonnets of an Immigrant

Chicago and St. Louis were the main urban centers to which most first-generation Greeks in the Midwest initially gravitated. Chicago in the early twentieth century had the second largest Greek community in America and thus is an integral thread in the story of Greek immigration to the United States and to central Illinois. Theodore Saloutos wrote extensively about the city in his early work and noted that it was an immigrant destination because work was available and "almost every province of Greece was represented here."[1] Over time, in the late 1800s and early 1900s, as the early Greek immigrants acquired an increased knowledge of the English language and American customs, they sought new opportunities in different work venues and in other cities and towns across the Midwest. But Chicago also became a destination in itself, for Greek immigrants saw it as a place to work, at least for a time, earn some money and learn a trade, meet up with fellow Greeks, and determine whether or not the city was the place to remain.

In Chicago, Greek immigrants primarily settled in the neighborhood that is today known as "Greek Town," along Halsted Street around Hull House, Jane Addams's famous settlement house. As one pillar of community life, Hull House met many of the Greek immigrants' social and cultural needs. Thousands of Greeks utilized the services and classes at Hull House as it became known as the place to go for Greeks to receive assistance and education and to participate in recreational and cultural activities.

Founded in 1889, Hull House fulfilled the needs of Jane Addams as well. She attended Rockford (Illinois) Seminary for Women (and there became friends with my maternal great-grandmother), where she developed a more liberal and progressive world view. After visiting the English settlement house Toynbee Hall in London in June 1888, Jane Addams found her life's work and established Hull House the following year.[2]

Jane Addams's concern for "the Greek immigrants and her espousal of Greek culture . . . quickly endeared her to the Greek community as a patroness of Hellenic arts and ideals. It did much to help solidify ethnic solidarity and pride among the Greek immigrants of Chicago."[3] In May 1930, the Greek government bestowed upon Addams the "Gold Medal of Military Merit," one of its highest awards normally reserved for Greek military officers, in recognition of "her Phil-Hellenic spirit and the encouragement and consideration extended to the Greeks of Chicago for the last forty years." A year later Addams received the Nobel Peace Prize.[4]

Hull House has a distinct place in the history of my family as well. Since I was a child, my non-Greek mother, a product of a Chicago upper-class family of English and German ancestry,[5] shared stories about Jane Addams, a contemporary of my mother's grandmother.[6] As an adolescent, my mother volunteered at Hull House, teaching new immigrants in the early 1930s how to handle American money and finances. Coincidentally, some of my father's Greek relatives also spent time at Hull House on the receiving end of this volunteerism.

Hull House offered a variety of services to Greek (and other) immigrants coming to Chicago, with multiple clubs for both men and women. Sunday evenings found an average of four hundred men attending social functions. There was an active athletic club with an emphasis on wrestling. The Hellenic League for the Molding of Young Men was founded at Hull House in 1910. Partly run by former Greek army officers, one of the many activities of this group was the drilling and training of young Greek men to fight in the Balkan Wars. Educational activities at Hull House included English-language instruction, music, dancing, and crafts as well as lectures from University of Chicago professors and other famous visitors.[7] In 1905 the Greek newspaper the *Greek Star* announced that the first public lectures in Greek, under the auspices of the Pan-Hellenic Society, would be given on Sunday, November 26, at Hull House. This was an all-day affair, after church, and was to end with the singing of the "Hymn of the Turk-Fighting Greek."[8]

Hull House became the "safe place" for Greeks to express themselves and to share accounts of the hostility they encountered daily in Chicago. Overall, they believed this criticism was unfounded due to the historical legacy and traditions Greeks brought with them to America, despite their supposed differences in language and customs.[9] They called for public meetings to be held in English where Americans could learn Greek history. Other meetings, held in Greek, would discuss ways for the immigrants to navigate the various duties and requirements related to being an American. There were usually multiple sessions held during these programs, and newspapers reported that capacity crowds were in attendance. Thus, "due to Jane Addams' ceaseless dedication, Hull House became the spiritual and cultural hearth of the Greek immigrants—their veritable second home."[10]

Addams also spearheaded studies of immigrant living conditions and fought for years to improve housing and raise sanitary standards in poor neighborhoods. In 1909, Grace Abbott, a social worker and director of the League for the Protection of Immigrants, conducted a study of Chicago's Greeks, supported and assisted by Hull House. Abbott's report focused on housing conditions, occupations, and family life and aspirations. Over 1,400 Greeks were interviewed at 350 residences. These residences were not confined to one neighborhood and thus represented a range of family circumstances.[11]

From the 1908 school census in Chicago, Abbott determined that there were 3,521 foreign-born Greeks out of 4,218 Greeks in the city. School censuses were taken in May after the railroad workers had left for the summer, so that population number was probably lower than if it had been taken in the winter. Of the 424 Greeks living near Hull House, 205 hailed from Sparta, 102 from Tripoli, and only 5 from Athens. Thus, as I have noted before, the majority of the immigrants coming to Chicago and then downstate hailed from the central Peloponnese, between Tripoli in the north and Sparta in the south. Abbott herself observed that "most of the Greeks who come to the United States are from the Peloponnesus" and that "most of those who say they came from Sparta and Tripoli have not really lived in those towns but in the country villages near by." She also noted that "like all pioneers who come from various countries of Europe to the United States the Greeks expect to return." And, at this time, of the 790 men over the age of twenty in the study, only 124 had become naturalized citizens.

Greeks settled primarily in the neighborhood of the Nineteenth Ward, where Hull House was located. A Greek Orthodox Church was there with a Greek school, where the focus was on teaching some English, some Greek, "much of the achievements of Hellas, and the obligation that rests on every Greek to rescue Macedonia from the Turks and the Bulgarians." The neighborhood contained a holistic community with the necessary amenities for survival in this new world, such as a bank, a steamship ticket office, multiple coffeehouses for the men, and Hull House, which provided a safety net for families.

Abbott's comments on the character of the new immigrants are telling, for they appear to represent an educated native American's perception rather than stereotypical notions of what Greeks should be like. She wrote, "With the glory of ancient Greece and Byron's romantic championship of the modern Greek in mind, one is shocked when he meets for the first time a representative of that people in the thrifty, good natured, and polite keeper of a fruit-stand or 'shoe-shine parlor.'" She suggested that average Americans expecting Greeks to represent Apollo and Pericles would conclude that "the race has degenerated and constitutes a most undesirable addition to our population." She added, however, that such a characterization would be unfair and that the Greek immigrant should be accepted and assisted in his development in America. Abbott noted that a very large proportion of the Greeks were males and that they were desirable immigrants. Of the almost 1,000 Greek men in her study, 195 were laborers, 178 were peddlers, and approximately 400 were engaged in the food business as waiters or owners of ice-cream parlors or restaurants.

Abbott concluded that once a man had earned some money, perhaps on the railroad, he could then become a peddler or start a business and that "during the short time that he has been in Chicago the Greek has established his reputation as a shrewd business man." Abbott predicted that the Greeks would become great business and professional men because they were willing to do any kind of work. She added that the compulsory education in Greece contributed to over half of those interviewed being literate in Greek, and of those included in her survey, 348 could read and write in English. Greeks were also attending adult education classes at a public school and at Hull House.

Abbott underscored the unsanitary conditions in which many Greeks lived, particularly the single Greek males who inhabited rooms above barns and feed stores. As an example of these cramped and unsanitary conditions, she described a situation where fifteen young peddlers were living above a barn, all unmarried and earning an average of ten dollars per week: "This place is not clean. There is no furniture except beds and a long table in an inside room which serves as a dining-room. Here the boys were found one night between half-past nine and ten o'clock. They had just returned from work and were eating their supper of soup and stewed corn."

In 1915, Natalie Walker, with the Chicago Schools of Civics and Philanthropy, conducted an updated study, which found that within the Hull House neighborhood the Greek population by 1914 had grown to 1,881, "the largest colony of that race in Chicago, and one of the largest in the United States."[12] Describing the neighborhood in which they resided, she noted that the sidewalks were lined with Greek newspapers, bookstores, groceries, saloons, and pool halls, as well as the offices of professional men such as dentists, physicians, and businessmen.

Walker's focus was on sixteen blocks in the Nineteenth Ward, an area in which there were over ten thousand inhabitants. More than half of these people lived in families, approximately 30 percent were children under the age of twelve, and over 10 percent were lodgers, mostly male and somewhat transitory. Within this district the Italians were the largest immigrant group, making up 72 percent of the residents, followed by the Greeks at 13 percent. The remaining 15 percent of the population comprised twenty-seven other nationalities. Most heads of families were either unskilled laborers or employed in various trade occupations, including barbers, bakers, confectioners, cobblers, saloonkeepers, peddlers, and tailors. The women who were employed held jobs as housekeepers, seamstresses, tailoresses, and laundresses.

Walker also reported that only 9 percent of the population owned their homes and that over half had lived in the neighborhood fewer than two years; 25 percent had lived there fewer than six months. The houses themselves were primarily frame buildings and in a slow state of disintegration. They were built to accommodate one family, but many held three or four. She devoted a significant amount of her report to describing specific conditions, such as overcrowding, poor ventilation, inadequate lighting, and the deplorable state of indoor plumbing. Walker noted that despite these conditions, some of the residents endeavored to keep their homes clean and attractive. One Greek painter, while unemployed for a brief time, stenciled the walls of his apartment, and sometimes in good weather, window boxes of flowers could be seen or vegetable gardens were planted.

The story of Georgia Bitzis Pooley (b. January 20, 1849), one of the first Greek women known to have settled in Chicago, offers an insight into the world of immigrant women at the end of the nineteenth century.[13] Georgia Bitzis was educated at an academy in Corfu, where her paternal grandfather had migrated from Epirus. She studied multiple languages in addition to other subjects, a formal education that was rare at the time. She married Peter Pooley (b. 1841) (Pangiotis Poulis), and they arrived in Chicago in 1885. Georgia gave birth to seven children, beginning in 1886. The couple and their children lived in Greek Town along Halstead Street, and Pooley ran a confectionery business next door to their home. He died in 1914.[14]

When Georgia arrived in Chicago, the Greek community was made up of approximately one thousand males who worked long hours for low pay and lived in unsanitary conditions. Georgia was appalled at the deplorable state of these living arrangements and organized some older Greek men and their (mostly) non-Greek wives of Italian and Irish descent to assist with improving the financial and social situations of the young immigrants.[15] She pushed to establish Greek Orthodox Church services, and a Greco-Slavonic Brotherhood was formed in 1885 that provided religious structure. This arrangement eventually resulted in the establishment of the Annunciation Greek Orthodox Church in 1892.[16] Pooley used Hull House as the vehicle to reach out to the Greek women who were, for the most part, illiterate and unemployed. She also encouraged them, their husbands, and their children to learn English.

As we have seen, Hull House was the Greek focal point for recreational, educational, and health programs. Pooley was instrumental in creating the Philoptochos (Friends of the poor) Society of Greek Women at Hull House, which aided indigent Greeks. During this time as well, Pooley encouraged women to leave their homes and—following the establishment of the first Greek school in Chicago in 1905–6 and the Socrates School in 1908—to become more formally educated.[17] During the Second World War, when Pooley was in her nineties, her concern over the suffering of her compatriots in Nazi-occupied Greece drove her to participate in the Greek War Relief Association to raise funds for the homeless and starving back in her homeland.[18] Georgia Pooley lived to be ninety-six years old—she died on June 1, 1945—and clearly left an indelible mark for women in particular but also for young men through her philanthropic endeavors and partnership with Hull House.[19]

Grace Abbott and Natalie Walker both noted that male and female Greek immigrants were employed in a wide range of occupations once settled in Chicago. Although those who were illiterate had limited possibilities for work, there were many more opportunities for those who had some trade skills and education. Recall that the strong sense of *philotimo*, or individual self-esteem, was the catalyst that propelled many Greek immigrants to gravitate toward entrepreneurship as soon as they were able. In a somewhat idealized account, the *Greek Star* offered this version of the process: "According to our investigators, [around 1885] the Greeks began to arrive in Chicago. Unlike other aliens, the Greek did not seek work on the railroads, . . . nor did he attach himself to any other form of day labor. As far as we have been able to learn, he avoided all heavy work and used his brains instead. We find him first associated with Italian merchants as helpers in a fruit store or a market, and because he was thrifty, industrious, and quick to learn, it was not long before he was peddling produce on his own account."[20] Thus, one might rightly conclude that "these street peddlers were the pioneers of Greek-American business."[21]

The earliest Greeks immigrants in Chicago gravitated to fruit and vegetable peddling for a number of reasons. Street vending appealed to the new immigrants because there was a minimal amount of capital expense for start-up, and one did not need to know that much English. Working in the open air and keeping one's own hours was also attractive. In Chicago, the Greeks butted up against the Italian peddlers, who had entered the fruit and vegetable trade earlier and in large numbers. The *Greek Star* credited the Greeks' success to "being at the market with their wagons just a little earlier than their competitors, and thus reaching the trade before their less diligent rivals appeared."[22] An editorial in the Greek newspaper *Loxias* in 1911 took the independent merchant ideal one step further and called for Greek fruit peddlers to buy their fruit from Greece, for "there are no better lemons, pears, citrons and apples than those that come from Greece." The editorial noted that the "Greek steamship lines approve of the idea and the cost of transportation isn't much."[23]

Both the Greek and Italian peddlers were competing with neighborhood merchants, however, and in 1904 the Grocers' Association took action against street peddling and petitioned the city council to either prohibit selling on the streets or to impose a heavy tax. The city council refused the petition, but in 1909 the city raised the license for peddlers from twenty-five dollars to two hundred dollars per year and the Greeks took this increase personally, which galvanized them to become citizens and voters.[24] As late as 1929 Chicago's grocers were still complaining about the competition from Greek fruit and vegetable peddlers and wanted "the Greek leeches off the street."[25]

An increase in peddlers' license fees was not the only problem Greek sellers faced. In 1908 the *Greek Star* noted the formation in that year of a Peddlers' Protective Association by some Greek fruit and vegetable street traders to protect themselves against "shameless and dishonest enforcement [police] officers" who intimidated the peddlers and forced them to pay small fees to avoid harassment and arrest.[26]

It was the confectionery trade where Greeks found the perfect niche at just the right time. From the middle of the nineteenth century, the evolution of the American attraction to sweets, and thus candy, was slow and sporadic. Heretofore, candy had been a luxury item with its consumption limited to those who could afford special treats. It was not until the late 1800s that domestic cookbooks and encyclopedias included sections about candy, candy recipe books appeared, and candy began to be consumed by the masses. George Frye's book for housewives, for example, contained numerous recipes for treats such as caramels, chocolate logs, and cream mint drops.[27] Americans were familiar with chocolate, however, and had been using it in desserts such as cakes, creams, pies, custards, cookies, puddings, syrups, and tarts since the Civil War. With the advent of ice cream and soda fountains, chocolate was used to make syrups, ice creams, and frappés. By century's end, confectioners were using chocolate to create chocolate drops, bonbons, and fudge. The transformation from desserts to individual pieces of delight was complete.[28]

Initially, advertising and marketing focused upon women, who were the main consumers of candy. In May 1895, the "new age of candy" was proclaimed by the Walter M. Lowney Company in Boston, which ran consecutive monthly ads of a smiling young woman enjoying chocolate bonbons. Candy eating by women, particularly white middle-class women, was becoming an increasingly popular, and proper, indulgence.[29]

By 1910, candy consumption had become one of America's leisure time activities.[30] Men and children were now included in marketing strategies. In 1907, Dr. D. C. Abbott, chief of the Pennsylvania State Bureau of Health, asserted that "men have been deserting alcohol for candy, . . . and . . . women have taken up alcohol in place of candy. . . . The appetite for candy and the desire for liquor were now substantially the same."[31] In January 1910, the *New York Times* published a story about America's annual candy bill—estimated at around $500,000,000, up from only $125,000,000 four years before—and noted that Americans ate more candy than all the rest of the world combined. The author bemoaned America's increasing obsession with candy and the excessive amounts of money expended that could be spent in other ways, such as the cost of all New York's subways and river tubes. Interestingly for our study as well, the article also maintained that "the foreign immigrant is the greatest eater of candy in America. In New York fully one-half of the city's candy bill is purchased by the men, women, and children of the east side tenement districts."[32] The inclusion of America's soldiers as candy consumers solidified the total validation of candy as a cultural phenomenon. Since 1899, the US government had included candy, such as chocolate creams and lemon drops, in soldiers' rations. Candy was fed to the soldiers before going into battle, elevating it from a woman's pastime to a manly action. "Real men eating candy on foreign battlefields was too powerful a notion for the American people to ignore," scholar Jane Dusselier points out.[33]

Well before this candy consumption surge, however, pioneer Greek confectioners were busy at work in Chicago. Eleutherios Pelalas of Sparta and Panagiotis Hatzideris of Smyrna established a Chicago candy shop in 1869 and provided employment and confectionery training for some of the early immigrants from Sparta. Pelalas later moved to Springfield, Massachusetts, and opened more stores, while Hatzideris formed a partnership with another associate in New York and sold popular, commercially produced brands of candy. Although Hatzideris eventually returned to Smyrna, his associate formed the Haggis Greek-American Confectionery Company that produced candies in New York, Memphis, and Pittsburg.[34]

Steve Frangos gives much of the credit for the early establishment of Greek candy kitchens in the Midwest to Christos Tsakonas. Tsakonas came from Tsintzina, northeast of Sparta, and immigrated to America in 1873. He initially sold fruit and candy confections from a cart, first in New York and then in Chicago. Around 1875 Tsakonas went back to Greece and returned to Chicago with five young villagers accompanying him. He then trained the five men in the confectionery business. Frangos writes, "Over the rest of his professional life, Tsakonas followed this pattern of establishing then handing over to his extended relatives or fellow patriots the business as he traveled south and east down through Illinois, across Indiana, Ohio, and Pennsylvania into the upper Mohawk Valley of New York state. Once each store was successfully established Tsakonas would sign over part partnership to those he left behind and then move on to found yet another store."[35]

In the mid-1880s, Tsakonas founded the Greek American Fruit Company and began importing pineapples and bananas from Tsintzinian fruit dealers in California and Hawaii. After the fruit arrived in Chicago, Tsakonas distributed it to the confectionery stores. Frangos argues that "it was this collectivist model that impressed later Greek immigrant businessmen. A long over-looked aspect to Greek mercantile success in the United States is their readiness to join networks to purchase in bulk. This form of purchasing raw goods allowed the individual Greek businessman to undersell his local competition." Frangos estimates that Tsakonas brought some 1,000 young Spartans to Chicago between 1870 and 1880.[36] Perhaps one of Tsakonas's protégés was James A. Benekos. He was born in Tsintzina, Greece, and arrived in Chicago in 1881. Here he first learned the confectionery trade and then became a confectionery store proprietor himself and taught others the trade. Benekos later took his candy-making skills to Pennsylvania and New York State.[37]

Chicago soon became "the Acropolis of the Greek-American candy business."[38] The *Greek Star* reported in 1904 that "Chicago, not New York, has the credit of being the city of candy-makers. Practically every corner in Chicago was occupied by a Greek candy store. Seventy percent of the Greek candy-merchants in America were originally citizens of Chicago. After they had learned the trade from fellow-Greeks for whom they worked, and by saving had accumulated enough capital, they bade Chicago farewell and scattered to the four corners of this great country . . . which is sweetened by the exquisite art of the Greek confectioner."[39]

In August 1906, a *Greek Star* editorialist observed that "one out of every four Greeks living in Chicago is in business of some kind, but the Greek confectioner predominates among Greek business men with the restaurateur second." These Greek confectioners, "because of their great numbers and the tremendous business which they do[,] have untold power in their hands, whether they know it or not." And, the writer counseled, "such power and such influence, if properly and wisely used, will bring honor and credit to them and to the Greek community."[40] In a 1915 review of the Greek confectionery business, another Chicago Greek newspaper reported that "the confectionery business employs about fifty thousand Greeks throughout the United States. It is estimated that in every major city—for example, New York or Chicago—there must be over ten thousand candy stores . . . which are a creation of our native Greek sense of beauty. For the establishment of these fine, clean, and luxurious stores, which are an adornment and a thing of beauty on the main streets of our American cities, the Greek confectioners certainly deserve more profits and greater recognition."[41] An editorial a week later in the same paper noted that the majority of Greeks in the confectionery line were from Sparta and the surrounding provinces of Laconia and Arcadia and that they accounted for "almost two-thirds of the confectionery business of Chicago." Together with the ice cream, sodas, cigars, cigarettes, and fresh fruit that were sold in these stores, the "annual sales made by Greek candy stores amount to many millions of dollars. Business conditions in Chicago are determined, to a large extent, by the progress and prosperity of our many enterprises, especially of the Greek-owned confectionery and restaurant businesses."[42]

In his book of recipes, *We Make Our Own Candy*, Theodore Zaffer recounts the poignant story of his father, John, a Chicago Greek immigrant confectioner who first learned the confectionery trade while working for a large candy company. He then worked for a time in a smaller candy shop and learned how to run a business and speak better English. Armed with this knowledge and a collection of recipes, John was prepared when, after three months, the shop's owner was unable to pay him and offered him the store. "By now Dad knew not only how to make the finest quality chocolates, peppermint sticks, and hard candies, but fudges and creams as well. He was becoming very adept to this life in the New World and he immediately took over." Over time, John Zaffer expanded his candy empire and purchased the store of his dreams, which he called the Ting-

A-Ling Chocolate Shoppe after a popular chocolate confection. It was replete with wood carvings on the candy cases, hand-carved booths with marble tables, and cut-glass windows. With the store's opening in the late 1920s, the Ting-A-Ling at 42 West Division Street became reality, and, Zaffer's son recalled, "Now the long hours began." Success followed until the 1929 economic depression in America hit Chicago hard. Zaffer responded by adding food to the confections offered. "Of course, the dinners were of seven courses with a special homemade fudge sundae for dessert, all for thirty-five cents. . . . Instead of the old twelve-hour day it became an eighteen-hour grind." But hard work and long hours made the shop succeed. In 1936 John married Angeline Nicholas, and they had four children, all of whom grew up working in the store at young ages. The shop was open for forty-two years until the family sold out in the 1970s. Theodore's collection offers delightful recipes for candies and ice cream treats as a tribute to his family.[43]

Alexander Rassogianis's history of the Greek entrepreneurial spirit highlights several Greek confectioners and restaurateurs in Chicago who became famous for their delicious treats and the shops they owned. One example is the De Mets Candy Stores. From a small shop on the South Side, this enterprise expanded into one of the most successful chain candy stores in the city. By the mid-1920s De Mets had opened several stores in the Loop. These stores' claim to fame were their caramel nut "turtles," a staple of many confectioneries. Another Greek confectioner success story was that of the Gallanis brothers. Their company, Temptation Chocolates, "became the largest of its kind in the United States by 1921. The chocolates were made in their airy and immaculate plant by expert candy makers who not only used superior ingredients in the products but made a certain type of chocolate that did not melt in warm weather."[44] One Chicago favorite founded in the 1920s and still in business is Margie's Candies. In 1921 Peter George Poulos opened an ice cream parlor on the North Side, and in 1933 his son George Peter Poulos married Margie Michaels. To honor her the store became Margie's Candies.[45] Andrew Kanelos founded Andes Candies also in 1921. Having arrived in the United States at the age of twelve, Kanelos first operated a newspaper stand. Then, while serving in World War I, he saved $1,500 with which he opened his first candy shop. His homemade chocolates enticed enough customers that, over time, the number of stores grew to more than fifty in the metropolitan Chicago area.[46] Andrew's son, George, developed the small but ubiquitous "after-dinner" Andes mints (in the green foil wrapper) known and loved by so many. George also reorganized the business, moving from making assorted chocolates by hand to manufacturing the mints in Delavan, Wisconsin, with nationwide distribution.[47] This company was sold to a Swiss company in 1980 and then to Tootsie Roll Industries in 2000.[48]

One other "larger than life" Greek confectioner springing from Chicago, but who later moved on to Davenport, Iowa, and the Quad Cities, is Charles Bookidis. I include his story as another example of Greek entrepreneurship that manifested itself within one generation, as Bookidis took advantage of the time and opportunities the candy industry had to offer. Bookidis came to America, and Chicago, in 1903, a penniless fifteen-year-old who initially sold newspapers and shined shoes. He went to high school and studied English. While working as a traveling salesman for a few years, he improved his English and learned about the American culture. In 1920 he joined with relatives in Davenport who were already in the retail candy business. They began a manufacturing plant named the Ucanco Candy Company, and from most accounts, it was one of the first companies to make and wrap the penny candy bar.[49] The company's most popular item, the Pecanola Bar, was one of the top sellers of its day. During World War II, Bookidis gave free bars to those who purchased war bonds, which resulted in the sale of more than $9 million worth of bonds.[50] Subsequent generations of the family were not interested in continuing the business, however, and it faded away during the 1960s.

Chicago became the center not only of established small and large confectioneries but of providers of materials and necessities to make candy. Hundreds of salespeople traveled throughout Illinois and the Midwest supplying confectioners who had learned their trade and then moved from Chicago to open new stores in smaller communities. An article in the *Saloniki-Greek Press* in 1915 estimated that "many thousands of Greeks throughout the United States are employed in the manufacture and sale of confectionery products."[51] Greeks also added soda fountains to their shops and became ice cream vendors as well. By the 1930s Liquid Carbonic, the makers and installers of soda fountains across the Midwest, was reporting an increase in sales of almost 57 percent.[52]

An ice cream soda fountain was the perfect complement to the confectionery business, and again the Greeks capitalized on that invention. The soda fountain industry in America began with primitive attempts to disperse "medicinal" carbonated water in pump rooms, drugstores, and coffeehouses in the early 1800s. Chicago's first soda fountain opened in 1848 when the population was around twenty thousand. From the time of the Civil War until the Great Chicago Fire in 1871, there were approximately two hundred soda fountains in operation.[53] By the late 1870s a merchant could buy a small soda fountain outfit for $345 or spend ten times that amount for a larger apparatus.[54]

The transformation of soda fountains from medicinal and utilitarian uses to highly decorative mechanisms for distributing tasty ice cream concoctions led them to become one of the icons of America's social pastime activities.[55] The simple introduction of flavored carbonated water catapulted the soda fountain shop into "a fashionable social center," and these magnificent pumps became an integral part of confectioneries.[56] This affordable aspect of adding variety to one's shop allowed Greek confectioners to be up-to-date with the latest trends in sweets of all kinds.

By 1919 there were enough Greek confectioners in Chicago to organize the Greek Confectioners' Association, with its object to "elucidate the methods and ways of the Confectionary man and thoroughly Americanize the confectionary business."[57] The *Loxias* newspaper proudly proclaimed that there were now "6,000 candy stores under one roof. Bravo!"[58] In 1926 more than two hundred Greek storeowners joined together to pool their resources and help each other with the challenges of doing business in America. The advent of chain drugstores and their soda fountains, lunch counters, and less expensive candies were beginning to cut into their business. In 1929 small Greek businessmen voiced concern about the threat from these chain stores that were a "combination store of candy, grocery, book, tobacco, hardware, jewelry, restaurant and haberdashery stores."[59]

Even though Chicago had at one time perhaps as many as 3,000 Greek-owned candy stores or more, by the mid-1940s that number had dropped to an estimated 350–400 shops with 80 percent of candy manufacturers located within the city center.[60] Certainly the Great Depression severely impacted Greek businesses, but the first-generation Greeks' tenacity and flexibility enabled many of them to survive, some even into the second half of the twentieth century.

The restaurant business was another notable niche for Greeks. A 1909 editorial in *Loxias* claimed that "the largest number of restaurants in Chicago are owned and run by Greeks." The editorialist then warned, however, that "recently a small number of Americans entered this field. . . . The Greek restaurateurs in Chicago must organize immediately. They must protect themselves from this unsuspecting menace. When an American opens up a restaurant, a Greek loses one. . . . Someday all the Greeks will be thrown into the streets."[61] Given the debate over Americanization and Greek identity, it is interesting to note this differentiation between Greeks and "Americans." The article's real aim seemed to be to create anxiety among the Greek restaurant owners so they would attend an organizational meeting. That same year an editorial in the *Greek Star* encouraged the formation of a Greek Restaurant Association, which would include confectioners as well.[62] Greek restaurant owners formed such an association in Chicago less than a year later, and a Greek restaurant employees' union was formed in 1916.[63]

Initially the immigrants served their own communities with native "comfort" food. Indeed, Donna Gabaccia notes that, "lacking cosmopolitan palates, American consumers at the turn of the century bought much of their food from entrepreneurs of their own kind."[64] Greeks quickly adapted, however, to the Americanization of the restaurant business by serving more mainstream foods and fewer dishes that were popular only among themselves. Katherine Turner notes that historically, working-class folks in urban areas ate primarily in cafeterias and small restaurants and from food carts. She estimates that a century ago, half of Chicago's working class ate away from home.[65] The advent of hamburgers, hot dogs, and other "blue plate" types of quick dinners soon became the daily fare in restaurants owned and operated by Greek immigrants. Gabaccia argues that this evolution of Greek food to "American" was driven by customer demand: "Even in cities with substantial immigrant populations, like New York and Chicago, the sale of 'American' foods from lunch stands and diners became a Greek niche." She contends that one key to the growth of Greeks in the restaurant business was the ethnic channeling of wage labor—new immigrants could be hired cheaply, trained, and encouraged to open their own businesses with more migrant labor, thus maintaining the chain. This pattern would be repeated over and over.[66]

As with candy, success in the food business was "hardly the product of a national talent," since most of the Greek immigrants were originally small peasant farmers. A *Greek Star* article examined why Greeks seemed to find their calling as restaurateurs and confectioners, noting that "of the Americans of Greek birth or extraction in this country over 75 percent are in some kind of food business." Thus, the "question naturally arises, Why? Is it racial tendency, instinct, natural ability, or what?" The writer decided "it is hardly racial tendency, for the average Greek immigrant . . . was either a farmer or a shepherd in his native land. If . . . instinct, we think . . . it would certainly have manifested itself before his arrival in this country. As to natural ability, there is no evidence to show that the Greek has any finer 'food-sense' than any other foreign-born Americans."[67]

This article then considered how the Greeks ended up in the food business. As early as 1900, it noted, Greeks in urban areas quickly learned what their customers wanted, and they created profitable businesses not involving burdensome overhead costs or too much reliance on skills that required extensive training. The Greeks' initial success was with the lunch wagon as the means and the factory worker's patronage as the ends. About 1900, "the dinner pail was the emblem of the American workingman, and it seemed likely to continue to be so, because no one had thought of the idea of creating a restaurant to serve this man. Then the Greek came. He drove his lunch wagon at the noon hour to the factory district and was popular from the start. Later he opened restaurants close to the factories, serving food at prices which appealed to the laborers, and eventually he won a reputation for himself."[68]

Having all the family members work in the restaurant or confectionery—as my sister, brother, and I did growing up—also contributed to cost savings, as did leasing space until enough funds were saved to purchase property. In Chicago, groups of peddlers would sometimes band together, pool their resources, and open joint-owned restaurants, illustrating the old adage "When two Greeks meet, they open up a restaurant."[69] In 1909 the *Loxias* editor reflected on this practice and called on confectionery and restaurant owners to follow more professional business practices, remarking sarcastically, "A few Greeks think that the only thing necessary to open a store is $50, $100, or $200 borrowed from Paul or Gus."[70]

Greek restaurant owners also organized to push back against attacks on their success, particularly from more "native" Americans who opposed "foreigners" who prospered in business. One common accusation was that Greek restaurants were unsanitary places.[71] In 1917 the Municipal Council of Chicago passed an act to deny business licenses to aliens who had not applied or gained American citizenship. The city alderman who introduced the act "declared that aliens are rapidly taking the place of the men who enlisted in the army." It was estimated that up to six thousand non-declarants would lose their licenses.[72] The act passed and was to go into effect on May 1, 1918. The Greek newspapers raised an alarm about the consequences of this legislation for Greek merchants in Chicago.[73] Before it took effect, foreign embassies weighed in, raising the question of treaty obligations, as the act threatened "to precipitate international complications," which could bring complaints from the federal government. Chinese businessmen, for example, could not meet the requirements because the Chinese Exclusion Act of 1882 prevented them from becoming citizens. Because of these conflicts with international treaties, the municipal council announced the act would not be enforced, the day before it was to take effect.[74]

Of course, these attacks on Greeks and others not considered "100 percent American" were part of the evolving xenophobia of post–World War I America. In 1919 the American Association of Greek Restaurant Keepers tried to encourage its members to meet these attacks by raising their standards of cooking, sanitation, working conditions, and service. The association also tried to aid its members in complying with local health regulations. It sponsored a program of naturalization, aiming to have all owners and employees become American citizens, and it urged its members to conform to American ideals and institutions.[75] As we will see in chapter 5, however, in the 1920s the attacks were only going to become worse.

Although St. Louis was also an important stop for Greek immigrants who eventually moved to central Illinois, it was not usually a primary destination like Chicago. Gary Mormino cites multiple factors that limited immigration to St. Louis at the end of the 1800s and into the early 1900s. Large numbers of Slavs had settled across the Mississippi River to the east, in Illinois, which evolved into "an industrial matrix of iron foundries, oil refineries, slaughterhouses, and leather tanneries."[76] Land on the Illinois side was less expensive, the government was more compliant regarding the needs of industrialists, the coal was plentiful, and rail and barge access was easy. Factories were built in East St. Louis, Alton, Belleville, and other Illinois cities along the Mississippi. By 1920 there were over 25,000 immigrants in Madison and St. Clair Counties. Granite City had the distinction, prior to 1910, of containing "Hunky Hollow," where lived the largest Bulgarian population in the United States. Nonetheless, Greeks did gravitate to St. Louis, along with Italians, Jews, and Slavs.[77] And Germans made up the largest immigrant community in St. Louis.[78] The 1880 census showed that approximately 30 percent of the St. Louis population was foreign-born.[79]

Immigrant experiences in St. Louis were not unlike those in Chicago. In 1916, sociologist Ruth Crawford submitted a report that attempted to determine the size and ethnic identity of St. Louis's immigrant population. By 1880, according to Crawford, the majority of immigrants were German and Irish settlers with a significant number of people identified as "Bohemians." There was already a large settlement of Italians as well. No Greeks were listed in the 1880 or 1890 censuses, and only 38 in 1900. The 1910 census, however, contained over 1,300 Greeks.[80] In addition, in 1910 there were 15,000 Russians and 7,000 Italians. At the onset of the Balkan War in 1912, the registry of the Greek consul estimated the number of Greeks in the city at 5,000, with 2,000 returning to Greece to fight in the war. World War I caused a brief halt in immigration, but that resumed when the war ended.[81]

The train trip from New York to St. Louis in the early 1900s usually took two days. Immigrants traveling across the country often rode in special train cars no longer used for regular service.[82] In 1913, the St. Louis YMCA hired a "foreign" secretary whose role was to meet all of the immigrant trains and assist settlers in navigating their way through their new environment. On February 9, 1915, the city council passed a municipal ordinance establishing a City Immigration Bureau in St. Louis's Union Station. A former mayor of St. Louis, Bryan Mullanphy, also bequeathed funds to establish the Mullanphy Fund, which was for "the relief of all poor immigrants and travelers, coming to St. Louis on their way 'bona fide' to settle in the West."[83]

The US Immigration Commission report of 1911 included information on immigration to cities such as Chicago, Philadelphia, Boston, and Cleveland but omitted St. Louis.[84] To try to compare St. Louis's immigrant population with similarly sized cities that the Immigration Commission did include, Crawford turned to a study conducted by the Civic League of St. Louis in 1908 on the Jewish and Italian districts in the city. This report, authored by Charlotte Rumbold, revealed overcrowding in dwellings and the transitioning of homes from "native" St. Louisans and Germans to occupation by the Irish, then Jews, then Italians, and then Poles. "The Negroes," the report concludes, "have held on through all the changes." This report also noted that "there are a few Hungarians, a few Roumanians, a few Greeks" in these districts, but "these races . . . have formed colonies elsewhere in the city." Rumbold found that "of the Greeks there are said to be some 3000 in the city, and only about ten families among them; nearly the whole number being unattached men, who help complicate the lodger problem."[85] In her 1916 report Crawford noted that a 1914 study of the Italian/Jewish area of the city found that Greeks and Turks were "fast wedging their way into these same premises vacated by the removal of families to a better part of town."[86] Crawford concluded that "the strong endure their surroundings with but one idea—that of escape" and that immigrants were "inordinately desirous of better surroundings" for themselves over time.

Crawford's investigation led the city to enact a housing code in 1908. Outdoor plumbing was prohibited and running water was to be accessible on every floor of a building. Lighting was to be placed in hallways and a janitor was to be provided for tenements housing eight or more families. Cellar leasing for living space became illegal.

The US Immigration Commission's failure to include St. Louis in its report also meant that Crawford had little data on industries and employment to add to her study. Thus, she asked the St. Louis Business Men's League to submit a list of firms employing large numbers of foreign-born employees. Another list was obtained from the "factory inspector of smaller establishments such as tailors, restaurants, and shoe shining parlors." Thirty-seven firms were then selected as most representative of industries employing foreign labor, and they were asked to submit employment information. Eight refused to participate; three had closed; but twenty-six firms reported employing almost 23,000 people. Seven of the twenty-six businesses indicated that they did not employ many, if any, non-English-speaking immigrants or those from southern Europe.

The breweries, started by Germans, employed over 6,000 men and women in 1913–14. Brewery workers were unionized, which required American citizenship. "For this, among other reasons, Germans and Austrians, who have been in the country for many years, are almost the only types found" in the brewery industries. The shoe industry employed local native whites, Germans, and Irish but, with the influx of southeastern immigrants, engaged Italians in 1900, followed by Bohemians and Poles in 1902, Greeks, Armenians, and a few Turks in 1904, and small numbers of Swedes and Maygars in 1905. There were 212 males and 2 females working in the shoe industry at the time of the study. Greeks and Turks "were found in supply plants where there is packing and heavy work, or in the most unskilled departments, such as heel cutting. They also build heels, which, in the cheap shoe . . . consists of merely sticking the 'lifts' together with cement." Greeks and Italians also worked in the brick and tile industry along with "white labor" and a few blacks. Crawford noted that, for the most part, the neighborhood in which a plant may be located drove the employee composition, but officials agreed that overall, recent immigrants made up only approximately 16 percent of the total employee population.

Greeks in St. Louis, as in Chicago and other urban areas, gravitated to entrepreneurship. The approximately five thousand Greeks living in St. Louis by 1915 had established over four hundred business concerns representing over $1 million worth of investment. These included moving picture theaters, multiple restaurants and confectioneries, coffeehouses, and shoe-shining parlors. Crawford noted that a report by the National Consumers League in 1915 found that the preparation of food in Greek restaurants was "done under sanitary conditions." She then observed that "the shrewd business sense of the Greek made him glad to incorporate any changes suggested by the inspector." These Greek businesses did come under criticism, however, in regard to "moral issues." Young girls from the YWCA hired as waitresses in some Greek restaurants or coffeehouses had suffered negative experiences in the form of sexual advances and mistreatment, "although it is almost impossible to find girls who will produce on the witness stand the evidence necessary for conviction." The coffeehouses, frequented by Greeks themselves, had a "particularly unsavory reputation."

Greek ice cream parlors also came under scrutiny as sites for immoral behavior and even recruiting grounds for white slavery. Bill Ellis argues that ice cream parlors, being still a rather "ethnic novelty" in 1910, were associated with foreignness and that "like other urban interzones such as movie theaters, buses and trains, and amusement parks," they were "culturally dangerous places precisely because they were sites in which ethnic groups met, mingled, held social intercourse, and sought out common forms of entertainment, recreation, and food."[87]

In her study Crawford also noted the existence of the padrone system in St. Louis with regard to the shoe-shining businesses. Crawford reported on one case where thirty-five boys were kept in one loft for the entire winter in horrible conditions. One padrone operating parlors on Sixth and Seventh Streets paid the Greek parents of each boy $150 to send them to St. Louis for work. This money was used to pay wedding dowries for daughters back in Greece. One boy escaped his peonage and testified against his padrone, freeing the padrone's other charges from their sad existence.[88]

A comparison of the Italian community with the Greek migrants in St. Louis during this period suggests that the Italians lived in a distinct enclave, whereas Greeks were dispersed throughout the city as they engaged in the entrepreneurial undertaking of restaurants, confectioneries, shoeshine operations, and entertainment. The St. Louis Greek community was small and could support only a "limited number of endeavors, hence the Greek population became geographically decentralized."[89] The Greeks also had specific business interests, like confectioneries and restaurants, that were catalysts for them to be more mobile, serving as apprentices before moving to the city or moving out of the city to other areas.[90] One study of 167 Greeks who had petitioned for naturalization revealed that only 37 percent had immigrated directly to St. Louis upon their arrival in America. In addition, 75 percent of the Greeks were single males and therefore able to be more transitory.[91]

Immigrant women did work in St. Louis, but specific information about the lives of individual Greek immigrant women is sparse. Perhaps this is because there were relatively few of them or they too had very little formal education and left behind few written records. No doubt they generally remained in the home or assisted in their family restaurants or other private businesses. Gary Ross Mormino observes that the Greek population was the most celibate of the immigrant groups, the men traditionally marrying late in life after establishing themselves in business. The *St. Louis Globe-Democrat* noted, "The early Greek colony was overwhelmingly masculine. One report placed fifteen hundred men and six women at the 1907 Greek Orthodox Easter Services." Even as late as 1930, the St. Louis census showed that Greek males outnumbered Greek females 1,207 to 377.[92]

Two confectioneries stand out in the history of Greeks and St. Louis. The Crown Candy Kitchen was founded in 1913 by Macedonian Greeks Harry Karandzieff and his cousin Pete Jugaloff, from Krystallopigi (old Smardesi), right on the northern border with Albania. This St. Louis institution houses the city's oldest soda fountain and has provided sweet delicacies throughout three generations. Mavrokos Candies, in business until the mid-1980s, was another famous St. Louis confectionery. The founder, John Mavrokos, distributed his confections all over the city, not only in his own shop but in department stores and across the river in East St. Louis. Both places employed fellow immigrants and nurtured those who ventured out on their own.[93]

Chicago and St. Louis were the two main midwestern destinations where recently arrived Greek immigrants began their new lives in America. In these cities they linked up with relatives who had come before, they learned their first words of English, and they became Americanized. Here also they discovered the opportunities available for Greek immigrants in America and where the Greek business niches were. Armed with this knowledge, some of them spread out across the Midwest and started their own businesses in smaller cities and towns. But opening a shop did not guarantee automatic success, nor did it imply acceptance into the local community. As we shall see next, these first-generation Greeks, like my grandfather, faced many more obstacles as they struggled to open and remain in business.

CHAPTER 5

GREEKS VS. GOBLINS

> The Greeks in some towns may not live up to our standards, but the attack was unfair to the Flesor boys who conduct the Candy Kitchen in Tuscola.
>
> —*Tuscola Journal*, December 8, 1923

The backlash against "foreigners" that had been building throughout the war years erupted into openly ugly and vicious attacks in urban centers and small towns across America in the early 1920s. The "anti-hyphen" xenophobia that developed after the Great War had real, often violent, and sometimes tragic consequences for immigrant communities. Helen Zeese Papanikolas recalled how when she was "an immigrant child growing up in eastern Utah in the 1920s . . . the American Legion, the Ku Klux Klan, and daily newspapers vilified immigrants from southern Europe, the Middle East, and Asia."[1] She vividly recalled one popular Klan song, the words for which Klansmen printed on cards and passed out at election polls:

When cotton grows on the fig tree
And alfalfa hangs on the rose
When the aliens run the United States
And the Jews grow a straight nose
When the Pope is praised by everyone
In the Land of Uncle Sam

THEN—the Ku Klux Klan won't
be worth a damn.[2]

"Nativist" Americans accused Greeks (and similarly all southern European immigrants) of being un-American because they established Greek schools, sent great amounts of money back to their homelands, read Greek newspapers in their coffeehouses, became involved in labor strikes, and did not immediately forget their language and customs.[3] In the West the term "Greek" became linked to monikers such as "alien," "troublemaker," "inferior," and "not white."[4] In this chapter we explore how the anti-immigrant policies of the US government and the activities of the Ku Klux Klan and other "100 percent American" organizations affected Greek settlement in America in general, particularly in the Midwest, and how the immigrants resisted these efforts to intimidate them or even drive them away.

As millions of southeastern European immigrants arrived in the late nineteenth and early twentieth centuries, they increasingly became the targets of racist and xenophobic attacks across the country. Greeks were not immune to these outpouring of hatred. One of the earliest large-scale attacks aimed at Greek immigrants in the United States occurred in July 1907 in Roanoke, Virginia. Here "mobs of hundreds" attacked Greeks and their businesses. Although "law and order was quickly restored . . . and not permitted to get out of hand,"[5] this was only a precursor to far worse incidents. In February 1909, anti-Greek riots broke out in South Omaha, Nebraska, after a young Greek immigrant, John Masourides,[6] was accused of killing a policeman. Born near Kalamata, Greece, in the Peloponnese, Masourides had come to America in 1906 when he was thirty-six, leaving behind a wife and four children. He and his brother, Gust, opened a grocery and confectionery in Omaha around 1907–8.[7] From the beginning, however, it was clear that the riots were aimed not at Masourides alone but at the entire Greek community. There were between two thousand and three thousand Greeks in Omaha and South Omaha[8] combined, tending to the higher number in the winter months when the unemployed railroad gangs swelled the population.[9]

South Omaha Greeks were viewed as "clannish, immoral, unclean, and un-American, especially after they had begun to move into the Irish neighborhood."[10] Greek laborers were willing to work for lower wages, and local "native" businessmen faced strong economic competition from a group of successful Greek business entrepreneurs. These Greeks had "established their own grocery stores, confectioneries, shoeshine parlors, and coffee houses," where the language was Greek. The Greeks were thought to keep "very much to themselves," and "few Greeks were interested in learning English because most were waiting for the day they would return to their poor native land to live luxuriously on their American earnings. Often their earnings went home to support their families and to furnish dowries for their daughters and sisters."[11]

Most South Omaha Greeks were young single males, and they were naturally attracted to women in the city. Thus, "too often . . . they insulted, or it was thought they insulted, women as they passed the Greek rooming houses, and brawls between Greeks and the other men of the community were not uncommon."[12]

On the evening of Friday, February 19, John Masourides, in the company of Lillian Breese, a seventeen-year-old woman of "questionable virtue," was confronted by an Irish policeman, Ed Lowery, and arrested for vagrancy. Masourides later testified that on the way to the station he tried to throw away a pistol that he was carrying illegally. Lowery then started firing at him and Masourides returned the fire, killing Lowery and being wounded himself.[13]

The following day, an anti-Greek petition, published in two of South Omaha's three major newspapers, attacked Masourides and the city's Greek community. It characterized the "so-called quarters of the Greeks" as "infested by a vile bunch of filthy Greeks who have attacked our women, insulted pedestrians upon the street, [and] openly maintained gambling dens and many other forms of viciousness."[14] It portrayed Masourides as a Greek whose "life was filled with the brightness of freedom and his pockets filled with the easy gold. He was made to feel that he was a human being. He grew fat in arrogance and pushed aside the native sons or used them as mere rungs of his ladder of success. . . . And when a gentle hand sought to restrain him for a moment from wrong doing his thought was only to kill, to kill craftily. And he killed."[15]

The petition called on city hall "to . . . rid the city of the Greeks, and thereby remove the menacing conditions that threaten the very life and welfare of South Omaha."[16] The anger and hostility toward Greeks stirred up by this yellow journalism led to "a vindictive mob causing injury to scores, inflicting thousands of dollars in personal damages, resulting in the flight of some twelve hundred Greek citizens and immigrants from

South Omaha, and straining the United States' relations with Greece, Austro-Hungary, and the Ottoman Empire, all three of which demanded indemnities and received them."[17]

The Greek community remaining in Omaha rallied, and its leaders urged calmness.[18] They hired an Omaha law firm to represent riot victims and to sue for damages. The Greek diplomatic representative in Washington, DC, sent an attorney to South Omaha to conduct an external investigation and report his findings to the Greek government. The investigation proved that John Masourides was responsible for the policeman's death but was not having an illicit affair with a prostitute because, upon medical examination, Lillian Breese was found "virtuous." Moreover, Breese had in fact simply been giving Masourides English lessons. The attorney concluded that Masourides had no motive for opening fire upon the policeman,[19] and he placed blame on local authorities, citing inflammatory rhetoric from city leaders that fueled the riot. Mary Demos, co-owner of the Demos Brothers Confectionary, later testified that when she called the local police for help during the riot, they "laughed at her over the telephone." Her business was subsequently wrecked and looted by a group of men that she said included police officers.[20] Greek property owners such as Demos had no real recourse in recovering damages to their property. The investigation proffered that such acts of mass violence could happen again and to other European ethnic groups as well.[21] This violent episode triggered at least two other anti-Greek riots, in Kansas City, Kansas, and Dayton, Ohio, within the week.[22]

These anti-Greek riots in 1909 were random events for the time,[23] but the hatred and bigotry unleashed on the Greek immigrants were precursors to the xenophobia that developed during and after the Great War. The anti-immigrant, anti-hyphen, "100 percent Americanism" campaigns encouraged by America's leaders beginning with presidents Theodore Roosevelt and Woodrow Wilson, by America's newspapers, and by various national organizations such as the Ku Klux Klan and the American Legion created a hostile, threatening environment for anyone not of "old stock" and Protestant.

Sparked by the "heroic image of the Reconstruction Klan as the defender of white womanhood and Christian civilization" in D. W. Griffith's 1915 silent film, *The Birth of a Nation,* the Ku Klux Klan was reborn in that year at Stone Mountain, Georgia.[24] But, as one historian of this "second-era" Ku Klux Klan notes, the Klan had very little presence on the American scene until 1921.[25] An in-depth history of the second-era Ku Klux Klan is beyond the scope of this study, but the strong Klan presence in Illinois in the 1920s does deserve some discussion, because its members attacked Greek confectioners, including, as we shall see, my grandfather.[26]

In studying the Klan in the Midwest, it is the "ordinariness" of the organization that is most striking. "Its taste for vigilantism, and well-publicized cases of Klan violence in the 1920s, marked the Ku Klux Klan as sinister and extremist," but there was also an "ordinary, everyday quality to the Klan's presence in the still-dominant white Protestant America of the 1920s."[27] Studies of Klan membership rosters of the second-era Klan "have shown that Klansmen were ordinary Americans representing an occupational cross section of the local white Protestant society" and that "the secret order recruited those who had taken an active part in the community's civil and political affairs."[28] The traditional view of Klan membership is that it "attracted its share of 'low status' individuals, men prone to violence, and many thousands from rural communities and small towns who felt threatened by urban America and might have wished for nothing better than to see the great cities and their 'unAmerican' inhabitants disappear from the landscape." But it is also clear that "the Klan was composed primarily of average citizens representing nearly all parts of America's white Protestant society."[29] As an example of Klan infiltration in Illinois, a study of the Ku Klux Klan in downstate Williamson County, Illinois,[30] found that the "Invisible Empire of Williamson County was in fact highly visible. . . . The *Herrin Semi-Weekly Herald* declared that it was 'owned by Klansmen, edited by Klansmen, and printed by Klansmen.'" The paper's editor, B. E. Green, wrote, "We shall state plainly that we belong to the Klan and we are proud of it, just as proud as we are of our church membership."[31] Indeed, the pastor of the First Christian Church of Mattoon described the Ku Klux Klan as "the 'masculine part' of the Protestant Church in action."[32]

While supposedly secret, "Klan membership in many communities . . . included public officials, Protestant ministers, and ordinary and prominent citizens alike."[33] A typical Klan meeting "resembled one any other organization might hold: minutes read and approved, new members voted in, dues collected, plans laid for a recruitment campaign, an educational discussion, and even niceties: members received thanks [from one member] for having visited him when he was sick, and from the board . . . of a local church for having attended its recent revival meeting with a contribution."[34] And, although the Klan in Indiana had a larger membership, the following description could apply to many small towns in Illinois and across the Midwest: "The Invisible Empire in Indiana was so tightly interwoven into the fabric of society that newspapers regularly advertised Klan events, [and] Klan members there felt comfortable marching in public without masks."[35] Thus, in an advertisement in the southern Illinois *Eldorado Daily Journal*, the Illinois Furniture Company announced the arrival of a "large shipment of K.K.K. Records and Player Rolls" and the "very latest numbers in Klan music." Songs included "Women of the Ku Klux Klan," "Why I Am a Klansman," "Uncle Sammy's Melting Pot," "Midnight Roll Call," "100% March," and "Daddy Swiped Our Last Clean Sheet and Joined the Ku Klux Klan." There was also available a recorded lecture on "America's Task," by Dr. Hiram Evans, Imperial Wizard of the Klan.[36]

The second-era Klan was quite different from the post–Civil War Klan. It was "both a product and a reflection of the distinctive patterns" of post–World War I America. The Klan revival built upon such twentieth-century developments as "mass entertainment and leisure, patriotic voluntary associations, advertising and the go-go economic style of the 1920s."[37] No surprise, then, that the Klan continued to use *The Birth of a Nation* for recruiting into the 1970s. In 1924 a high school near Marion, Illinois, included a full-page Klan advertisement in its yearbook.[38] Moreover, the "cultural balkanization of the urban, industrialized, pluralistic United States into a racialized, religious tribalism . . . produced a greater range of potential enemies for the new Klan to confront."[39]

Klan membership appealed to those in downstate Illinois and in other small towns in the Midwest who were middle-class, nativist, nationalist, and Protestant and who longed for some active response to the new immigrants.[40] The aftermath of World War I "generated a lingering postwar suspicion of labor unionists, political radicals, recent immigrants, Southern black migrants, and other Americans then considered marginal."[41] Becoming a Klan member was, for many, equated with Americanism and not aligned with any exclusionary doctrine or discrimination.[42] Congressional hearings on the Klan in 1921 showed, however, that

> a central core of beliefs . . . held the Klan together. As the organization's constitution and other Imperial documents indicate, Klansmen advocated "pure Americanism" and "the faithful maintenance of White Su-

premacy." The Klan viewed with suspicion those who owed "allegiance of any nature or degree to any foreign Government, nation, institution, sect, ruler, person, or people," and proudly asserted that Anglo-Saxons were "the only race that has ever proved its ability and supremacy and its determination to progress under any and all conditions and handicaps." The order also advocated strict enforcement of the law, particularly the various prohibition statutes.[43]

One might consider another view as well, though, one that argues against "the traditional view of the Klan as an extremist organization devoted almost exclusively to the persecution of Catholics, Jews, immigrants and blacks." While "there can be no argument that the Klan's racist, anti-Catholic, anti-Semitic ideology was offensive and threatening to many Americans during the 1920s . . . to describe such ideas as extremist and pathological . . . is to paint a rather distorted picture of mainstream racial and ethnic attitudes." One must also recognize that "blatantly discriminatory immigration restrictions were enacted during this time not by the Ku Klux Klan, but by a bipartisan coalition in the United States Congress. And if anti-Catholicism was the code of radical fringe groups, it was also the most important single factor in Herbert Hoover's victory in the presidential election of 1928."[44]

Moreover, in many places, like Indiana, where the Klan was most popular, racial and ethnic minorities were tiny or even nonexistent. To focus on the Klansman's anxiety over the distant urban immigrant is to "preclude the possibility that local events and circumstances played any important part in the Klan's popularity."[45] This position asks that one look beyond the blatantly racist and bigoted behavior and activities of the Klan as reasons for Klan membership and focus on the group's economic and political messages. After studying Indiana membership data, one author concluded that while Klan leaders would not have "promoted the supremacy of white, Protestant, '100 percent Americanism' if these cultural appeals were not meaningful to the people they intended to recruit," the Klan's economic and political rhetoric also must be considered.[46] In fact, "the Klan's rise is best understood as a response to the sudden devaluation in the economic and political 'purchasing power' of the Klan's recruits." The Klan used its cultural appeals to the anti-immigrant, anti–African American, anti-Catholic prejudices in its targeted membership "to stimulate demand for what its members had to offer in exchange with economic and political markets. It also used cultural attacks to restrict the supply of competitors."[47] Interestingly, however, while Protestantism was a key component of these cultural appeals, more than one-third to one-half of Klan membership comprised Protestants without a religious "home."[48]

There was also a social aspect to the Klan that gave its members, particularly those in rural areas and small towns, a chance to come together, socialize, and be part of a larger movement. "Spectacle was a device for establishing the Klan as a mysterious presence and for winning converts to the Invisible Empire, but it was also a continuing tool for community-building among white Protestants," notes historian Thomas R. Pegram.[49] Public demonstrations, such as visits to Protestant churches and cross burnings, were augmented by elaborate parades and speeches.[50] During the "great summer of Illini Klandom," in 1923, "the members turned out by the tens of thousands for a succession of enormous outdoor Klan rallies at Joliet, Rockford, Springfield, Oak Forest, and Urbana. Zenith Klan No. 56 of Champaign-Urbana bought the old Illinois Theater, which seated over a thousand, to use as a Klavern." When Hiram Evans, the Klan's Imperial Wizard, came to Champaign-Urbana that fall, "a mammoth open meeting was staged in the University of Illinois armory."[51] At one gathering in Kokomo, Indiana, on July 4, 1923, there were at least fifty thousand people gathered who were entertained with "boxing matches, a pie-eating contest, a beautiful baby competition, a parade featuring Klansmen towering on twelve-foot stilts, and everywhere the extravagant display of American flags."[52] In Muncie, Indiana, "one Jewish man . . . took his son to watch Klan parades for their entertainment value."[53] These public gatherings were akin to those held in the previous decade by Progressives, determined to invite membership with music, picnics, and speeches.[54] By the mid-1920s approximately four million men and women had enlisted as members of the Klan.[55]

White Protestant women joined the Women of the Ku Klux Klan, as many as half a million or more in the 1920s. In some states women made up nearly half of the Klan membership.[56] Klan women "drew on familial and community ties—traditions of church suppers, kin reunions, and social celebrations—to circulate the Klan's message of racial, religious, and national bigotry."[57] Factors that made the Klan appealing to women at this juncture in American history included the recent passage of woman suffrage and wide-reaching participation in the temperance movement.[58] These activities empowered women, and they looked to the Klan as another vehicle for the expression of agency. Some Klan chapters became social service agencies for young women seeking employment and housing in urban areas while making them swear never to vote for those who were not American-born, white, or Protestant or to consider such for positions as teachers, governesses, or instructors of children.[59]

Women seemed ready for a public sphere of activity and power, and by November 1923, thirty-six states had established chapters of the Women of the Ku Klux Klan.[60] Although the Klanswomen aligned themselves with the national KKK tenets, they also articulated their own agenda to achieve equality with men for white Protestant women.[61] In time, however, the women's Klan chapters, especially in Indiana, collapsed through internal strife.[62] With the general decline of the Klan in the Midwest, women's Klan membership also ebbed considerably by 1928.[63]

Leonard Moore, in a review essay of major studies of the Klan from the 1920s to 1990, concludes that "a single term may not be adequate as a label for the 1920s Klan, but if a single label is needed . . . 'populist' seems best. Certainly it is better than 'extremist,' 'terrorist,' 'nativist,' or the other terms historians have traditionally employed." Moore argues that

> the Klan appears to have acted as a kind of interest group for the average white Protestant who believed that his values should be dominant in American society. Prohibition represented the great symbol of that desire, and support for Prohibition seemed to bond together the nation's Klansmen more tightly than any other single issue. The crisis of Prohibition enforcement, in fact, may have been the most powerful catalyst of the Klan movement and during the early 1920's the Klan may have been the most popular means of expressing support for the Noble Experiment. . . . The reformist attacks on political and economic elites . . . make the term "populist" appear particularly credible. . . . The Klan became a means through which average citizens could resist elite political domination and attempt to make local and even state governments more responsive to popular interests. . . . The Klansmen were too much a part of America's social mainstream to be dismissed as an extremist aberration. Their movement spoke to too many social and political concerns to be understood through ideology alone.[64]

The Klan was not allowed, however, to carry on its activities in a vacuum. Anti-Klan activists challenged the Klan through the law and in the courts, with public exposure of Klan members, by staging boycotts, by forming organizations to oppose the Klan, and sometimes with violence.

"Even in an age when assumptions of white supremacy, unembarrassed ethnic chauvinism, and religious intolerance toward Catholics and Jews were commonplace, the Klan's expression of these themes was deemed incendiary and objectionable," observes Pegram.[65]

In Chicago during the early 1920s, the Invisible Empire began to come under continuous attack. One of the key organizations leading the attack on the Klan was the American Unity League (AUL). Founded in Chicago in 1922 with Patrick O'Donnell, a criminal lawyer and Irish Catholic, as its chair, the AUL was dedicated to the eradication of the Ku Klux Klan not only in Chicago but nationally.[66] The AUL's newspaper, *Tolerance*, boldly proclaimed, "We HATE the Ku Klux Klan and everything it stands for," and its goal was to "smash the Invisible Empire."[67] It advocated "true Americanism" as opposed to the Klan's "pure Americanism" and sought to be inclusive of Catholics, African Americans, the foreign born, and Jews. The AUL did not always receive the full cooperation or participation of those groups, however, and its initial supporters were priests, allowing the Klan to brand the organization as "an Irish, Roman Catholic clique."[68]

The American Unity League was effective because it "infiltrated the Klan, staged break-ins at Klan offices and gathered information supplied by disillusioned former Klansmen."[69] It then published the names, addresses, and occupations of thousands of Klansmen in Chicago and elsewhere in *Tolerance*,[70] often under the heading "Who's Who in Nightgowns."[71] O'Donnell boasted in 1923 that the AUL had "exposed over 23,000 Klan members in Illinois and Indiana alone."[72] With Klan identities now revealed in states across the Midwest, the AUL organized massive boycotts. Once a Chicago bank president, Augustus E. Olson, was exposed as a Klan member, for example, the resulting boycott led to a dramatic decline in deposits and Olson's resignation from the Klan.[73] Klansmen also found themselves being barred from grand jury duty, aldermen called for the firing of city employees who belonged to the Klan, and some Klansmen's business establishments were bombed.[74] A *New York Times* article in November 1922 began, "To be a member of the Ku Klux Klan in Illinois, particularly in Chicago, these days is to invite social ostracism and business disaster. The fact is slowly but surely being driven into the minds of the 50,000 or so members of the secret organization in and around this city."[75] The *Chicago Defender* newspaper also publicly engaged in vanquishing the Klan, rallying voters to vote against a Klan candidate.[76]

The American Unity League went bankrupt within a year of its founding, primarily because of the many lawsuits filed against it.[77] But other anti-Klan organizations took its place, and across the north these groups began to use "considerable violence . . . far more violence than the Klan had ever employed in the North."[78] In April 1923, for example, "a bomb destroyed the office of *Dawn*, the chief organ of the Chicago-area Klan."[79] Although the Klan in Chicago and elsewhere appeared to be on the rise in 1923, it was actually at its zenith.[80] Eventually its activities waned, and "by early 1925, many members who had rushed to join were rushing to get out."[81]

Kenneth Jackson asserts that the Chicago KKK met its demise due to internal disputes but also from the efforts of the American Unity League and its publication of membership lists.[82] Another historian, David Goldberg, contends that the Klan's downfall came about partly as a result of the violence used against it. He writes, "[The Klan] attracted its share of hatemongers, but for the most part, its rank and file consisted of ordinary, naive, fearful, gullible citizens. These were not the American equivalent of Blackshirts or Brownshirts . . . anxious to spill blood in the streets. . . . Intimidated by the violence and unprepared to respond in kind, the Klan discovered that it could not hope to organize in any community where a significant number of those ineligible to join the KKK had decided to take the law into their own hands."[83] Although "deep-seated and powerful social movements do not generally fall apart overnight," a combination of factors led by 1926 to the Klan having only a token presence in the North.[84]

The Ku Klux Klan had mixed success in Illinois during the four or so years—1922 to 1926—when it was most active. Kenneth Jackson's innovative work, *The Ku Klux Klan in the City, 1915–1930*, focuses on Klan development and activities in urban areas. It was groundbreaking in that Jackson challenged the traditional interpretation, prevalent since the 1920s, of the Klan as primarily a small-town, rural phenomenon, consisting largely of illiterate, "backward" rustics. He demonstrated that while Klan membership numbers were divided about equally between rural and urban areas, state headquarters were nearly always located in urban areas, and from here Klan leaders directed activities for the rest of the state.[85]

In Chicago the Klan was most successful in recruiting members on the south side of the city, drawing support "primarily from lower echelon white-collar workers, small businessmen, and semi-skilled laborers, many of whom resented the economic, social and political pressure of the city's

Catholics and second-generation immigrants, and were equally alarmed by the rapid influx of Negroes."[86] Jackson found that Chicago Masons "joined the organization by the hundreds, and Masonic Halls were frequently utilized for Klan meetings."[87] There were eighteen Klans operating in the city and twelve outside of Cook County by 1922.[88] Their influence went all the way to the governor's election in 1924, when they claimed credit for the reelection of Governor Len Small.[89] By 1925, however, as we have seen, "the Invisible Empire was virtually inert in Chicago."[90]

Despite its being a main Klan headquarters of the Grand Goblin of the Domain of the Mississippi Valley and home to two King Kleagles, the Invisible Empire never got traction in St. Louis. It got off to a bad start when, shortly after organizing in 1922, the Klan made a $10,000 pledge to a Boy Scout troop and then raised only $1,000. Membership was never more than two thousand, and between 1915 and 1944, total Klan membership in St. Louis totaled only five thousand.[91]

In Illinois on the whole, "the Klan did better downstate," particularly in the southern part. Here, "for generations, the mountain people of Kentucky and Tennessee" had peopled the land, "forming a backwater of rural, fundamentalist, old-stock America." After coal was discovered in the 1890s, "a flood of foreigners began to pour in," opening the way for Klan activity by citizens "concerned about foreigners, Roman Catholicism, saloons and roadhouses, gambling, prostitution, and widespread public corruption."[92] Bootlegging contributed to the "downstate" Illinois perception that bootleggers and gambling operators, spawned from Chicago's "underworld" of foreign influence, were working in alliance with Catholics to infiltrate rural areas. The Klan played on these perceptions, portraying members as the "self-appointed defenders of public morality."[93] In addition, "an almost endemic struggle raged between the unions and anti-labor mine owners."[94]

Anti-immigrant prejudice was widespread in southern Illinois even before the rise of the Klan, and so were acts of mob violence against immigrants.[95] From 1914 to 1920 there were several attacks on Italian migrants in southern Illinois. In Willisville in October 1914, for example, Italian poolroom operator Albert Piazzia and his brother got into a scuffle with two "Americans." Guns were drawn; the brother was killed and the two Americans wounded. As Albert was being transferred from the local jail to the county jail, a mob stopped the party and shot Piazza several times, killing him. In nearby Johnston City in June 1915, Joseph Stranzo, an

Italian mine worker, was accused of killing a local mine superintendent's father-in-law. Upwards of a thousand residents broke into the jail, seized Stranzo, and hanged him.[96] In August 1920, West Frankfort witnessed three days and nights of mob rioting, directed at the local Italian population. This resulted in tens of thousands of dollars of damage, mainly by fire; hundreds of Italian Americans being made homeless; some deaths; and scores injured. After the West Frankfort incident, at least 250 Italians departed for St. Louis.[97]

Once the Klan started recruiting in southern Illinois, it found a receptive audience. Williamson County, in particular, a coal mining region fewer than a hundred miles from St. Louis with a long history of violence, had a strong KKK presence. The Klan here vowed to eradicate bootlegging and gambling and focused upon Italian coal miners. Klan antipathy toward the Italians was neatly summarized as opposition to "chianti, Catholicism, and crime."[98] Williamson County was the scene of the famous "Herrin Massacre" in June 1922, in which union miners killed nineteen of fifty strikebreakers and nine mine guards. Three union miners also died. It was also, from December 1923 to April 1926, the site of a "civil war in which Klan and anti-Klan factions engaged in fierce battles over Prohibition enforcement on the streets as well as at the polls."[99] Both the National Guard and state troopers were called in to maintain order, but the battles continued. They ended with the "election day riot" of April 13, 1926, won by the bootleggers, putting "the hooded organization out of existence in 'Bloody Williamson'" County.[100] The end of the Klan did nothing, however, to lessen anti-immigrant sentiments.[101]

Violence continued in southern Illinois. In *Sundown Towns: A Hidden Dimension of American Racism*, James Loewen asserts that in the 1920s, coal miners in Zeigler, Illinois, drove all the Greek migrants out of town at gunpoint, but only for two days, and also forced all of the African Americans out. He contends that African Americans are still unwelcome into the twenty-first century.[102] He maintains that these "sundown towns," which seek the total exclusion of African Americans, in particular, or at least for them to be out of town by sundown, "provided fertile recruiting fields for the Ku Klux Klan in the 1920s and still do today."[103]

The end to the bloody violence in Williamson County and elsewhere "failed to ameliorate the economic misery in southern Illinois." In one scholar's words, "King Coal had simply collapsed."[104] Hundreds of Italians fled southern Illinois to St. Louis as a result of the attacks and the economic hardships. It appears the Italians rejoined family members in the city, demonstrating internal migration from rural areas in America back to an urban setting. During the 1920s and 1930s as much as 15 percent of St. Louis's Italian population growth was the direct result of Italian migration from central and southern Illinois. As one example, one man immigrated from Buscate, Lombardy, in Italy to St. Louis, then to Herrin, Illinois, in 1905 to be a miner. He then moved to Christopher, Illinois, in 1912, to Belleville, Illinois, in 1920, and back to St. Louis that same year.[105]

Greek communities across the heartland, and indeed across America, were frequent targets for the overt racism, bigotry, and violence directed at African Americans, Jews, and eastern and southern European immigrants in the mid-1920s. On a national level, Greeks responded to the Klan by forming the American Hellenic Educational Progressive Association, but individual Greeks in cities and towns across America all had to deal with racial prejudice in their own way. Some closed their stores and returned to Greece. Others, as had happened in Omaha in 1909, simply moved to another city or state where the climate was less threatening.

Between the two World Wars, the "greasy spoon Greeks" were very often "attacked or at the least frequently harassed by those around them."[106] Studies have shown that "many Greek-owned confectionaries and restaurants failed financially or were sold at sacrificial prices to non-Greeks because of boycotts instigated by the Klan. Greek establishments doing as much as $500 to $1000 a day business, especially in the South and Midwest, dropped to as little as $25 a day. The only recourse was to sell or close. The Klan often bolstered its boycotts by openly threatening or attacking customers entering and leaving."[107]

Many incidents and references from Klan speeches and literature underscore the fact that the Klan targeted Greeks. A Klan spokesman in Spokane called for Mexicans and Greeks to "be sent back to where they came from so that white supremacy and the purity of Americans could be preserved." He noted that a Klan affiliate, the Royal Riders of the Red Robe, was a patriotic organization for "approved naturalized citizens unluckily born outside the United States," but immigrants from Greece, Italy, and the Balkans were not eligible to join.[108] At a massive rally attended by several thousand Klan members near Creve Coeur Lake outside of St. Louis in May 1923, the main speaker was the Reverend C. C. Crawford, pastor of the Fourth Christian Church in St. Louis. Dressed in full Klan attire, Crawford condemned immigration, "using as an example the establishment of Greek restaurants in recent years. He said he hoped the time would come when no restaurants in this country were operated by Greeks."[109] At another rally in Maplewood, also near St. Louis, the Reverend James Dunleavy, a KKK organizer, told how "the Pope planned to control the next presidential election; how Jews controlled the newspapers; [and] how white women were not safe working in Greek candy kitchens." He added that "our women, forced to work in their candy kitchens, are unsafe if they remain three weeks."[110]

One of the common accusations made about Greeks was that they were involved in white slavery, run through their restaurants and candy kitchens. A particularly spurious and vicious attack on Greeks during these years appeared in *The Fraternalist*, a newspaper devoted to news from fraternal and secret organizations that was filled with positive stories about the Klan. In January 1925 the newspaper published a long article titled "Greeks Are Worst Criminals. Greek Law Violators Out Number Negroes 2 to 1, Population Considered." The article, which took nearly four full columns over two pages, accused Greeks of white slavery. Supposedly using Chicago police records, the paper declared, "Greeks are by far the most criminal race on earth." Regarding white slavery, the paper claimed that Greek immigrants had no love or respect for womanhood and that, although they constituted only about one-third of 1 percent of Chicago's population, they controlled prostitution there. And how was this traffic conducted? "Logically then, the Greek restaurants and ice cream parlors are the recruiting stations of the white slave traffic." Moreover, the paper noted, when the police raided the Greek establishments, the traffickers simply moved the business to Greek restaurants or ice cream parlors in other cities. These and other similar attacks made Greeks the easy targets of Klan violence.[111]

George Leber contends that violence against Greeks was greatest in the South. "Young Greek men working in the kitchens of restaurants in the South were taken, along with black workers, by the Ku Klux Klan on lynching 'parties' into the woods, where the Greeks were roughed up and released, but the blacks were lynched." Leber says he has no evidence that any Greeks were ever lynched by the Klan, but "they were intimidated and told to leave town." Another favorite Klan warning directed at the Greeks was to not be "seen with a white girl."[112] One specific example of these attacks occurred in Guntersville, Alabama, where, one night in July 1924, a band of masked men wearing Klan regalia abducted Greek restaurant proprietor Martin Zuckas. They took him to a nearby woods and warned him to "be out of town in two weeks." Zuckas left town, but only to travel to Washington, DC, where he met with the Greek minister to the United States to ask for protection.[113] It seems Zuckas then did leave Alabama, but he may have relocated to Atlanta, where he owned, or at least worked in, a restaurant in 1926.[114]

As Klan and other anti-immigrant organizations' violent attacks on Greek immigrants increased, Greek leaders felt a need to respond, and on July 26, 1922, they formed the American Hellenic Educational Progressive Association (or Order of AHEPA).[115] Through no coincidence, their founding meeting was held in Atlanta, home of the national Imperial Headquarters of the Klan.[116] The critical figure in this history is George Poulos, who "was employed by the Imperial Palace of the Ku Klux Klan [in Atlanta] in a confidential capacity and . . . was present and participated in its secret meetings and conferences. . . . In this capacity he was in a position to have advanced knowledge of the plots and plans of the clans. . . . This advance information was constantly used to the best advantage of the unsuspecting victims."[117] It appears that Poulos's "contact with the Klan was nothing short of terrifying" and that while his "role as Klan consularrie [*sic*] is never explained in detail, . . . his role at the Palace was unquestionably as spy and not a fellow conspirator."[118]

Poulos and the other AHEPA founders had to frame a response to this "wave of hostility which had almost drowned them" and chose "to create a patriotic fraternal order espousing undivided loyalty to the United States, American citizenship, proficiency in English, active participation in the civic mainstream, economic stability, social unity, and the pursuit of education."[119] Through their knowledge of business corporations and how "fraternal organizations can link lone individuals to a wider network of other Americans," the Greek founders of AHEPA "sought to gain moral and political influence through collective efforts." Thus, "from this perspective the Greeks are far from hapless peasants bumbling about America."[120] AHEPA became then "the most influential Greek fraternal organization in the history of the United States."[121] And, as the second-era Klan died away at the end of the 1920s, AHEPA remained and remains active today supporting Greek American causes, communities, and charities. AHEPA positions were not without controversy, of course, as they placed the organization squarely in the middle of the debate discussed previously over the desire to maintain one's culture and heritage or to drop the hyphen and become "100 percent American." But as the *Greek News* reminded its readers in 1935, its original purpose was "to protect the Greeks from the attacks of the K.K.K."[122]

Many Greeks, individually, simply chose to stay where they were and resist. Steve Frangos recounts a personal anecdote about one such Greek family. While a student at Indiana University, Bloomington, in the early 1980s, he met an elderly Greek woman who said her father had owned a candy store in the town. She told him that when she was a little girl, "every Friday night the Ku Klux Klan would ride horses around and around the main square in a torch light parade. Many times the windows in her parents' store were broken." They refused to close, however. This woman was almost certainly the daughter of Gus C. Poolitsan, Catherine, who was seven in 1920. Gus, born in Sparta around 1880, operated a candy store, along with his wife, Angelika (Zaharkos), and their four children. Besides the candy store, Poolitsan also owned the iconic Book-Nook, a student hangout where Hoagy Carmichael (an IU alum) wrote the classic melody "Stardust."[123]

Another wonderful story of Greek confectioners resisting the Klan, although somewhat anecdotal for now, took place in Sac City, Iowa. It seems that in the hot summer of 1924, as the Sac County Fair was in progress, two Greek cousins, who may have been Daniel and James G. Cosman,[124] were celebrating the grand opening of their new Kandy Kitchen on Main Street. In protest, hooded Klansmen stood on the street and surrounded the building, intending to block anyone from entering. The Greeks then announced they were offering free ice cream to children, so Sac City's youngest began to wiggle their way through the line of Klansmen, and their parents of course followed. Helpless to stop them, the Klansmen drifted away.[125]

My grandfather also resisted the Klan, in a unique and humorous way. By the mid-1920s Gus had already been in business in Tuscola for twenty years, but still not everyone accepted him as a rightful member of the community. Here is how I learned about the Ku Klux Klan and how our family became a target.

Growing up I worked every day at the Candy Kitchen after school. If we did not have a scheduled official school activity, my brother, sister, and I had to be at the store at 4:00 p.m., without excuse. One day I was working behind the soda fountain with my father mixing and serving phosphates and sodas to our customers. My grandfather (by then in his eighties) was in his usual spot at the end of the counter in the corner sitting on top of two cardboard cartons of Coca-Cola syrup. An elderly man came in for refreshment. He called out to my grandfather with a wave and a "Hello, Gus!" My grandfather replied, "Hello," and then inserted a Greek moniker for this man, who beamed at being specially recognized. This was a Greek word I did not know, so I asked my father what name Grandfather was calling our customer. My father took my arm and led me to the back of the store so no one could hear us. "It means 'horse's ass' in Greek," he whispered. So I queried why Grandfather would call anyone by that name, and my father explained that this man had been in the Ku Klux Klan and had participated in burning a cross in Grandfather's yard and in the downtown area. So, after pondering this for a while, and knowing a bit about the KKK, I concluded with great satisfaction that not only had Grandfather retaliated in his very personal way every day for almost fifty years, sometimes twice a day, but he had also taken this man's money while doing it. The man never asked Gus what the name meant; he just assumed it was a special Greek nickname. Indeed. And I decided, good for Grandfather. Of course, we were all then complicit participants in this behavior, we never questioned it, and we never said a word about it.

The *Tuscola Journal* began reporting about Ku Klux Klan activities nationally as early as 1921, when it ran a story about Virginia schoolteachers asking children to donate a hen or some eggs in exchange for Anti-Tuberculosis Christmas Seals. If they donated a hen, they could become charter members in the KKK, and if they gave eggs, they could become active members. The article left the impression that this was an innocuous activity that engaged whole families.[126] Although the newspaper did generally portray the Klan as a "sinister organization," that did not prevent it from continuing to run stories about its activities.[127] It was not until around 1923 that the KKK became overtly active in central Illinois.

Although Tuscola is the county seat, local lore has placed the locus of Klan activity in Douglas County in Atwood, a small town directly west of Tuscola on Route 36. Unfortunately there are few primary records of the Klan's activities in Douglas County in general, but there was plenty of newspaper coverage of them. Article after article reported how the organization attracted hundreds to its rallies and filled its membership rolls with its unique blend of midwestern racism, bigotry, community "values," anti-corruption and bootlegging crusades, "100 percent Americanism," and showmanship. The *Tuscola Journal* reported, after a large cross was burned in Ervin Park north of town, that it was "generally known that there is a large Klan of Ku Klux followers in and around Tuscola" and that meetings were held in large halls and outdoors in fields, especially in nicer weather.[128] Villa Grove is a town in Douglas County northeast of Tuscola, and in July 1923 a local church hosted a religious revival there.

At one point, in a display of typical Ku Klux Klan bravado, thirteen men in white robes marched down the church aisle and handed the speaker a sealed envelope containing a twenty-five-dollar offering from the Klan.[129]

The Mattoon Klan chapter in Coles County also appeared to have a large membership and notable influence in central Illinois. The local paper reported on multiple public Klan demonstrations there, including one on a Saturday night in May 1923, where more than five hundred hooded members walked down Broadway Street between 9:00 and 10:00 p.m. Thousands lined the route to view the parade, and banners proudly proclaiming "100 Per Cent American" were on display all around. Showing their support, members of the Champaign Klan sent a letter to their fellow Klansmen in Mattoon indicating that they shared the goal of eradicating the area of bootleggers and the need to "clean up the city." Cars in the parade hailed from Paris, Newton, Champaign-Urbana, and Shelbyville, reflecting the multicounty participation in the rally.[130] Also in July 1923, the Mattoon newspaper ran an informational piece, not on the Klan but on the plight of thousands of Greek immigrants and other natives from "Asia" attempting to enter the country at Ellis Island. The article noted how the Greek immigrant quota had been exhausted already for the year.[131]

Klan rallies were held throughout the summer of 1923 across central Illinois. At the end of July a major Klan rally took place in Paris, Illinois, in Edgar County. Thousands of visitors were on hand to witness or participate in an all-day Klan celebration at the county fairgrounds. The minister of the First Baptist Church gave the welcome address before the Universalist Church minister spoke briefly.[132] Five thousand people gathered in Villa Grove in August to hear Reverend McMahan of Mattoon, who had become a noted regional Klan leader and spokesperson for the Klan's xenophobic and supremacist agenda. McMahan spoke for two hours, "explaining to the crowd the mysteries of the Klan as understood by him."[133] The humorously titled article concluded with a notice that the next Klan meeting would be held in Tuscola, where a speaker would be expounding upon the ideals of the KKK and teaching about 100 percent Americanism.[134]

As promised, the Klan held a rally in Tuscola the following week, and it was a large one.[135] The rally began on Saturday night with a "bomb explosion" at the west end of Sale Street. The explosion came from the lighting of a huge "fiery Cross" that blazed in the night sky and was witnessed by a large crowd, including approximately five hundred carloads of "country people" who had come to Tuscola to shop. The next day, on Sunday afternoon at the Frahm grove south of Tuscola, hundreds of automobiles filled the park and surrounding roadsides. An estimated five thousand people gathered to hear two Christian ministers, James "Jack" Masters, formerly of Danville, and the Reverend Mr. Hollingsworth of Villa Grove, offer the benediction, followed by speeches. The newspaper reporter remarked that "who called the meeting, who sponsored it, and who were the moving spirits remained a mystery." "Pierson's band" from Mattoon provided the music.

The Reverend Hollingsworth, the featured speaker, was "a practiced talker and threw off his coat and then jerked his collar and tie away." He was a "young man and rather given to imitating the Reverend Billy Sunday. Stomping his feet, clinching his fists, and slinging slang, he startled his audience from the first." "The Klan," the speaker railed, "stands for the election of judges, and for the complete separation of the white and the colored people in church and school, and in marriage."

The next speaker, the minister Jack Masters, was particularly energetic. He began with an attack on the Catholic Church that "was vitriolic. He complained that Woodrow Wilson had seventy percent of his appointments to political office from this church." Masters then made "a most seething denunciation of foreigners and especially the Greeks." Stung by this polemic, the newspaper writer felt an immediate need to respond, allowing us a rare insight into how Tuscola's citizens felt about my grandfather and his brothers: "The Greeks in some towns may not live up to our standards, but the attack was unfair to the Flesor boys who conduct the Candy Kitchen in Tuscola. These boys are all naturalized citizens; one of them was a soldier in the late war, and all of them have saved their money and invested it in Tuscola property. They are prominent Masons and highly respected in Tuscola."

The writer might also have mentioned that my grandfather sent his children to the Presbyterian church. Everyone in town probably knew this because family legend holds that Grandfather would stand outside the store on the corner of Main and Sale and watch every Sunday morning

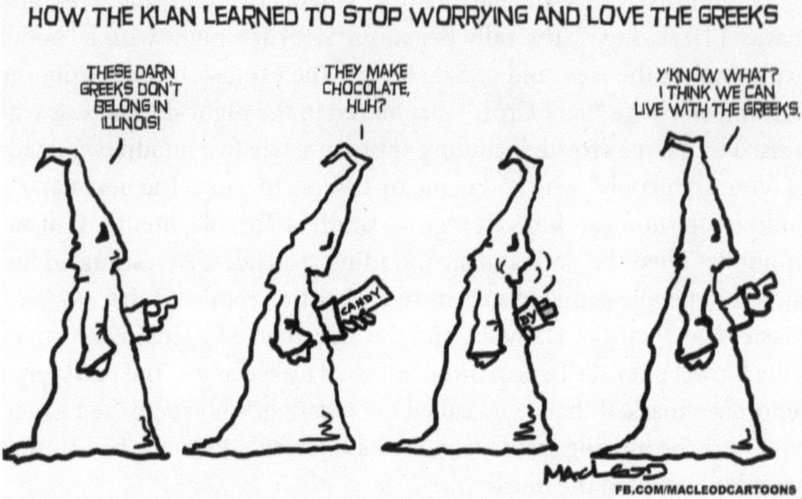

PHOTO 2. "How the Klan Learned to Stop Worrying and Love the Greeks" cartoon. (Courtesy of James MacLeod, FB.com/MACLEODCARTOONS.)

as his children left the house two blocks north of the store and paraded past to the church, two blocks south. At any rate, my grandfather was appreciative of this local public support, and he did not forget it, something he shared with me in his later years.[136]

The summer passed, and my grandfather remained in Tuscola and continued to advertise his business. On December 4 and 8, 1923, he ran a large ad for his open house celebration of the Kandy Kitchen remodeling (note that it was styled with a *K* at this time). "Our Remodeling Work is now nearing completion and we are planning to have a Grand Opening" headed the advertisement. The grand opening was scheduled for December 15, 1923, and all were welcome.[137] On December 4, when the first ad appeared, there was also another Klan attack. Three explosions were heard after a huge cross was erected and burned near the Presbyterian church. A car then came from East Sale Street toward the Kandy Kitchen on the corner. Two men "with their coat collars turned high to hide their faces alighted from the car and planted a cross at the street intersection and set it afire and hurried on northward."[138] Grandfather and my uncles carried on undaunted, and the *Tuscola Journal* encouraged everyone to attend the reopening celebration. "Tommy, Nick and Gus will be there with that big welcome smile and feed you on candy and ice cream or pass the best cigars. Visit Douglas County's most beautiful store . . . on December 15th, just in time for the holidays."[139]

By the summer of 1924 the Klan had begun to lose its appeal and its power, at least in Tuscola. In June 1924 a "Klantauqua" was held in Villa Grove.[140] There was also a band concert in Tuscola at Ervin Park in July, but the concert, given by the Danville Klan, primarily attracted members from Champaign, Decatur, Mattoon, and other towns in Douglas County.[141] After 1925 the Klan receives almost no mention in the Tuscola newspaper. Through it all, the Flesor brothers had gone about their daily business at the Tuscola Kandy Kitchen.

We have discussed why Greeks came to America, where they initially settled in urban areas, how acculturation evolved within the rapidly changing political, cultural, and social American landscape, and what types of resistance they met and overcame. The next part of the journey brings all the elements of our story together as, over the next three chapters, we discuss the Greek confectioners in central Illinois.

CHAPTER 6

MY GRANDFATHER AND HIS MENTORS

It's hard to believe how he ended out here in the cornfields.
—James Vaky, second-generation Greek American

Most Greek immigrant confectioners in central Illinois first passed through Ellis Island and then headed west, generally to Chicago, less often to St. Louis. Some then traveled farther west to work on the railroads for a handful of years before returning to Illinois. The money they earned and saved was used to open a business, marry, and start a family. The micro-history of my grandfather Gus (or Constantine) Flesor serves as the primary case history for this study.[1] His journey contains elements of all the stories of these Greek pioneers that I will discuss.

Greek immigrants in Chicago traveled "downstate" following the railroad lines or main highways south. They generally had three options when deciding where to settle. First, they could stop in a town where there was already an established Greek business and go to work for those Greeks. Second, they could go to a town where they had relatives and join them in their business. Third, they could settle in a town where there were no Greeks and set up their own business. St. Louis Greeks spread out across Illinois in the same manner and for the same reasons. The networking among the Greeks was extensive and demonstrates the pat-

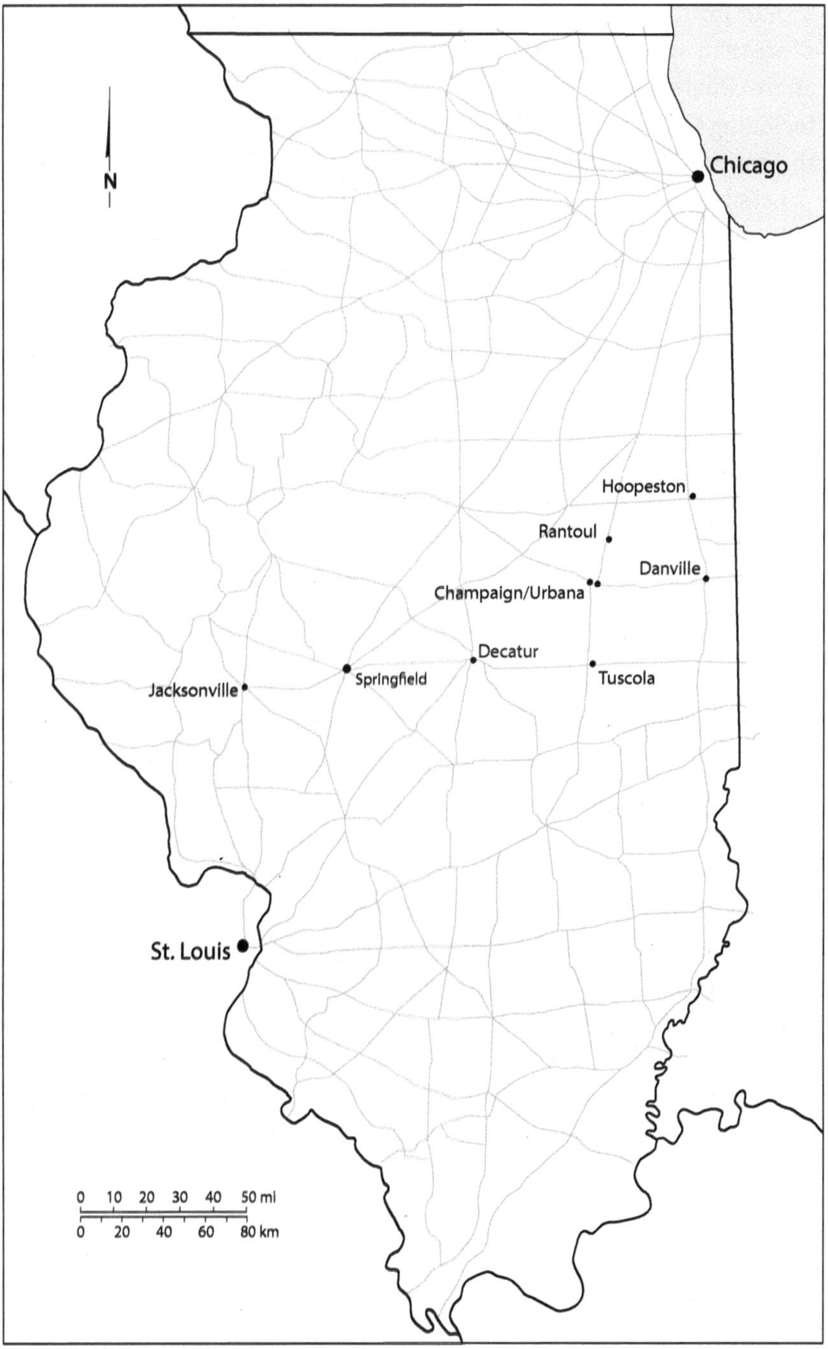

MAP 2. Chicago, St. Louis, Large Towns in Central Illinois, and Tuscola. (Courtesy Bill Nelson.)

tern of immigration and settlement that the first generation employed. More than seventy significant Greek immigrant confectioners settled in approximately forty-five small cities and towns across central Illinois, including Champaign-Urbana, Decatur, Danville, and Springfield, during the period from around 1880 through the 1920s.

Let's begin with the Greek confectioners in Champaign-Urbana who were my grandfather's mentors, Peter George Vriner and George Vaky.[2] Vriner (b. March 20, 1864, in Pigadakia) came to America in 1889 or 1890. After working in Chicago for a few years, he moved to Champaign and opened a confectionery and fruit store, the Champaign Candy Company, in 1898 at 55 Main Street. George Vaky was his junior partner. Some of their first customers "were soldiers waiting for the Illinois Central to carry them to the Spanish-American War."[3] The shop later became known simply as "Vriner's." In 1901 Peter and George also opened what became Flesor's Candy Kitchen in Tuscola, taking the opportunity to fill a niche south of Champaign. Although over the years Peter opened other stores in both Champaign and Urbana that were also called "Vriner's," the one on Main was his first and his base.

Peter first rented and then bought the building at 55 Main Street. By 1908 he had completely revamped the storefront and remodeled and refurnished the interior, which remained essentially the same until Vriner's closed in 1997. The building is on the National Register of Historic Places.[4] The old saying about the three keys to business success being "location, location, and location" certainly holds true for Vriner's. Located in Champaign, one of the moderate-sized twin cities that were the home of the state's largest university, the shop sat on Main Street next to a vaudeville theater and just across the street from the Champaign-Urbana railroad station.[5]

Local legends about Vriner's customers are colorful and impressive. During Prohibition, for example, "Al Capone came to Vriner's regularly to conduct business with his partners from St. Louis. It's said that the chubby criminal would put away one, two, and sometimes three chocolate marshmallow sundaes while planning out heists and murders." Another story goes that "First Lady Eleanor Roosevelt demanded a soda upon her arrival in Champaign in 1942. She proclaimed Vriner's to be the finest she had ever tasted." In 1960, during a campaign stop, local lore has it that "someone offered JFK a Vriner's candy cane" and that "he scarfed it down faster than you could say 'peppermint.'" REO Speedwagon, the American rock band formed in 1967 by three University of Illinois students, used a press photo of themselves sitting at Vriner's soda fountain for their second album, *R.E.O./T.W.O.*[6] Finally, the late film critic Roger Ebert, who grew up in Urbana, went to the University of Illinois, and took his first job with the *News-Gazette* in 1963 when he was fifteen, later recalled how "the paper was put to bed every day at noon, and the city room cleared out for Vriner's, across the street."[7] Vriner's truly was the iconic candy shop, opened for a hundred years, that everyone remembers.[8]

PHOTO 3. Champaign Candy Company. First Vriner's store at 55 Main Street, Champaign, about 1904, before Peter George Vriner completely remodeled the front and interior of the store around 1907–8. The man wearing the hat is Vriner. His partner, George Vaky, is to the right in the white apron. (Champaign County Historical Archives, The Urbana Free Library, Urbana, Illinois.)

Peter George Vriner was the patriarch of the Vriner clan in Champaign-Urbana. He was the first of many Vriners, and later the Flesors, who, through chain migration, came from Pigadakia, where their Greek name was Vrinios.[9] Peter married Chresula (Christine) Mouyios (b. August 12, 1884) in Chicago in 1905. She had emigrated from Greece in 1895.[10] They had three children: George Peter (b. April 8, 1906), William Peter (b. July 24, 1910), and Sammy P. "Tyke" (b. May 5, 1912) Vriner.

George Peter's daughter Diana Vriner Krandel told me that in 1929 her father married a non-Greek woman, Juanita Creighton (b. January 17, 1909),[11] whom he had met at a coffee shop he frequented. Sadly, he died in 1953.[12] She never knew her uncle William, as he was killed in action in Germany in 1944.[13] I asked her if there had ever been any derogatory acts or speech against them for being Greek. Diana recalled that her mother told her that one day while walking with baby Diana in a stroller, a neighbor gazed into the carriage and commented, "She's not so dark after all."[14]

Another early Vriner in the Champaign-Urbana confectionery and restaurant business was Peter's nephew George John Vriner. George was born in Pigadakia (March 7, 1887) to John (Joannis) G. and Stella G. Vriner.[15] He was ten years old when he came to the United States with his father, who was forty years old, in June 1896.[16] They went first to Chicago and then down to Champaign, where George was living with his uncle Peter G. Vriner in 1900.[17] In 1904 there was a small news item in the *Champaign Daily News* that mentioned that "J. Vriner of Tuscola, brother of P. G. Vriner of this city," was returning to Europe.[18] It could be that John Vriner, George J.'s father, brought the boy over and then went down to Tuscola to help run the Vriner/Vaky Candy Kitchen there. In 1904, when my grandfather bought the store, John perhaps went back to Greece, for he does not appear again in the record. George J. married Stella Pappaganes (b. 1898 in Felatra) in July 1921. They had no children.[19] George J. did have a brother, Louis J. Vriner, whom we will discuss below.

In 1912, there were three Vriners working at the three Vriner's Confectioneries (407 E. University and 55 Main in Champaign and 132 West Main in Urbana): Peter G. Vriner, George J. Vriner, and a James Vriner, about whom I have little information regarding his relationship to Peter. James and Peter sold the confectionery at 132 West Main in Urbana in 1917 to Nick, George, and Peter Mouyios, perhaps the brothers of Peter Vriner's wife, Christine (Mouyios). James then moved to New Orleans. The Mouyios brothers (about whom there is no other information) renamed the store the Apollo and operated it until October 1927, when they sold it to George J. Vriner.[20]

There was also a George P. Vriner (b. February 22, 1879) who was living in Tuscola and working for my grandfather when he registered for the draft in September 1918. On his Great War registration card he gives his nearest relative as Thomas P. Vriner (b. May 2, 1887, in Tripoli) in Chicago.[21] As with my grandfather's brother Nick, George P.'s draft registration for World War I lists his nationality as "Oriental (Asian)." George signed his last name as Vrinios.[22] It is not clear how this George P. and his brother Thomas are related to the other Vriner/Vrinios or Flesor families or what became of him. He is not the same person as Peter G. Vriner's oldest son, George Peter.

In 1914, Peter G. Vriner bought a building at the corner of Main and Market Streets (132 West Main), opposite the courthouse, in Urbana. The *Urbana Daily Courier* speculated that the purchase price was $25,000. Mr. Vriner's intent, the newspaper stated, was to "remodel the building into one of the most magnificent confectioneries in this part of the state."[23] This became the Olympia Confectionery, which opened on September 10, 1914. Although Peter owned the building, his nephew George J. was the proprietor of the store. George had managed two of his uncle's stores, and now he had "decided to give up his interest in the other two places to start in business for himself, with the backing furnished by his uncle."[24] The newspaper article announcing its opening proclaimed it just as grand as advertised—"one of the finest of its kind in Illinois, for one could hardly imagine more expensive fittings for such a business." There was "over $12,000 worth of marble, metal and glass installed" in the store, including a "twenty-five-foot onyx marble beautifully trimmed liquid carbonic fountain with an all-marble back-bar with German silver doors and trimmings."[25]

Peter also made his own ice cream at this first Urbana store at 132 West Main.[26] He continued this ice cream business at the Olympia and in 1919 made plans to build a separate ice cream factory behind the Olympia, which he opened in 1921.[27] By 1923 there were three ice cream manufacturers and twenty-two confectioneries in Champaign-Urbana.[28] After Peter G. Vriner died on June 11, 1929, at the age of sixty-five or sixty-six,[29] his youngest son, Sam Vriner (or "Tyke"), took over the Vriner's confectionery business. Sam died in 1993.[30] One of Sam's sons, Pete, had helped his father with the business and then kept it going until 1997, when the last Vriner's, at 55 Main, closed. With Pete's retirement, the Champaign-Urbana Vriner candy dynasty ended as well.

The other branch of the Vriner family is that of Louis (or Lambros) John Vriner (b. October 7, 1891, in Pigadakia), who was George John's brother and Peter George's nephew.[31] He immigrated to America through Ellis Island in December 1906, intending to join his "brother George Vrinios of Champaign Candy Co. Champaign (Il)."[32] Louis later helped his brother George manage the Olympia Confectionery and eventually took it over.[33]

Louis and his wife, Athanasia (b. 1888), had four children (George, Dina, Maria, and John) who were all born in Pigadakia. Athanasia was born in Alepochori, which is very near Pigadakia.[34] Only their fifth child, Anna, was born in America. Louis's son John Vriner wrote his family history while in eighth grade after moving to Champaign, and his recollections of life in both Greece and America are revealing. According to John, the family name originally was Vrinios, and the family lineage could be traced to 1821 and the Greek war with Turkey. The Turks killed all but one of the Vriners. If John's story is true, we can thank the sultan for sparing the last remaining male, who then married and had two sons. Their descendants ended up making chocolates in Champaign-Urbana.[35]

George Vaky (b. 1871) was the other pioneer confectioner in Champaign-Urbana. George Vaky's son James (b. November 3, 1911)[36] said his father was born in Paradisi, near Sparta, and migrated to America in 1887, when he was fifteen, with a younger brother. George had heard that in America the streets were paved with gold.[37] He came not only for the great adventure but to earn money to send to his widowed mother, who made a suit for George to wear on the journey. After passing through Ellis Island, George traveled on to Chicago, where he sold bananas in a pushcart. The growth of Greek confectioneries in Chicago in the late 1890s may have caused George to realize that there was a future in candy making. James recalled that his father wanted to improve his chances for success, so he went to Boston to learn the confectionery trade. After a while some Greek friends told him about opportunities for confectioners in the "downstate" region of Illinois, and he headed to Champaign. There he met Peter Vriner, and together they established the Champaign Candy Company in 1898 in Champaign.[38]

Soon after setting up their first store, Vriner and Vaky opened the Urbana Candy Company, and in 1901, they opened the Candy Kitchen confectionery in Tuscola. Vaky married a German American woman, Cinnia

Oden (b. 1873), in Tuscola in 1904.[39] Vaky then heard of an excellent store location at the intersection of Main, Neil, and Church Streets in Champaign and established his own business, the Frat Confectionery, there in 1908. This was his "home" business for the remainder of his life, managing it for thirty-six years.[40] Vriner and Vaky, however, maintained their business partnership until they mutually agreed to dissolve it in 1925.[41]

George Vaky seems to have been a bit of a maverick. He did not marry a Greek woman, and although he supported the Greek Orthodox Church,

PHOTO 4. The Frat Confectionery, Champaign. George D. Vaky's store at 3 Main Street, about 1909. Vaky is nearest the camera. (Champaign County Historical Archives, The Urbana Free Library, Urbana, Illinois.)

he was not a regular member. He was instrumental in organizing the AHEPA lodge in Champaign-Urbana, perhaps because the Klan was very active there. The Champaign County Klan began in the fall of 1921[42] and held a conclave in August 1922.[43] Champaign-Urbana businessmen who were members of the Klan were supposed to identify each other with lapel pins, and anyone caught doing business with non-Klan members were liable to possible marginalization or retribution.

Although they were living in a community with a large university, Greeks faced overt discrimination because of their ethnicity. James Vaky recalled his sister, Alpha (b. April 9, 1908), being excluded from a university (Greek!) sorority because she was Greek.[44] Decades later this event still obviously deeply troubled him:

> Now my sister, you talk about discrimination, . . . she was a beautiful young lady and was of course rushed to the various sororities. Then there was this private session, when they go over the young ladies' names. . . . A wonderful family friend was present at this time and later told my mother [that] my sister's name came up, [and a woman who later became an] English teacher at Champaign High, whom I had later, this English teacher made the comment that, "Oh yes, Al was a very beautiful girl, but you know her father owns a confectionery. He's a Greek." That was the end of that.[45]

James Vaky also remembered being part of a choir that sang at the funeral of a Klan member in Champaign; gazing upon the audience, he saw that all the participants were wearing their robes.[46]

Like most of the second generation we have discussed, the Vaky children worked in their father's store but had different dreams for their futures. James Vaky recalled working on Saturdays, but he was drawn to the arts, which he pursued in college and throughout his life. James told me that his older brother, Theodore (b. September 22, 1906),[47] attempted to enter the business and even took ice cream making and hotel management courses at the University of Illinois, but his real passion was for flying. George Vaky supported that endeavor and paid for his son's flying lessons.

George Vaky sent his widowed mother fifty dollars per month for the rest of her life, but he never returned to Greece. When he died in 1944, Vaky's Confectionery died as well.[48] James Vaky later reflected that "it's hard to believe how he [his father] ended out here in the cornfields, but he had heard that there's a chance to start a business on your own in the

Midwest."[49] That observation could have been made about all the Greek confectioners we discuss in this study.

Peter Vriner and George Vaky helped many other Greek relatives and immigrants, not just my grandfather, across east-central Illinois. For example, Vaky influenced Tom Lessaris's decision to come to Champaign-Urbana, according to Tom's son Peter.[50] Thomas John Lessaris (b. October 23, 1878) was born in Geraki, about twenty miles southeast of Sparta.[51] It is not clear when he came to America, but he appears to have been working as a confectioner in New Haven, Connecticut, in 1900 and 1901.[52] Thomas first opened the Blue Fountain in Champaign near Vriner's, selling candy and food. He then established the Elite Restaurant in 1923 or 1924, and that store remained opened until 1936. Tom also made candy there for a few years. In 1936 he moved the store's location to 116 North Neil, where it remained in business until the 1980s.[53]

Thomas married Dina Kontoyiannes (b. August 23, 1897, in Geraki). The three Lessaris sons, Peter, John, and George,[54] carried on in the food business after Thomas's death in 1951 and expanded into Top Boy Drive-Ins, the first of their kind in the area.[55] They eventually operated twelve stores in different states. Thomas's son George met Sophia Lenardos (b. February 27, 1929), from Aurora, Illinois, while they were attending a funeral, and they were married in 1951.[56] Sophia, like many wives who were employed in the businesses, was very integral to the success of the Elite.

When I asked Thomas's son Peter whether he was aware of any discrimination against Greeks because of their ethnicity, Peter shared a story, known to all the Champaign-Urbana Greek community, about Mr. Vaky. George Vaky wanted to purchase a "nice" brick home near Prospect and University. When word got out, a local doctor bought it out from under him so that a Greek would not "infiltrate" the neighborhood. Despite the prejudice, and like the Vakys and Vriners, the Lessaris brothers were very successful. Peter was very proud of his Greek heritage, and yet proud to be an American as well.[57]

Another Vriner family chain migration connection is with the Samaras family in Champaign-Urbana. There were four Samaras brothers: Nick (b. 1891), Paul, George, and William. In my interview with Alexander "Lex" Samaras, George's son, he shared that Peter Vriner was a great-uncle (or uncle) on the Samaras brothers' mother's side, as she had been a Vrinios before her marriage.[58] The Samarases came from the village of Lygoudista, Greece, near Tripoli and Pigadakia in the Peloponnese. According to Lex, the four boys had become orphans, and their great-uncle Peter Vriner took it upon himself to send for them and have them join him in Champaign-Urbana. Nick came over first, in 1902, when he was eleven.[59] Peter later paid for Nick's brothers Paul and George to join him. William remained in Greece.

The SS *Martha Washington* manifest list shows that on April 26, 1911, the Samaras brothers Nicolas, Georgios (b. December 15, 1896), and Apostolos (Paul) (b. July 24, 1898), from Lygoudista, Greece, arrived at Ellis Island. Nick is listed as a "confectioner" and as having already lived in Champaign from 1902 to 1910. His brother Georgios is a "farmer." Apostolos is a "pupil." The manifest notes "parents dead." They were traveling on from New York to join their uncle Panagiotis (Peter G.) Vrinios, at 55 Main Street, Champaign, who "has store Champaign Candy Co." From this it seems that Nick spent eight years in Champaign working for Peter Vriner as a confectioner and then returned to Greece in 1911 to bring back two of his brothers.

When America entered World War I, George Samaras enlisted in the army and served in France. Discharged in 1919, he returned to Champaign and married a local non-Greek woman, Edna (Hullinger); they had four children. His brother Nick, after learning the trade, moved to Hoopeston, Illinois, in 1927, where he opened a confectionery named the Ritz. George joined Nick in 1933. In 1936, George bought the business from his brother, who then moved to Lansing, Michigan, and opened a business there. Proud of his confectionery lineage, George was quoted as saying, "There are easier ways to make candy, but I have always maintained that quality is the most important factor in a good finished product."[60] The store was completely remodeled in 1940 to reflect a more modern feel, and by the mid-1940s annual candy production reached over four thousand pounds.

Lex Samaras, like his father, proudly served America in the US Navy, landing his ship on Utah Beach on D-Day, participating in the invasion of Okinawa, and finally being a member of the occupation forces of Japan at the end of World War II.[61] After his discharge, he studied and taught music for a few years, but his confectionery heritage was too strong, so he returned to Hoopeston and first partnered with his father and then bought the business from him. He became very active in the community, serving on the school board and as a member of multiple service organizations.[62] Lex's mother, Edna, died in 1964 and his father George in 1977.[63]

Lex remained in Hoopeston until the late 1950s, when he opened another Ritz in Watseka. Having no offspring of his own who were interested in continuing the business, Lex closed the Ritz in the 1970s. As Lex related his life experiences with me, he obviously took great pride in the fact that the first-generation Greeks came to America at such young ages, worked hard, learned a trade, and became successful despite being labeled "greasy Greeks." He had his father's and uncle's immigration records, and

PHOTO 5. The Ritz Confectionery, Hoopeston. George Samaras works behind the counter at the Ritz. The photo is undated but was taken before the remodeling began in the mid-1940s. (Courtesy of Lex Samaras.)

it was clear that he cherished his connection to Lygoudista and took great pleasure in sharing his family heritage.[64] Sadly, Lex died in October 2017, marking the loss of another second-generation Greek confectioner.[65]

The Tomaras family in Champaign-Urbana is another link in the local chain migration network, in this case through both the Vakys and Vriners. The Tomaras story begins with Pangiotis (Pete) Tomaras (b. July 15, 1888), who immigrated to America in 1903. Pete's journey closely mirrors many of the first-generation narratives. We know a good deal about him as his son Peter wrote a family history that he generously shared with me.[66]

> My father arrived at Ellis Island in September 1903. He had a 6th grade education and less than $20. He and an uncle had been watching a steamship prepare to sail for the U.S. and, almost on the spur of the moment, the uncle bought his passage and put him on the ship, [as] there was little future for Pangiotis Tomaras at his home village of Paradisi, Korinth, Greece, which is high on a mountain above the gulf-side town of Kiato. As with most immigrants, my dad had the name of a cousin or uncle in NY who took him in at first. He shined shoes. He washed dishes. At some point, he began work on the railroads. . . . He was on the gangs, who took rails from flat cars and laid them on ties, building the lines West. . . . For a time, he worked in coalmines around Benld [Illinois]. I believe he did not like working underground, and probably went back to the railroads, teaching himself English by reading newspapers and saving money as he could. (p. 1)[67]

In the mid-1920s Pete left the railroads, and around 1928 he found a food business opportunity in Champaign.

> Now, how did these men know where to look? As I said, they had a support system of friends with whom they communicated. So, on the brink of the Great Depression, he learned of a 10-seat counter diner, owned by a Greek, that was broke. The First National Bank had seized it. My dad went to the banker and said, "I will take over the operation, pay the debts of the previous owner, and then pay back the loan you give me to get it going." The bank thought that sounded like a deal. He named the place Pete's Annex. The Annex was a one-man operation; Pete cooked on the grill, plated, and served customers who sat at the C-shaped counter. He paid all the back debts, including suppliers, and put himself in position to make an offer for Grindley's (another restaurant) in 1929. (pp. 2–3)

At this point, George Vaky stepped in and loaned Tomaras $5,000 to enable him to purchase Grindley's (p. 3).

Pete Tomaras returned to Greece in 1930 to marry, and family tradition has it that eligible village girls were paraded before him. He realized while in Greece, however, that he was in love with his hostess/worker, Julia Creighton (b. 1/12/1902), a non-Greek woman who was running Grindley's while he was away. Pete mentioned this to an uncle, who urged him to return to America and marry her, since she could be his business partner as well (pp. 3–4).

Julia and Pete married, renamed Grindley's the Quality Café, and lived above the business. Son Peter remembers working at the restaurant during World War II, when, despite good business, it was difficult to obtain staples, such as meat, sugar, coffee, and chocolate. Christos Bartges, a Danville confectioner and restaurant owner and best man at Pete and Julia's wedding, had somehow cornered the market on sugar and had hundreds of pounds on the second floor of his business. He supplied his fellow Greeks with sugar throughout the war for barter or cash (pp. 3–4).

At the end of World War II, Pete planned to purchase a lovely home on a large lot at the corner of University and Prospect Avenue but was unable to close the deal. Peter learned the truth many years later from Kyle Robeson: "'You know why your folks didn't get that house, don't you?' I was clueless. 'They wouldn't let them,' he replied. That is, the country club set, the 'good' people of Champaign, did not want an immigrant restaurant man to have that property. Would simply not be acceptable" (p. 4). In 1947 Pete Tomaras purchased an even grander house and the surrounding Old Orchard Farm south of Champaign on Hwy. 45. Here in 1956 he and Julia built the Paradise Inn Motel and Restaurant, named for his Greek village. The motel was enlarged in 1961, and the family operated the dual businesses until they sold the restaurant and home in 1977 and the motel in July 1981, a year after Pete Tomaras passed away (pp. 5–6).

I discussed in chapter 1 how important the Orthodox Church was in providing a community for Greek immigrants in America. As an integral and active member of the Champaign Greek community, Pete was instrumental in establishing the Champaign Greek Orthodox Church. Before this, Greeks who wanted to attend church drove to the one in Decatur, which "was difficult, especially for those whose businesses operated on Sunday. AHEPA finally bought a frame house at the corner of Green and Locust Streets in 1953, thinking it would be a good location . . . [as] they wanted it close to campus for U. of I. Orthodox students. Once in a great while a priest (from Decatur) would hold a Liturgy there on a Saturday."[68]

The frame house was eventually demolished in 1960, and the next year Gus Leo Furla, John and George Lessaris, Pete Tomaras, and John Trebellas, a "new" Greek in town who owned the Pepsi franchise, contributed $5,000 to build a "center," not yet a formal church. In time, an altar was positioned and the church board of directors formed, with Pete Tomaras as president and Furla as treasurer.

In 1965 a permanent priest was assigned, Father Yalouris, who came down from Chicago for Sunday Liturgy only. The Greek women formed the Champaign Ladies' Philoptochos Society, and there was a Hellenic Student Organization at the University of Illinois. The current Three Hierarchs Greek Orthodox Church was built in south Champaign in 1985

PHOTO 6. The White & Gold Confectionery, Urbana. John D. Pelafos and his wife, Georgia, proudly stand in their store at 106 West Main in the 1930s. (Photo courtesy of Jeni Pelafos Mechalas.)

with a generous donation of $2 million by John Trebellas. Today the church serves approximately 100 member families and 150–200 Orthodox persons of varied ethnicities and is active in reaching out to 40–70 Orthodox University of Illinois students.[69]

The Pelafos family also ran a Greek confectionery business in Champaign-Urbana. Jeni Pelafos Mechalas shared her family story and experiences as a daughter growing up in a Greek confectionery business in central Illinois. Her father, John Pelafos, owned the White & Gold Confectionery. It was located two doors over from Louis Vriner's Olympia Confectionery and Café. Jeni remembers that "the White & Gold sold homemade candy, chocolates of all kinds, peanut brittle, caramels, taffy apples, candy canes, roasted peanuts, . . . [all] made using copper kettles. The chocolates were hand dipped by my father. Marble slabs were used for the peanut brittle and candy canes."[70]

John Peter Pelafos (b. 1887) was born in Arvanitokerasia, Greece, just to the northwest of Pigadakia.[71] He immigrated to America in 1904 and went on to Chicago, where he worked for the railroad for a time and then learned the candy business from a relative in the city. Jeni was not sure how her father found his way to Champaign-Urbana because her parents rarely discussed family history with their children. She knows her mother was a seamstress in Greece and had her own shop in her family home. By 1912 John was working as a dispenser for George Vaky at the Frat Confectionery,[72] and by 1919, in an article noting that John Pelafos was a cousin of the Greek premier, Eleftherios Venizelos, he was described as a proprietor of the White & Gold Confectionery at 106 West Main in Urbana.[73] In the 1920s John Pelafos also took over the Palace of Sweets in Champaign. John's first wife, Antonia, died in 1924, and he returned to Greece to remarry in 1927, coming back to Urbana with his bride, Georgia, in 1928. While in Greece, his Palace of Sweets failed due to poor management. When he returned, then, he began again with just the White & Gold Confectionery.

John Pelafos was a friend of my grandfather, and Jeni recalls visiting the Candy Kitchen in Tuscola when she was a child. Like my grandfather and many other Greek businessmen, John also invested in land, buying an eighty-acre farm north of Rantoul in 1932 for seventy-one dollars an acre.[74] With the farmland providing extra income, the White & Gold Confectionery continued as a thriving business until John's death in 1951.[75]

Jeni remembers that her parents, John and Georgia, ran the business together and that all the children worked in the business. "In my family, we ran the cash register, bussed tables, waited on customers, ran the soda fountain, and washed dishes. We were allowed to have ice cream, candy made by Dad, but no soft drinks nor wholesale candy. That was hard to take."[76] John's grandson Mark Pelafos believes that the Pelafos family initially lived above the store, as an investment in store property would have been more important than a house.[77] One childhood memory that stands out in Jeni's mind occurred on July 4, 1939, when she was ten years old.

> For the Fourth of July, White & Gold and Vriner's had fireworks of all kinds, rockets, Roman candles, sparklers, bombs, etc. for sale. We had a table set up in front of the store, and so did Vriner's. Vriner's also had fireworks in their window. Something happened and the Vriner's fireworks ignited and rockets, Roman candles, sparklers, etc. shot all over Main Street! You can imagine the chaos. I was frightened and ran down to the Princess Theater and took cover in the lobby. Downtown was lit up brighter than the Northern Lights! Fire engines, police, and ambulances were on the scene. After that incident, fireworks were not allowed on Main Street.[78]

Jeni and I discussed these family businesses and how once the first-generation Greek male died, the widow and children would sometimes carry on for a while, but that would not last long as the offspring left to pursue other interests. So it was with the White & Gold, which faded from Champaign-Urbana's business scene after John's passing:[79] "We, Mom, I, and my two brothers, kept the place for a while and later rented to other businesses until we sold the building in the '60's, and it is now the Heel and Toe shoe store."[80]

Diana Vriner Krandel, Peter G. Vriner's granddaughter, told me that her grandfather sponsored many Greek males so they could come to America. Some stayed and worked in his store for a time to learn the trade and to determine whether they wanted to be confectioners. Some established their own businesses in Champaign, while others moved on to other cities or towns. For example, Nick Somers was a dispenser at Vriner's Confectionery, who left in 1915 to open a new confectionery in Olney, Illinois, with his brother.[81] A year later, another dispenser at Vriner's, Thomas Callas, resigned his position and left for Iowa to start a business for himself.[82] It is not clear how successful Nick and Thomas were, but one former employee who did have success was Paul Angel. He first worked for Peter Vriner.[83] By 1931 he was running the Apollo Confectionery,[84] which eventually evolved into the Apollo Restaurant on Main Street in Urbana.[85]

Many more Greek candy stores and soda fountains soon sprang up all over the region, as Greek immigration increased in the early 1900s and Greeks spilled out of Chicago or St. Louis to establish their own businesses downstate, marry and raise families, and become part of small-town America. With some individual variations, their stories were like that of my grandfather, and, like him, they belonged to a larger relational web, or network, of Greek immigrants whose lives wove together over time and place.

So let us now travel south from Champaign-Urbana and learn more about my grandfather and his store, the Tuscola Kandy Kitchen (now Flesor's Candy Kitchen) at the corner of Main and Sale, which he purchased from Vriner and Vaky in 1904.

In April 2010 Fred Ross, a Tuscola native, recalled for me his favorite Tuscola Kandy Kitchen memory:

> In February 1962, I had a Gusburger[86] on my mind on a train ride all the way from San Diego, California to Tuscola. My family were members of the Presbyterian Church in Tuscola and friends with Bill and Helen Skinner. Bill was married to Helen, Gus Flesor's daughter. Bill influenced my decision to join the Navy in 1959. While frequently drinking "green rivers" [lemon-lime soda] and visiting with Bill about his experience in the US Navy in WWII, I knew I wanted to serve my country. I enlisted. When I had completed my active duty, I returned to Tuscola. (In those years, the passenger trains from Chicago to New Orleans stopped in Tuscola.) I was home! I picked up my seabag (which is still in our attic), and got off the train. Even before I called my folks, Virgil and Mary Ross, I walked from the depot to the Kandy Kitchen and ordered a Gusburger. Immediately Bill said, "It's on me!" He soon served up two Gusburgers and two green rivers.[87]

For Fred Ross and so many others in Tuscola, Flesor's Kandy Kitchen was that downtown corner touchstone for seventy-plus years.

My grandfather arrived in Chicago in 1901 and traveled from there to Champaign and then on south to Tuscola, where he worked in Vriner and Vaky's Candy Kitchen. Peter Vriner and my grandfather, both from Pigadakia, were possibly first cousins. My grandfather's mother's maiden name was Viola Vriner, so she may have been Peter's sister or aunt.[88] Their journeys to central Illinois illustrate the chain migration process of the time: they both traveled from Pigadakia to Ellis Island to Chicago to Champaign-Urbana and finally to Tuscola.

According to my father, Paul (b. December 24, 1921), my grandfather worked at the store for about a year and then left in 1902 to work on the railroads out west to save enough money to purchase the business for himself. He received a letter from George Vaky in 1904, which said that if he wanted the business, Vaky and Vriner would sell it to him for $500. My grandfather earned only $1.10 per day working on the railroad but still had saved enough to make the purchase. Gus returned to Tuscola, and the Kandy Kitchen became his.[89]

PHOTO 7. Flesor's Candy Kitchen, 1913. Nick Flesor is on the right, and employee Jack Boyles is on the left. Owner (and my grandfather) Gus Flesor can be seen in the reflection in the mirror behind Nick. This is the store as it originally looked before it was completely remodeled in 1923. (Personal copy, Ann F. Beck.)

Eventually Gus sponsored his brothers' immigration to America. Nick (b. February 25, 1880) arrived in Tuscola in 1908[90] and Tom in 1912. Nick later opened his own candy and camera shop, Nick's, across the street from Gus's store in 1945. Nick sold Kodak and other camera brands and camera supplies in his store. Although chocolates and cameras may seem a strange combination, many Greek candy stores sold cigars (as my grandfather did), magazines, even phonograph players.[91]

Tom left Tuscola and moved north to Elmhurst, Illinois, after 1930. I have only recently learned why. Constance Constant, author of *Austin Lunch,* told me that the aunt of her brother-in-law Jim Constant was married to Tom. Her family history has it that Aunt Marigoula Papadakos Flesor supposedly did not like Tuscola and persuaded her husband to leave![92]

Viola ("Milia"), Gus, Nick, and Tom's sister, had remained in Greece, but in late 1954 or early 1955, the brothers were reunited with her. Viola had three sons, and all three had careers in education. One of the sons had received a special award from the Greek government to study teaching methods in the United States for six months, so Viola came to visit her son, her brother Tom in Chicago, and Gus and Nick in Tuscola. For Gus, it was the first time he had seen her since 1901, for, unlike many of the Greeks, he never returned to Greece.[93]

In 2010, I interviewed my great-aunt Viola's granddaughter Christine Katris Kockler, who revealed to me even more about my family and Flesor immigration to Illinois.[94] Christine told me that Viola had married an Orthodox priest, Father Soteras, and they had seven children. Two of the daughters, Maria and Paula, and a son, Nick, immigrated to America.[95] Maria Soteras, Christine's mother, traveled from Greece with another woman, Agnes Tzanopoulos, who came to Tuscola and married my grandfather's brother Nick, thus becoming another of my great-aunts.[96] Agnes came from Agios Vasilios, a small town east of Tripoli. I do not know if this was an arranged marriage, but Maria's marriage to Chris Katris, of Chicago, was. Chris owned a grocery store, which he bought after first working on the railroad to make money.

During the Depression, Chris Katris's grocery was in the Swedish neighborhood on Clark and Berwyn Streets. The Katris family, which included three children, lived in the back of the store. Christine was the oldest and had a sister, Betty, and a brother, Nick. Christine told me that she herself did not marry a Greek man, causing a cultural rift in the family.

As a result, her mother, Maria, did not speak to her for seven years, until Christine had her first child.

Another example of Flesor chain migration, and Greek confectioneries, is illustrated by two families: we Flesors with one *s* are second cousins to the Flessors with two *s*'s who came from Alepochori, a village near Pigadakia.[97] The Flessors' story begins with Helen and Jim Papageorge, brother and sister, who immigrated to Chicago in the early 1900s. Jim Papageorge came first, by himself, in 1904 at the age of fifteen. His mother had mortgaged her property in the village for ten thousand drachmas to send her son to America. He later paid her back. When Jim arrived in Chicago, he was employed in the ice cream business. Jim never married but brought his nephews into the ice cream and confectionery business. In 1920, he bought a building on Ninety-Second Street and Commercial and named his establishment Gayety Candies.

Helen Papageorge immigrated to Chicago in 1916. She married Tom Flessor in 1920, when she was sixteen. This marriage was for love, not an arranged marriage. Tom and his brother George were from Alepochori and were second cousins of my grandfather. Their brother John Flessor remained in Alepochori, where he married Georgia Tzanopoulos, my great-aunt Agnes's sister.[98] George Flessor was the godfather to my aunt Viola, my father's oldest sister, and to my uncle George, my father's older brother. The Pigadakia/Alepochori-Chicago-Tuscola connection therefore stayed strong.

Helen and Tom Flessor had four children: Lee, Nick, Bea, and Art. Lee Flessor worked with his uncle Jim Papageorge in the Gayety Candies store and eventually took it over. Gayety's moved from downtown Chicago, after the steel mills closed, to Torrence Avenue, where the rent was more reasonable. Lee did well and soon opened a second candy and ice cream store. Lee met his wife, Angie Chiou, at the Greek church, and they had three children. Their son Jim was the third generation to own and operate Gayety Candies in Lansing, Illinois. In 2018, after Gayety's had been in business for ninety-eight years, Jim took a different path, and Gayety's closed.[99] Fortunately, however, new owners bought the business and reopened the Lansing store in April 2019, so the tradition continues.[100]

Lee and his brother Nick visited my grandfather upon occasion, and the two, in their eighties, came down to Tuscola in 2009 to wish me and my sister well in the reopening of our grandfather's store. They have both

PHOTO 8. Gus and Sophia Flesor. This photo was taken on their wedding day in June 1914, Danville, Illinois. (Personal copy, Ann F. Beck.)

passed on now, but they were very proud men and proud of the Flesor/Flessor heritage.

In early 1914 my grandfather spread the word to the wider Greek community that, as he had established his confectionery and soda fountain business and had also purchased a house,[101] he was looking for a wife. In June 1914, he married Sophia Tingus (b. September 16, 1897?) in an arranged marriage.[102] They were married in Danville, where she was then living with relatives.

Sophia was born in Boston to Greek immigrant parents and was the eldest of five children—four daughters and one son. In 1910 Sophia's mother, Dimitra, was a housewife and her father, James, a molder in a Pittsburgh, Pennsylvania, foundry.[103] According to family history, my grandmother's family moved frequently. Considering that my grandmother's family had many daughters, I am sure they were happy to have one leave the nest but sad that she would not be able to assist her mother with her younger siblings.

Unfortunately, Sophia died in 1927, not long after the birth of her eighth child, named Sophie. At this time, Sophia's mother was in Chicago, and my grandfather took baby Sophie to Dimitra in Chicago for her to care for during that first year. The Tuscola newspaper reported that Sophia Flesor was "a woman who had friends everywhere, in spite of the fact that she was essentially a home woman and spent most of her time there with her housework and children, to whom she was passionately devoted." As the news of her death became known, "there was sadness all over the city."[104] Her funeral services were held at home, with the local Presbyterian minister officiating, not a Greek priest. "The spacious home was filled with friends of the family and the many there attested to the high regard in which she had been held by people who had known her during her residence in Tuscola."[105] My grandfather never remarried. Five children survived infancy: Viola, George, Paul (my father), Helen, and baby Sophie. Sadly, Sophie died on June 1, 1942, a week before her high school commencement.[106]

When one thinks of my grandfather, now a widower with five children to raise, who came from a tiny peasant village in Greece where there was no chocolate, no ice cream, not even cows, one has to ask, how did he learn the confectionery business? Few, if any, first-generation Greek immigrants arrived in America as confectioners or ice cream makers. One answer is that he learned from those who came before, such as George Vaky and Peter Vriner, who taught many of the central Illinois Greek confectioners how to make candy and set up their businesses. In 2011, James Vaky, a year before he died, shared with me that indeed his father and Peter Vriner had taught my grandfather the business after he arrived in America.[107]

My grandfather also used the book *Rigby's Reliable Candy Teacher* as a guide,[108] and there are still notations in my grandfather's copy that we use today for our own candy manufacturing. Most confections made by the first-generation Greeks were from recipes handed down or shared orally or copied from recipe books, such as *Rigby's*.

Mr. Rigby (as we have always referred to him) said his impetus for compiling recipes and the "straight from the shoulder tips" of the confectionery and soda fountain businesses was his own personal interest and that, at that time in the late 1890s, "there was only one recipe book on the market, and it was very poorly written, unauthentic and impractical to give information to beginners."[109] *Rigby's* remains an invaluable source still today, as many of the confectionery tools and ingredients have not changed in over one hundred years. Core confections include caramel, fondants, and hard candies, which one can embellish with nuts, flavors, and different chocolate coatings. One notable recipe is for "Old English Toffee," consisting of sugar, corn syrup, cream, and a bit of salt. The formula was modified by many confectioners with the addition of nuts or varying cooking temperatures, making it a softer or harder candy.[110] We will see in chapter 8 how this "trail toffee" recipe could also be the basis for the famous Heath Bar.

With George Vaky and Peter Vriner's help, my grandfather, at first on his own and then with his two brothers, worked hard to make his business a success. According to my father, in 1910 or 1912, Grandfather purchased the Union Building on the corner of Main and Sale Streets in downtown Tuscola, in which his store was (and is still) located. The price was $25,000, but $1,200 was deducted from that because the basement had to be excavated. This is important because the Flesors manufactured candy in this basement until the 1970s, which seems to have been a fairly usual practice among Greek candy makers. My father remembered freight coming on the railroad and being delivered to the store, including big barrels of Coca-Cola syrup. He also shared that in Tuscola in the first decades of the 1900s there was a small downtown that included the Kandy Kitchen, Mr. Cox's hardware store, a men's clothing store, the movie theater, and other retail shops. He recalled that, from his childhood perspective, Tuscola, being a farm community, was excitingly active on Saturday night. Farmers with their families would come into town with their produce to barter with others for theirs. They would park their cars or trucks, have dinner, take in a movie, and enjoy an ice cream soda on the corner of Main and Sale.[111] My grandfather would roll the combination popcorn popper and peanut roaster out to the sidewalk and dispense goodness in a bag for a nickel.

In the small towns outside of Champaign-Urbana, Decatur, Danville, and Springfield, there were no Greek communities of any size. Often, as was the case with the Flesors, there were but one or two Greeks, generally male, in town. All the Flesor brothers were in the store seven days a week and demonstrated what would be viewed as a great Protestant work ethic, but unless they married and had families, they usually remained foreigners and outsiders. My grandfather and his brothers, however, made every effort to integrate themselves into the community, given the time constraints imposed by operating a small business. They all married and had children. My grandfather and great-uncle Nick remained in Tuscola their entire lives. Nick served in the army in World War I. Still, on his draft registration card, Nick was listed as an "Oriental (Asian)."[112]

One strategy for becoming a respected business community member was to join the Masonic Lodge. My grandfather was asked to join the Masons and received his first Masonic degree in 1909. He utilized his tutoring in learning the degrees to improve his English. His brother Tom also joined the Masonic Lodge in 1918.[113] This attempt to extend themselves into the public realm of the English-speaking community was planned; only Greek was spoken at home and among the brothers and family at the store. My father always said that he did not speak English until he went to public school at the age of five, thus illustrating the tension between the "home" Greeks, who maintained some aspects of the Greek culture in their homes and among themselves, and the "public" Greeks, who assimilated fully into American society and culture.

The Masonic Lodge was an integral part of life among the nativist populations in the Midwest, and the Tuscola Lodge was an important part of my grandfather's life as well.[114] Greeks in general were active in Masonic Lodges across the state, including in Chicago. There is, of course, a long history of Freemasonry in Greece, not to mention the references to ancient Greece in Freemasonry symbolism. The Greek organization AHEPA was organized along Masonic lines. This relationship between Greeks and Freemasonry has received little attention, however, from scholars. The Masons served as one means by which Greek immigrants were Americanized and learned English.

The Tuscola Masonic Lodge had first been convened on March 5, 1860.[115] It had been organized "at a time when the surrounding area was open territory and brethren felt the need of banding together, not only for survival but for social reasons as well." The most famous of its members was

Joseph G. "Uncle Joe" Cannon, who entered politics as Douglas County's first state's attorney. He was elected to the U.S. House of Representatives in 1873 and, with the exception of two terms, served in Congress for fifty years, including eight years as Speaker of the House (1903–11).

Tuscola Masons meet today at 107 North Main Street, which my grandfather purchased from the Knights of Pythias Lodge in 1937. "In turn," says Paul White, author of a history of Masonry in Tuscola, "Mr. Flesor gave the second story half of the building to the [Masons], free of conditions or obligations, for as long as it is needed for Masonic purposes." For my grandfather and great-uncle, as "foreigners," to be accepted as Masonic Lodge members meant acceptance into the community. For that, and for helping him to learn English, my grandfather showed his thanks by buying them a building in which to meet.

My grandfather was self-taught, having only four years of formal education, and managed to learn about America from various sources throughout his life. His knowledge was on full display one summer Sunday morning in 1950 when a young reporter from Chicago, Norma Lee Browning from the *Chicago Daily Tribune*, was "wandering through" central Illinois and stumbled into the Tuscola Kandy Kitchen.[116] As the sole customer that morning, the reporter got a unique insight into a man who was at home in his domain. She wrote, "I have just had the honor of meeting Gus, a Greek philosofer [*sic*], whose fame has spread across the corn belt of Douglas County. His bailiwick is the village sweet shop in Uncle Joe Cannon's home of Tuscola, population slightly under 3000."[117]

Her trip turned into more than a simple visit to the village sweet shop, however. My grandfather quizzed her on facts from the Bible to American history. He had the answers on his pad of penciled notations listing American "facts," in his world atlas, and in newspapers, some dated but still useful. While impressed Ms. Browning had attended college, he chastised her for not attending church that morning and not knowing basic American history, such as the number of votes in the electoral college, or facts from the Bible. On her way out the door, Gus gave her a stick of gum and some peanuts. In her article Browning listed some of Gus's accomplishments. He was a 33rd degree Mason and had recently donated funds for the new Masonic Hall in Tuscola. He was also a director of one of the banks, had raised five children as a single parent, and had "adopted" another boy to keep him out of an orphanage. Browning concluded her article by observing that "Gus came to this country . . . to work in an

PHOTO 9. Gus Flesor. My grandfather, some time in the 1950s, with his ever-present cigar. (Personal copy, Ann F. Beck.)

uncle's confectionery for $70 a year. He couldn't speak English. Nearly everyone in Douglas County agrees that Gus has done all right. But what pleases him most is to put the bee on a college graduate, because Gus went to school only thru the fourth grade."[118] Gus did do all right, keeping the store going right through the anti-immigrant, Ku Klux Klan era of the 1920s and the Great Depression.

My grandfather took great pride in his business and in the store's interior. Over the years, he invested funds to keep improving the fixtures, as did most of the Greek candy and soda fountain store owners. These additions and renovations always made headlines. Newspaper articles and advertisements frequently mention the amount that owners spent on a new tile floor or new pressed tin ceiling or new soda fountain and proclaim that theirs is now the "grandest store in the land" or some similar pronouncement. In 1921 Grandfather installed a new parquet tile floor that cost $2,000 and can still be seen in our store today. When one studies the photos of all the early Greek candy stores in central Illinois and beyond and almost invariably sees the same style of parquet tile floor as in our store, one can imagine that a tile floor salesman swept through the region in the early 1920s and sold all the Greeks the same tile floor!

The soda fountain bar grandfather purchased (still used today) was marble and was manufactured by Liquid Carbonic, the "one-time General Motors of the soda fountain business." Gus bought his soda fountain from the Chicago Soda Fountain Company, begun by Sam Schy. His grandson Phil and his sister Terry now own and operate the business, renamed the American Soda Fountain Company. This business was responsible for installing hundreds of soda fountains all over the Midwest, including the "new" one we bought (made in 1947). We are happy the third generations are able to work together to keep the soda fountain tradition alive.[119] Soda fountains are reminders of small-town downtown meeting spots across the nation, and the Greek confectioneries in particular became, as Sinclair Lewis recalled in his classic tale of middle America, iconic symbols of Main Streets in America, where teenagers gathered "at the counter of the Greek Confectionery Parlor."[120]

Maintaining the Tuscola Kandy Kitchen was a family affair, and as we have noted, my great-uncles Tom and Nick worked with my grandfather until they established their own businesses, one across the street in Tuscola and one in Elmhurst, Illinois. After his brothers left, my grandfather employed his two sons-in-law, my uncles Bill Skinner and Chris Voltis, husbands of my aunts Helen and Viola, respectively. My father's cousin George, one of Nick's three children, took over Nick's as the owner, and he and his wife, Irene, managed it until their retirement in the 1970s. In the mid-1960s, my family returned to Tuscola from the East Coast, and my father reentered the business with my grandfather. This resulted in some family disruption, but as a child, I was not privy to the process.

The question of whom one married, another common thread that appeared in many of the Greek immigrant stories, also impacted my family. My aunt Viola's marriage was semi-arranged. My father's version of the story is that my grandfather put out "the word" that his eldest daughter was eligible to be married. Grandfather had sent both my aunts to college for at least a year or two, so they were more formally educated than many Americans at the time. Chris Voltis became the prospective bridegroom; he and Viola were married by a Greek priest in the Tuscola Presbyterian Church.[121]

My father was also expected to marry "a good Greek girl," but he went to Eureka College where he met my mother, Margaret "Betty" Leonard (b. June 12, 1922), a product of a wealthy Chicago WASP family.[122] My mother knew my Aunt Helen at Eureka, and that is how she met Paul Flesor. They eloped to Missouri in 1942, which caused a scandal at the time in both families. Consequently, my mother was disinherited for marrying the son of a Greek immigrant, and my father was in trouble with his father, at least for a time, for not marrying a Greek girl. When my mother came to Tuscola for the first time, she was relegated to the kitchen with the Greek women while the males ate in the dining room. "I thought I had landed on the moon," she told me. "Here I was in a small town in the middle of nowhere, Greek ladies chattering away in their language, no smoking for women allowed in the house or in public, and the men in the other room laughing and having a good time. I could not believe my fate." She always told me, however, that as she became a master chocolate dipper, that skill put her solidly in Gus's good graces.

Betty and Paul's union did, however, clear the way for my Aunt Helen to marry her Tuscola sweetheart, Bill Skinner. While Helen was being courted, my parents had to chaperone them on their dates. My mother said she and my father would just sleep in the back seat of the car.

After my father returned from serving in Europe in World War II, my parents moved to the East Coast, where my father had two confectionery stores over the course of twenty years, one in Maryland and one in Pennsylvania. He also tried the insurance business for a time but missed being a confectioner. We gravitated back to Illinois in the mid-1960s and settled in Tuscola. As children, my brother, Scott, and sister, Devon, and I were required to work at the store in the afternoons when school was over if we had no school activities, and of course we worked Saturdays and Sundays. Our wages were paid "under the table." Many afternoons I completed my school homework at the counter while I served coffee and sodas, and during the holidays I packed hundreds of boxes of candy.

We were fortunate that my grandfather still came into the store every day. He called Scott, Devon, and me "half-breeds," since our mother was not Greek, but that never really bothered me personally. We did not discuss what it meant to be Greek, although my father and grandfather spoke Greek often during the day with each other. My father's cousin George, son of Nick from across the street, came in everyday to get ice; he and my father spoke Greek then as well. We learned "store Greek," or specific words for things like the numerations of money, shoplifting, or one's capability to complete a task. My great-aunt Agnes was still living as well, and both she and my grandfather spoke with pretty thick accents into their senior years. My grandfather always scared me, yet he was approachable. He was filled with great axioms of life lessons and shared his words of wisdom at every opportunity. When I was a teenager, though, I must admit, much of it was lost on me. I did understand, however, what it had taken to immigrate to America, establish a business, become successful, and survive the Depression, two World Wars, and the changing entrepreneurial climate.

I remember the local businessmen, in the 1960s and 1970s, meeting every afternoon at our corner store for a drink and gossip. Before e-mail and the internet, our store was the hub of information gathering and dissemination. I learned quite a bit from just observing. At that time there were two banks in downtown Tuscola, two newspapers, and many shops. The businesspeople, bankers, lawyers, and others would come in with their news, political views, and candid opinions about local and world events. Farmers, if not in the fields, would come into town for shopping and would also make their way into our store. We were the neighborhood repository of all that was happening in our world at that moment. It was heady stuff for a young person to absorb; perhaps that is what I missed the most as an adult, and it motivated me in the decision to return to Tuscola. Of course, there was also just the visceral feeling of the place. My memories are similar to those of Constance Constant, author of *Austin Lunch*. Like her family's restaurant for her, the Candy Kitchen for me was the safe place where I could go every day; I could have ice cream or chocolate; my family was all together. Though working at the store was very hard, the Candy Kitchen was that familiar and constant element of my life.

That was not enough at the time, however, to keep the three third-generation Greeks there on the corner. My siblings and I all knew how to make our products from beginning to end, but none of us had any desire to continue in this business after high school, nor did my parents encourage it. We all went off to college and had left Tuscola behind by the end of the 1970s and early 1980s. This was also a time when fast-food chains, big box stores, and small retail shops were spreading from less busy downtowns to new shopping malls and the suburbs. Small-town "downtowns" died. This sounded the final death knell for first- and sometimes second-generation-owned soda fountains and candy stores, such as ours. My father retired, and our building was sold. It remained empty for almost thirty years until my sister and I resurrected it in 2004 and Flesor's Candy Kitchen reopened on the corner of Main and Sale.

Peter Vriner and George Vaky and my grandfather were three of the earliest Greek confectioners in central Illinois. Thousands more Greeks were soon to immigrate in the first two decades of the twentieth century, however, and many of them would make their way to Chicago or St. Louis and then to central Illinois. It is their stories I want to tell now, both of those who went to the larger cities, like Springfield and Decatur, and of those who, like my grandfather, settled in the small rural towns.

CHAPTER 7

SMALL-CITY GREEK CONFECTIONERS

He had fourteen dollars pinned to his underwear.
His "luggage" was a paper bag of meager possessions.
—Phyllis Bartges Bayles

While Champaign-Urbana was the original center of Greek confectioneries in central Illinois, Greek-owned shops soon opened in cities such as Springfield, Decatur, and Danville and in other towns across the region, thanks to the pioneering efforts of George Vaky and Peter Vriner. Many of these Greek entrepreneurs initially passed through Champaign to receive training in candy making, a quick education in how to run a business, and sometimes financial support, with Vaky's and Vriner's blessing. Though in many ways their experiences were like my grandfather's, each of their stories is also different, in intriguing and interesting ways. For the Greeks in the small cities, there was usually a Greek community and sometimes even an Orthodox church. Here they did not have to go it alone, as did the single Greek confectioner in the rural towns. One thing they all had in common, however, was a strong determination to succeed.

I have had the good fortune to visit with Phyllis Bartges Bayles and hear the poignant story of her Greek immigrant father, Christos Bartges (b. 1905 in the Bay of Corinth), who grew up in a tiny village.[1] In 1918 the

Greek army needed more soldiers, so the Greek military began going from village to village to force young men and even boys to fill the ranks. Phyllis said her grandfather was concerned that his eldest son would be conscripted, so he smuggled him to a coastal port and placed young Christos on a ship bound for America. This was in 1919.

> He had fourteen dollars pinned to his underwear. His "luggage" was a paper bag of meager possessions. He was scared and lonely and missed his family. He wondered if he would ever see them again. During his voyage, the passengers kept busy trying to pass the time. They visited. They prayed. They walked around the decks of the ship. The women would sew, and the men would smoke and discuss politics, the war, and the rumors they had heard about America. At night, they would find ways to keep their spirits up. There were passengers not only from Greece, but from several other countries. Each nation had its own type of music, and each group had at least one person who had brought along a musical instrument. So, the people would play their native songs and dance to their music. My dad told me that, although he cried every night from being scared and lonely, listening to the music, and watching the dancing, helped lift his spirits and take his mind off things.

A lovely Greek woman befriended Christos on the crossing and looked after him. When Christos landed in New York, he was met by an uncle, who took him to Boston. There he worked as a busboy. Christos and his uncle then traveled to Chicago, where Christos was surprised to find the kind Greek lady from his ship—she had married Christos's uncle! In Chicago, Christos worked in a factory for less than one week and decided that was not the job for him. He attended classes at Northwestern University for approximately one year. An uncle, George Variames, suggested Christos go stay with relatives in Lansing, Michigan. In Lansing he met his wife, Margaret Baryames, and they then moved to Danville, Illinois. Christos began business, albeit briefly, as a confectioner but quickly moved into the food business, opening the Deluxe Restaurant around 1937. As mentioned in chapter 6, Christos Bartges was instrumental in supplying the Greek restaurant and candy store owners in central Illinois with sugar during World War II.

Phyllis stressed that the Greek community in Danville was quite tight-knit. There were approximately twenty families, and everyone got along, especially the women. She did not remember any Ku Klux Klan activity, but she did recall her mother telling her the non-Greek townspeople sometimes called them "the dirty Greeks" and that first-generation Greeks knew that many in the community were prejudiced against them. Because the Danville Greeks were so close, they were one of the first communities in downstate Illinois to establish a Greek Orthodox Church, St. Barbara's, in 1927.

In 2011 Phyllis published an essay about Greek identity and community strength titled "Memories of a Church Bakery." In it she discussed women's roles in the Greek community and the three mainstays of their lives: home, church, and the business. In St. Barbara's, "the chapel's *kitchen* [her emphasis] was where the strength of the Greek community was at its finest. The women ruled. This was their domain—and nobody in his or her right mind would ever question, doubt, or argue that fact."[2] The ladies raised funds with bake sales for church repair and maintenance. Other old country traditions for women prevailed as well. Most second-generation Danville Greek women, for example, married Greek men, while, conversely, only two or three male members married Greek women. Phyllis's brother Dean[3] recalled how important family was—their great-uncle and great-aunt, the lady from the boat, lived upstairs in their house. Phyllis agreed, noting that "you knew what your dad did and your friends knew what their parents did. That engendered respect."[4]

Education was the key to success for the second generation. Phyllis, Dean, and their younger brother, Art, all left home to attend college and have professional careers. Dean said his father hinted to him that perhaps he might consider staying in the restaurant business, but Dean had different aspirations, and his father supported him. Phyllis and Dean both related, however, that through their time spent at the family restaurant as children, they learned a great work ethic and understood what it took to make a living. Despite the hard work required, most second-generation Greek youngsters later appreciated having been an integral part of their parents' businesses.

Decatur had one of the most important Greek communities in central Illinois. Like several other "downstate" cities, Decatur owed much of its rapid growth to the railroads. After the mid-1800s, it was positioned as a "processing point for agricultural products, a transportation link to larger markets, and a retail goods distribution center to the surrounding hinterlands."[5] In 1920, Decatur's population stood at almost fifty thousand, approximately twice the size of Champaign-Urbana in the same year.[6]

Decatur was the center for farm produce processing in central Illinois for export. After World War I, soybeans became second only to corn as the favored crop of Illinois farmers. My grandfather, who bought a farm in the 1930s, recalled how representatives from the large Decatur-based agribusiness A. E. Staley came to Tuscola to try to convince him and other Douglas County farmers to plant soybeans instead of corn. They offered free seed to those who tried it. It was a radical move at the time, but it turned out to be profitable.

Decatur became known as the "Soybean Capital of the World."[7] Its burgeoning growth and accessibility to the railroads and newly built highways, such as Route 36, beckoned immigrants, like the Greeks, to establish businesses there. In 1930 there were 104 native-born Greeks in Decatur, the largest foreign group in the city after the Germans and English. Virtually all were naturalized citizens.[8] These Decatur Greeks created several migration networks, connecting with Greeks in Mattoon, Cairo, Greenup, Jacksonville, Champaign-Urbana, Springfield, Litchfield, and Pana and even over in Iowa. They were an enterprising group.

John Papadopulos and Louis George Nichols were the first Greek confectioners in Decatur. Papadopulos (b. 1855) came to America in 1884 and became a naturalized citizen in 1886. Where he lived between then and 1899 is not clear, but in that year he is one of three confectioners in Decatur, along with Louis George Nichols and a non-Greek, John F. Somerville.[9] By 1902 Papadopulos had moved to Mattoon, Illinois, where he had a candy store,[10] and then, around 1905, he moved again, this time to Cedar Rapids, Iowa.[11] He and his wife, Lucretia, lived above their confectionery store.[12] By the 1920s many other Greek names appeared in Cedar Rapids connected to the food business, suggesting that a large Greek entrepreneurial community was evolving there. Sadly, however, in 1922, Lucretia asked the court to appoint a guardian for John as he was now of "unsound mind." John died in Chicago in May 1923. Lucretia disappears from the record after that.[13]

Louis Nichols (b. March 18, 1872, in Athens) came to America in 1890. By 1900 he was living in Decatur, rooming with non-Greeks, and working as a candy maker,[14] in partnership with John F. Somerville.[15] In 1905 he married a non-Greek woman from Mt. Zion, Illinois, Lillian Burrows, in Chicago,[16] and they returned to Decatur to establish a family.[17] Around 1907 Louis opened the "Nicholas Candy Co.," one of eight retail confectioneries then with addresses on North Water Street.[18] Nichols sold his store to the Bacopuloses in 1914, which they renamed the Princess Confectionery.[19] Sometime between then and 1920, he moved with his family to Delaware, Ohio, and took up farming.[20] One might speculate that, like my grandfather, Nichols maintained a love for the land and had saved his candy business earnings to eventually purchase a farm. However, by 1930 Nichols had returned to candy making, now in Schoolcraft, Michigan. His son John was a salesman in the candy store they owned.[21] Louis Nichols died in Schoolcraft in 1934 at age sixty-two, and Lillian in 1968 at age eighty-one.[22]

Sam J. Malleos (b. January 15, 1886) came directly to Decatur from San Nicholas, Greece, in 1903. Sam worked in Louis Nichols's confectionery for five years and then opened his own confectionery, Sam's, in 1908. He must have rolled his peanut roaster out on the sidewalk as my grandfather did, for in July 1909 he was charged with "taking up the sidewalk with his peanut wagon."[23] When this store was destroyed by fire (not from the peanut roaster), he opened a new store at 114 Merchant Street on Lincoln Square in 1909.[24] Sam's brothers Thomas J. (b. July 4, 1884), Peter J. (b. August 15, 1889), and Nickolas J. (b. April 3, 1894) all came with him to America in 1903.[25] Nick and Peter went into the confectionery business with Sam as the "Sam J. Malleos Brothers Co." Brother Thomas worked for the railroad as a section foreman, employment agent, and interpreter.

Tragically, Sam and Thomas died in 1923 within two months of each other. Sam died from surgical complications, and Thomas was electrocuted while assisting with wiring for a city festival.[26] In his obituary, Sam was described as "a good businessman and progressive, always endeavoring to make his place the most attractive in the city. Only recently he spent several thousand dollars in remodeling his place on Lincoln Square. He was known to practically everybody in Decatur."[27] Within days of Sam's death, Nick and Pete assured Sam's customers they were keeping the business going, and there "will be no change except for the better, if that is possible."[28] They maintained it together until Peter died in 1945,[29] after which Nick ran the store himself until 1948 when he retired. Nick died in 1952.[30] Sam's was a Greek-owned mainstay of the Decatur downtown for over forty-five years.[31]

Two other longtime Greek ice cream and candy makers in Decatur were Peter J. Balamos and James Kareotes. They both came to America around 1903–4 and went almost directly to Decatur where, in 1909, they established the American Ice Cream Company.[32] Peter Balamos (b. June

1885 in Argos) not only was a successful business leader, but he also was instrumental in founding the Annunciation Greek Orthodox Church in Decatur, which drew Greeks from across central Illinois to its services.[33] James Kareotes (b. August 1881 in Nemea)[34] and Peter were partners until October 1948, when Peter died suddenly of a stroke. James kept the company going until his retirement in 1962. James had an uncle, Gus. D. Kareotes, who also came to America in 1903, spent some time in Chicago and Springfield, and then headed to Decatur, where he became a confectioner.[35] James Kareotes was in partnership with Greek immigrants Gust Pappas and Thomas, Andrew, and George Greanias in the Central Park Confectionery. The American Ice Cream Company and the Central Park Confectionery were both located on North Water Street in Decatur.[36]

The Greanias brothers, Thomas (b. 1883), Andrew (b. 1893), and George (b. 1895), all came from Masklena, Arcadia, Greece. Tom immigrated to America in 1899, initially going to Chicago and then moving to Decatur. In 1914 he opened the Lincoln Square Café and later also worked at the Central Park Confectionery. Along with Peter Balamos, Tom was instrumental in the establishment of the Decatur Greek Orthodox Church and was also active in the World War I Red Cross food drive.[37] Tom's brothers followed him to America. Andrew immigrated in 1906 at the age of twelve and went directly to Decatur.[38] George came to America in 1912, when he was seventeen. He joined his brothers in Decatur in 1916, helping to run the restaurant.[39]

Another Greek candy institution in Decatur was the Princess Confectionery, run by the Bacopulos cousins Peter G. (b. August 25, 1888) and Basil (Bill) (b. January 1, 1891). They came to America in 1903 from Dara, Greece, and first lived in Jacksonville, Illinois, west of Springfield, where they had an older cousin, Basil John Geanetos.[40] In late 1914, the Bacopuloses moved to Decatur, bought Louis Nichols's store, and renamed it the Princess Confectionery.[41] In March 1918 they installed a "new and sanitary tile floor," which they promised would make theirs the "most sanitary confectionery in the state."[42] Two months later they announced they had used store sales from the past week to buy $1,400 worth of Liberty bonds.[43] And, interestingly, they closed the store on May 8, 1921, so everyone could attend Peter's marriage to Anthe Karakathona (b. July 28, 1896) at Hull House in Chicago.[44] Around 1924, Basil and his brother, another Peter G. (b. August 15, 1894), moved to Monticello, Illinois, where they opened Bill and Pete's Restaurant.[45]

Peter and Anthe had five children, one of whom, Gregory, sacrificed for his country by serving in World War II and returning paralyzed from the waist down.[46] Peter kept the Princess open until 1946.[47] He died in February 1968 after living a successful and benevolent fifty-three years in Decatur. He belonged to AHEPA and served at various times as president, treasurer, and chanter at the Decatur Orthodox Church.[48]

Peter Haikalis, Basil Geanetos's grandson, described to me how the chain migration from Dara, northwest of Tripoli, to Jacksonville came about and the network from there to Decatur.[49] Peter's grandfather Basil (b. January 1, 1871) came from a very poor family, so he decided to immigrate to America in 1901 or 1902. His steamship ticket, however, took him only as far as Marseilles, France. He was not allowed to continue to America, so he remained in France for four or five years, apprenticed with a confectioner, and earned enough for passage to America. He passed through Ellis Island and then went to Eau Claire, Wisconsin, where he knew that others from his village had settled. Basil then returned to Greece and married Vassiliki (Bessie) Chekos (b. 1884) around 1910. Her father was Dara's mayor and was in the grain business, so this apparently was a good match with a dowry.[50] The couple returned to America and settled in Jacksonville, Illinois. Basil registered for the draft on September 12, 1917, but did not have to serve because of his wife and family.[51] With the help of his Bacopulos cousins, Basil opened the Jacksonville Ice Cream and Confectionery Company store around 1920. His grandfather's store, Peter reflected, looked like the Tuscola Candy Kitchen, which he and his brother visited in 2012.

The Geanetos family took pride in their Jacksonville store and even ordered ice cream chairs from Austria. Basil and Bessie had five children.[52] Although Peter claims his mother, Jennie (b. March 12, 1911), was the favorite, she was still expected at the store after school to do her homework and work in the shop as needed, as were her siblings. In 1929 Jennie graduated from high school and was sent to Illinois College in Jacksonville. Her mother, Bessie, was illiterate, and she wanted her daughter to be educated. According to Peter, his mother was to have an arranged marriage; appropriate suitors came to court, but the men did not want to marry a woman who had attended college. As a result, she went to Decatur to stay with an aunt and there met her husband, Dennis Haikalis (b. January 27, 1895), who owned a grocery store.[53] They were married in 1931 and stayed in Decatur until 1964, when he sold his businesses and moved to California. As none of Basil Geanetos's children were interested in taking over the business, the Jacksonville Ice Cream and Confectionery was sold following his death on February 11, 1938.[54]

Another landmark Decatur confectionery in the 1910s and 1920s was the Empress, owned by James K. Dovekas (Demetrios Konstantinos Ntovikas) (b. June 17, 1889, in Katompolios) and Gust Constantopulos (b. January 9, 1891, in Tripoli).[55] Dovekas immigrated through Chicago, heading first to Springfield, where he opened a confectionery in 1914, and then moving to Decatur.[56] Constantopulos came to America in 1911 and to Decatur in 1913, after working at a confectionery in Lincoln, Illinois, for a year. He then worked in Louis Nichols's confectionery and the Bacopulos's Princess Confectionery for three years.[57] When it opened in April 1916, the local news reported that "hundreds of Decatur folks were delighted Saturday, when they attended the formal opening of the new Empress Confectionery." The new store was next to the Empress theater.[58] Meanwhile, Gust's older brother, Christ George Constantopulos (b. September 6, 1890) arrived in Decatur in 1915 and in 1917 registered for the draft.[59] In February 1921, Christ and a Greek partner from Chicago, William Chagoures, opened the Butterfly Confectionery, initially making their candy at the Empress.[60]

Similar to the way my grandfather and others invested in land, Gust and Christ took their profits and went into the theater business.[61] In 1924 they bought the Avon Theater and later the Rogers Theater.[62] This caused a split between Gust and James Dovekas and the end of their partnership. Gust sold Dovekas his half-ownership in the Empress, but the business lasted only three more years until Dovekas declared bankruptcy. He then moved to Chicago and died there in 1976.[63]

In 1922 another Constantopulos brother, Angelo (b. 1895), immigrated in 1922, and in 1925 the youngest brother, Theodore George (b. 1900), came to Decatur. In 1928 Gust and Christ Constantopulos partnered with James Dalmares (b. 1895) to establish another store, the Chocolate Shop.[64] The brothers Gust, Christ, Angelo, and Theodore now worked together managing the Chocolate Shop, the Butterfly Confectionery, and the Decatur theaters.[65] Gust later acquired the Castle Theater in Bloomington and the Times Theater in Danville.[66]

Interestingly, in 1924 Gust and Christ Constantopulos became citizens and changed their name to Constan (or Constant). Thereafter they used both spellings.[67]

Like many of our Greek confectioners, once Gust had established himself in business, he returned to Greece, in 1935, to marry a Greek woman, Vasula Platopulou. She was a family friend of another Constantopulos brother, Anastasios, who was an Athens lawyer.[68]

In 1944 the Constantopulos brothers sold the last of their confectionery enterprises, the Chocolate Shop, to three other Greeks—Peter Stavropoulos of Chicago (a cousin), Napoleon Lekas of Peoria (formerly with the Sugar Bowl there), and James Dalmares of Rantoul (who had worked at the Chocolate Shop for several years).[69] They kept possession of their theaters until 1966, a year after Gust's death in February 1965. On the day of his funeral, "out of respect to the memory of our founder, Gust Constan," the Avon, Rogers, Castle, and Times theaters were all closed.[70] After he died, Gust's estate was valued at over $350,000. The Avon and Rogers theaters were later taken over by another Greek theater family, the Kerasoteses, whom we will discuss when we come to Springfield.[71]

Christ's death in 1978[72] and Theodore's in 1992 marked the true end of the confectionery and theater empire the Constantopulos brothers had run successfully for more than five decades. Over this time they were some of Decatur's most successful businessmen, even branching out into Danville and Bloomington. They were all active members of AHEPA and various civic organizations. Gust was another of the founders of the Decatur Greek Orthodox Church in the 1920s, and all the brothers were active church members. Gust, with his brothers' help, also led the local Greek War Relief fund during World War II.

By the middle of the 1920s, other Greek confectioneries had established businesses in Decatur. There was the Candyland Confectionery Company, operated by G. P. Stamas, James Sanas, D. A. Regiokos, and Pete Moukas,[73] which remained open until around 1938.[74] Paul Dalamas and Peter Mitrakos had set up the Eureka Confectionery,[75] which Paul Dalamas's son, Paul T. Jr., kept open into the 1950s.[76] Theodore Athas was a confectioner on East Eldorado Street.[77] In 1935, Pete Moukas opened his own shop, the Rainbow Confectionery, and remained in business at least until 1960.[78]

Although this research is focused upon the first three decades of the twentieth century, there were later Greek immigrants who also operated confectioneries in Decatur. These would include James Dalmares of the Chocolate Shop, which he ran from 1944 to 1961,[79] and Kyros Ashemos, who ran the Ashemos Candy Shop from 1935 to 1966. Kyros Ashemos and his brother Gus were born in Kastanochori, Arcadia, Greece. Kyros became a very prominent member of the Decatur community. He was active in the Masons as well as in the Greek Orthodox Church.[80] His brother Gus owned the Charleston Confectionery for two or three years and also operated a restaurant in Decatur before moving to Champaign.[81]

The original Greek confectioners in Decatur, while maintaining a small ethnic conclave, integrated into the established Decatur business community and served a variety of customers, including young people. During the first two decades of the twentieth century, the Greek confectioners advertised heavily in the Decatur High School yearbook, the *Decanois*. As with many advertising efforts by first-generation Greeks, the ads revealed a rich narrative about pride in their businesses, the desire to emphasize cleanliness and accessibility, and the fact that they were all in competition with each other despite the affinity they had in maintaining their local and home country networks.

Sam Malleos advertised that his store, Sam's, was "The Original Confectionery"[82] and that "our place is the cleanest, coolest and most sanitary place in the city. All interurbans and trolley cars stop in front of our store at the transfer house."[83] The Bacopulos cousins, Peter and Bill, advertised their "up-to-date and sanitary shop," the Princess Confectionery, and also, in competition with Sam's, staked their store's reputation on being "the coolest and most sanitary place in town."[84] James Dovekas and Gust Constantopulos emphasized the Empress Confectionery's location in the Empress Building and proudly proclaimed that their confections were "clean and fresh."[85] These and similar ads were repeated over the course of several years through the 1920s, and one can assume that the emphases on sanitary conditions and the modernization of their stores was an effort to eradicate any anti-foreign characterizations of Greeks as having unclean environments and old-fashioned modes of operation. During one of the Ku Klux Klan's more active years, Sam's invited all patrons in because "our place is always open to public inspection."[86] Christ Constantopulos, in contrast, simply advised teens in 1923 to not forget the Butterfly Confectionery during the summer months.[87]

High school yearbooks and newspapers were not the confectioners' only means of advertising. The Annunciation Greek Orthodox Church, founded in 1927, not only served its parishioners in Decatur but also touched most central Illinois Greek communities. The church published two histories, one completed in 1945 and a second in 1997, which celebrated its seventieth anniversary. The Annunciation Church's histories include pages advertising, congratulating, memorializing, announcing, recognizing, remembering, and honoring families and businesses in Decatur, Springfield, Champaign-Urbana, Pana, Mattoon, Charleston, Taylorville, Clinton, and other towns across central Illinois. Many of these celebrated the regional growth and success of the Greeks and the Greek business community. On April 14, 1919, the state of Illinois had recognized the "Hellenic Society of Decatur, Illinois."[88] Founding trustees were familiar names: Sam Malleos, Nick Spell, Peter Balamos, James Dovekas, Gust Constantopulos, Peter Bacopulos, George Calfas, and George Davis. They began to raise funds to build a church, and the project was completed in 1927. The Reverend Emmanuel Papapanagiotou was the first priest to say the Divine Liturgy, on Christmas Day. The first church officers were Tom Greanias, Nick Malleos, William Frank, and William A. Chiagouris (Chagoures). The first Greek Language School was established in 1931,[89] and most second-generation Greek children were enrolled.

The Greeks in Springfield are the last of the city confectioners to discuss before we turn to the Greeks in the small towns. Over one hundred years ago, some of the state capital's leading businessmen were Greek confectioners and restaurant owners, and one Greek gentleman began by making candy and ended up selling it in his chain of movie theaters that eventually stretched across the country.

Springfield's first Greek confectioners were Peter Coutrakon Jr. (b. November 17, 1875) and Constantine ("Gus") Kerasotes. Peter came from Karaspai (modern Lefkokhoma, southeast of Sparta) to America in 1889.[90] In 1900 there were four male Coutrakons living together at 215 South Fifth: the head of the household, Peter Sr., age fifty-five; Peter Jr., his son, age twenty-five; John, Peter Sr.'s brother, age forty-four; and Peter Perikle, Peter Sr.'s nephew and John's son, age sixteen.[91] Peter Jr. is listed as a "candy maker." As 215 South Fifth was the future address of the Coutrakon–Kerasotes confectionery, it appears that Peter Jr. was already making candy in this location before his partnership with Gus Kerasotes, and the four relatives were living above the store.

John Coutrakon came over first, in 1887, and in 1900 worked as a day laborer in Springfield. He must have received some confectionery training, however, because in 1902 he moved to Lawrence, Kansas, and opened Coutrakon's Candy and Ice Cream Shop (later changed to Boston Confectionery). Peter Sr. had accompanied his teenage nephew Peter Perikle over in 1898 but then returned to Greece shortly after 1900. Peter P. was working for his father by 1917 and in 1920 bought the Boston Confectionery from him, while John opened the Lawrence Confectionery.[92]

Peter Jr. came over in 1889 and went first to Chicago, where he was a fruit peddler. He then moved to Springfield when he heard about a demand there for food service workers. Peter Jr. had a semi-arranged marriage in 1905 with Isabelle Hattoon (b. 1890). She was a Lebanese Christian, born in the Ottoman Empire (after World War I, Lebanon/Syria), who came to America in 1893.[93] Peter Jr. and Isabelle had two sons, George and Basil.[94]

Peter Coutrakon Jr.'s partner, Gus Kerasotes (b. August 1873 in Sparta), was first a confectioner before he moved into the theater business. Gus came to America in 1893 and first met Peter Jr. in Chicago. Coutrakon family history says that Peter told Gus he should come to Springfield, so Gus moved there around 1902.[95] That same year Peter and Gus founded the C&E Confectionery at 215 South Fifth. Gus's half-brother Louis George Kerasotes (b. 1884) immigrated in 1900[96] and initially worked as a clerk at the store.[97]

By 1908 there were over twenty other confectioners in Springfield, but none were Greeks.[98] In 1914 Sam Malleos from Decatur opened the Gaiety Confectionery, which had a common entrance with the Gaiety Theatre. It was managed by James Dovekas and Angel B. Nases (b. March 25, 1886, in Argus).[99] Dovekas moved on to Decatur in 1916, partnering with Gust Constantopolus at the Empress Confectionery. Angel Nases, along with his brother Thomas (b. July 14, 1893), appears to have managed the Gaiety well into the 1930s. It is not clear if Thomas and Angel bought it after Malleos's death in 1923. Angel died in 1942.[100]

The number of Greek confectioners continued to grow in the 1910s. Peter Coutrakon Jr.'s brother Charles (Constantine), who came to Springfield in 1905 and who first learned the confectionery and ice cream trade at the C&E, opened the Buffalo Confectionery in 1910 in partnership with Louis Kerasotes, who had moved over from Charleston.[101] Stephen and William Mastorakas opened Boy's Candy Shop in 1915.[102] They were joined by George Satiropoulos in 1919,[103] and in 1923 the three opened another place, the Oaks.[104] Around 1917 Charles Coutrakon went out on his own and opened the Avenue Confectionery at 813 North Grand. In 1924 Peter Coutrakon Jr. sold the C&E to the Greek Presvelos brothers, Nick and Chris. They named their new place the Elite Luncheonette and

Confectionery. Peter then joined Charles over at the Avenue, until they sold it around 1950. Peter died in 1951, Charles in 1956. Both brothers remained active businessmen and community members until their deaths.[105]

In 1919, after returning from service in World War I, Theodore ("Teddy") Gray (b. February 9, 1892, in Corinth) took ownership of the Sugar Bowl at Eleventh Street and South Grand Avenue and operated it and Gray's Restaurant for decades.[106] Gray, born Theodorus Anastasios Georgiou,

PHOTO 10. Avenue Confectionery, Springfield, c. 1928. Charles and Peter Coutrakon's iconic confectionery at 813 North Grand. Standing in the doorway, second from left, is Virginia Coutrakon, Charles's daughter, with friends Loretta, Toots, and Mildred. (Photo and information courtesy of Laura Catherwood and Laurel Rice.)

came to America around 1907, possessing a fourth grade education.[107] It appears that he apprenticed with Coutrakon and Kerasotes.[108] He married Mary Schrock in April 1920.[109] Gray is credited with opening the first drive-in restaurant in Springfield in 1926. In 1927 Gray and Alex Karon opened a second Sugar Bowl at State Street and South Grand.[110] Gray was also part-owner of two local theaters, the Pantheon and the Southtown. He was eighty-five years old when he died in 1977, having resided in Springfield for almost seventy years.[111]

Just as Coutrakon and Kerasotes helped Theodore Gray get into the confectionery business, so Gray then helped another new immigrant, James P. James (b. January 11, 1893, in Corinth), learn the trade. James's Greek name was Dimitrious Papadimitrious. It is not clear what year he immigrated to America, but family tradition says he came over with a brother (or half-brother) who then returned to Greece. Initially James went to St. Louis before then coming to Springfield in 1906 at age thirteen.[112] He initially worked as a bootblack, first on his own and then in partnership with the Kokenes brothers. He served in France during World War I, and in 1920 he met and married Antonella Konrad in Springfield. They had two girls, Helen and Katherine.[113] He began his confectionery career in 1921 when he became a clerk at Theodore Gray's Sugar Bowl Confectionery but eventually ventured out on his own.[114] Around 1923 he opened his own business, the James Confectionery, at 616 South Grand Avenue East. During the Great Depression he also acted as a private financier and provided money for investors. The James Confectionery remained open until 1942, when, because of the war, he was unable to find enough help. As a result, he closed the store and went into the real estate and development business.[115] By the time of his death in May 1960, he was recognized not only as a successful businessman but also as an active member of St. Anthony's Greek Orthodox Church, American Legion Post 32, and AHEPA. Katherine James, who graduated from St. Mary's at Notre Dame in South Bend, Indiana, married Peter Coutrakon Jr.'s son Basil. Interestingly, James's four sisters and a brother all remained in Greece.[116]

The food business is never easy, and the competition in larger cities like Springfield and Decatur made survival even more difficult. In Springfield during the 1920s, the number of retail confectioneries ranged from forty to fifty or more for any one year. In 1923, for example, there were forty-one retail confectioners in Springfield, and in 1928 there were fifty-one.[117]

It appears that the Greeks were pretty consistently represented, making up approximately 25 to 30 percent of the confectioners listed.

Charles Poulos's story (b. January 14, 1887) was a good example of the precarious life of a confectioner. Born in Sparta,[118] Poulos first appeared in Springfield in 1908, when he was a confectioner apprentice for Coutrakon and Kerasotes at the C&E. Charles worked for them until 1914, when he became a clerk at Coutrakon's Buffalo Confectionery.[119] In 1923 he established his own place, the Butterfly Confectionery on East Monroe, but closed by 1929.[120] Charles was then working as a soda dispenser at the

PHOTO 11. Theodore Gray (*right*) and James P. James (*left*), Springfield. James and Gray stand next to their delivery truck for the Sugar Bowl at Eleventh Street and South Grand Avenue in 1921. James opened the James Confectionery, at 616 South Grand Avenue East, two years later. (Photo Courtesy of Laurel Rice; also in Sangamon Valley Collection, Lincoln Library, Springfield, Illinois.)

Presvelos brothers' Elite Luncheonette and Confectionery.[121] A year later he was a clerk at Charles Coutrakon's Avenue Confectionery.[122] Poulos remained at the Avenue Confectionery until 1934, when he opened the Sherlock Confectionery, but he closed it[123] and opened the Enos Candy Kitchen on Enos Aveue in 1937.[124] Charles never married, and the Enos was his last venture. He ran it successfully until August 1945, when he tragically died in an automobile accident.[125]

In 1924, another Greek confectioner gained notoriety, not because of the quality of his sweets but because of his brutal murder. George Xamis was born in August 1895 in Moulki, on the Bay of Corinth, and immigrated to America in 1915. Early records described him as self-employed with his brother Gust (b. July 4, 1891) as a hat cleaner in Springfield.[126] They then opened the Xamis Brothers shoeshine parlor in 1919.[127] Four years later he took over the Princess Confectionery in Springfield, while another Xamis brother, Peter (b. 1889), was a barber.[128] Because of his diminutive build, George was known as "Shorty." Tragically, only a year after opening the Princess, late in the evening on October 16, 1924, an unknown assailant beat Xamis to death with a two-foot length of gas pipe outside of his home.[129] The newspaper described him as one of the best-known members of the local Greek colony and noted that he had served America in the Great War.[130] After George's death, Gust and Peter took over the running of the Princess Confectionery, but it closed by 1930 and Gust was back shoe shining and Peter barbering.[131]

There were several other Greek confectioners who made their mark on downtown Springfield. Chris (b. 1888 in Argos) and Nick (b. 1896 in Argos) Presvelos owned the Elite Luncheonette and Confectionery in the 1920s.[132] Chris came over first, in 1902, and Nick followed in 1910.[133] It is not clear why, but Nick and Chris seem to have split apart by 1933, when Chris was running the Elite but Nick was an employee at the Coney Island Red Hot Restaurant.[134] The Elite did not remain open long after that. In 1937 Chris was working at the South Town Grill and then at a pastry shop in the late 1940s.[135] Perhaps Nick returned to Greece, as he disappeared from the Springfield record.

Alex George Karon (b. June 14, 1893, in Corinth) was another longtime confectioner in Springfield. Born Alekos Karahouzites,[136] he immigrated to America in 1907 and was a clerk for Louis Nichols in Decatur by 1911 before he moved to Vandalia and worked with James Seolas. According to Karon's daughter Mary Dash, his name change came about while in

Vandalia when his employer kept misspelling his name on his paycheck. One day the employer wrote "Karon" on the paycheck with a two-dollar raise. "So, for $2, my father changed his name," Dash said.[137]

Karon returned to Springfield in 1927, and he and Theodore Gray jointly opened the second Sugar Bowl in April.[138] By 1930 Gray was managing the original restaurant, Sugar Bowl I, on Eleventh Street and Alex was manager of Sugar Bowl II on State Street. Alex went back to Corinth in 1930 to marry Angeline Pappas. After they returned to America, the

PHOTO 12. Sugar Bowl II, Springfield. Alex Karon leans on the counter at the Sugar Bowl II, at the corner of State Street and South Grand, Springfield, in the early 1930s. (Sangamon Valley Collection, Lincoln Library, Springfield, Illinois.)

couple lived with Gray and his family for a time.[139] While Sugar Bowl I also had a restaurant, Sugar Bowl II was primarily a confectionery and ice cream shop. Dash remembered though that during World War II the sugar shortage forced her dad to serve more food, including a steakburger, called the Karon-burger.[140] I wonder how the taste compared with my grandfather's Gusburger?

In the 1930s and 1940s the Sugar Bowl was a teen "hangout" along with Coutrakon's Avenue Confectionery and Diana's Sweet Shop.[141] Nancy Drake, another Karon daughter, remembered how "we went through a lot of love lives at the Sugar Bowl. There were so many dates we fixed up." Teenagers were not the only patrons, however, as Illinois governors Henry Horner, Dwight Green, and William Stratton were all regulars.[142] Nancy also recalled that she started working at the Sugar Bowl in 1942, when she was twelve. "We were taught how to wash, sweep, how to waitress and carry things to the curb. Later on, I was the only carhop in town with a college degree."[143]

Alex Karon's compassion and values were displayed in July 1949 when there was a polio outbreak in Springfield and all children under sixteen were ordered off the streets. Playgrounds, teenage soda fountain hangouts, golf courses, and bowling alleys all were feeling the effect of the ban. Karon, however, "as he looked over his deserted high school hangout," declared, "But I'd rather lose a thousand dollars than lose a single kid on account of polio."[144] Sadly, Theodore T. Gray, the son of Karon's close friend Theodore Gray, was one of the earliest victims of the polio outbreak, dying of the illness at age twenty-eight on September 2, 1950.[145]

Springfield Greeks, established and respected in the community, were integral in assisting on the American home front during World War II. In 1941, the Springfield Greek community gathered with other city and state leaders, including the Illinois governor, to support the Greek war relief. More than two thousand people attended a midnight benefit at the Orpheum Theater, and over $1,000 was raised. Entertainment ranged from radio star "Pappy" Cheshire to first-run movies. Governor Green and Springfield mayor John Kapp spoke of their admiration for the courage of the Greek people; Mayor Kapp observed that, "when historians write of the Second World War, certainly the brightest chapter will be the bravery of the Greeks in their fight."[146] As "Pappy" Cheshire and his wife were traveling to Springfield for the show, they stopped at the Greek-owned

Ariston Restaurant on Route 66 in Litchfield. Upon finishing his meal, Cheshire went to pay his bill and was recognized by owner Pete Adam. "You're doing a great thing tonight in Springfield, going up there to help my countrymen," said the Litchfield businessman, with a tear in his eye. "I'm going to pay for your dinner."[147]

The Greek war against the Axis powers in World War II drew the attention of Greeks and non-Greeks alike in Springfield. *Illinois State Journal-Register* staff writer Joe Belair wrote about the Greek war with Italy, sharing that the Greek soldiers were defining it as "another Thermopylae."[148] This historical reference to the defense of Thermopylae by Leonidas and his Spartan soldiers in 480 BC against the Persian leader Xerxes publicly linked the Springfield Greek immigrants to this heritage. James P. James reported that his brother Milton had his heel shot off during fighting in the Albanian mountains. Milton was described as "a modern Achilles."[149] James Magas's son, a cook at Gray's Confectionery, wrote to his father that he would be proud to fight and die for liberty. Theodore Gray had two brothers in Greece who were waiting to be called up to service. Basil Caselas, brother-in-law of Alex Karon, wrote from Greece, "We are fighting for honor, liberty, and family, and if anything happens, remember the children; this may be my last letter."[150] Basil Spiropoulos, the nephew of George Satiropolos, manager of Diana's Sweet Shop, was convinced the Greeks would win because they had faith in their cause. Gus and Louis Kerasotes had four nephews stationed along the Bulgarian line; Gus Kerasotes's son Anthony died when a German submarine torpedoed his ship, the USS *Leary*, in the North Atlantic on December 24, 1943.[151] Charles Coutrakon had two brothers and two nephews fighting, but he had not heard from them since August 1940. Steve Cherekos and Frank Houleris, proprietors of Mo Coffee Shop, had several male relatives fighting, but they had not heard from them either, nor had Andrew Lekometros, of Nick's Hat Cleaning and Shoe Shining Shop, heard from his two brothers and two brothers-in-law serving in the war.[152] Greek American patriotism was on full display during the war, both for the country where they were born and for their adopted country, America.

After the war, many second-generation Greeks moved on to other occupations, and the confectioneries in Springfield, as elsewhere, slowly went out of business. By 1953, the remaining Greek confectioneries in Springfield were Boy's Candy Shop, Coutrakon Confectionery (the old

Avenue Confectionery), Diana's Sweet Shop, and the Sugar Bowl II.[153] Some first-generation Greeks had simply gone out of business, some had opened restaurants, and some had retired and no one took their place.

The one major exception was the famous Kerasotes family. Gus and Louis Kerasotes began as confectioners and, like the Constantopulos brothers in Decatur, seized on a great opportunity at the birth of the movie age to expand their business ventures. Gus and Louis started what was to grow initially into a chain of forty central Illinois theaters when they opened a nickelodeon, the Royal Theatre, in 1909.[154] Eventually Kerasotes Theatres would become one of the largest theatre chains in America.

The Kerasotes family never forgot their Springfield roots, however, and in 1956, Gus donated the ground for the new St. Anthony's Hellenic Orthodox Church, which was built in 1957 for approximately $75,000. The building fund committee comprised Gus's sons George and Louis Kerasotes, Mary Karon, Dr. Aristides Kufdakis, Mrs. Theodore Gray, Constantine Passialis, Harry Xamis, and Gus Xamis.[155] The church was instrumental in coalescing the Greek community in Springfield and the surrounding towns. Nick Adam, son of Pete Adam, founder of the Ariston Restaurant in Litchfield, told me that he attends when he is able and is happy that he does not have to travel to St. Louis for worship.[156] There is also an active AHEPA chapter in Springfield that remains an important part of the Greek community to this day.

As we have seen, in the early decades of the nineteenth century first-generation Greek immigrants settled and prospered in the larger cities across central Illinois—Champaign-Urbana, Danville, Decatur, and Springfield. Often earning their first wages as shoe shiners, railroad workers, and unskilled laborers, they evolved into confectioners, soda fountain and candy shop owners, restaurateurs, theater owners, and, in one case, a movie house mogul. They built Orthodox churches, invested in buildings and land, became leaders in local social organizations and government, donated to charities, and displayed their patriotism by serving in the military and encouraging the buying of war bonds. Their second-generation sons and daughters went to local schools, and many on to college, obtaining the educations that most of their parents never received. Their Greek communities grew through networking and chain migration, as the first arrivals paid for their family members and friends to follow them to America and then helped them to survive by providing acculturation, lodging, training, jobs, and even monetary support for them to establish their own businesses.

Along with Chicago and St. Louis, these central Illinois cities became the hubs from which Greek individuals, brothers, and single families radiated to the small towns. There, like my grandfather, they established confectioneries and became integral and respected members of their communities. It is their stories we now want to tell.

CHAPTER 8

SMALL-TOWN GREEK CONFECTIONERS

The place [Papadakos Confectionery and Soda Fountain] was so busy on Saturday night, they charged a ten-cent admission! It was quite the hangout.

—Paul Jacobs

It is not hard to imagine larger Greek communities in small urban centers like Springfield or Decatur. This chapter, however, tells the story of the first-generation immigrants who settled in small-town central Illinois, most often singly or accompanied only by a wife or sibling. Going into business for oneself is always difficult, even more so when a person is in a small town, is a foreigner, speaks little English, has little money or education, and is learning on the fly both how to make candy and ice cream and how to run a business. And yet there were Greek immigrants who did it, making new homes for themselves, raising families, and creating successful businesses in small rural communities. Like my grandfather, they persevered, overcoming prejudice, difficult economic times, and separation from their native homes and families. They are wonderful examples of the immigrant success story in America.

Due south of Decatur is Pana, once the Rose Capital of the country thanks to its extensive greenhouses of roses grown each year for the

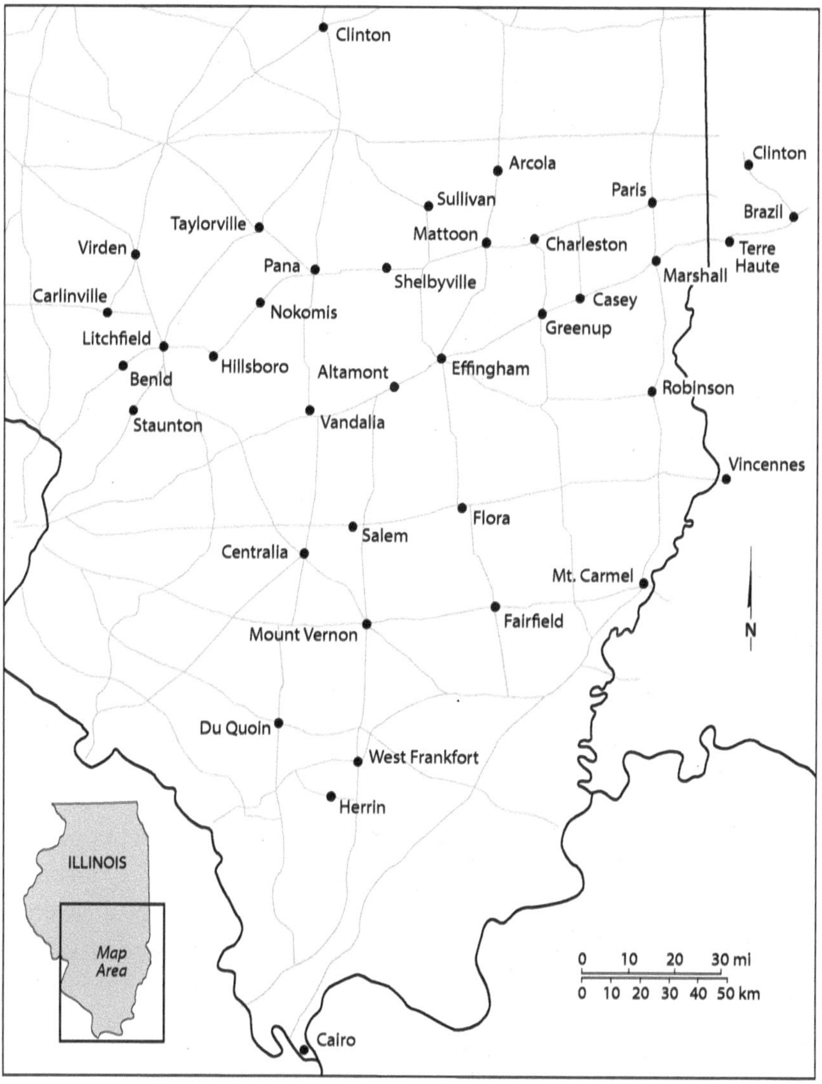

MAP 3. Smaller Towns in Central Illinois. (Courtesy Bill Nelson.)

Rose Bowl Parade in California. Here lived two of the most successful Greek confectioners in central Illinois. One was George Avgary Kehias (or Kehagias) (b. January 6, 1894), one of eight children who grew up in the village of Vamvakou, Lakonia, north of Sparta. His family lived in a valley and grew olives and oranges. George immigrated to America in 1909 and went first to Wisconsin, where he had cousins. From there he traveled to Chicago and then to Pana, where he arrived with only five dollars in his pocket.[1] An initial loan from a local bank allowed him to buy a soda fountain shop in 1914 that went by various names over the years but was commonly known as George's Candy Shop.[2] He then purchased ingredients to make taffy for Christmas and, having sold it all, decided that Pana would be a good place to make his home.[3]

Only three years after opening his store, George went to serve his new country in the Great War, attending baking and cooking school and then serving in France in the Quartermaster Corps.[4] George's oldest son, Avgary, later related that while his father was away, his father's cousin Louis ran George's store. In a 1983 newspaper article, Avgary fondly remembered receiving an English toffee recipe from Louis that included the temperature to which it should cook before pouring it out on the marble table, "but we know he didn't use a thermometer." Avgary recalled that candy recipes and flavor formulas were exchanged and shared among the Greek confectioners in Taylorville, Mattoon, and Champaign.[5]

George Kehias married Katherine Haynes, a non-Greek woman from Pana, on April 1, 1923. They met while attending the Pana opera and eventually had five children—Avgary, Stratton, James, Caroline, and Georgia.[6] Katherine embraced Greek customs, including cooking, and also found time to manage real estate properties. The family made multiple trips together back to Greece.[7]

George's innate business acumen seems to have been exceptional, because only eleven years after opening his store, George donated an entire city block to be developed into a children's playground, free of all taxation or indebtedness whatsoever. He also agreed to construct a wading pool in the park plus make other improvements before deeding it to the city and then to pay for any future improvements. The city council unanimously agreed to his proposal, and Kehias Park remains a popular green space in Pana today.[8]

George's love of children is evident in some wonderful memories that his youngest daughter, Georgia Kehias Hamilton, shared with me.

> [At Christmas] Dad dressed up like Santa in a beautiful crimson velvet suit my mother made for him; he would fill bushel baskets full of candy and fruit [and] take them to Assumption, Illinois, to the Kemmerer Home for Children. Dad would ride in on the fender of a car, waving to all the children, and then leave the gifts. Also, he hired someone to dress up like Santa (also the Easter bunny) and they would stand outside the confec-

> tionery handing out candy to everyone. In the summer he would invite all the Bible School children to walk (single file) to his store on their last day and treat them to his homemade ice cream. It was quite a sight to see![9]

In May 1929 George razed one of Pana's old derelict buildings downtown and constructed a two-story brick building that, ever proud of his Greek heritage, he named the Spartan Building. The building was completed the same week as the stock market crash that began on October 24, 1929, and set off the Great Depression. As one news reporter noted, "Probably no other Pana businessman . . . other than George Kehias, would have at this period undertaken so large an investment and undertaking as the erection of this beautiful business structure." But, the reporter added, one of George's mottos had always been, "There shall Be No Backward Step."[10] Intended for office and store space, the total cost for land and building was $35,000. As the building neared completion, George expressed his love and gratefulness to the city and people of Pana:

> I have faith in Pana. What little I am in a business way came from the people of Pana—they made me what I am today. I am not afraid of investing the money I have made . . . right back in Pana my hometown. I am not worried about the financial returns. I came here sixteen years ago . . . with a five-dollar bill in my pocket. Pana people . . . have been my friends and my patrons. My wife is a Pana girl and my [children] are Pana born.

The news reporter observed, "It would be well for Pana if this city had more business men and home loving and progressive citizens like George Kehias."[11] In 1940, after having operated George's Place on North Locust Street since 1914, he moved the shop to the Spartan Building.[12] George was only fifty-nine when he died in 1953 following a stroke. Demonstrating the high respect in which he was held, Pana businesses closed during the hour of his funeral.[13]

Georgia remembers that, like many second-generation Greek children, they all worked in the store—she "from the time I could see over the counter." The family lived above a store across the street from George's, which was open every day, even Christmas.[14] George's son Avgary took over the business after his father's death, partnering with Auggie Kronshagen, a childhood friend who had worked in George's from an early age. Avgary had attended the University of Illinois and Wayne State University in Michigan and had served in India during World War II, but his heart was back in Pana. He and Auggie transitioned into the management and then ownership of George's Place in 1949 and ran the shop for the next forty-two years, until June 30, 1991.[15] Because of Avgary, George's Candy Shop remained open for more than seventy-six years, which was phenomenal for small-town confectioneries and soda fountains.

The other Greek confectioner in Pana was George H. Lecas (b. August 1899), who started the Lecas Candy Company around 1930 and remained in business for over thirty years. His was not a candy shop but a factory that manufactured candies for mass distribution in Illinois, Indiana, Missouri, Wisconsin, and Minnesota.

Born in Paxos, Lecas came to America in 1914. He married German-born Edith Bank in Pana in 1920.[16] A company history written around 1950 says Lecas first worked in a confectionery store in Peoria, where he learned candy making from the store's owner, his uncle Christ Lecas. George then worked for a time in a confectionery store in Joplin, Missouri, then in Champaign for a year, and finally he moved to Pana. He first ran a combination restaurant and candy store but then began manufacturing candy. By 1950 he had contracts with S. S. Kresge 5&10, F. W. Woolworth, and "thousands of retail outlets." Two of his biggest sellers were peanut brittle and coconut brittle.[17] The plant used 15,000–16,000 gallons of corn syrup every week. For Christmas in 1948 the company produced 300,000 pounds of peanut brittle and had Easter orders for 500,000 candy baskets and 15,000 pounds of chocolate Easter eggs for 1949.[18] Lecas died in 1971 and Edith in 2000. The Parthenon is engraved on their gravestone.[19]

Because it remained open into the 1960s, the Greenup Candy Kitchen on Old National Road 40 is as fondly remembered by residents of that area as my grandfather's store is in Tuscola. It belonged to Thomas (b. 1880 in Sparta) and Angela (Kominos) Loomis (b. 1881), who opened it around 1915. Thomas immigrated to America in 1907,[20] having left Angela (known as "Lil") behind in Greece to take care of their children, Nicollette and John.

Thomas was not the first of his family to immigrate, however. His brothers Peter (with wife Annie) and then George had come over in 1888 and 1896[21] and had opened the Greek Candy Factory in Burlington, Iowa, by 1900.[22] Peter and Annie left Burlington in 1900, though,[23] leaving George to run the shop, now the Elite Confectionery. In 1908, by which time there were thirty-three confectioners in Burlington, George moved to Keokuk, Iowa, where he first owned a bowling alley[24] and then opened a confectionery, selling candy, fruit, and ice cream.[25] Peter reappears as a confectioner in Decatur in 1905,[26] but as Decatur had three "manufacturing confectioners" and twenty-two "retail confectioners" by 1907, he, Annie, and their four children relocated again, to downstate Cairo, Illinois.[27] There he opened the North Pole Candy Kitchen.[28] When Annie died in 1928, Peter left the confectionery business.[29] He died in 1944.[30]

After immigrating in 1907, Thomas Loomis initially went to Burlington to visit his brother George. He then operated a confectionery in Clinton, Illinois, for a short time around 1909.[31] In 1912 he was helping his brother Peter as a confectioner in Cairo. Angela and the children came over in 1913. The family then moved to Greenup, opened the Candy Kitchen, and made their home above it.

In 1925, Tom and Lil remodeled and updated the Candy Kitchen, where they served delicious ice cream, taffy, and triple-dip sundaes. Their frequent domestic spats, staged in their native tongue, were "almost as celebrated as their sweets."[32] One anecdote has Lil chasing Tom around the store with a butcher's knife![33] Tom died in 1954,[34] but Lil and another son, Sam, kept the store open until the early 1960s, when Lil's health declined. Her daughter, Niki, then took Lil back to Greece, and they never returned. Sam then closed the Candy Kitchen after approximately forty-five years in business and returned to Greece as well.[35]

To the north of Greenup is Mattoon, where George Sheopoolos (b. around 1880) was the first Greek confectioner. He opened the Buffalo Candy Factory in 1905 at 1708 Broadway, promising that, having remodeled the space, it would be "one of the best and most up-to-date stores in the city . . . with all kinds of Home-Made Candies Always in Stock."[36] Sheopoolos advertised regularly in the local paper, including an ad in June 1913 for "fireworks . . . that will suit your fancy for your celebrating—everything in colored lights, roman candles, fire crackers, powder, noise-makers . . . prices, of course, always the lowest."[37]

Besides selling fireworks and confectioneries, Sheopoolos also branched out into other businesses. In 1909 he bought a fruit store at 1714 Broadway, one of three such stores George owned in Mattoon.[38] In that same year George married a local girl, Cuddy "Cora" Montgomery (b. 1875), who cashiered at a local restaurant.[39] Sheopoolos ran the Buffalo Candy Factory for twelve years, and then, after being in poor health for over a year, he sold it to a non-Greek in August 1917. When asked if he planned to leave Mattoon, he said, "No, Mattoon is my home and I intend to remain here. I own my residence."[40]

Interestingly, George's story does not end here, however. Despite his promise to stay in Mattoon, a year later he moved to Chicago, where he registered for the draft in 1918, giving his occupation as self-employed confectioner.[41] George had an uncle in Chicago, John Stephanou, which may have influenced his move.[42] George remained a confectioner into the 1940s and died in Chicago in May 1954.[43]

Like many of the Greek confectioners, George helped newly arrived immigrants learn a trade and find a home. One of the immigrants he helped was Thomas Deligianis (b. September 17, 1890, in Manari). He immigrated to New York in January 1907[44] and then headed directly to Mattoon, where he went to work for Sheopoolos in the Buffalo Candy Factory, rooming at the back of the store. The naturalization hearing judge in 1914 said Deligianis's "hand-writing was better than the average natural born citizen."[45]

Thomas left Mattoon when Sheopoolos sold the store and moved south to Centralia, where he registered for the draft in June 1917, giving his occupation as a self-employed confectioner.[46] Thomas served in France as a cook during the Great War.[47] He returned to Centralia in September 1919 and took up the confectionery trade again.[48] His brother John (b. March 3, 1895, in Manari) came to America in 1912 and was working as a soda dispenser at the College Inn in Centralia in 1918 when he registered for the draft.[49] Another Deligianis, Louis (also Elias) (b. May 18, 1886), the oldest brother, immigrated somewhere around 1907.[50] Louis and John were rooming together in Centralia by 1920 and partnering together in a confectionery.[51] Sometime between 1920 and 1940 Louis took his family—wife Bertha (Apostolon) (b. August 15, 1897, in Tripoli) and four children—to Chicago, where he worked as a factory laborer,[52] and then returned to Centralia around 1940 and purchased a confectionery.[53]

Meanwhile, Thomas Deligianis was one of the College Inn proprietors in 1927.[54] In that same year, the thirty-seven-year-old returned to Greece, married the twenty-two-year-old Stavronla (Stella), and returned with her to Centralia.[55] By 1930 Thomas co-owned the Centralia Candy Kitchen with his brother John.[56] When Louis returned to Centralia around 1940, he and John took over the Candy Kitchen, and Thomas and Stella ran the Deley Tavern.[57] Thomas received an American Legion honor in 1947 (to "Thomas Deligianis") for his service in World War I, and he died in 1951.[58] John and Louis may have kept the Candy Kitchen going until John died in 1942, but this is unclear. Louis died in 1971.

Like many Greeks, including my grandfather, the Deligianis brothers changed their name at some point. Louis and John were already using the name Deley by 1920, but somewhat confusingly, they also seem to have continued to use both names interchangeably the rest of their lives. All three brothers and their families appear in the 1940 census under the name Deley, but both names are engraved on all three brothers' tombstones.[59]

Let us now return to Mattoon. We have seen how Louis Kehias, George's cousin, ran George's Pana store while George served in World War I. Louis immigrated to America in 1904 and resided in Chicago for a while, where he was a candy maker. He boarded there with his future business partner, Peter Lehares, who was a cook in a restaurant.[60] The two then traveled south to Mattoon and together established a restaurant/confectionery business, the Blue Bird Candy Shop, in 1919, with some help from George Kehias.[61] Even during the worst of the Klan years, they proudly proclaimed theirs the "Coolest Place in Town," urging all to stop in for ice cream and a soda.[62] Louis ran the confectionery and Peter the restaurant ("the Annex") until Louis's retirement in 1946, when the Blue Bird was sold. Peter helped the new owners until 1953.[63]

Peter was a Mason and a member of the Decatur Greek Orthodox Church.[64] He was married to Stella Rezinas, the sister of the Shelbyville Greek confectioner Tom P. Rezinas.[65] Peter died in 1966.[66] Louis Kehias never married but was active in the Mattoon community. He was a member of the Masons and also the Elks Lodge in Danville.[67] After retiring, he moved to McAllen, Texas, where he worked as a real estate agent and owned a fifteen-acre citrus tree grove.[68] He also remained fiercely proud of his American citizenship. Two years before his death in 1972, a photo in the McAllen newspaper showed him proudly displaying the American flag in front of his house during Flag Week. The caption noted, "He was the only one in a seven-block stretch . . . to have a flag on display."[69]

While not a confectioner, another early Greek immigrant in Mattoon, Peter J. Sutter (Sotiropoulou) (b. April 1, 1890 in Aegeon), deserves some mention in his own right and because of the central Illinois links to the Katsinas family in Springfield and Champaign. Peter owned and operated the Victory Café in Mattoon. The Victory was the type of roadside restaurant from yesterday that Will Anderson later eulogized in *Where Have You Gone, Starlight Café?*[70]

According to Peter's daughter Patsy Sutter Carney, Peter immigrated to America in 1903.[71] A tag attached to his clothing said he was destined for

St. Louis. In St. Louis he worked at the Mayflower Hotel for three dollars per week, beginning as a bus boy and then rising into more advanced positions of waiter and assistant chef, learning the food business from the ground up. Peter's brothers Anthony and Michael immigrated to America several years later. Peter and Michael both worked in St. Louis until going off to fight in World War I. Anthony later became a confectioner in Peoria, Illinois, working at the Lekas Candy Store and Restaurant. After returning from the war, Peter met John Katsinas in St. Louis. They formed a partnership and moved to Decatur, where they opened a restaurant. They then took their partnership to Mattoon in 1919, where they opened the Victory Café. The business prospered, and they relocated to larger quarters in 1923. Having established himself, Peter returned to Greece in 1923, to the village of Gropa near his home village of Aegeon. There he married Photula Marantis (b. April 6, 1897).[72] They went back to Mattoon and began a family. During the Depression years, Peter and John Katsinas dissolved their partnership, and John moved to Champaign-Urbana, where he became famous for his restaurants.

Peter Sutter's Victory Café was well-known and beloved by Mattoon citizens. Pete was a good community participant and volunteer, holding office in the local American Legion post. He was in the Illinois State Restaurant Association, serving as president at one time, which demonstrates his more prominent involvement and reputation outside of Mattoon. Unfortunately, in 1950 Pete suffered a cerebral hemorrhage. The Victory Café was sold in 1957 after thirty-eight years in business. Peter Sutter died on February 13, 1962.[73]

Charleston lies another few miles east of Mattoon, and there Gus Kerasotes's half-brother Louis owned a confectionery at 505 Seventh Street around 1906 or 1907 before moving back to Springfield and opening the Buffalo Confectionery with Charles Coutrakon in 1910.[74] Around 1916 another Greek, Nicholas George Alexander, opened the Charleston Confectionery at 623 Monroe, which was purchased by Gus Ashemos in 1919.[75]

At about this time, William A. "Bill" Panas (Panagiotopolos) (b. March 18, 1892) arrived in Charleston. He had immigrated to America by stowing away on a ship bound for New York and received aid from a Greek Orthodox Church there before joining relatives in Milwaukee. In Milwaukee he worked in a grocery store and managed to save his money to become a partner in the business. We know he went to Springfield, where he apprenticed with the confectioners Charles Coutrakon and Louis Kerasotes in 1918,[76] and to Decatur as well, "with the goal of starting an ice cream and candy store. After looking over several communities in the Central Illinois area, he purchased an existing store" in Charleston and reopened Louis Kerasotes's former confectionery there around 1918.[77] He called it the "Candy Shop." John and Ida Snyder (who owned a farm outside of town) managed the store for him. The following year he bought the Charleston Confectionery from Gus Ashemos,[78] which he renamed the Corner Confectionery. The "Candy Shop" appears to have closed in the late 1930s.[79] The Corner Confectionery, however, was a Charleston institution for over half a century.

I first met Bill Panas while I was an undergraduate student at Eastern Illinois University; he knew my father and grandfather. His place on the

PHOTO 13. The Candy Shop, Charleston. William Panas's first store was on the east side of the square in 1921. Panas is behind the soda fountain, and the couple standing by the cash register are probably John and Ida Snyder, who managed the store for him.

northeast corner of the downtown square looked like most of the Greek confectioneries, including ours, replete with the parquet tile floor that is still in place today, in what is now the Uptowner Bar.

In a 1971 interview with Panas, conducted by Candy Hoem, an Eastern Illinois University student, he described the gaslights that used to illuminate the shop and the different types of confections that he created and sold: taffy, caramels, pecan rolls, and peanut brittle, all standard fare for Greek confectioners. For the original price of twenty cents per pound, folks could enjoy the bounty of homemade goodness. Panas installed an air conditioner in 1934 that he claimed was the first one in town. Other than the electric lighting, Hoem reflected that in the early 1970s the store looked much the same as it might have when it opened, were it not for Panas's advancing age, the decline of the downtown retail business community, and the booths and dusty shelves along the back of the store, all of which made her realize that the Corner Confectionery was a dying testament to another era. It seemed a sad foil against the newer fast-food restaurants then popping up across the region.

Panas told Hoem that until the late 1960s the candy was still manufactured in the store's basement, which was where we did it at Flesor's Candy Kitchen until my father, encouraged by the local public health department, moved the candy making upstairs into a more sanitary location. Panas also mentioned that his recipes were "acquired from other candy shops and other candy makers. 'Not everything can be learned from books,'" he said, reflecting the ongoing connections and communications among Greek confectioners in the region.[80]

Panas's obituary noted that "memories of his ice cream and candy store will remain with many former EIU students and Charleston residents."[81] His Corner Confectionery was one of many properties he had acquired in his fifty-plus years in Charleston. He owned the Lincoln Building and founded the Charleston National Bank, an indication of his great financial success and what the newspaper dubbed a "rags to riches" life. Burl Ives, the famous actor and folk singer and a former EIU student, is said to have been one of his best customers. Panas died in May 1977 a very wealthy man. He had no family in Charleston but did have a sister and several nieces and nephews in Greece. He left his entire, and considerable, fortune to them.[82]

Stavros (Stephen) John Papadakos (b. September 14, 1874, in Lacedaemon), a Greek confectioner in Paris, Illinois, immigrated to America in

1893.[83] He may have stayed in New York for a time and learned candy making there. We do know that he is described as a confectioner in Philadelphia for at least one year, in 1898.[84] By 1901 he moved to Terre Haute, Indiana, right across the Illinois state line, where he partnered with a Greek man, James Zarafonetis, in the Papadakos and Zarafonetis Confectionery at 676 Wabash Avenue.[85] James had come to America from Sparta in 1887, and his younger brother Nicolas followed in 1893. They may have met Papadakos in Philadelphia, for in 1900 the brothers were living there together. James was a flower dealer and Nick a fruit dealer. They had also left Philadelphia by 1901.[86] Perhaps James Zarafonetis and Stephen Papadakos went together directly to Terre Haute and started their business.

It seems that soon after opening the Terre Haute confectionery, James Zarafonetis went to Brazil, Indiana, and opened a Candy Kitchen there. Papadakos and Zarafonetis Confectionery, therefore, did not last long, and in 1903 or 1904 Papadakos partnered at the same location in Terre Haute with James and Peter Georgopoulos.[87] This business too lasted just a year or so.

Papadakos's obituary says that he returned to Greece in 1904, where he married Mary (Panagiota) Rallis (or Rollis). They came back to America, and he opened the Papadakos Confectionery and Soda Fountain in Paris in 1906 or 1907.[88] It was a popular place for decades, and although Stavros passed away in May 1947,[89] the business continued for approximately ten more years before it closed. One Paris native, Paul Jacobs, a teen in the 1930s, remembered that "the place was so busy on Saturday night, they charged a ten-cent admission! It was quite the hangout."[90]

In 1906, James Zarafonetis (b. September 14, 1871) revisited his birthplace in Sparta, where he married Mary Vlahos (b. May 16, 1888).[91] The family story then goes that when they returned to Brazil, Mary complained about the cold winters, so James asked a man where there might be milder winters. The man recommended Vincennes, Indiana. James then went there to look for a place to rent for a confectionery. He found an appropriate building and sealed an agreement with the building's owner with a handshake. James then closed the Brazil store after six years in business, and he and Mary headed to the warmer climate seventy-four miles to the south in Vincennes in 1908. Mary and James's son Louis recalled that as children, "all we spoke was Greek. We lived above the store. If I asked Mother for something in English, she'd turn a deaf ear.

I had to re-ask in Greek." This knowledge came in handy, for when his father died in 1950, Louis had to translate the "candy recipes his father had written in Greek on the restaurant walls . . . done so his father could not possibly lose a recipe."[92]

James's brother Nick (b. around 1876) reappeared as a confectioner in Vincennes in 1908.[93] By 1910 Nick and James were living the Greek immigrant American dream, having gone from fruit and flower sellers in 1900 to owning the Zarafonetis Brothers Candy Kitchen at 233 Main in Vincennes. In May 1910 they received a new double soda fountain, lined with marble and the exterior built of onyx, costing $2,500. It was "one of the very finest in the state."[94] And they were not done. Around 1918 the brothers opened another Zarafonetis Brothers Candy Kitchen in Clinton, Indiana, and Nick moved there to run it.[95] He became ill soon after, however, and returned to Greece.[96] He never came back to America, dying at his home in Amykles, Sparta, in August 1934.[97] Mary Zarafonetis died in 1945 and James in 1950.[98] Their sons Peter and Louis kept the Candy Kitchen going until 1959, when they closed it after fifty-one successful years in business.[99]

Let us return to Illinois. Due south of Tuscola is Arcola, which was home to Greek confectioner Mike Poulos, my father's godfather. Dr. Robert Arrol, longtime Arcola resident, described Mike as "tall and strong and [he] had an accent; he was well-liked and made great candy. He was a great kidder. On April Fool's Day he would dip onions in chocolate as a joke!"[100] Like many others, Mike Poulos was another Greek immigrant business success story. He purchased farmland during the Depression and utilized income from that to augment his business. He kept in constant communication with the Tuscola Greeks as well as the Champaign contingent.[101]

Mike (b. August 25, 1888, in Chios)[102] immigrated from Patras to America in 1908. After arriving in New York, he traveled first to Baltimore and then to Chicago and somehow made a connection with George Vaky in Champaign. Mike worked for Vaky, learning the confectionery trade, and when he was ready, Vaky helped Mike get started in Arcola, another town on the north-south railroad line with a main road, Route 45, that went to Chicago. Mike Poulos opened the Arcola Candy Kitchen on February 4, 1915. According to James Vaky, after one early visit to assess his latest batch, his father judged Mike's candy as similar to "mudballs" and helped him improve his technique. James recalled that on Sunday afternoons his father would visit his Greek protégés in Tuscola, Rantoul, Danville, Decatur, and Springfield to give them encouragement and to make a "Greek" connection, since some lived far from their compatriots.

Mike retired on February 14, 1951, and died on September 8, 1965.[103] Mike's son Mike P. Poulos Jr. was not interested in continuing in the business, and Ben Bushu, a local Arcola resident who had worked for Mike since 1945, took over the store. The business continued until August 1965, when Ben died and the store closed.[104]

Mike Jr. told me that his father often sent him to buy butter for the English toffee and would dip his hand into the copper kettle, pick up a bit of boiling hot toffee in his fingers to determine if it was done, and then run his hand under cold water.[105] Mike Jr. had many fond memories of working in the Candy Kitchen with his father, doing everything from making candy, cleaning dishes and tables, and making delicious ice cream treats at the soda fountain.[106]

Speaking of English toffee, the most important of all confectionery questions in east-central Illinois is, "Who really taught the Heath family, famous for the nationally known Heath Bar, how to make toffee?" To find an answer, we must travel southeast to Robinson, home of the Heath Bar, where initially in 1911 the Souris brothers, John, Peter, and Theodore, operated the Original Robinson Candy Kitchen west of the downtown square. They lived above the store.[107] We know John Souris had immigrated from Greece to Peoria and worked there for confectioner James Basil in 1906 but little else about the brothers.[108] They did not remain in Robinson long, however, as they sold their confectionery to B. G. Olwin in 1912.[109] John Souris eventually moved to Alton, Illinois.[110] He and a relative, perhaps a younger brother, Paul Souris, ran the Venardos Candy Company there in the 1920s and 1930s.[111]

After B. G. Olwin purchased the Robinson business, he sold it to L. S. Heath in 1914.[112] Heath gave the confectionery and soda fountain to his sons Bayard and Everett, who ran it until 1931 as the Heath Brothers' Store before closing it and opening a joint business with their father out of his dairy factory.[113]

The principal confectioner in the Heath store was Maurice Andrew Jonquet (b. June 3, 1885), an intriguing and somewhat mysterious figure born in South Bend, Indiana, to a French father and a Swiss mother. The question arises then as to whether the original toffee recipe came from Jonquet or from Greek confectioners. One story suggests that the Heaths were given the recipe for "trail toffee" by a traveling salesman, who was said to have acquired it from a Greek confectioner—perhaps George Vaky or Peter Vriner or my grandfather![114] According to the official Heath Candy literature, L. S. Heath's eldest son, Bayard, took the basic toffee recipe and developed it into what is now known as the Heath Bar. It was first offered for sale in 1928. "The confection grew in popularity and word quickly spread that the Heath Brothers Confectionery was the one and only place to get delicious 'English Toffee.' This was the era of the oil boom in southern Illinois, and many travelers passed through the city. It was traditional to take Heath English Toffee with them when departing."[115] If only the Greek confectioners had had the foresight to recognize how valuable their recipe was, they might have made that fortune rather than Mr. Heath.

We know little about the other possible inventor, Maurice Jonquet,[116] except that his father was a cook.[117] We can assume he honed his skills under his father's guidance, because by 1912 he was married, living in Mishawaka, Indiana, and making candy for Solari and Company.[118] He then moved to Robinson to work with the Heath brothers and then to Decatur by 1920.[119] Here he settled down with his wife and children and made his living as a wholesale confectioner there for many years.[120] The origins of the Heath Bar remain a mystery!

In the early 1900s Effingham was the county seat of Effingham County, with a population of around five thousand. Several Greek confectioners passed through Effingham, but only Thomas Kores (b. around 1873 in Sparta) stayed any length of time. Kores had owned a candy store at the turn of the twentieth century in Greenup before coming to Effingham.[121] By 1910 he had opened the Effingham Candy Kitchen. Tom, his wife, Aderta, and their daughter Amanda came together to America in 1902 and became naturalized citizens in 1907. The couple had five more children, all born in America.[122] Living with them in 1910 was Georgios Louis Kores (b. 1886), perhaps Thomas's brother, who arrived in America in 1909.[123]

Kores advertised his store in 1912 as the "Effingham Candy Kitchen, Home-made Ice Cream and Candy."[124] Of the six confectioners in Effingham in the 1910s, Kores was the only Greek. Peggy Pulliam, in a two-part newspaper article about the business (and using a *K* instead of a *C* in its name), wrote in 1970, "Of the many stores in the Loy Building, the best remembered is the Kandy Kitchen. A Greek by the name of Tom Kores made mouth-watering delicacies. At that time the Austin Building [next door] (now Jansens) had been a movie theater, so the Kandy Kitchen was a very popular place."[125] Kores sold the Effingham Candy Kitchen in the early 1920s and returned to Greece with his family. They came back to the United States in 1930, but not to Effingham.[126]

The last Greek confectioner in Effingham was James John Potakes (b. 1898 in Athens), who in 1938 placed a Christmas newspaper ad announcing he was now the owner of the Effingham Candy Kitchen.[127] Potakes came to America with an uncle when he was nine.[128] He first appeared in Vandalia in 1918 when he registered for the draft and gave his occupation as "clerk" in the Vandalia Confectionery.[129] In 1920 he and Alex Karon (whom we met in Springfield in chapter 7) were rooming with Greek confectioners James G. and Mary Seolas.[130] Potakes moved to Champaign-Urbana in 1928, where he linked up with George Vaky and got a job at Vaky's as a soda dispenser.[131] He remained in Champaign and lived with the George Samaras family, another familiar name.[132] When he moved to Effingham in 1938 he was still single, but he married Emma Alwardt in 1941. He then went off to World War II and closed the Effingham Candy Kitchen for good.[133]

Farther west along National Road 40 is Vandalia, once the Illinois state capital. Here there was a candy kitchen,[134] and sometime in the 1910s James (b. February 4, 1889, in Corinth) and Mary Seolas (b. 1897 in Illinois) took it over.[135] James and Mary had no better luck than the original owners, however, and closed the business in the 1920s.[136] This was perhaps because of competition from the Matalas brothers, Gus (or Gust, b. January 19, 1890, in Karyai) and John (b. around 1892 in Karyai), who owned and operated the Vandalia Confectionery for many years.[137]

It appears the patriarch of the Matalas family, Nicholas George Matalas (b. around 1862), immigrated to the United States in 1909 from modern Arachova (formerly Karyai), Greece, with his sons, Constantinos (Gus) and Joannis (John); wife Penelope was left behind in Greece for the time.[138] The Ellis Island manifest form said father and sons were going to stay with a cousin who owned a Chicago restaurant.[139]

Nicholas moved to St. Louis in 1910, where he and John were living together as "candy makers."[140] We next find Nicholas Matalas in West Frankfort, Illinois, where he was a confectioner and where he died July 12, 1917.[141] Nicholas's wife, Penelope (b. May 30, 1874, in Tripoli), had immigrated to West Frankfort in 1914 and still lived there in 1920 with her two sons, Gus and John, and daughter, Anna.[142] Previously, though, the sons had migrated to Paducah, Kentucky, either from Chicago or St. Louis, to establish their own confectionery business.[143] John's World War I draft registration shows he had moved back to West Frankfort by 1917.[144] Both sons had joined their mother by 1920 to continue their father's business, and they had also opened stores in Herrin and Salem.[145]

John Matalas then branched out alone. He took over the Candy Kitchen confectionery in Mt. Carmel in September 1922 that was originally owned, as we will discuss further below, first by the Ginos brothers and then by the Govits brothers. The latter left the city after their store was destroyed by fire in October 1921. In January 1925 Matalas moved the entire business to Casey, Illinois, and opened the Candyland Confectionery, replete with a grand opening featuring an orchestra and the dispensing of carnations. The Candyland was described as "one of the best appointed in this part of the state. The interior was blue and white with a flashing sign said to have cost $500."[146] This venture did not last long, either. John was the only Greek confectioner in Casey, but Bertram's Fresh Candies had been an established institution since 1904 and remained in business until 1955. Perhaps in a small town such as Casey, one confectionery was enough.[147] John Matalas then moved to Vandalia around 1930 to partner with his brother, Gus. John, Gus, and their families, including their mother, Penelope (age sixty-seven), remained in Vandalia until 1942, when they all migrated to Henderson, North Carolina.[148] Thus ended the journeys of the Matalas brothers in Illinois.

Returning to Mt. Carmel, we find that attempts by Greek migrants to establish a confectionery there evolved over a period of approximately twelve years. The first Greeks in Mt. Carmel were Spyros (William "Bill") (b. September 25, 1891) and Nicholas (b. August 20, 1889) Ginos, two of five Ginos brothers who had immigrated to Hillsboro, Illinois, in the first decade of the century and already owned a confectionery there.[149] On December 23, 1911, Spyros and Nickolas opened the doors of the Mt. Carmel Candy Kitchen on Market Street, where they lived above their store.[150] At their opening they announced they had a large supply of candy on hand and hoped "to get their portion of the Christmas trade, even though opening at a late date."[151] In their 1914 Christmas ad, they proclaimed, "The Mt. Carmel Candy Kitchen has had for some years the well-deserved reputation of [having] . . . every Christmas the most complete line of Candies in Mt. Carmel. . . . Visit Ginos Bros. and let them help you select your gift."[152]

A newspaper article in December 1916 noted that "Zissis Ginos of Hillsboro, Ill., an uncle [incorrect; he was a brother] of the two Ginos brothers of this city, arrived in the city last night, and will remain during the holidays. Mr. Ginos is an expert candy maker and will aid the firm in their preparation for Christmas. William [Spyros] Ginos of the local firm, will remain in Hillsboro while his uncle is here."[153] In June 1917 Zissis came again to Mt. Carmel for several days to show "the other Ginos boys how to conduct a candy kitchen. Zissis is the bell-weather of the Ginos flock and was the pioneer member of the family to leave Greece and seek his fortune in this country. He hopes to become an American citizen this fall."[154] Spyros had already become a naturalized citizen in 1915, and Zissis (b. August 27, 1875) was naturalized on November 17, 1919.[155]

Although the Ginos brothers were in Mt. Carmel for only eight years, they clearly made a good impression and were well-liked by the townspeople. On September 24, 1919, Spyros married a local girl, Eunice Lela Brines (b. September 8, 1895), whose family had lived around Mt. Carmel for four generations.[156] Like most Greek confectioners, the Ginos brothers were very patriotic. As the United States entered the Great War in 1917, they announced that on August 8, they would "give forty per cent of their gross proceeds of this day to the local . . . Red Cross." The citizens of Mt. Carmel were encouraged to support "this worthy undertaking," and "ladies of the Red Cross in uniform will serve the tables and wait on you that day."[157] Both brothers also publicly bought Liberty bonds.[158] At least three of the Ginos brothers registered for the draft in World War I.[159] We know that Spyros served as an army cook and was honorably discharged in January 1919.[160]

The Ginos brothers were still operating the Candy Kitchen in 1918[161] but faced competition from other candy stores in town. One was run by longtime resident Guy H. Hadley, who owned the Quality Drug Store. He regularly took out large ads in the newspaper with bold headlines such as, "Candies Made Fresh Every Day. Largest Soda Fountain in the State." The Ginos brothers were up against one of the town's most prominent citizens.[162]

In February 1919, Nick and Spyros sold the Candy Kitchen to another pair of Greek brothers, Gus B. (b. February 26, 1896) and James (b. February 17, 1898, in Thessaly) Govits, and another man named Steve Frank.[163] The sale announcement noted that the Ginos brothers were returning to Hillsboro, where they owned a candy kitchen and had recently acquired a restaurant and wanted to "devote their whole attention" to these enterprises. They were described as "excellent young men." The new owners, the Govits brothers, were "competent young business men and no doubt will continue to make the business a big success."[164]

Only a month after buying the Candy Kitchen, its new proprietors ran ads announcing that the store was now "in new hands," that they were "experienced metropolitan candy-makers, confectioners and fancy drink dispensers," that they had had "years of big city experience," and that they wanted to "get personally acquainted with every man, woman and child in the town and county." Directly addressing the old stereotype, they also proclaimed their motto to be "Cleanliness, Quality, and Courtesy" and "Purity and Cleanliness."[165] Later they also started selling the new Pasco Phonograph player, which, at the time, was quite the item.[166] In November 1919, Steve Frank sold his one-third interest in the Candy Kitchen to the Govits brothers and returned to Hillsboro, "where he was employed before coming to Mount Carmel," to work with the Ginos brothers.[167]

Gus and James Govits had immigrated to America in 1912 and 1914 respectively. They went initially to St. Louis[168] and then moved to Mt. Carmel, where they roomed with a family that took in boarders.[169] In February 1921, Mick (or Mike) Govits, perhaps a cousin, joined them in Mt. Carmel, also coming from St. Louis. He was said to be "well experienced in the confectionery business."[170] Unfortunately, on Sunday, October 23, 1921, faulty wiring started a fire in the back room where candy was made and then spread to the whole store. Damage to the store was "exceptionally heavy," and the back room was "practically destroyed." The total value of the store's contents was estimated at $10,000 and the loss was $6,000, including "a large stock of cigars in the rear." As the brothers had only $4,000 of insurance,[171] they abandoned the business and Mt. Carmel. Gus gravitated to Evansville, Indiana, where by 1930 he was selling confectionery fixtures.[172] James Govits moved to Owensboro, Kentucky, and in 1926 was a clerk with Mike Callas, another Greek, at the Progress Candy Company. Mick Govits returned to St. Louis.[173]

The burned-out building was owned by a local businessman, Charles Bonham, and he and another businessman, Fred Harnish, neither of whom were confectioners, restored it and opened a confectionery in April 1922.[174] They then sold it in September 1922 to John Matalas. He was described as an "experienced candy and ice cream man, [who] looks forward to a great business in Mount Carmel," and the store as "modern in every detail, and one of Mount Carmel's show places." The new owner now had four confectioneries: one in Mt. Carmel and "one at West Frankfort, one at Herrin, and one at Salem."[175] Matalas renamed his business "Candyland," but, as we discussed above, he remained open for just over two years before relocating to Casey.[176]

By the mid-1920s, all the Greeks had departed Mt. Carmel. The question arises then as to why, after more than twelve years of successful Greek candy stores in Mt. Carmel, John Matalas would pick up and leave the town so suddenly. The mid-1920s were the years of the greatest Ku Klux Klan activity; was his departure related to some sort of threat from the Klan? There is no indication either in the article announcing his moving or in any local newspapers for these years that Klan activity or threats might have been the reason. Matalas might have simply moved to Casey because he believed there was more opportunity there. In the 1920s there was an oil boom around Casey, and the town's population and wealth were expected to increase substantially. Perhaps Matalas intended to take advantage of that potential.[177]

Mount Vernon is southwest of Mt. Carmel and on the southern edge of our central Illinois focus. Greeks begin to navigate there after the Great War, and several of them became its leading citizens. They offer some interesting differences and some familiar similarities to our study of Greek migration to small-town America. In 1915 Mount Vernon had a population of 11,300 and was growing, as was true for many towns in central-southern Illinois, as coal mines multiplied and coal miners (many of whom were immigrants) arrived to work in them.[178]

The Greek story in Mount Vernon begins with John Notaras and his brother Louis, who in 1908 were confectioners at 906 Main,[179] calling their store the Olympia Palace of Sweets.[180] By 1912 John Notaras had sold the store to another Greek, Nick Cheolas (or Cholas, Chilos, or Chiolos), who changed the name to the Queen Bee Candy Kitchen.[181] John Notaras then left town but showed up farther south in Du Quoin, Illinois, in 1920, running the Candy Kitchen there with his brother Tom.[182]

Born in Greece, Nick Cheolas (b. March 9, 1860) came to America in 1903, then brought his wife, Katherine (b. June 15, 1872), and daughter Alexandria (b. November 17, 1896) over in 1914. Around 1918 Alexandria married a Greek Mount Vernon businessman, John Louis (b. May 1, 1881), and together they had a daughter and a son.[183] John Louis came from Larissa and arrived in America in 1905. He initially owned a pressing and dry-cleaning store in Mount Vernon. Nick's other daughter, Kristefelia (b. May 5, 1892, in Kazaklar), also married a Greek man, Jim Zarkadas (b. March 29, 1888). The couple and their one-year-old daughter, Helen, were living with Nick and his wife, as were the Louises, when Kristefelia died in March 1920.[184]

Nick Cheolas and Jim Zarkadas ran the Queen Bee for a while, along with Aristides (Aris) George Zicos, who bought half-interest in the store in the late 1910s. Around 1920 Zicos took ownership of the Queen Bee. In 1923, John Louis, along with his father-in-law, Nick, opened a new confectionery that became the Deluxe Candy Kitchen at 1003 Broadway.[185] John Louis ran the Deluxe until his death in 1959.[186]

Aris Zicos (b. December 7, 1877) was born in Albania to Greek parents and had an elementary school education.[187] A stonemason and skilled marble cutter, he came to St. Louis in 1903 as a craftsman to work on the 1904 St. Louis Exposition.[188] In the 1910s he moved to Mount Vernon and in 1920 brought his wife, Alexandra (b. September 20, 1882), and two sons over from Greece after he had purchased a home and furnishings.[189] The Queen Bee Candy Kitchen "became a household name in Mt. Vernon. It was quite the thing to get all dressed in your best, go downtown, walk around the square and stop in at the Queen Bee for a coke ice cream soda, sundae, or a few candies."[190] In January 1930 the Queen Bee burned to the ground.[191] Although Aris rebuilt the store at the same location, it became the Queen Bee Café. Along with his wife, "Mama Zicos," and Jim Zarkadas, Aris ran the Queen Bee Candy Kitchen, and later Café, until his death in 1942.[192] His son George (b. December 22, 1902, in Greece) then took over from him.[193]

The Hassakis brothers were the other prominent Greeks in Mount Vernon for several decades. Nicholas Hassakis (b. August 17, 1881), born in Zaverda (now Paleros) Greece, came over first, arriving through the port at New Orleans in 1907, with twenty-five dollars to his name. He initially worked in the sugarcane fields and on the railroads around the city. He also went to Beaumont, Texas, for a time to work as a dishwasher in a Greek restaurant there.[194] He then traveled to St. Louis, where in 1910 his brother John (b. 1892) joined him, followed in 1912 by brother Spiro (b. December 13, 1895) and cousin Denny (b. December 17, 1886).[195] In that same year, Nick went off to Greece to fight in the Balkan War, returning in 1914, while brother John went to work on the railroad out in Montana for a while.[196]

In 1914 the three Hassakis brothers and their cousin Denny moved to Mount Vernon and partnered with Zissis Ginos of Hillsboro to open the Rex Restaurant. Nicholas later said that when he opened the restaurant he had "$7 in my pocket and $13 in the cash register."[197] In 1919 Nick returned to Greece and married a Greek woman, Efstathia Karpouzi (b. January 25, 1892); to them a daughter was born, Despo. The family then came back to Mount Vernon in 1922. Nick and his brothers were good citizens and gave willingly of themselves and their resources to help their adopted country. Before he left for Greece in 1919, Nick deposited funds in his bank and left instructions that they be donated to any fund created at Christmas for helping the poor that year.[198]

While Nick was away, John and Spiro opened the Acme Candy Kitchen in 1920, and cousin Denny opened the Blue Goose Café and Tavern. The Mount Vernon newspaper in May 1920 carried ads, all on the same page, for the Rex Restaurant and Soda Fountain, the Acme Candy Kitchen, and the Queen Bee Candy Kitchen. The Rex ad proclaimed, "We serve to please and are pleased to serve." The Queen Bee announced, "Get this thought—Ice Cream *IS* a Food!" Its new competitor, the Acme, called on customers to "Eat at the Newest, Most Attractive Candy Kitchen in the City" and added the standard Greek pledge, "Everything New, Clean, and Sanitary."[199] Over the next thirty years the Hassakis brothers and their cousin Denny, along with other family members (wives, sons, daughters, grandchildren), established several food businesses that Mount Vernonites fondly remembered years after they had closed. Denny, who was the last of the four to die, in 1974, operated the Blue Goose Café and Tavern from the late 1920s until his death.[200] John died in 1951, having been a partner with his brothers over the years in the Rex Restaurant, the Rex Café, the Acme Candy Kitchen, the Gem Café, the West Shell Café, and the North Shell Café.[201] Spiro passed away in 1969. At the time he ran Spiro's Buffet and was a member of the Lions, the Elks, and AHEPA. All the brothers were members of the Saints Constantine and Helen Greek Orthodox Church in East St. Louis.[202] Nick, who became one of Mount Vernon's "most successful and respected businessmen from a humble start," died in 1970. Many old-timers remembered how he welcomed "all of his customers with a cheery 'Hello, my friend.'"[203]

Most Greeks in central Illinois were in contact with each other, and this networking landed Tom P. (Athanasios Panagiotis) Rezinas (b. December 23, 1898, in Sparta) a home and business in Shelbyville. Rezinas immigrated to the United States in 1912 with his uncle George Tsourunis and two others, his father, Peter (Panagiotis), and sister Stavroulas. Their initial destination after arriving in New York was Ipswich, Massachusetts, where they had cousins and where Tom worked in a shoe factory.[204] From there he traveled to the Midwest and first learned the confectionery trade in Flora, where he worked for Sam Cheorvas, and in Effingham.[205] While in Effingham Tom decided to go west to Litchfield and open a candy shop, but it did not work out. While taking the train back to Effingham he realized he had only enough fare to get to Shelbyville, so there he detrained and stayed. He then asked his uncle George Tsourunis, who was living in Terre Haute, Indiana, at the time, to come and join him. By 1920 George and Tom had opened a confectionery in Shelbyville and were single boarders in the same rooming house.[206] George was married, but his wife had remained in Greece. After about five years he sold his share of the business to Tom and returned to Greece. The same is probably true for Tom's father, Peter, who seems to have accompanied his two children to America and then immediately returned home.[207]

Tom married a local woman, Reatha Kimlel (b. March 9, 1903), and they were the parents of four children.[208] George Kehias of Pana was son William's godfather.[209] William told me that the store was open seven days a week, that his father made the candy, his mother ran the store out front, and that he worked there as a boy. Besides the train fare story, William also said that when his father arrived in Shelbyville, he applied for a bank loan to start his business. A salesman from Effingham was in the bank at the time and vouched for Tom, so he got the loan.[210]

The Shelbyville Candy Kitchen was similar to most Greek confectioneries and soda shops during this time period. Tom was self-taught in English, learned to make candy from other Greeks, and then put those skills to use by making his own candies and ice cream. Tom invented a machine in the mid-1920s that accelerated a process for making hard candy Easter baskets, which were popular and sold around the country. S. S. Kresge 5&10 was his largest customer. The family lived above the shop in the wintertime so they could continue to make candy and serve their customers despite the weather. In the summer, they lived in a home on Broadway Street.[211] In the 1940s the business expanded with food service for lunch, made in the family kitchen above the store and sent downstairs in a dumb waiter. Tom also put in a jukebox to lure evening customers into the shop for treats. Tom's son William was kind enough to share with me one of his father's recipes, written in both English and Greek, as was a common practice with the first-generation Greek confectioners.

Tom Rezinas, George Kehias in Pana, my grandfather in Tuscola, and many other Greeks who had established successful businesses by the mid-1920s carried on despite a very active Ku Klux Klan in the area. Shelbyville was home to the Chautauqua, a large gathering site for various religious and civic organizations, including Klan Day. From the end of July 1924 through the middle of August, multiple Klan events invited community participation.[212] Through all of this activity, Tom Rezinas continued to advertise, exhorting the townspeople and visitors alike to "Refresh Yourself with one of the Delightful Drinks we serve at our Fountain, You'll find our store restful, neat and home-like . . . Shelbyville Candy Kitchen 'Home of Sweets.'"[213] Klansmen even opened a stand at the Chautauqua rally and bought their ice cream from Tom![214] Perhaps because he had married a local woman, Tom did not experience overt Klan threats.

Tom operated the Candy Kitchen from 1919 to 1955, when he retired. None of his children wanted to keep the business going, and it closed. Tom died, a successful businessman and prominent citizen, on August 17, 1980.[215]

In July 2013 I received a note from one of our Tuscola customers, Jean Attebery, a Fairfield native, who recalled that Fairfield, between Mount Vernon and Mt. Carmel, had a thriving Greek confectionery for many years. She wrote that the store contributed at one time to the town's identity, and she forwarded a long article on the history of the Greeks in Fairfield.[216] William Pappas (b. 1894)[217] and another Greek, Constantine "Gus" Theofanopoulos (b. 1892) each had a candy shop in Fairfield around 1930—a difficult time to run a business, considering this was at the beginning of the Depression. Gus Theofanopoulos was born in Frousina, Argos, Greece, the hometown, as we will see, of Sam Cheorvas in Flora. Gus immigrated to America in 1911 and married Helen Chrysovergis (b. 1900 in Stenon, Tripoli) in 1924.[218] His Corner Candy Store opened in Fairfield in June 1930, in a building he commissioned: "The building was very strong. The floor was six inches thick with terrazzo marble embedded in it. The ceiling was twelve feet high; the countertop was imported green marble from Italy."[219] A Fairfield resident, Otis Brach, remembered five-cent sodas and fifteen-cent milkshakes. "A well-known candy to the rural people was horehound. Gus hand made the candy by boiling the horehound plant. The women packaged the candy and cleaned the store."[220] Brach also remembered that Bill Pappas's Banner Candy Kitchen was not as successful as Gus Theofanopoulos's Corner Candy Store, perhaps, Brach thought, because Gus was located near the Greyhound bus stop. Gus had also added a second floor to his building and rented out office space to a doctor and dentist.[221]

Brach worked for another Greek, John Verdulas, who was not a confectioner but a wholesale distributor. During World War II Verdulas supplied Gus and other confectioners in the area with cigarettes, soda for the fountain, and eventually beer and liquor—high profit margin items, even though Fairfield was a dry town then. Brach recalled that "'The Greeks' at that time was 'the place.' Gus had a big trade. . . . Sophia, George, Eugenia [Jeanie] (Gus' children) worked there all the time, behind the counter. Lordy, the work was all he and Helen ever did—the hours and hours they put in. The kids grew up in the store. Gus was everywhere . . . behind the counter usually."[222] These memories recall those of Constance Constant growing up in her parents' restaurant, Austin Lunch; the reminiscences others shared in my interviews with them; and my own memories of growing up in the Candy Kitchen! It is fascinating to hear similar stories repeated over and over into the second and third generations.

Otis Brach mentioned that Bill, Gus's son, went to Greece while serving in the army. "He said he couldn't understand how his mother and dad ever got together. One village was on one side of the mountain, the other village was on the other side. It took them all day with a donkey to walk to the other village in the mountains."[223] Brach remembered Gus's wonderful sense of humor and his April Fool's Day jokes, similar to Mike Poulos's in Arcola, such as candy with garlic infused. Eventually sons George and Bill became confectioners.[224]

Brach also commented both on Gus's success and on his unfortunate death. "Gus amassed a fortune. He had a big dairy farm, apartment buildings, the Greek Candy store. Then he got killed in a car wreck. I understand they were going to church. Sophia and George were in the front seat, Helen and Gus in back. They stopped for road construction and got rear-ended. Everybody got out and seemed alright, but I guess it broke Gus's neck. He keeled over."[225] Gus was fifty-six when he died in 1949.

Gus's son-in-law, Jack Frank,[226] who married Eugenia, grew up in Centralia and graduated from the University of Illinois as a civil engineer. He went to work for the Illinois Highway Department and had an office above the Candy Kitchen, where he met Eugenia, who worked there occasionally. They fell in love, and although it was "a big deal" for Eugenia to get married to a non-Greek boy, they were wed by the Greek priest from Decatur in the Fairfield Methodist Church, and eventually all was forgiven. Jack recalled from family lore that Eugenia's mother, Helen, had two brothers in Chicago and Gus went there to marry her. Jack also added to the central Illinois Greek networking/chain migration narrative by discussing how Gus Theofanopoulos first worked in Altamont, a town near Effingham, perhaps with Peter and Tom Granupulos. They along with their wives, Ina and Eva respectively, owned a confectionery there.[227] Gus then went to Fairfield with Bill Pappas. Eugenia's sister, Sofia, remained single and kept the confectionery in Fairfield going for a while after Gus's death, but the third generation of the family did not pursue the business. Jack did not recall any anti-Greek sentiment, and as far as he knew, the whole family was very much an integral part of the community.[228] If the article on the "Sweet Memories" of the Fairfield Greeks is any indication of the townspeople's fond remembrance and respect, then, indeed, the Greeks were very much an important part of Fairfield's history.

Flora is another small town where Greeks settled before 1920. Sam Cheorvas and his wife, Panagiota, or "Pota" as she was known, established the Flora Candy Kitchen there in 1918. Pota was the aunt of both Peter and of his wife, Stella (Rezinas) Lehares, of Mattoon.[229] Sam (b. February 1881 in Frousiouna [?], Argolis) immigrated to St. Louis, where he met and married his wife.[230] They then moved to Illinois to go into business for themselves. They had five children who worked in the store when they were old enough to help. One of these, Sophia, married Peter Chagares of Richmond, Indiana, in Flora in 1936. Peter, along with his brothers Nick and William and father, James, were co-owners of the Olympian Ice Cream Parlor in Richmond.[231] The Flora Candy Kitchen, and later a café, was in business for several decades,[232] until Sam sold it in 1948.[233] He died in 1955 and Pota the following year.[234]

Continuing the journey west across central Illinois, Nokomis and Taylorville were two towns linked by Greek immigrants in surprising ways. The Greek Candy Kitchen in Nokomis was founded in 1919 when brothers George (b. May 25, 1892) and Phillip (b. February 1893 in Tripoli) Kouchiveris and George Ellis (Eliopoulos) (b. June 24, 1890, in Tripoli) formed a partnership to open the business. Ellis sold his interest in 1921 to the Kouchiveris brothers and left Nokomis. The brothers ran the store until around 1932, when they purchased a confectionery in nearby Taylorville. They sold their Nokomis store to Joe Viola, a second-generation Italian,[235] who, with his sister Mary, had worked there since its inception.[236] The Violas sold the popular Nokomis Candy Kitchen in 1965, and it closed for good in 1967.[237]

Before we move on to Taylorville, we must ask, How did the Kouchiveris brothers and George Ellis learn to make candy?

It seems that George Ellis learned from James Zarafonetis, the Greek confectioner in Brazil, Indiana, who himself may have learned his confectionery skills from Stephen Papadakos, before Papadakos went off to Paris, Illinois, and Zarafonetis moved to Vincennes, Indiana. When enlisting for the Great War, Ellis said he was a confectioner for Zarafonetis in Vincennes.[238] Ellis and George Kouchiveris both registered for the draft in Clinton, Indiana, where Nick Zarafonetis had opened the Zarafonetis Brothers Candy Kitchen in 1918 and Nick might have brought Ellis with him from Vincennes to help. George Kouchiveris was a self-employed hat cleaner and blocker in Clinton.[239] Perhaps they were related or had known each other in Tripoli, but sometime in late 1918 or early 1919 Ellis and Kouchiveris were opening their new store in Nokomis. Ellis married Lena Sanders, a non-Greek woman in Terre Haute in March 1919.[240] As George Kouchiveris seemingly had no candy-making experience, Ellis must have taught him what he had learned from Zarafonetis in Vincennes. Meanwhile, brother Phillip Kouchiveris was in Chicago registering for the draft while working as a candy store clerk.[241]

So, one might draw a line representing the handing down of Greek confectionery skills from Stephen Papadakos to James Zarafonetis to George Ellis and then to George Kouchiveris, thereby illustrating some of the major themes in this study: chain migration, networking, and the Greek immigrant entrepreneurial evolution in small-town America.

Ellis sold his part of the business to the Kouchiveris brothers in 1921. He and Lena moved to Aurora, Illinois, in 1924, where he first worked for T. C. Paulos in his confectionery,[242] and then he established his own confectionery and ice cream business.[243] The Kouchiveris brothers relocated to Taylorville around 1932, but Greek candy stores in that town were well-established long before they arrived.

The Taylorville story begins with two other Greek brothers, Peter (b. around 1885) and Louis (b. around 1882) Apostle, who operated the Apostle Bros. Candy and Ice Cream Company in that city on South Washington, and by all accounts it was a beautiful place.[244] The Apostle brothers immigrated to America early—Louis in 1902 and Peter in 1905—and had opened their confectionery in Taylorville by 1910.[245] It appears that Louis had moved on by 1912 and became the proprietor of a candy store in Marquette, Michigan.[246] That same year, another Apostle brother, Frank, joined Peter in the business.[247] Their advertising proclaimed the same purity theme we have noted before: "Apostle Bros. Candy and Ice Cream Stands for Purity."[248] Peter and Frank left Taylorville around the end of 1914, though, and sold their interest to Gust Moucoulis and Thomas Orfanos (b. February 14, 1886) of Decatur. Frank moved to Chicago; by 1916 Peter Apostle had joined Louis in Marquette; and by 1920 James, John, Louis, and Peter, perhaps all brothers, were all working at Louis's confectionery.[249]

Gust Moucoulis (b. January 17, 1890) and Orfanos, later joined by Moucoulis's brothers George B. (b. February 23, 1894,) and John B. (b. November 18, 1893), transformed the Apostle Bros. confectionery into the new Royal Confectionery. Gust Moucoulis had immigrated to the United States in 1906 at the age of sixteen; his father had been born in Bulgaria and his mother in Greece. In 1910 he was residing in Stonington, Illinois, where he was employed as a laborer on the railroad.[250] Later that same year Gust was working in Decatur, Illinois, as a driver for another Greek, George Stamatopoulos, a grocer and baker.[251] The local paper reported that after buying the Taylorville confectionery in 1914, the brothers were spending time and money on renovations: "The Royal Confectionery today closed the deal that will, as soon as new fixtures that come to them as a result, arrive, give them the most up to date ice cream parlor in this section of the state."[252] The improvements were to include a new sixteen-foot fountain made of marble and mahogany, two new candy cases of marble and glass, and "an artistic mahogany arch that will act as a division between the front or candy store, and the fountain and the back part of their room, which is the ice cream parlor with 18 tables."[253] In June the new fixtures arrived and the renovations took place. Manufactured by the Progressive Mercantile Manufacturing Company in Pana, Illinois, the new fixtures cost $7,000.

> Gust and George Moucoulis and Thomas Orfalos [*sic*] have been in the city but nine months, since purchasing the Apostle store and have made good in every way in that time. The . . . new fixtures in the front part of the store is the third step of progress made by them. . . . They first remodeled their front window; later they concreted their ice cream factory in the

basement. Cleanliness has been their watchword all the time and with the improvements . . . they need doff their hats to no store in the city.[254]

It was interesting to note the advent of concrete basement floors and again an emphasis on cleanliness, perhaps not just because they were Greeks but because of the new expectations of sanitation with food and dairy products. In one entertaining advertisement in 1919, the Royal Confectionery was described as "The Most Up-To-Date and Best Ice Cream and Confectionery Parlor," and the owners celebrated their new improvements with a poem:

The Song That Everybody Will Be Singing
For ice cream and candy that can't be beat
Go to the Royal—the house of sweet.
It's the place you ought to know
It's where all the ice cream lovers go.[255]

Despite all the renovating, celebrating, and poetry writing, the Moucoulis brothers evidently had sold the Royal by 1926,[256] for in that year George, Gust, and John opened a different store at 100 South Main, called the Eureka, or sometimes simply Moucoulis Brothers. Orfanos had moved to Indiana and was working in a restaurant.[257] Gust and George were still confectioners in Taylorville in 1929 but seemingly not owners.[258] In 1928, George Kehias, of Pana, took a ten-year lease on the Eureka confectionery, after creditors had closed it. He paid nearly $10,500 for all the fixtures and reopened it as "George's Candy Shop," like his place in Pana. Although George and his brother Louis Kehias were now operating three confectioneries—in Pana, Mattoon, and Taylorville—the Moucoulis brothers must have stayed around and helped them with the Eureka.[259] Sometime before 1934, though, Gust and George Moucoulis left Taylorville and traveled to Rockford, Illinois, where they were manager and clerk of the Northern Lights Ice Cream Company in that year.[260]

George and Phillip Kouchiveris now enter the Greek confectionery narrative in Taylorville, taking over George's Candy Shop in 1932, after having sold their Nokomis confectionery. The brothers retained the name, George's, and it was "one of Taylorville's most popular hangouts for many years."[261] Dan Farrimond worked at George's for a year at an hourly pay rate of eighty-five cents. He remembered that George was the chief candy maker, which was done in the basement, while Phil was the "out front" man, running the shop and keeping the peace.[262]

George's was an integral part of downtown Taylorville. The Kouchiveris brothers were good community citizens and beloved by Taylorville residents. Most everyone I have encountered who lived there during the 1950s and 1960s remembers George's with fondness. Interestingly, the Kouchiveris brothers never married and retired back to Peristeri, Greece, where they had at least four sisters and a brother. Phil died there in May 1969 at the age of seventy-six and George in October 1974 at eighty-two.[263]

Hillsboro, Illinois, was the home of the Hillsboro Candy Kitchen, originally owned and operated by the Ginos brothers.[264] We first met Nick, Spyros and Zissis Ginos in Mt. Carmel, where they operated the Candy Kitchen there from 1911 to 1919. There were five Ginos brothers altogether: Zissis (Zissos), Spyros (also called William or "Bill"), Nicholas, Paul D. (Apostole) (b. June 30, 1886, or 1887?), and Thomas (b. around 1887).[265] They were all born in Kazaklar (now named Ampelonas), Larissa, Greece. In 1910 Zissis, Spyros, and Nicholas were confectioners in Hillsboro, after which Zissis and Paul remained there, while Nick and Spyros moved to Mt. Carmel.[266] The fifth brother, Thomas, was tragically killed by a streetcar in March 1913.[267]

In 1926 Nicholas, Paul, and Spyros Ginos were together again making candy in Hillsboro, while Zissis owned a restaurant. All the brothers were now married.[268] Zissis Ginos had returned to Greece in 1921 to marry and then came back to Hillsboro with his new wife, Nikoletta.[269]

In 1930 Paul Ginos and wife Bessie moved to Brooklyn, New York, where he was a confectioner, but he died there only two years later. Although Paul's body was brought back to Hillsboro to be interred, neither Bessie nor their children came back to Hillsboro to live.[270] Zissis Ginos returned to Greece to live in 1930 and died in Larissa on May 2, 1931.[271]

Spyros (Bill) and Nick Ginos kept the Candy Kitchen going. Dorothy Bliss, in her book, *Hillsboro: A History*, shared that her husband, Tom, recalled how "Bill and Nick, who operated the family business for years, were generous with their 'samples.' Often, they called me in to try a treat, especially when they saw my nose pressed against the front window. Their Heavenly Hash [chocolate, walnuts/pecans, marshmallow] was ambrosia."[272] Spyros's son Bill evidently took over the business for some short time after his father died in 1963, but the Ginos brothers' decades-long confectionery odyssey in central Illinois effectively ended with Nick's and Spyros's deaths.[273]

Several small towns with southeastern European ethnic histories and Greek confectioners lie west of Hillsboro. At the end of the 1800s, south-central Illinois had many coal mines, and the workers displacing the early English, Irish, Welsh, and Scots as lower-waged miners and as strike-breakers were Italians, Greeks, and Slavic immigrants. These southeastern European immigrants working as miners in Benld, Carlinville, Gillespie, Girard, Mt. Olive, Staunton, and Virden created a new environment in the mines and mining communities. The ethnic diversity was captured by a story about a young girl moving from Missouri to Macoupin County, Illinois, around 1910. A family friend told her that she might have trouble understanding the speech of people in her new location.

> The child couldn't comprehend that, but she soon learned. There was a babble of tongues spoken on the streets of most any mining community in the early 1900's, and teaching English to all these people was another problem of the period. The men slowly learned to speak it from those with whom they worked, boarded, or did business. . . . Enterprising people, who were anxious to become citizens, often banded together and paid a small fee to some local ex-teacher or other educated person in the community for evening lessons in reading and understanding English material pertaining to the Constitution and government of the United States.[274]

How the little town of Benld came to be in 1904 is another fascinating tale. "A local businessman at the time in Benld [told the story], 'When they opened the new mine south of Gillespie, a large group of Italians and Greeks came to work there. Gillespie did not welcome us so we built our own city.'"[275] The immigrants wanted to honor a local man who had befriended them, Ben L. Dorsey. They were not keen on naming it Dorsey or Dorseyville, however, because there were some Dorseys who were not supportive of the immigrants, so they took pieces of his name and created Benld.[276] Of particular note, the immigrants in Benld, particularly those of Russian descent, built a Russian Orthodox Church in 1907, which at its peak had a membership of approximately two hundred families. This was significant as the only other central Illinois Orthodox churches were in larger towns: Springfield, Champaign-Urbana, Decatur, and Danville. For a small town to commit resources and build a church like this was no minor accomplishment.[277] According to the church's pastor Reverend Waters, over time attendance dwindled as second- and third-generation family members left town to pursue professional careers, and the church became a monastery. According to the *Illinois State Journal-Register*, "Many of the first- and second-generation miners the church served were determined to see their children college-educated."[278]

In this study the Benld, Virden, Carlinville, and Litchfield narratives intersect, beginning with Peter Markos (b. November 21, 1878), a confectioner in Virden. According to Gene Markos, a great-nephew of Peter Markos, family legend relates that "Uncle Pete" emigrated from Greece and first traveled to St. Louis. From there he ventured north to Virden, though for unknown reasons.[279] From his draft registration in 1918 we know that Peter Markos was working in Virden as a self-employed confectioner.[280] He was still in Virden in 1920[281] but then sold his store to his nephew George Markos (b. February 12, 1895). Peter moved north to Chicago, and the family lost track of him.

George Markos was the son of an Orthodox priest, born in Pyrgos, Greece, on the west coast of the Peloponnese. He immigrated to the United States in 1912. George was working for his uncle Peter when he registered for the draft in 1918.[282] George kept the confectionery going until the Depression years between 1930 and 1932, when he was forced to close. His investments in the local bank disappeared, no doubt along with the savings of other townspeople, after the bank president committed suicide. George had married a local Virden woman, Mittie (Harris), who had worked in the store. After the business closed, George worked odd jobs and gravitated toward Litchfield and the Ariston restaurant, owned by another Greek, Pete Adam, whom we shall discuss next. Pete took George in and helped him. Eventually George became the head chef at the Elks Club in Litchfield.[283]

Panos, or Pete, Adam (b. October 9, 1890, in Zacholi) founded the Ariston restaurant, a famous landmark still in existence, in Litchfield along the equally famous Route 66, south of Springfield, Illinois.[284] I had the great pleasure of meeting Pete's son Nick, for many years the owner and manager of the Ariston. With great zeal and pride, he shared with me his father's story and also a copy of his father's autobiography.[285] Pete was the first son in his family to leave Greece. On his first attempt to immigrate he got only as far as Naples, Italy, before being turned back for some unspecified reason but then made it to America on a subsequent attempt in 1905.

In his autobiography, Pete describes his extensive travels around America looking for work before he finally settled in Litchfield in 1930.

His story is a wonderful illustration of the desire and determination immigrants brought with them to America in hopes of having a new, better life. After passing through Ellis Island, Pete went to St. Louis, where his sponsor lived and where people from Zacholi had already settled. A sample of Pete's travels and jobs over the next seven years, in chronological order, include washing dishes at a St. Louis restaurant; shining shoes in Baltimore; working in different St. Louis factories; cleaning rooms in a St. Louis hotel; herding sheep in Roswell, New Mexico; working in a steel mill in Pueblo, Colorado; working above ground at a coal mining camp in Delagua, Colorado; co-owning a bakery in Delagua; and laboring as a coal miner in Dawson, New Mexico. When the First Balkan War began in October 1912, Pete returned to Greece and joined the army. He fought in both the First and Second Balkan Wars and remained in his home village for a bit, running a coffeehouse after the wars ended, and then his father gave him the money to return to America. His sister had immigrated after World War I and married a barber in St. Louis, so Pete headed there. He worked in a factory by day and attended barber school at night but soon decided barbering was not for him.[286] Pete then heard from a cousin about mining jobs in Benld in the late 1910s, so off he went. It was there he made some new career choices.

In 1920, Pete and his cousin Tom Bouclamon (b. around 1893) were boarding together in Benld and had a confectionery.[287] Nick believes that his father and Tom had originally met, possibly among the Zacholi Greeks, in St. Louis. Tom had learned candy making while working in a St. Louis candy shop, which explains where Pete learned to be a confectioner. Tom paid the up-front money to get the business going. By 1922 Pete and Tom had sold their shares of the business to another Greek, Andy Golfinopoulus, and moved on; Tom became a barber.[288]

In 1922, Pete partnered with Chris Chrisakis (b. 1894 in Andronianous),[289] who emigrated from Greece in 1916. The two opened a confectionery in Carlinville, Illinois, on Route 4, the main road at the time between St. Louis and Chicago. As the town had no "decent" (Pete's word) restaurant, a local doctor offered to loan him $2,000 if he opened one. So he did, adding a partner, who was also a cook, from St. Louis. Chris and Pete's partnership lasted for a few years, with Chris making candy and Pete managing the restaurant.[290] In 1930 Pete noted that a new north-south road was to be built through Litchfield—Route 66. Pete found a gasoline station for sale on the new route and ran this until, on March 15, 1931, he opened a restaurant. In recalling how his father chose the name for his place, Nick noted how Greek businessmen were never shy—his father named his restaurant "Ariston," Greek for "the Best."[291]

Pete opened his Litchfield business at the height of the Great Depression, but with hard work and a willingness to take risks, he managed to survive. In 1935 Pete partnered with Tom Cokinos, a Greek immigrant who also ran a billiard parlor[292] in Litchfield, but then bought out Tom's portion of the business in 1937. On October 27, 1937, Pete married Emily Bartsis (b. October 17, 1909), a first-generation Greek woman from Chicago, and they had one son, Nick.[293] Pete's Ariston restaurant is the longest continuously open restaurant along Route 66. Nick Adam sold the Ariston to new owners in June 2018, and they are keeping the tradition alive.[294]

Tom Cokinos (b. May 25, 1898, in Sparta) came to America in 1909. After selling his partnership to Pete, Tom remained in Litchfield and owned the Blue Danube café. In 1954 he opened the Ranch Inn just outside of Litchfield.[295] He died in 1956.[296] Tom was not the first Cokinos in Litchfield, however, as brothers John (b. April 18, 1877) and Stephen (b. March 20, 1881) Cokinos had already settled in Litchfield by 1907, working as confectioners. By 1911 they were calling themselves the Litchfield Candy Company, and in 1912 they bought a new $2,000 soda fountain.[297] They were both "Born in Sparta, Greece," as is proudly engraved on each of their gravestones.[298] John's obituary in 1941 says that he first ran a candy kitchen in Staunton, Illinois, before moving to Litchfield.[299]

Around 1914 another Greek confectioner, Konstantinos "Gus" Skeadas, along with his brother-in-law Gust Vapos, bought the Litchfield Candy Company from the Cokinos brothers. Born in Sparta between 1880 and 1884,[300] Gus immigrated to the United States around 1900.[301] According to his obituary, when he arrived in the United States, he worked for a time in New York City as a barber. He then migrated to Philadelphia, Boston, and finally White Plains, New York, where he was a confectioner. After returning to Greece and marrying Annie Vapos, Gus and his new bride went back to the United States and settled in Litchfield around 1913 and bought the candy company.[302] In 1931, Gus sold his interest in the confectionery to his brother-in-law Anthony Vapos (b. January 17, 1892, in Sparta) and took the entire family to Greece to live for several months. When they returned to Litchfield, Gus bought his share of the business back from Anthony Vapos. In February 1939, he bought out Anthony's share and was operating the candy company on his own when he died in November 1939. A Greek Orthodox priest from East St. Louis conducted Gus Skeadas's funeral, and, like the Cokinos brothers, Gus's tombstone proudly reads, "Born in Sparta, Greece."[303] Son James (b. August 1, 1919) managed the business through the 1950s until it finally closed.[304]

In one final amazing example of the interconnectedness of the central Illinois Greeks, Pete Adam's partner in Carlinville, Chris Chrisakis, remained there for some time after Pete Adam moved to Litchfield. By 1940 Chris had relocated to Mattoon, where he was a candy maker at Louis Kehias's Blue Bird Candy Shop.[305] Chris later migrated to Champaign-Urbana and opened his own business, Chris's Candy Shop, on Neil Street. Chris never married and died in Champaign in December 1966.[306] By this time, his nephew Gus had become the Candy Shop manager, and he ran it for many years. Gus Chrisagis (note that the *k* became a *g*) was a contemporary of my father, and my mother, a master candy dipper, once worked a short while for Gus. Gus was one of the founders of the Three Hierarchs Greek Orthodox Church in Champaign. When he was in his eighties, Gus came to Tuscola and helped my sister make candy when we reopened in 2004, standing over the copper kettle and stirring the hot caramel with a wooden paddle in one hand. Following the old Greek candy maker tradition, we also watched him dip his fingers in cold water, then into the boiling caramel to pull out a bit to test its texture. Through his presence, we had another direct connection with the generations of Greek confectioners described in this history.[307] Sadly, Chris Chrisagis died only a few weeks after our reopening.[308] We still remember him fondly and are so grateful for all he taught us about candy and the candy business.

Of the many small towns and small cities explored within this rural study, despite the amount of research conducted, there is so much more that could be done. These fascinating stories of Greek immigration, networking, and settlement can be replicated in every state in America. They should be recovered, for they beautifully illustrate our country's immigrant heritage and celebrate the hardworking Greek immigrants who carved out new lives in their adopted land's rural areas. It has been an honor to share my family's story and those of the first generation of Greeks in central Illinois.

CONCLUSION

Thank you for the opportunity to share the vibrant stories of first-generation Greek immigrants to Illinois, tales that still resonate today.

Their stories seek to deconstruct what Paul Spickard has called the "Ellis Island Model," a formulaic approach to immigration. In the Ellis Island Model, immigrants are poor and oppressed, determined to come to the United States on a one-way trajectory, hoping to find freedom and riches.[1] That particular model usually focuses upon urban settlement. Here I have focused on individual male or singular family immigrants in a rural environment. This has allowed me to identify common themes in both the urban and rural immigrant experience but also to delineate the differences. This micro-level approach could serve as a model for further studies of the Greek immigration experience in different communities or regions outside of central Illinois or for exploring the experiences of other distinct ethnic groups in small towns. The model could also be utilized to research current immigration to America and the entrepreneurial enterprises and networks more recent immigrants have established in this country. Immigration as a fluid concept incorporating self-efficacy and networking easily lends itself to the discourses of diaspora, transnationalism, and transculturalism.[2]

As we conclude our journey, some aspects of immigration theory and history can be highlighted. Education, identity, generation succession, and gender are all areas that should be considered for further exploration.

This research, as a rural study, delineates aspects of formal and informal education and the development of entrepreneurial pursuits in the niche occupation of confectioners in small towns. It additionally traces the wider networks of support and training between and among first-generation Greek immigrants. While Theodore Saloutos extensively chronicled the history of Greek immigrants in Chicago, including the rise of the Greek confectioner in that city, it is clear from my study that the urban experience was only part of the story. We must also examine the lives of those who left the urban communities and attempted to make their way in the small towns and cities. The first generation of Greek immigrants in central Illinois and across the Midwest began their journeys along paths similar to those of their urban compatriots in Chicago or St. Louis, but perhaps because they were more independent, or adventurous, or entrepreneurial, they struck out on their own. It is this last leg of their life's journey that offers such a unique and rich topic for study and allows us, from the vantage point of the immigrant, to consider this experience at the local and rural level. Redefining "place" by the sole Greek male or Greek family in a small town, claiming one's "space" with a newly outfitted soda fountain and candy counter display, and projecting one's "agency" amid overt Ku Klux Klan resistance are the components that distill the rural immigrant experience into one of daily reality. It is indeed the creation of a "new space" that transcends the Greek village, the urban transition, and life in a small midwestern town. It projects the tension of the shifting patterns of conformity between and among the Greek immigrants and the "majority population" but also between and among themselves.

The issue of identity has been one that Greek American historians have frequently considered between and among the generations. Alice Scourby addresses the question of what it means for first-, second-, and third-generation Greek Americans to "be Greek." She suggests that for some, identification with cultural indices, such as music, dance, or food, is enough, while for others it is membership or affiliation with the Greek Orthodox Church. She quotes George Stephanopoulos, President Clinton's former communications director, who responded to a question about his ethnic identity with the affirmation, "'I am American, but I am Greek Orthodox.'"[3] As first-generation Greek immigrants claimed identity with their respective villages in Greece, Scourby contends that the second generation would have absolutely aligned itself with the Greek church as the defining marker of "being Greek." How the third, fourth, and fifth generations define their ethnicity can be a topic for further research.

Of course, the issue of race and the evolution from the first generation of "in-between" people to the second generation's "white" identity are also integral components of this narrative. Yiorgos Anagnostou, in his extensive treatise on Greek identity, proposes looking to the past as "a resource for organizing ethnic identity and as a venue of containment and domination." This requires the observer to assign a hegemonic meaning to the acquisition of cultural practices. Over time, Anagnostou suggests that this effort will contribute to a powerful and dynamic pluralistic society.[4] Anagnostou urges researchers to recognize the past as a constructed process and that the context of its definition assists in the recovery of the past that may have been erased or excluded from public memory. Underscoring the fact that some pasts are more privileged than others, he contends that whiteness studies in particular "have been effective in showing that race talk permeates social discourse even when not making explicit references to race or racism" when it employs the construction of "being white" as opposed to "not being black."[5] This allowed the "in-between" southeastern immigrants to eventually privilege their ethnic identities as being white, despite initial resistance from majority populations and sociocultural labeling as "Oriental," "Octoroon," or "Black."[6] If we accept this argument, we could possibly extend Scourby's research and further explore the third-generation Greek construct of individual or collective identity.

The matter of the longevity of my grandfather's business also serves as an entry point into a much larger discussion of why nearly all the old Greek confectionaries eventually closed. What factors might have served to bring about their demise? Based on data taken from the 1980 US census, Scourby suggests that the trend of upward economic mobility across generations among individuals of Greek descent was demonstrated in male movement from being shopkeepers and laborers into more managerial, sales, and administrative occupations. In addition, females also moved into a wider workforce that required more education and different skills from those needed in the candy store.[7] She argued that within the Greek family structure, the strong emphasis on formal education as a vehicle for upward mobility was manifested in the second and third generations.[8] Whether or not higher education was the primary factor in the decline and demise of the existing confectioneries in east-central Illinois after the 1970s is not easily demonstrable, but it is clear that few of the second-generation Greeks wanted to remain in the family businesses established by their immigrant fathers.

Of course, the demise and decimation of small city and small-town "downtowns" must also be considered as a significant factor in the decline of the Greek confectioneries as well as other retail enterprises. My research shows that by the 1960s, only a handful of confectioneries, managed by second-generation Greeks, were surviving in central Illinois. Often with the death of the father, and particularly after World War II, businesses closed due to lack of interest on the part of the second generation. Concurrently, with the advent of the interstate highway system and the burgeoning development of malls and "big box" all-purpose stores, downtowns across America began their rapid decline after 1970. Tristan Donovan, in his treatise on soda, states that after World War II, "the postwar economic boom led to an explosion in car ownership, and as Americans became motorists they left the inner cities and headed for the greenery, space, and peace of the suburbs. To supply their needs came new types of retail environments: shopping malls, supermarkets, drive-in movie theaters, fast-food chains, and gas stations—all offering convenience and copious parking. Main Street with its soda fountains and mom-and-pop stores was left behind as America headed for the highway."[9] He notes that before the war, most small towns hosted at least one soda fountain, but by the mid-1960s, only half of them did.[10] Most of the small towns I visited in the course of this study had whole blocks of empty buildings that once held thriving unique retail shops serving the community. While some efforts are being made to revive downtowns with governmental and private funding, it has been a slow process. Yet, it is the romance of small-town America that still holds many of us in its grip. Miles Orvell, in *The Death and Life of Main Street*, suggests that despite the reality that "Main Street" has been "battered for decades . . . the idea of the small town lies at the heart of the American ethos, with a strong and continuing appeal for Americans."[11] Indeed, particularly after the attacks of 9/11, the attraction of a neighborhood, that safe place to shop and meet, has continued to resonate with the public, when in reality there are few of those spaces left in small towns. Jane Jacobs must be cited as the voice from the urban wilderness with her admonition that neighborhoods that are lived in and utilized are "typically strong proponents of peace and order," and it is the stores and public places close to each other that promote and perpetuate an orderly society.[12]

Luckily for all of us, there are some Greek confectioneries still operating in the Midwest. Worth noting is one founded by the Zanetos family in Columbus, Ohio. The patriarch, Antonios Tzanetopoulos, came to Columbus in 1907 from Andritsaina, changed his name to Zanetos, and apprenticed as a candy maker. Son Tom returned from World War II and joined his father as a confectioner, and the multiple Anthony-Thomas Candy Company stores were formed in 1946. They continue today serving the greater Columbus area.[13] The Olympia Candy Kitchen in Goshen, Indiana, is a step back in time. Owned by the Paflas family, Nicholas Paflas began there in 1912, making candy and running the soda fountain. In 1920, he purchased the business and added a diner. It has remained a family business and still serves homemade treats made by third- and fourth-generation relatives.[14]

My favorite Greek sisters in Minnesota, Pamela Canelake Matson and Patricia Canelake, are another third-generation family who reopened their grandfather's confectionery. Their grandfather Gust Canelake was born in Sikea, Laconia, Greece, and immigrated to America in 1896, arriving at Ellis Island when he was twenty. From there he traveled to Waukegan, Illinois, and worked in a foundry. Gust had an older brother, Chris, who had come to America a few years earlier and learned to make candy in Providence, Rhode Island, from other Sikea immigrants there. Chris then moved to Green Bay, Wisconsin, and opened a store but was urged to move to Minnesota by a salesperson. In 1905, Chris, Gust, and another brother, Tom, opened the Virginia Candy Kitchen in Virginia, Minnesota. Chris and a fourth brother, Nick, initially opened two confectioneries in nearby Hibbing, Minnesota—the Hibbing Candy Kitchen (1907) and the Arcadia Candy Kitchen (1912). In 1920 they combined them into a restaurant and confectionery called Canelake's Café and Sweet Shop (closed in 1968). Tom also opened and ran the Olympia Candy Kitchen in Virginia from 1914 to 1951. The Virginia Candy Kitchen moved several times until its permanent location at 414 Chestnut Street. The name changed to Canelake's Candies in the 1940s and has been in business for over one hundred years. In 2007, third-generation confectioners Pamela Canelake Matson and Patricia Canelake opened Great! Lakes Candy Kitchen in

Knife River. Their father, John, shared his recipes and knowledge until his death in 2012. The sisters also bought back the original Canelake's Candies in Virginia in 2018.[15]

Some few confectionaries remain open in the Midwest, in urban centers and a few small towns, but they are anomalies in the world of sweets. The three Greek Zaharako brothers founded Zaharakos in 1900 in Columbus, Indiana, where tasty confectioneries and ice cream are still served, and there is also a soda fountain museum. Regina's Candies in St. Paul, Minnesota, was founded by Frank Elliot (Eliopoulos), from Xilokastro in the Peloponnese, in 1926[16] and continues to offer real high-fat ice cream and artisanal chocolates. Crown Candy Kitchen in St. Louis is an institution still producing delicious treats since 1913.[17]

In a real-world experience at the micro-level, my sister and I have seen a resurgence of downtown Tuscola as a result of reestablishing our business on the corner of Main and Sale Streets. Several other retail businesses have opened in the past ten years, bringing the locals and "out-of-towners" to our four-block area. Children can safely park their bicycles at the bike rack on the corner and come in for a soda or sundae, knowing they will be greeted by name and listened to when they share stories about their escapades. We hire high school students to work, and it has been a valuable experience for most. My sister's children also work if there are no school activities, repeating the cycle begun by our grandfather. While this life may sound romantically lovely and bucolic, the owning and operating of a candy/food business remains hard work. It is not for the faint of heart; this type of business requires commitment, capital, and a bit of crazy passion.

My sister and I represent the third generation of Greek confectioners, but as female owners and entrepreneurs we also exemplify the changing gender roles that second- and third-generation Greek women have experienced. In particular, marriage patterns in the Greek Orthodox Church moved from the traditional Greek-only spousal arrangements to intermarriage among non-Orthodox and non-Greeks by the second generation. As I have also shown, many Greek males, particularly in the small towns in central Illinois, frequently married non-Greek women from their local community. Among the second-generation Greek women I interviewed, their views on taking traditional Greek husbands varied, from agreeing to an arranged marriage, to making every effort not to marry a Greek man. Educational endeavors, exposure to life outside of their hometowns, and the absence of a nearby Greek Orthodox Church all impacted the marriage unions among first- and second-generation Greeks in central Illinois. This was especially true for those residing in small towns whose Orthodox church attendance in relatively faraway Danville, Decatur, Champaign, or Springfield was sporadic and usually relegated to holidays.

The Greek Orthodox Church claims to be "the One, Holy, Catholic and Apostolic Church" and holds a deep reluctance to ascribe to any other church this "ecclesial reality."[18] Statistics around the year 2000 kept by the Greek Orthodox Archdiocese of America revealed that two out of three marriages, or 66 percent, were "inter-Christian," which represented a tremendous growth of such interfaith unions over a time span of sixty years of records.[19] Indeed, in the years following World War II, the Greek Orthodox Church in the United States became "American." A study conducted in 1976 revealed that the Greek Orthodox Archdiocese of North and South America had evolved into one that incorporated more "professional" American-trained clergy, the inclusion of English into the Liturgy and church governance, the utilization by some parishes of organ music, and the continued multipurpose use of church buildings for events other than formal church services.[20] By 2012 the intermarriage rate among Greek Americans had risen to between 75 and 85 percent along with a projected attrition rate of church attendance greater than 60 percent over the next generation. The archdiocese reports that 90 percent of Americans with Greek roots are "no longer in communion with the Church."[21]

This study of first-generation Greek confectioners in central Illinois touched on the journeys of hundreds of people, but there are many tales yet to be uncovered. I hope that this initial exploration into local, rural, and public history will encourage others to build upon my work here and thereby ensure that the neglected but fascinating lives of other generations of immigrants will be illuminated so that they, too, may be justly remembered and honored.

NOTES

ABBREVIATIONS

A.c. Ancestry.com
DDR Decatur Daily Review
DH Decatur Herald
DHR Decatur Herald and Review
DRC Draft Registration Cards
Find A Grave The proper format for these citations is: Find A Grave.com, *Find A Grave,* database and images (https://www.findagrave.com: accessed DD/MM/YYYY), memorial page for NAME (Date of Birth–Date of Death), Find A Grave Memorial no. 136004001. However, the entries below will be abbreviated to: *Find A Grave*, NAME, (MM/DD/YYYY-MM/DD/YYYY), memorial no. (access date).
MJG Mattoon Journal Gazette
NARA National Archives and Records Administration
NLC Newberry Library, Chicago
NYPCL New York, Passenger and Crew Lists (including Castle Garden and Ellis Island), 1820–1957
TJ Tuscola Journal
US United States
USFC United States Federal Census
WW World War

INTRODUCTION

1. "George Flesor Makes a Big Hit at Rotary," *TJ*, April 3, 1930, 1.

2. See both George D. Vaky and Peter G. Vriner, 1900 USFC, census place: Champaign Ward 3, Champaign; roll: 240; p. 9A; enumeration district: 0006.

3. "Why Tuscola?," *TJ*, August 15, 1957, 1.

4. "Why Tuscola?," 1.

5. "Railroad Gives Tuscola Lead," *TJ*, August 15, 1957, 1.

6. "Why Tuscola?," 1. See also J. King, *History of Douglas County*, 634.

7. Handlin, *Uprooted*, 3. Emphasis in original.

8. "Why Tuscola?," 16.

9. "Candy Kitchen Oldest Business," *TJ*, August 15, 1957, 16.

10. Hansen, *Immigration*, 9.

11. Indeed, there are few studies of any of the different immigrant ethnic groups in rural America, and this remains a wide-open field for further research.

12. Force, "House on Bayou Road," 23.

13. Thelen, "Memory and American History," 1127, quoted in E. Lewis, "Connecting Memory," 117.

14. R. White, *Remembering Ahanagran*, 3.

15. R. White, 4.

16. R. White, 6.

17. Kaufman, *Place, Race, and Story*, 5.

18. Kaufman, 22.

19. Constant, *Austin Lunch*, 9.

20. Constant, 30.

21. Constant, 41.

22. Constant, 46.

23. Constant, 147.

24. Hamilton, *Complete Arithmetic*, 187.

25. Gildemeister, *Minnesota Course of Study*, 43.

26. Steve Frangos, "Pioneers of Confection in America," 1.

27. WPA Writers' Program in New York State, *New York*, 110.

28. Hansen, *Problem of the Third Generation Immigrant*, 9.

CHAPTER 1. FOUNDATIONS

1. Budin, *Ancient Greeks*, 11.

2. Budin, 11–12.

3. Budin, 12.

4. See Hughes and Thirgood, "Deforestation, Erosion, and Forest Management."

5. Budin, *Ancient Greeks*, 12.

6. Freeman, *Greek Achievement*, 22.

7. See Clogg, *Concise History*, 111.

8. Higgins and Higgins, *Geological Companion to Greece and the Aegean*, 40–64.

9. Kremezi, "Greece and Crete," 151–52.

10. Kremezi, 152.

11. Kremezi, 212–13.

12. Dalby, "Greece, Ancient," 149.

13. Dalby and Dalby, *Gifts of the Gods*, 170–71.

14. Dalby and Dalby, 171.

15. Kremezi, *Foods of Greece*, 18–19.

16. Freeman, *Greek Achievement*, 23.

17. Saloutos, *Greeks in the United States*, 20.

18. Saloutos, ix. See also Dakin, *Unification of Greece*, 2–5; and Anagnostou, "'That Imagination Called Hellenism,'" 247–48.

19. See Shelmerdine, *Cambridge Companion to the Aegean Bronze Age*, 19–76.

20. Shinn and Keefe, *Greece*, 3.

21. For this history, see Castleden, *Minoans*.

22. Freeman, *Greek Achievement*, 28–32.

23. Garland, *Daily Life of the Ancient Greeks*, 1–3; Budin, *Ancient Greeks*, 53–54. See also Freeman, *Greek Achievement*, 28–32; and Cartledge, "Peoples," 37–46.

24. Castleden, *Mycenaeans*, 1–2.

25. Garland, *Daily Life of the Ancient Greeks*, 9–12, 24–30; Budin, *Ancient Greeks*, 78–79.

26. Shinn and Keefe, *Greece*, 9–10. See also Fisher, "Rich and Poor," 82–89; and Budin, *Ancient Greeks*, 72–77.

27. Freeman, *Greek Achievement*, 24. See also Cartledge, "Peoples."

28. Budin, *Ancient Greeks*, 62–67; Shinn and Keefe, *Greece*, 10.

29. See E. Hall, "Literature and Performance"; and Arafat and Morgan, "Architecture and Other Visual Arts."

30. Dean-Jones, "Philosophy and Science"; Budin, *Ancient Greeks*, 363–99.

31. Fox, *Pagans and Christians*, 282; Freeman, *Greek Achievement*, 324–37, 341–71; Cartledge, "War and Peace," 186–92; and Budin, *Ancient Greeks*, 80–88.

32. Budin, *Ancient Greeks*, 19.

33. Erickson, *Orthodox Christians in America*, 8.

34. Erickson, 8.

35. H. Papanikolas, *Amulet of Greek Earth*, 3. See also Anagnostou, *Contours of White Ethnicity*, 37; and Anagnostou, "Forget the Past, Remember the Ancestors!"

36. Herrin, *Byzantium*, 262–63; Shinn and Keefe, *Greece*, 15.

37. Herrin, *Byzantium*, 270–80.

38. Shinn and Keefe, *Greece*, 18.

39. Shinn and Keefe, 18.

40. Scourby, *Greek Americans*, 2.

41. Clogg, *Concise History*, 17–21; Shinn and Keefe, *Greece*, 16–17; H. Papanikolas, *Amulet of Greek Earth*, 3.

42. Clogg, *Concise History*, 21.

43. Scourby, *Greek Americans*, 17. See also Clogg, *Concise History*, 21–27.

44. Clogg, *Concise History*, 25, 27.

45. Jusdanis, *Necessary Nation*, 111.

46. Jusdanis, 112.

47. Jusdanis, 112–13.

48. Greece's romantic appeal during this period is discussed in Howarth, *Greek Adventure*. For the "Grecian Fever" in America, see Steve Frangos, "1821."

49. Brown, *International Politics*, 52. See also Cassimatis, *American Influence in Greece*, 2.

50. Quoted in Howarth, *Greek Adventure*, 73.

51. Hatzidimitriou, "American Response."

52. Woodhouse, *Capodistria*, ix.

53. The definitive English biography is Woodhouse, *Capodistria*, but see also Clogg, *Concise History*, 41–45; Dakin, *Unification of Greece*, 55–63; and Woodhouse, *Modern Greece*, 148–56.

54. Woodhouse, *Capodistria*, 488–507; Koliopoulos, *Brigands with a Cause*, 67; Dakin, *Greek Struggle*, 238–301.

55. Dakin, *Greek Struggle*, 310–12; Woodhouse, *Capodistria*, 504–7.

56. McGrew, *Land and Revolution*, 57.

57. McGrew, 161–62.

58. Greek land use and peasant farming is discussed in Gallant, *Modern Greece*, 91–97.

59. McGrew, *Land and Revolution*, 175.

60. Scourby, *Greek Americans*, 3.

61. Fairchild, *Greek Immigration*, 60–63.

62. McGrew, *Land and Revolution*, 175.

63. Shinn and Keefe, *Greece*, 21–22.

64. Clogg, *Concise History*, 49; Gallant, *Modern Greece*, 107–12.

65. Benjamin of Lesvos, *Elements of Metaphysics*, quoted in Clogg, *Concise History*, 32.

66. Clogg, *Concise History*, 46–55; Dakin, *Unification of Greece*, 82–86; Gallant, *Modern Greece*, 54–60.

67. Gallant, *Modern Greece*, 45; Clogg, *Concise History*, 55–57, 240–41.

68. Clogg, *Concise History*, 162–63; Gallant, *Modern Greece*, 203.

69. Woodhouse, *Modern Greece*, 172; Shinn and Keefe, *Greece*, 26.

70. Shinn and Keefe, *Greece*, 24–25.

71. Dakin, *Unification of Greece*, 95–96; Shinn and Keefe, *Greece*, 25; Gallant, *Modern Greece*, 107–12.

72. Dakin, *Unification of Greece*, 100.

73. Constantinou, "Profiles of Greek Americans," 93.

74. Moffett, "Notes," 612.

75. Fairchild, *Greek Immigration*, 64.

76. Cranshaw and Redak, *Bugs Rule!*, 237–38.

77. Saloutos, *Greeks in the United States*, 28.

78. Fairchild, *Greek Immigration*, 76–77.

79. Cranshaw and Redak, *Bugs Rule!*, 238; Fairchild, *Greek Immigration*, 76–77.

80. Saloutos, *Greeks in the United States*, 29.

81. Fairchild, *Greek Immigration*, 77–78. See also Saloutos, *Greeks in the United States*, 29.

82. Fairchild, *Greek Immigration*, 65.

83. Gallant, *Modern Greece*, 50; Dakin, *Unification of Greece*, 96, 253–55.

84. Saloutos, *Greeks in the United States*, 7.

85. Dakin, *Unification of Greece*, 144; Gallant, *Modern Greece*, 51; Shinn and Keefe, *Greece*, 27.

86. Lennartz and Wassong, "Athens 1896," 20–21, 24.

87. Scourby, *Greek Americans*, 4.

88. Woodhouse, *Modern Greece*, 183–85; Dakin, *Unification of Greece*, 107–14.

89. Clogg, *Concise History*, 71, 255–56.

90. Lloyd George, *Truth about the Peace Treaties*, 2:1216, quoted in MacMillan, *Paris 1919*, 354.

91. Woodhouse, *Modern Greece*, 187–93; Shinn and Keefe, *Greece*, 30–32; Dakin, *Unification of Greece*, 199.

92. Clogg, *Concise History*, 75–76; Gallant, *Modern Greece*, 116–17, 123–25.

93. Fairchild, *Greek Immigration*, 30.

94. Saloutos, *Greeks in the United States*, 30; Fairchild, *Greek Immigration*, 30.

95. Clogg, *Concise History*, 77–82; Gallant, *Modern Greece*, 125–29; Dakin, *Unification of Greece*, 190–200.

96. Shinn and Keefe, *Greece*, 32–36.

97. Seligman, *Victory of Venizelos*, 31.

98. As we shall see in chapter 2, it also divided Greeks in the United States.

99. Seligman, *Victory of Venizelos*, 33; Tucker, *Great War*, 121–23; Clogg, *Concise History*, 83–91; Gallant, *Modern Greece*, 129–34.

100. Tucker, *Great War*, 121–22; Gallant, *Modern Greece*, 133–34; Clogg, *Concise History*, 89–91.

101. Tucker, *Great War*, 122–23; Clogg, *Concise History*, 91.

102. Shinn and Keefe, *Greece*, 34–37; Clogg, *Concise History*, 143, 170.

103. Kalogeras, "Narrating an Ethnic Group," 14–15.

104. Moskos, "Growing Up Greek American," 65.

105. Anagnostou, *Contours of White Ethnicity*, 37. See also Anagnostou, "Forget the Past, Remember the Ancestors!"

106. Myres, *Who Were the Greeks?*, 538–39.

CHAPTER 2. THE JOURNEY

1. Petrakis, *Odyssey of Kostas Volakis*.

2. Petrakis, 3.

3. Kalogeras offers an overview of Greek immigrant historiography in America written during the early twentieth century. See "Narrating an Ethnic Group." The primary studies of early Greek American history are Fairchild, *Greek Immigration*; Burgess, *Greeks in America*; Xenides, *Greeks in America*; C. Malafouris, *Hellenes tes Amerikes*; and Saloutos, *Greeks in the United States*. See also Spear, "Marcus Lee Hansen"; and Scourby, *Greek Americans*.

4. "Greeks in Chicago in 1890," *Illinois Staats-Zeitung*, January 25, 1892, 1.

5. Hecker and Fenton, *Greeks in America*, 6–10; Saloutos, *Greeks in the United States*, 20–25.

6. Moskos and Moskos, *Greek Americans*, 11.

7. Gallant, *Modern Greece*, 114.

8. Gallant, 114–15.

9. Gallant, 114–15.

10. Gallant, 80.

11. Gallant, 86.

12. Gallant, 114–15.

13. Saloutos, *Greeks in the United States*, 3.

14. Repouli, *Study of Immigration*, 57, cited by Saloutos, *Greeks in the United States*, 33. See also Saloutos, *They Remember America*, 3–4.

15. Vlachos, *Assimilation of Greeks*, 58–59.

16. Fairchild, *Greek Immigration*, 81. See also Saloutos, *Greeks in the United States*, 33–36.

17. Kourvetaris, *Studies on Greek Americans*, 20.

18. Gallant, *Modern Greece*, 115.

19. Saloutos, *They Remember America*, 29–32; Sandis, "Greek Population of New York City," 68.

20. Vlachos, *Assimilation of Greeks*, 69; Saloutos, *Greeks in the United States*, 110–17.

21. Saloutos, *They Remember America*, 29–32.

22. Saloutos, *Greeks in the United States*, 85.

23. Saloutos, 31.

24. Saloutos, 31–32.

25. Steve Frangos, "Picture Bride Era," 4–5.

26. Saloutos, *Greeks in the United States*, 32.

27. Saloutos, *They Remember America*, 45.

28. Callinicos, *American Aphrodite*, 21–24.

29. H. Papanikolas, "Greek Immigrant Women," 26.

30. H. Papanikolas, 29.

31. H. Papanikolas, 24–25.

32. H. Papanikolas, 26.

33. Steve Frangos, "Picture Bride Era," 4.

34. Frangos, 4.

35. Frangos, 4.

36. Drachsler, *Intermarriage in New York City*, 44–45.

37. H. Papanikolas, "Greek Immigrant Women," 32.

38. H. Papanikolas, 33.

39. See H. Papanikolas, 17.

40. H. Papanikolas, 26–27.

41. H. Papanikolas, 20.

42. H. Papanikolas, 21.

43. H. Papanikolas, 23.

44. H. Papanikolas, 23.

45. Ekonomidou, "Greeks in America," 35.

46. H. Papanikolas, "Greek Immigrant Women," 31.

47. Ekonomidou, "Greeks in America," 37.

48. Lefkada is a Greek island off Greece's central west coast.

49. Ekonomidou, "Greeks in America," 40.

50. Ekonomidou, 41.

51. Ekonomidou, 42.

52. Chock, "'Self-Made Woman,'" 243.

53. Chock, 240.

54. Steve Frangos, "Picture Bride Era," 8.

55. Frangos, 4–5.

56. Saloutos, *Greeks in the United States*, 24.

57. Scourby, *Greek Americans*, 27.

58. Saloutos, *Greeks in the United States*, 86.

59. Saloutos, 32.

60. Saloutos, 39.

61. Saloutos, 33.

62. Scourby, *Greek Americans*, 27.

63. Saloutos, *Greeks in the United States*, 36.

64. Saloutos, 39.

65. Saloutos, 40–41.

66. Saloutos, 41–42.

67. Drachsler, *Intermarriage in New York City*, 11. See also Moskos and Moskos, *Greek Americans*, 12–15.

68. Peck, "Reinventing Free Labor," 849.

69. Peck, 851.

70. "The Labor Question," *Saloniki-Greek Press*, May 4, 1915.

71. H. Papanikolas, "Greek Immigrant Women," 27.

72. Georgakas, "Greek-American Radicalism," 214.

73. Biles, *Illinois*, 60.

74. Biles, 62–63.

75. Biles, 130–31.

CHAPTER 3. ACCULTURATION AND AMERICANIZATION

1. Wilson, *Reunion and Nationalism*, 98–99.

2. Kopan, *Education and Greek Immigrants*, 8.

3. Dimitri Tassiopoulos notes that at the beginning of the twenty-first century "the Greek economy is notable for having the highest density of small and medium-sized businesses per 1000 inhabitants in the European Union." See Tassiopoulos, "Greek Christian Orthodoxy and Entrepreneurship," 122. Of course, Greek entrepreneurship is not limited to the United States or to the twenty-first century. See Minoglou, "Toward a Typology."

4. United States, Department of the Interior, Bureau of Education, and Commissioner James Eaton, *Education in Italy and Greece*, 7–8.

5. See Handlin, "Education and the European Immigrant," 3.

6. Kopan, *Education and Greek Immigrants*, 75.

7. The quote is from R. Carlson, *Americanization Syndrome*, 1. The famous phrase "city upon a hill" comes from the Reverend John Winthrop's sermon "A Model of Christian Charity," 10.

8. R. Carlson, *Americanization Syndrome*, 3. Franklin first used the phrase "Happy Mediocrity" in his essay "Information to Those Who Would Remove to America."

9. R. Carlson, *American Syndrome*, 3.

10. See Wood, *Americanization of Benjamin Franklin*, 3.

11. Wood, 1–13.

12. Wood, 71. See Franklin's essay "Observations Concerning the Increase of Mankind." See also Lee, *America for Americans*, 17–18, 25, 33, and 34–35. This stimulating, comprehensive, and timely study of the history of xenophobia in America appeared too late for me to use in the writing of this book, but it touches on many of the same themes, such as racism, anti-immigration, and Americanism, that are discussed here.

13. A. Carlson, *"American Way,"* 19.

14. Gleason, "American Identity and Americanization," 31, quoted in A. Carlson, *"American Way,"* 19.

15. Handlin, "Education and the European Immigrant," 6.

16. Handlin, 8.

17. Handlin, 7.

18. R. Carlson, *Americanization Syndrome*, 3–5.

19. See Goodwin, *Bully Pulpit*. Two classics on the Progressive Era are Hofstadter, *Age of Reform*, and Mowry, *Era of Theodore Roosevelt*. For a more recent discussion of progressivism, immigration, and the Americanization process, see Pickus, *True Faith and Allegiance*, particularly chapter 4, "Americanization and Pluralism in the Progressive Era."

20. Daniels, *Not Like Us*, 47.

21. Burkholder, *Color in the Classroom*, 16–18. See also Handlin, "Education and the European Immigrant," 10–11.

22. Burkholder, *Color in the Classroom*, 16. Her emphasis.

23. Handlin, "Education and the European Immigrant," 6.

24. Handlin, 6.

25. Pickus, *True Faith and Allegiance*, 73.

26. Addams, "Americanization," 210, 213–14.

27. Addams, *Second Twenty Years*, 217.

28. Daniels, *Not Like Us*, 48. For a comprehensive discussion of these issues see chapter 3, "Hyphenates, *Hausfraus*, and Baby-Saving: The Peculiar Legacy of German America," in A. Carlson, *"American Way."*

29. Roosevelt, *Newer Roosevelt Messages*, 1079.

30. See M. Friedman, *Rethinking Anti-Americanism*, 11–12, 14, 55.

31. See American Legion, *Americanism Manual*, 3, 4.

32. Quoted in Luebke, *Bonds of Loyalty*, 174.

33. Roosevelt, *Fear God*, 19, 361, 362.

34. See Alexander, *Ethnic Pride*, 16–19; and A. Carlson, *"American Way,"* 17–18.

35. "Our Societies and Clubs," *Loxias*, May 2, 1917.

36. "Our Duty," *Saloniki-Greek Press*, September 19, 1917

37. "Business and Americanism," *Saloniki-Greek Press*, July 16, 1921.

38. R. Carlson, *Americanization Syndrome*, 5.

39. Addams, *Twenty Years at Hull-House*, 200.

40. Kopan, *Education and Greek Immigrants*, 141.

41. Kopan, 197.

42. Kopan, 199. See the role of settlement houses within the Mexican community in Innis-Jiménez, *Steel Barrio*, 5; and the Catholic settlement houses depicted in Barrett, *Irish Way*, 86–89. For a discussion of modern Greek Americans and education, see Orfanos, Psomiades, and Spiridakis, *Education and Greek Americans.*

43. Hirschman, "America's Melting Pot Reconsidered." See also Park and Burgess, *Introduction to the Science of Sociology.*

44. Hirschman, "America's Melting Pot Reconsidered," 400.

45. Hirschman, 397. See Harper, *Course of the Melting Pot Idea.*

46. Roediger, *Colored White*, 147–48. See also Knight, *Citizen*, 11–12.

47. Roediger, *Colored White*, 148.

48. Roediger, 138.

49. Kraut, *Silent Travelers*, 224–25.

50. Curry, *Modern Mothers*, 39.

51. Curry, 40.

52. Davis, "Racism, Birth Control, and Reproductive Rights," 20. See also "Birth Control," *Saloniki-Greek Press*, December 6, 1934.

53. Engelman, *Birth Control Movement*, 54.

54. Engelman, 135.

55. Kraut, *Silent Travelers*, 225.

56. Kraut, 225.

57. Kraut, 222–23.

58. Curry, *Modern Mothers*, 41–42.

59. Curry, 45.

60. Curry, 65.

61. Curry, 66–67.

62. Curry, 68.

63. Illinois State Board of Health, "Typhoid Fever at Tuscola," 143; Curry, *Modern Mothers,* 28.

64. Illinois State Board of Health, "Typhoid Fever at Tuscola, 143. In the Tuscola case, nearness of the livery stable led the "public health officials who investigated the outbreak to presume that the disease originated with a traveller passing through the town." Curry, *Modern Mothers*, 28. The infected traveler may have come from or gone to Pana, some seventy miles away, which had an outbreak of typhoid at the same time, with thirty-eight clearly defined cases. See Anonymous, "Communicable

Diseases during May," 461; and also Anonymous, "Medical News, Typhoid Dangers," 1862.

65. Anonymous, "Communicable Diseases," 461.

66. Kraut, *Silent Travelers*, 96–103.

67. R. Carlson, *Americanization Syndrome*, 93.

68. R. Carlson, 96–97.

69. Fairchild, *Immigration*, 402–3.

70. R. Carlson, *Americanization Syndrome*, 96–97.

71. R. Carlson, 98–100.

72. Treudley, "Formal Organization," 47–48.

73. Treudley, 47–51. See also Doukas, "Story of Ahepa"; and Steve Frangos, "Origins of AHEPA."

74. Xenides, *Greeks in America*, 153.

75. Saloutos, *Greeks in the United States*, 88.

76. "Hellenic Post Elects New Officers," *Greek Star*, January 6, 1928, 1. See also "The Legion," *American Hellenic World*, June 1928, 9.

77. See, for example, the issue of the *Greek Star* for February 7, 1928, 8.

78. "Americanism," *Greek Star*, November 14, 1919, 6.

79. See "The Greek as a Restaurant Man," *Greek Star*, November 14, 1919.

80. "Greek as a Restaurant Man."

81. "Greek as a Restaurant Man."

82. McLean, "Summary of Important Finds and Recommendations, August 31, 1916."

83. McLean, 385.

84. McLean, 385–86, 393.

85. McLean, 404.

86. Crawford, *Immigrant in St. Louis*, 51–53.

87. Crawford, 56.

88. Crawford, 61–63.

89. Crawford, 64–65.

90. Theobald, *Call School*, 163.

91. See F. Turner, *Frontier in American History*; Turner and Faragher, *Rereading Frederick Jackson Turner*; James, *Pragmatism*; and Veblen, *Theory of the Leisure Class*.

92. Theobald, *Call School*, 164–66.

93. Theobald, 168.

94. Theobald, 170–71.

95. Balk, "Economic Contributions," 270.

96. Balk, 270.

97. Kourvetaris, *First and Second Generation Greeks*, 68.

98. Kourvetaris, 73.

99. Balk, "Economic Contributions," 271.

100. Balk, 271.

101. Kourvetaris, *First and Second Generation Greeks*, 51.

102. Kourvetaris, 60.

CHAPTER 4. FINDING A NICHE IN CHICAGO AND ST. LOUIS

1. Saloutos, *Greeks in the United States*, 51.

2. Addams, *Twenty Years at Hull-House*, 77–78. See also Knight, *Citizen*, 166–76.

3. Kopan, *Education and Greek Immigrants*, 121.

4. "Miss Jane Addams Decorated by Greek Government," *Greek Star*, May 23, 1930. See also "Greek Community Pays Homage to the Late Jane Addams," *Saloniki-Greek Press*, May 30, 1935, for a moving tribute following her death on May 22, 1935.

5. When my parents, Paul Flesor and Margaret Leonard, married, my father's relatives commented on how he had married a "white" girl.

6. In 2002 I recorded an oral interview with my mother about her experiences at Hull House and deposited a copy in Hull House's collection. See Special Collections, box 3, folder 30, "Margaret Leonard Flesor," Hull House Oral History Collection, 1974–2002, University of Illinois, Chicago.

7. Hull House Yearbook, 1913, p. 23; *Hull House Bulletin* 6 (Autumn 1904): 23–24.

8. "First Public Greek Lectures at Hull House," *Greek Star*, November 24, 1905. For a report on another Sunday of lectures, see "The Greeks of Chicago," *Greek Star*, November 22, 1907.

9. *Hull House Bulletin* 6 (Autumn 1904): 23–24.

10. Kopan, *Education and Greek Immigrants*, 123–24.

11. Abbott, "Study of the Greeks in Chicago," 379. The following discussion comes from this article, pp. 379–93, unless otherwise noted.

12. Walker, "Chicago Housing Conditions," 286. The following comes from Walker's study, pp. 285–316, unless otherwise noted.

13. See the *Greek Star*, January 10, 1941, 6; and Kopan and Kopan, "Georgia Bitzis Pooley." See also Kopan and Kopan, "Pooley, Georgia Bitzis."

14. Kopan and Kopan, "Georgia Bitzis Pooley," 10.

15. Ibid.

16. Ibid., 11. See also *Greek Star*, April 9, 1937, 1.

17. Kopan and Kopan, "Georgia Bitzis Pooley," 11; Kopan and Kopan, "Pooley, Georgia Bitzis," 708.

18. Kopan and Kopan, "Pooley, Georgia Bitzis," 709; Kopan and Kopan, "Georgia Bitzis Pooley," 11.

19. Kopan and Kopan, "Georgia Bitzis Pooley," 11–12.

20. "The Greek as a Restaurant Man," *Greek Star*, November 14, 1919.

21. Koken, Constant, and Canoutas, *History of the Greeks*, 96.

22. "Greek as a Restaurant Man."

23. See "The Fruit Business," *Loxias*, March 25, 1911.

24. Saloutos, *Greeks in the United States*, 260–61.

25. "Chicago Grocers against Greek Peddlers," *Saloniki-Greek Press*, December 4, 1929.

26. See "The Greeks of Chicago. The Fruit and Vegetable Business," *Greek Star*, September 25, 1908.

27. Dusselier, "Bonbons," 15–16.

28. Smith, "Chocolate Confections," 130.

29. Dusselier, "Bonbons," 17–20.

30. Dusselier, 28–29.

31. "Sugar and Alcohol," *Chicago Tribune*, August 10, 1907, 8. Dr. Abbott's comments were published in newspapers across America.

32. Anonymous, "The Nation's Annual Candy Bill and What the Money Would Do If Expended in Other Directions," *New York Times*, January 2, 1910, magazine section, 8.

33. Dusselier, "Bonbons," 36.

34. Saloutos, *Greeks in the United States*, 262.

35. Steve Frangos, "How the Tsintzinians Conquered America," 1, 7.

36. Steve Frangos, 1, 7. I have found no direct connection between Tsakonas and the Greek confectioners I have studied, although many of them came from the Sparta region and some from villages northeast of Sparta.

37. *Greek Star*, June 26, 1934, 4.

38. Saloutos, *Greeks in the United States*, 262.

39. "The Greek Confectioners. Chicago the Mecca of the Candy Business," *Greek Star*, April 1, 1904.

40. "A Word to the Greek Confectioners of Chicago," *Greek Star*, August 24, 1906.

41. "The Greek Confectionery Business," *Saloniki-Greek Press*, May 29, 1915.

42. "A Confectioners' Corporation," *Saloniki-Greek Press*, June 5, 1915.

43. Zaffer, *We Make Our Own Candy*, i–iv.

44. Rassogianis, *Entrepreneurial Spirit*, 43–44.

45. See http://www.margiesfinecandies.com (accessed July 28, 2018).

46. See "A. G. Kanelos, Andes Candies Founder, Dies," *Chicago Tribune*, December 4, 1959, 29; and "Andes Candies Rents Dearborn-Madison Corner," *Chicago Tribune*, March 2, 1941, 22.

47. "George Andrew Kanelos," obituary, *Chicago Tribune*, April 29, 2010, 28.

48. "The Lasting Contributions of Greeks on the World of Confections in America," *National Herald*, December 21, 2014, https://www.thenationalherald.com/69705/lasting-contributions-greeks-world-confections-america/ (accessed August 21, 2019).

49. Gene Raffensperger, "Penniless Immigrant at 15 Thrived on Candy-Making," *Des Moines Register*, June 17, 1962, 15; "Lions Cite Candy King," *Quad-City Times* (Davenport, IA), February 13, 1969, 25; "Local Candy Factory Is Well-Known," *Quad-City Times*, December 31, 1925, 4; "Former Civic Leader," obituary, *Quad-City Times*, July 1, 1979, 14.

50. Raffensperger, "Penniless Immigrant," 15.

51. Saloutos, *Greeks in the United States*, 262–63; "Greek Confectionery Business."

52. *Greek Star*, February 16, 1934, 7.

53. Funderburg, *Sundae Best*, 20.

54. Funderburg, 23.

55. Funderburg, 53.

56. Funderburg, 34.

57. See "The Greek Confectioners' Union," *Saloniki-Greek Press*, May 10, 1919; and "The Greek Confectioners' Association," *Saloniki-Greek Press*, October 15, 1927.

58. "Greek Candy-Makers," *Loxias*, March 7, 1918. The article's author later admitted that actually, "the exact number of Greek confectioners is not known. Some wholesalers claim that there are 6,000 or 7,000, others say there are over 10,000; anyway, it is a tremendous force . . ."

59. See "Greek Trade Is in Peril," *Greek Press*, July 1, 1929.

60. Saloutos, *Greeks in the United States*, 264–65.

61. "The Restaurants," *Loxias*, October 9, 1909.

62. "The Greek Restaurant Association, Editorial," *Greek Star*, October 8, 1909.

63. See "By-Laws of the Greek Restaurant Association of Chicago," which appeared in *Loxias*, April 23, 1910; and "Greek Restaurant Employees' Union," *Saloniki-Greek Press*, July 8, 1916.

64. Gabaccia, *We Are What We Eat*, 65.

65. K. Turner, *How the Other Half Ate*, 70.

66. Gabaccia, *We Are What We Eat*, 116.

67. "Greek as a Restaurant Man."

68. "Greek as a Restaurant Man." See also Saloutos, *Greeks in the United States*, 264–66.

69. Saloutos, *Greeks in the United States*, 265–66.

70. "Progress and System," *Loxias*, May 20, 1909.

71. See "To the Greek Business Men in Chicago," *Greek Star*, May 17, 1907.

72. "No Citizenship, No License, May Be New City Law," *Chicago Tribune*, December 14, 1917, 5.

73. "Six Thousand Aliens Will Be Refused the Right to Do Business," *Saloniki-Greek Press*, March 30, 1918.

74. See "Treaties Clash with City Law against Aliens," *Chicago Tribune*, April 18, 1918, 5; and "Licenses," *Chicago Tribune*, May 1, 1918, 11.

75. Saloutos, *Greeks in the United States*, 267–68.

76. Mormino, *Immigrants on the Hill*, 19.

77. See Burnett and Luebbering, *Immigrant Women*, 126.

78. Mormino, *Immigrants on the Hill*, 19–20. See also Lee, "Chinese Exclusion Example," 43.

79. Crawford, *Immigrant in St. Louis*, 12–13.

80. Crawford, 12–13.

81. Crawford, 14.

82. Crawford, 16.

83. Crawford, 16–17.

84. Crawford, 17–18. See US Immigration Commission and Dillingham, *Immigrants in Cities*. See also Hourwich, *Immigration and Labor*. Hourwich's extensive study, drawing from among other sources on the Immigration Commission's report, fails even to mention Greeks.

85. See *St. Louis Globe-Democrat*, June 28, 1907, magazine section, 4; and Rumbold, *Housing Conditions*, 64.

86. Crawford, *Immigrant in St. Louis*, 18–19. The following is taken from Crawford's report, pp. 18–42, unless otherwise noted.

87. See Ellis, "Whispers in the Ice Cream Parlor," 71.

88. Shoeshine parlors and shoe repair shops were a significant early niche for the Greek entrepreneurial spirit and should be included in any discussion of Greek businesses, along with confectioneries and restaurants. They existed in central Illinois, even in the smaller towns. For my discussion, see Beck, "Greek Immigration to, and Settlement in, Central Illinois," pp. 43–47; and also Z. Papanikolas, "To a Greek Bootblack."

89. Mormino, "Immigrants on the Hill," 63. See also Burnett and Luebbering, *Immigrant Women*, 12; and the St. Nicolas church website, http://www.sngoc.org (accessed September 1, 2019).

90. Mormino, "Immigrants on the Hill," 63.

91. Mormino, 64.

92. Mormino, 107.

93. Steve Frangos, "Oh, Those Sweet Greek Americans!," 18.

CHAPTER 5. GREEKS VS. GOBLINS

A Greek documentary filmmaker, Thoma Lamprini, is currently completing a project on the Greeks in America. She sent me a YouTube link to a fascinating excerpt from the film, titled "Between Black and White: Greek-Americans in the 20th Century" (© 2020 Barricade M.I.K.E.), https://www.youtube.com/watch?v=DziGTSRMQic. The link arrived too late to incorporate the material into this book, but the film offers a number of personal narratives about many of the book's themes, and particularly those in this chapter.

1. H. Papanikolas, *Amulet of Greek Earth*, ix.

2. H. Papanikolas, 161. For the printed cards, see Scofield, "Winning the Battle against Bigotry," 5. Scofield also notes how it is supremely ironic that "the six organizers of the original Klan in 1865 created the words Ku Klux from *kuklos*, a variation of the Greek *kyklos* meaning cycle or circle, and applied it to their little circle." Scofield, "Final Triumph of Hellenism," 17.

3. H. Papanikolas, "Greek Immigrant Women," 27.

4. Karampetsos, "Nativism in Nevada," 62.

5. Bitzes, "Anti-Greek Riot," 201.

6. Bitzes, 200.

7. Bitzes, 200, 204.

8. South Omaha was a separate metropolitan area until it joined with Omaha in 1915.

9. Bitzes, "Anti-Greek Riot," 200, 204. See also Saloutos, "Cultural Persistence," 85–88; and "Our Laboring Class," *Saloniki-Greek Press*, October 25, 1913.

10. Bitzes, "Anti-Greek Riot," 201, 203. See also Saloutos, "Cultural Persistence," 85–86; and "The Strike in Chicago Ended. The Greek Strike-Breakers Ousted. Union President Sympathetic," *Greek Star*, April 15, 1904.

11. Bitzes, "Anti-Greek Riot," 202.

12. Bitzes, 202–3.

13. Bitzes, 204–5.

14. *Omaha World-Herald*, February 20, 1909, quoted in Bitzes, "Anti-Greek Riot," 199.

15. *Omaha World-Herald*, February 21, 1909, quoted in Bitzes, "Anti-Greek Riot," 200.

16. *Omaha World-Herald* quoted in Bitzes, 200.

17. Bitzes, 200, 212. See also the editorial in the *Greek Star*, February 26, 1909.

18. Of the 2,000–3,000 Greeks in the Omaha area at the beginning of 1909, only a few hundred remained by year's end. The 1910 census lists 187 in Lincoln, 485 in Omaha, and 59 in South Omaha. See Bitzes, "Anti-Greek Riot," 214.

19. Masourides eventually served five and a half years and apparently then moved to Egypt. See Bitzes, 219.

20. Bitzes, 209.

21. Bitzes, 218–20. Barely ten years later Omaha experienced race riots again. See *Omaha Mediator*, September 19, 1919. Michael Lawson cites this passage in his article on the 1919 riots. See Lawson, "Omaha, a City in Ferment," 406.

22. *Kansas City Times*, February 22, 1909, and *Dayton Journal*, February 24, 1909, both cited by Bitzes, "Anti-Greek Riot," 200, 220n8.

23. Abraham Lincoln's hometown experienced a race riot in the summer of 1908, which led to the formation of the NAACP in January 1909. See Crouthamel, "Springfield Race Riot"; and P. Sullivan, *Lift Every Voice*, 1–14.

24. Pegram, *One Hundred Percent American*, 7.

25. Pegram, 7.

26. Research on the Klan in the 1920s is large and growing. A good overview of scholarship on the Klan is the review essay by Moore, "Historical Interpretations." Moore's long essay is a review of Bennett, *Party of Fear*, and Wade, *Fiery Cross*. Moore's emphasis is on the complex nature of the 1920s Klan and how difficult it is for scholars to arrive at any common consensus.

27. Pegram, *One Hundred Percent American*, 6–7.

28. Ayabe, "Ku Kluxers," 74. See also Angle, *Bloody Williamson*.

29. Moore, "Historical Interpretations," 353.

30. In 1925 a businessman from Marion (the county seat of Williamson County), John L. Whiteside was elected the "Great Titan of Province No. 7, Realm of Illinois." See "New Great Titan of Ku Klux Klan," *Marion Daily Republican*, February 28, 1925, 1.

31. *Herrin (IL) Semi-Weekly Herald*, November 7, 1924, quoted in Ayabe, "Ku Kluxers," 74.

32. Chalmers, *Hooded Americanism*. Chalmers's chapter on the Illinois Klan is titled "The Fighting Illini" (183–89).

33. Pegram, *One Hundred Percent American*, 6.

34. MacLean, *Behind the Mask of Chivalry*, 4. See also Moore, "Historical Interpretations," 353.

35. Pegram, *One Hundred Percent American*, 6. See also, for example, the ad for a "Parade and Open-Air Meeting of the Knights of the Ku Klux Klan" in the *Mount Carmel (IL) Daily Republican-Register*, September 23, 1925, 5.

36. "K.K.K.," *Eldorado (IL) Daily Journal*, December 19, 1924, 4.

37. Pegram, *One Hundred Percent American*, 6–7.

38. See Hale, *Williamson County*, 111. This advertisement, with the caption "This KKK advertisement appeared in an area high school yearbook in 1924," accompanied an article about "Bloody Williamson." I have been unable to identify the school in whose yearbook the advertisement appeared.

39. Pegram, *One Hundred Percent American*, 6–7.

40. There were large numbers of immigrants in rural Illinois whom the Klan might take exception to, beginning with German Catholics, particularly during and after the Great War. There were also many thousands of immigrants from the British Isles, Italy, Austria, Poland, Russia, and Greece, among others. The great majority worked in southern and central Illinois coal fields. For a detailed study of these immigrants and radicalism in the coal fields, see Booth, "Relationship between Radicalism and Ethnicity."

41. Pegram, *One Hundred Percent American*, 11.

42. Pegram, 22–23.

43. The quotation comes from U.S. Congress, House, Committee on Rules, *Hearings on the Ku Klux Klan*, 67th Cong., 1st sess., 1921, 67–68, contained in Lay, *Invisible Empire*, 9.

44. Moore, "Historical Interpretations," 346.

45. Moore, 346.

46. McVeigh, "Structural Incentives," 1490.

47. McVeigh, 1461. See also Horowitz, "Normality of Extremism," 77.

48. Pegram, *One Hundred Percent American*, 9.

49. Pegram, 28. Pegram discusses these spectacles on pp. 28–32 and communities on pp. 32–42.

50. Pegram, 28.

51. Chalmers, *Hooded Americanism*, 185. The Illinois Theater was "dedicated to the Klan" on the evening of November 23, during two days of Klan activities. See "Local Ku Klux Plan Host to Wizard Evans," *Urbana Daily Courier*, November 23, 1923, 1.

52. Pegram, *One Hundred Percent American*, 31.

53. Pegram, 29.

54. Pegram, 29.

55. Blee, *Women of the Klan*, 17.

56. Blee, 2.

57. Blee, 3.

58. Blee, 103. Blee notes that women in Indiana were drawn to the Klan through their involvement in the temperance movement. For a discussion of why contemporary women join the Klan and other extremist groups, see Blee, "Becoming a Racist."

59. Blee, *Women of the Klan*, 25.

60. Blee, 29.

61. Blee, 35.

62. Blee, 129. Internal dissension within local Klan organizations was a universal problem. See K. Jackson, *Ku Klux Klan*, 123.

63. Blee, *Women of the Klan*, 125.

64. Moore, "Historical Interpretations," 353–54. Horowitz, "Normality of Extremism," 77, argues that scholars must "abandon simplistic and elitist notions about mass movements like the Klan." For anti-German, anti-immigrant feelings and Prohibition, see Wellskopp, "Prohibition in the United States."

65. Pegram, *One Hundred Percent American*, xii.

66. K. Jackson, *Ku Klux Klan*, 102–3. See also Goldberg, "Unmasking the Ku Klux Klan," 36–42. For contemporary reaction to the American Unity League's formation, see "Move to Curb Ku Klux. American Unity League Is Formed for Nation-Wide Campaign," *New York Times*, August 12, 1922, 20.

67. Goldberg, "Unmasking the Ku Klux Klan," 39.

68. K. Jackson, *Ku Klux Klan*, 103. See also Pegram, *One Hundred Percent American*, 81–82.

69. Goldberg, "Unmasking the Ku Klux Klan," 40.

70. Jackson notes that "*Tolerance* represented the only major attempt in the nation to publicize the names of rank and file Klansmen on a systematic basis." See K. Jackson, *Ku Klux Klan*, 104.

71. Goldberg, "Unmasking the Ku Klux Klan," 40.

72. Goldberg, 41.

73. Goldberg, 40. See also K. Jackson, *Ku Klux Klan*, 104.

74. Chalmers, *Hooded Americanism*, 183–84.

75. "Chicago Opens War on Ku Klux Klan. Bankers and Business Men Known to Be Members Are Being Boycotted. Barred as Jurors by Judge. American Unity League Leads Fight against Klansmen and Makes Names Public," *New York Times*, November 12, 1922, 33.

76. K. Jackson, *Ku Klux Klan*, 111.

77. Goldberg, *Discontented America*, 135. There are no full-length studies of the AUL I have found, or even any articles devoted to it. K. Jackson's six pages on the AUL in *Ku Klux Klan*, 102–7, and Goldberg's "Unmasking the Ku Klux Klan," 39–42, are good starting places.

78. Goldberg, "Unmasking the Ku Klux Klan," 42.

79. Goldberg, 42.

80. K. Jackson, *Ku Klux Klan*, 116–17; Goldberg, *Discontented America*, 136–37.

81. Goldberg, *Discontented America*, 137.

82. K. Jackson, *Ku Klux Klan*, 125. See American Unity League, *Is Your Neighbor a Kluxer?*; and Goldberg, "Unmasking the Ku Klux Klan," 40.

83. Goldberg, *Discontented America*, 137; Goldberg, "Unmasking the Ku Klux Klan," 42–44.

84. Goldberg, "Unmasking the Ku Klux Klan," 44.

85. K. Jackson, *Ku Klux Klan*, 95.

86. K. Jackson, 126.

87. K. Jackson, 95.

88. K. Jackson, 97. See also Lay, *Invisible Empire*, 8.

89. "Mystery Solved; Klux Paper Says They Did It All: And, If You Please, for Clean Politics," *Chicago Daily Tribune*, April 22, 1924, 2.

90. K. Jackson, *Ku Klux Klan*, 125.

91. K. Jackson, 163.

92. Chalmers, *Hooded Americanism*, 185. As Klan membership was nearly equal between rural and urban areas and Chicago had a very large Klan membership, Chalmers's use of "better" here might refer to less organized opposition than was present in Chicago. He does not make this clear.

93. Biles, *Illinois*, 206.

94. Chalmers, *Hooded Americanism*, 185.

95. West-central Illinois had been the scene earlier of the "Illinois Coal Wars" (sometimes "Illinois Mine Wars") from 1898 to 1900 between white and black coal miners. See Hicken, "Virden and Pana Mine Wars." See also Dechenne, "Recipe for Violence," for a discussion of events in Macoupin and Montgomery Counties.

96. Watson, "Need of Federal Legislation," 561–62, 566–67.

97. Mormino, *Immigrants on the Hill*, 62-63; Maragni, "Riot of 1920."

98. Mormino, *Immigrants on the Hill*, 63.

99. Ayabe, "Ku Kluxers," 73. The standard work on these events is Angle, *Bloody Williamson.*

100. Ayabe, 74.

101. Biles, *Illinois*, 207.

102. James Loewen, *Sundown Towns*, 158.

103. Loewen, 339.

104. Mormino, *Immigrants on the Hill*, 63.

105. Mormino, 63.

106. Steve Frangos, "Origins of AHEPA," 16.

107. Scofield, "Winning the Battle against Bigotry," 8.

108. Scofield, 8, for these two examples and others. See also Scofield, "Final Triumph of Hellenism," 15.

109. "Initiation Held by Ku Klux Klan Near Creve Coeur Lake," *St. Louis Post-Dispatch*, May 31, 1923, 1.

110. "U.S. at the Mercy of Catholic Army and Navy, Klan Organizer Asserts," *St. Louis Star*, February 5, 1925, 3.

111. "Greeks Are Worst Criminals," *The Fraternalist* (St. Joseph, MO), January 8, 1925, 1 and 4.

112. Leber, *History of the Order of Ahepa*, 100.

113. "Greek to Seek Protection from Klan by His Country," *St. Louis Star and Times*, July 10, 1924, 1.

114. Entry for "Zuckas, Martin, restr," *1926 Atlanta City Directory* (Atlanta: Atlanta City Directory, 1926), 1109.

115. See Steve Frangos, "Origins of AHEPA," 6, for one of the best summaries of how AHEPA was formed.

116. Scofield, "Winning the Battle against Bigotry," 6–7.

117. Steve Frangos cites "a series of *National Herald* articles on the foundation of AHEPA published during October 1950" by V. I. Chebites for this quote. Frangos, "Origins of AHEPA," 14–15.

118. Frangos, 15.

119. Scofield, "Winning the Battle against Bigotry," 7.

120. Steve Frangos, "Origins of AHEPA," 16.

121. Frangos, 15.

122. "Editorial—The Work of AHEPA's Convention," *Greek News*, August 24, 1935.

123. Steve Frangos, "Origins of AHEPA," 15. See also Gus C. Poolitson (44), Catherine Poolitson (33), Chris Poolitson (18), Gus (also George C.) Poolitson (13), Peter Poolitson (11), Catherine Poolitson (7), and Nick Poolitson (5), A.c., 1920 USFC, census place: Bloomington, Ward 4, Precinct 3, Monroe, Indiana; roll: T625_457; p. 1B; lines 54–60; enumeration district: 178. In 1920 Gus C. Poolitsan owned the Greek Candy Store ("east side of square, opp. Court House") and the Book-Nook. See *1920 Bloomington City Directory* (Louisville, KY: Caron Directory, 1920), 7 passim (advertisements), 68 (listing), and 179 ("Confectioners").

124. Daniel (b. 1887) and James (b. 1898) are listed as candy makers at a Candy Kitchen in Storm City, Iowa, in 1920, which is about twenty-five miles or so from Sac City. See A.c., 1920 USFC, census place: Storm Lake, Buena Vista, Iowa; roll: T625_480; pp. 16A, 16B; lines 50, 51; enumeration district: 13. See also Daniel Constantinos Cosman, A.c., US WW I DRC, 1917–1918, June 5, 1917; registration state: Iowa; registration county: Buena Vista; roll: 1642912 (both accessed February 15, 2019).

125. Bree Ann Buckley lived in a building that housed a Chinese laundry from 1920 to 1930 run by Dea Sing and Pon Gong. The Klan also harassed them. It seems no Sac City newspaper for these years has survived. Several adults who as children stormed the KKK line for ice cream told Bree Ann about these events. E-mail correspondence with Bree Ann Buckley, January 30, 2018.

126. "Kluck Kluck Klan in County," *TJ*, December 8, 1921, 1.

127. "Kluck Kluck Klan in County," 1.

128. "Fiery Cross Glows in Park," *TJ*, May 19, 1923.

129. "Cash Offering to Evangelist," *TJ*, July 5, 1923, 1.

130. "Big Parade of Klansmen Saturday Night," *Mattoon Daily-Journal-Gazette and Commercial Star*, May 28, 1923, 1.

131. Jack Carberry, "Comedy and Tragedy on Ellis Island: Thousands of Immigrants Land on 12 Liners," *Mattoon Daily-Journal-Gazette and Commercial Star*, July 2, 1923, 1.

132. "Thousands Attend Klan Celebration," *Mattoon Daily-Journal-Gazette and Commercial Star*, July 25, 1923, 1.

133. "Villa Grove Vents Versions: Ku Klux Klan Knits Kith Kindly: Knocks Knights Keenly, Kindles Kount," *TJ*, August 16, 1923, 1. The alliteration is more extreme than most, but newspaper wordsmiths often had great fun with Klan article headlines. Of course, the organization itself practiced this type of absurd wordplay as their hierarchical structure included klaliffs, kludds, kligrapps, klabees, kladds, and klexters, down to their local chapters, known as klaverns.

134. "Villa Grove Vents Versions," 1.

135. The rally description comes from "Ku Klux Klan Hold Open Meeting. Burns Cross Saturday Night," *TJ*, August 23, 1923, 1, unless otherwise noted.

136. From what I gather from Tuscola newspaper articles, my grandfather and his family were held in high esteem. See, for example, "Viola Flesor at Hospital," *TJ*, November 15, 1923, 1.

137. "Grand Opening. Open House Celebration," *TJ*, December 8, 1923, 4.

138. *TJ*, December 4, 1923, 7.

139. "Kandy Kitchen Opening Saturday," *TJ*, December 23, 1923, 1.

140. "Villa Grove News," *TJ*, June 26, 1924, 7.

141. "Ku Klux Klan Holds Band Concert in Ervin Park," *TJ*, July 31, 1924, 1.

CHAPTER 6. MY GRANDFATHER AND HIS MENTORS

1. Kristen Hoganson's study of Champaign County beef producers utilizes local history to explain the "wider sets of relationships" in chain migration scholarship and how they form "larger relational webs." See Hoganson, "Meat in the Middle, " 1026–27.

2. James Vaky interview.

3. "Owner Needed to Reopen Confectionary in Champaign," *MJG*, April 25, 1995, 16.

4. See Betts, "Vriner's Confectionery."

5. Betts, 1–2.

6. Fein, "Vriner's Confectionary."

7. Ebert, "Roger Ebert's Journal."

8. See "Champaign Shop Get Sweet Reward," *The Pantagraph* (Bloomington, IL), August 22, 1983, A4. See also Steve Frangos, "Vriner's Confectionery"; Fein, "Vriner's Confectionary"; and Betts, "Vriner's Confectionery." See also "Vriner Rites Will Be Held Friday, 2 p.m.," *Urbana Daily Courier*, June 12, 1929, 2.

9. Ship manifest lists for immigrants arriving at Ellis Island include several Vriners, or Vrinioses, from Pigadakia.

10. Peter G. Vrinios, A.c., Cook County, IL, Marriages Index, 1871–1920 (accessed April 22, 2015). For Christine, see entry for Christina [*sic*] P. Vriner, A.c., 1930 USFC, census place: Champaign, Champaign, Illinois; p. 1A; enumeration district: 0008; FHL microfilm 2340144 (accessed June 22, 2018).

11. *Find A Grave*, Juanita Creighton Reid (1/17/1909–8/29/1995), 73029884, with obituary (accessed August 10, 2019). Juanita remarried in 1975 and died in Albion, Illinois.

12. *Find A Grave*, George P. Vriner (4/8/1906–12/8/1953), 136003847 (accessed March 10, 2013).

13. *Find A Grave*, William P. Vriner (7/24/1910–11/10/1944), 136004001 (accessed March 10, 2013).

14. Diana Vriner Krandel interview, November 4, 2013.

15. George J. Vriner, A.c., US Passport Applications, 1790–1825; NARA, Washington, DC; roll: 2739; volume: Certificates, 12300–12899, 3/30/1925–3/31/1925 (accessed April 8, 2018).

16. Joannis Vrinios and Georgios Vrinios, A.c., NYPCL; year: 1896; place of arrival: New York, New York; microfilm serial: M237, 1820–1897; microfilm roll: 660; lines 5, 6 (accessed June 22, 2018).

17. See George J. Vriner, A.c., 1900 USFC, census place: Champaign Ward 3, Champaign, Illinois; p. 9; line 43; enumeration district: 0006; FHL microfilm 1240240 (accessed September 2, 2019).

18. "J. Vriner of Tuscola," *Champaign Daily News,* February 12, 1904, 5.

19. "George Vriner Will Be Married Next Week," *Urbana Daily Courier*, July 1, 1921, 1; "Vriner Wedding," *Urbana Daily Courier*, July 5, 1921, 5; George J. Vriner, A.c., US Passport Applications, 1790–1825; NARA, Washington, DC; roll: 2739; volume: Certificates, 12300–12899, 3/30/1925–3/31/1925 (accessed April 8, 2018).

20. "Vriner Confectionery Has Changed Hands," *Urbana Daily Courier*, January 11, 1917, 2; and an ad, "For Easter Sunday—Apollo (Formerly Vriner's)," *Urbana Daily Courier*, April 3, 1917, 2. Then the ad, "Announcing—The Opening of The Apollo Confectionery under New Management," *Urbana Daily Courier*, October 28, 1927, 2.

21. The Chicago address George gives is 6 South Cranford. In 1917 there was a Thomas Vrinios living at this address, registering for the draft, who was born May 2, 1887. He had a shoeshine parlor and was married with two children. This must be George's brother. See Thomas Vrinios, A.c., US WW I DRC, 1917–1918, date: June 5, 1917; registration state: Illinois; registration county: Cook; roll: 1504081; draft board: 85 (accessed July 22, 2019).

22. See George P. Vriner, A.c., US WW I DRC, 1917–1918, date: September 12, 1918; registration state: Illinois, registration county: Douglas; roll: 1613181 (accessed February 18, 2013).

23. "Schlitz Co. Sells Out to Vriner: Greek Confectioner Buys Business Building." *Urbana Daily Courier*, May 7, 1914, 1.

24. "New Confectionery," *Champaign Daily News*, September 18, 1914, 9.

25. "New Confectionery," 9.

26. "Ice Cream Manufacturers," *1912 Champaign-Urbana City Directory* (Bloomington, IL: Pantagraph Printing, 1912), 570.

27. "The Ice Cream Season Is Now Open," *Urbana Daily Courier*, May 13, 1921, 11.

28. "Confectioneries," *1923 Champaign and Urbana City Directory* (Champaign: Flanigan-Pearson, 1923), 425, 469, 488.

29. "Services for P. G. Vriner to Be Held Tomorrow at 2 p.m.," *Urbana Daily Courier*, June 12, 1929, 2. The reverse side of Peter's tombstone has his Greek name in Greek letters—Panagiotis G. Vrinios. See *Find A Grave*, Peter G. Vriner (3/20/1864–6/11/1929), 136003473 (accessed March 10, 2013).

30. *Find A Grave*, Sammy P. "Tyke" Vriner (5/5/1912–11/16/1993), 136811790 (accessed March 10, 2013).

31. Louis J. Vriner, A.c., US WW II DRC, 1942; National Archives at St. Louis, US WW II DRC, 1942 (Fourth Registration), for the State of Illinois; Record Group title: Records of the Selective Service System, 1926–1975; Record Group number: 147; series number: M2097 (accessed April 22, 2018).

32. See Lambros Vrinios, A.c., NYPCL, year: 1929; date of arrival: December 29, 1906; place of arrival: New York, New York; microfilm serial: T715, 1897–1957; microfilm roll: 0815; p. 19; line 11 (accessed June 22, 2018).

33. John Vriner, private family history, pp. 6–7. Born in Greece while the family was visiting there in 1929–30, on December 28, 1929, John passed away on January 28, 1951.

34. Louis Vrinios, Athanasia Vriner, and children (George, Dina, Maria, John), A.c., NYPCL; year: 1930; date of arrival: July 1, 1930; place of arrival: New York, New York; microfilm serial: T715, 1897–1957; microfilm roll: 4768; p. 61; lines 5–10 (accessed June 22, 2018).

35. John Vriner, private family history, pp. 6–7.

36. *Find A Grave*, James Russell Vaky (11/3/1911–10/29/2012), 101486639, with obituary (accessed June 21, 2012). The following information, unless otherwise noted, is taken from these three sources: James Vaky, Oral History Project; James Vaky interview; and the typescript of a speech given by Russell Vaky in 1999. James Vaky died at age 100. As a young man, from 1925 to 1938, he worked at his father's confectionery. As James was quite elderly at the time of our interview, several details of his father's story are inconsistent or inaccurate. I have tried to construct as accurate a biography as I can for both Vriner and Vaky. See the obituary for James Vaky, *Champaign/Urbana News-Gazette*, November 6, 2012. The transcript of Russell Vaky's speech before the Champaign County Historical Society in November 1999 contains some interesting anecdotes but is also quite inaccurate in many places. See R. Vaky, *Vaky's Confectionery*.

37. Vaky roomed with Vriner in 1900. In that year's census, Vriner's birth date is given as February 1861, age thirty-nine, and immigration year 1890, but his birth year and age are incorrect. All other sources, including his tombstone, give his birth year as 1864. See n. 29 above. Vaky's birth date is March 1872, age twenty-eight, and immigration year 1887. Sources vary for Vaky's birth year: 1871, 1872, or 1873. His tombstone says his birth year is 1871 but his obituary says he was age seventy-one, which would mean he was born in 1872. See Peter Vriner and George Vaky, A.c., 1900 USFC; census place: Champaign Ward 3, Champaign, Illinois; p. 9; lines 40, 41; enumeration district: 0006; FHL microfilm: 1240240 (accessed June 22, 2018). See also "George D. Vaky, Ill over Year, Dies at 71," *Champaign/Urbana News-Gazette*, January 31, 1944, 3.

38. Vaky's obituary says he came to Champaign/Urbana in 1898. "George D. Vaky, Ill over Year, Dies at 71," 3.

39. Marriage of Cinnia Oden and George D. Vaky, May 2, 1904; Douglas County, Illinois; A.c., Illinois, County Marriage Records, 1800–1940; film number 001295956. See also Cinnie Oden, A.c., 1900 USFC; census place: Urbana, Champaign, Illinois; p. 13; line 93; enumeration district: 0032; FHL microfilm: 1240241 (accessed June 24, 2018).

40. "George D. Vaky, Ill over Year, Dies at 71," 3; *1900 Champaign/Urbana City Directory* (Bloomington, IL: Pantagraph Printing, 1900), 147; *1904 Champaign/Urbana City Directory* (Bloomington, IL: Pantagraph Printing, 1904), 363; *1906 Champaign/Urbana City Directory* (Bloomington, IL: Pantagraph Printing, 1906), 338.

41. "Partnership," *Urbana Daily Courier*, April 3, 1925, 4.

42. *Daily Illini* (student paper of the University of Illinois, Champaign/Urbana), October 4, 1921, 5.

43. *Daily Illini*, August 9, 1922, 1.

44. *Find A Grave*, Alpha M. Vaky Wingard (4/9/1908–6/6/1997), 187269570, with obituary (accessed September 15, 2013).

45. James Vaky interview. In this regard, Winton Solberg cites the remembrances of a UI Jewish student at this time, Samson Raphaelson, who "viewed the Christian fraternities as not so much Christian as they were in some obscure way American and only incidentally Christian. Snobbishness kept them from admitting Jews." See Samson Raphaelson Transcriptions: Family Tape, 1969–1971, 243, in Samson Raphaelson Papers, RS 26/20/38, University of Illinois Archives, cited in Solberg, "Early Years," 224.

46. James Vaky interview.

47. *Find A Grave*, Theodore G. Vaky (9/22/1906–1/6/1995), 84264034, with obituary (accessed March 15, 2013).

48. James Vaky interview. Theodore became a pilot for United Airlines and tested bombers during World War II, after which he worked for the Civil Aeronautics (later Federal Aviation) Administration. He died in 1995. See Theodore Vaky obituary, *Moline (IL) Dispatch*, January 11, 1995, 6. James maintained a lifelong interest in the arts and was an accomplished pianist, organist, artist, and poet.

49. James Vaky, Oral History Project.

50. Peter Lessaris interview.

51. Tom John Lessares, A.c., US WW II DRC, 1942; National Archives at St. Louis; US WW II DRC (Fourth Registration), for the State of Illinois; Record Group title: Records of the Selective Service System, 1926–1975; Record Group number: 147; series number: M2097 (accessed April 10, 2013).

52. "Thomas Lessaris," *1900 New Haven Directory Including West Haven* (New Haven, CT: Price and Lee Publishers, 1901), 365; *1901 New Haven Directory Including West Haven* (New Haven, CT: Price and Lee Publishers, 1902), 370. Family tradition has Tom coming to Chicago in 1889 or 1890 after first stopping in New Haven, Connecticut, where he worked as a dishwasher in a confectionery and ice cream store. In the 1901 directory, however, Thomas Lessaris is a "roomer" at 95 Congress Avenue in New Haven, in a confectionery and ice cream store (p. 370). On p. 689, Thomas Lessaris is listed under "Confectioners and Fruit Dealers" at 95 Congress Ave., and on p. 715 under "Ice Cream Mfrs." at the same address. He then went to Chicago around 1902. It is not clear when he came to Champaign, but he already knew the restaurant and confectionery business and could open the Blue Fountain soon after arriving.

53. Peter Lessaris interview.

54. *Find A Grave*, Peter Thomas Lessaris (10/18/1928–5/23/2017), 179660510, with obituary; John Thomas (3/14/1918–10/4/2001), 56879546; George Thomas Lessaris (12/6/1919–11/4/2005), 22022140, with obituary (accessed April 12, 2013).

55. *Find A Grave*, Thomas Lessaris (10/23/1878–1/23/1951), 57116048; Dina Lessaris (8/27/1897–2/15/1995), 56879836.

56. *Find A Grave,* George Thomas Lessaris.

57. Peter Lessaris interview.

58. Alexander "Lex" Samaras interview.

59. See Nicolas Samaras, Georgios Samaras, and Apostolos Samaras, A.c., NYPCL; date of arrival: April 26, 1911; place of arrival: New York, New York; microfilm serial: T715, 1897–1957; microfilm roll: 1668; p. 26; lines 03, 04, 05 (accessed November 2, 2018).

60. "The Ritz Enters 19th Year; Son Takes Over Ownership," *Hoopeston (IL) Chronicle,* April 13, 2011, 27. Reprinted article from 1946.

61. *Find A Grave,* Alexander George "Lex" Samaras (6/29/1921–10/28/2017), 184767694, with obituary (accessed January 14, 2019).

62. "The Ritz Enters 19th Year; Son Takes Over Ownership," 32.

63. *Find A Grave,* Edna Margaret Samaras (1/24/1902–6/29/1964), 29832436; George A. Samaras (12/15/1896–3/7/1977), 29832422 (both accessed January 14, 2019).

64. Alexander "Lex" Samaras interview.

65. *Find A Grave,* Alexander George "Lex" Samaras.

66. Tomaras, "Recollections." In the following account, Pete Tomaras is the father, and Peter Tomaras is the son. Page numbers refer to this unpublished manuscript unless otherwise noted.

67. George Vaky's birthplace was Paradisi, near Sparta. Pete Tomaris was born in Paradisi, near Korinth.

68. Tomaras, "Recollections," 7.

69. Three Hierarchs Greek Orthodox Church, Champaign-Urbana, IL, History, pp. 1–3.

70. Jeni Pelafos Mechalas phone interview, August 25, 2013, and in person, June 3, 2019.

71. See John P. Pelafos, FamilySearch.com (https://familysearch.org/ark:/61903/1:1:K68C-RBL), US WW I DRC, 1917–1918, database with images, Champaign County no. 1, US, NARA microfilm publication M1509 (Washington DC: NARA, n.d.); FHL microfilm 1,452,377 (accessed June 13, 2018).

72. "John Pelafos," *1912 Champaign and Urbana City Directory* (Bloomington: Pantagraph Printing, 1912), 410.

73. "Urbana Confectioner Is Cousin of Venizelos," *Urbana Daily Courier,* March 6, 1919, 1.

74. "Mack Land Near Rantoul Sells for $71 an Acre," *Urbana Daily Courier,* February 27, 1932, 1.

75. Jeni Pelafos Mechalas phone interviews, August 25, 2013, and September 18, 2013, and in person, June 3, 2019.

76. Jeni Pelafos Mechalas interview, June 3, 2019.

77. Mark Pelafos interview.

78. Jeni Pelafos Mechalas interview, June 3, 2019. See a short news item about this event—"Unruly Fireworks Thrill Urbanans," *Daily Illini,* July 4, 1939, 1. Louis Vriner estimated his losses at $150 to $250.

79. Jeni Pelafos Mechalas phone interviews and in person.

80. Jeni Pelafos Mechalas interview, June 3, 2019.

81. Diana Vriner Krandel interviews, November 4, 2013, and June 5, 2019.

82. Krandel interviews; "Thomas Callas," *Urbana Daily Courier*, February 11, 1916, 2; "Nick Somers," *Urbana Daily Courier*, January 14, 1915, 5.

83. Paul Angel, A.c., US WW I DRC, June 5, 1917; registration state: Illinois; registration county: Champaign; roll: 1452377; draft board: 2 (accessed December 2, 2018). "Paul Angelos," *1912 Champaign-Urbana City Directory* (Champaign: Pantagraph Printing, 1912), 110; Paul Angell, A.c., 1930 USFC; census place: Urbana, Champaign, Illinois; p. 17B; line 65; enumeration district: 75; FHL microfilm: 2340145 (accessed December 2, 2018).

84. "Paul Angel," *1931 Champaign and Urbana City Directory* (Champaign: Flanigan-Pearson, 1935), 12.

85. "East Central Illinois Deaths, Paul Angel, Sr.," *Champaign-Urbana Courier*, October 28, 1970, 20. Although he operated a business for many years in Champaign-Urbana, Angel's obituary was very brief. He was born in St. Peters, Greece, on December 26, 1899, and was married to Madge Johnson on May 30, 1930. She died in 1946. He died on October 27, 1970.

86. My grandfather did not serve lunch except for some hamburgers that he grilled each day and smothered with his own relish. The locals called these "Gusburgers," and we still serve them today.

87. Fred Ross private correspondence.

88. There is only one mention of this connection. My great-uncle Nick's obituary says he (and therefore Gus) "was a son of George and Viola Vriner Flesor." See "Attack Is Fatal to Nick Flesor at Age of 72," *TJ*, June 30, 1955, 5.

89. Paul G. Flesor interview.

90. *Find A Grave*, Gus Flesor (b. 1879–12/10/1978), 96286566, with obituary; Nick George Flesor (2/25/1880–6/26/1955), 96280871, with obituary (both accessed June 3, 2019). Nick may have come over in 1905 with Vassile P. Vrinios, also from Pigadakia, gone to Chicago, and remained there a year or two. See Nicola Flesuras, A.c., NYPCL, date of arrival: May 5, 1905; place of arrival: New York, New York; microfilm serial: T715, 1897–1957; microfilm roll: 0569; p. 100; line 13 (accessed November 21, 2018).

91. "Nick's Candy in Photo Business," *TJ*, August 15, 1957, 26. See the Govits brothers' advertisement for the "Pasco Phonograph" at the Mt. Carmel Candy Kitchen in the *Mount Carmel Daily Republican-Register*, December 3, 1920, 4.

92. Constance Constant, e-mail correspondence, February 11, 2018.

93. See "Reunion Occurs Here after over 53 Years," *TJ*, January 6, 1955, 1.

94. Christine Katris Kockler interview.

95. Greek Orthodox Church priests may marry.

96. I do not know if Maria and Agnes were related. See Argro [*sic*] Flesor, A.c., 1930 USFC; census place: Tuscola, Douglas, Illinois; roll number: 510; p. 19A; lines 29, 30; enumeration district: 0017; FHL microfilm: 2340245. See also Argero [*sic*] Flesor, A.c., 1940 USFC; census place: Tuscola, Douglas, Illinois; roll: m-t0627_00795; p. 7A; line 21; enumeration district: 21–17. In the mid-1920s Nick, Agnes, and their twin children, George and Mary, went back to Greece, returning to New York on November

7, 1928. On the ship's manifest, her name is Argero, and her father's name is Nick Tzanopoulos. Nick and the children are American citizens at this point, but Agnes is not. See Argero Flesor, Nick Flesor, George Flesor, and Mary Flesor, A.c., NYPCL, date of arrival: November 7, 1928; place of arrival: New York, New York; microfilm serial: T715, 1897–1957; microfilm roll: 4379; p. 26; lines 27–30. Nick and Agnes are buried in the Tuscola Township Cemetery. On her gravestone is engraved Agnes P. Flesor, June 30, 1900–May 6, 1977. Nick's tombstone has February 25, 1880–June 26, 1955. (All accessed December 5, 2018).

97. Lee Flessor interview.

98. Agnes's husband, my great-uncle Nick, was seemingly thus her distant cousin.

99. Rob Earnshaw, "A 98-Year Ice Cream Era Ends: Gayety's Owners Say the Sweet Shop Is Closed for Good," *Chicago Tribune*, October 24, 2018, https://www.chicagotribune.com/suburbs/daily-southtown/news/ct-sta-gayetys-closes-st-1025-story.html; Joseph S. Pete, "After Nearly a Century, Gayety's Closes for Good," NWI.com, October 23, 2018, https://www.nwitimes.com/business/lake-newsletter/after-nearly-a-century-gayety-s-closes-for-good/article_fa6d90db-e4cc-5b27-b118–1076682c5ad3.html (both accessed August 1, 2019); Jim Flessor e-mail.

100. Joseph S. Pete, "Sweet! Gayety's Chocolate & Ice Cream to Return under New Management," NWI.com, March 27, 2019, https://www.nwitimes.com/business/local/sweet-gayety-s-chocolate-ice-cream-to-return-under-new/article_a89fd80d-6af7–56dc-97d6–5745dfedcf33.html (accessed August 1, 2019).

101. "Ten Years Ago in 1914," *TJ*, June19, 1924, 2. "Gus Flesor has purchased the residence property on North Main Street from Fred Overstreet."

102. *Find A Grave*, Sophia Tingos Flesor (9/16/1898[?]-2/2/1927), 54939286 (accessed April 24, 2019). There is no birth or death info on Sophia's tombstone, and it is not clear where *Find A Grave*'s 1898 date comes from. Her newspaper obituary says simply 1897. See n. 105 below.

103. James Tingus, Dimitra Tingus, and Sophie Tingus, A.c., 1910 USFC, census place: Pittsburgh Ward 22, Allegheny, Pennsylvania; roll: T624–1306; p. 13A; lines 4, 5, 6; enumeration district: 0583; FHL microfilm: 1375319 (accessed July 21, 1912).

104. "Sad Death. Mrs. Gus Flesor Passes Away at Hospital after a Brief Illness," *Tuscola Review*, February 8, 1927, 1.

105. "Laid to Rest. Many Attend Funeral Services of Mrs. Gus Flesor Thursday Last," *Tuscola Review*, February 10, 1927, 2.

106. "Sophia Flesor, 15, Tuscola Senior, Dies," *DDR*, June 1, 1942, 22; *Find A Grave*, Viola Flesor Voltis (3/16/1916–4/23/1970), 99586354; Helen Flesor Skinner (7/12/1924–8/8/2009), 41936402, with obituary; Sophia Flesor (1927–6/1/1942), 148398557 (all accessed June 1, 2019). For George Flesor (4/20/1917–11/30/1952), see "Tuscola Bank Official Dies," *DDR*, December 1, 1952, 8.

107. James Vaky interview.

108. Rigby and Rigby, *Rigby's Reliable Candy Teacher*.

109. Rigby and Rigby, preface.

110. Rigby and Rigby, 153.

111. Paul G. Flesor interview.

112. See Nick G. Flesor, A.c., US WW I DRC, 1917–1918; date: September 12, 1918; registration state: Illinois; registration county: Douglas; roll: 1613181 (accessed July 8, 2012).

113. Lincoln, "History of the Tuscola, Illinois Masonic Lodge."

114. Interestingly too, the Masons were one of the largest single groups from which the Klan drew its members. Indeed, a Klan lecturer in 1922 "boasted that 75 percent of Klansmen were recruited from the Masons." Pegram, *One Hundred Percent American*, 8. In his study of the Klan in the West, Shawn Lay observes that "evidently the majority of initial contacts took place in fraternal lodges, particularly those of the various Masonic orders." Lay, *Invisible Empire*, 7.

115. Unless otherwise noted, the following information is taken from P. White, *100 Years of Masonry*, 1–12.

116. Norma Lee Browning, "City Girl Gets Soft Drink and a Sermon—Free; Gus Knows the Answers—and the Questions," *Chicago Daily Tribune*, August 1, 1950, 9.

117. Browning, 9.

118. Browning, 9.

119. Fitzgerald, "American Soda Fountain Company."

120. S. Lewis, *Main Street*, 102.

121. My grandfather gave my aunt Viola, his oldest daughter, a huge wedding, for which the *Tuscola Review* devoted two and a half columns. The Decatur Greek Orthodox Church priest came to Tuscola to officiate. "Viola Flesor and Chris Voltis Wed Sunday in Presbyterian Church," *Tuscola Review*, October 29, 1942, 6.

122. Margaret Flesor obituary, *MJG*, September 23, 2008, 11.

CHAPTER 7. SMALL-CITY GREEK CONFECTIONERS

1. Phyllis Bartges Bayles interview. This is the source for the quotes and info in the next few paragraphs. See also Christ Bartges, A.c., US Naturalization Record Indexes, 1791–1992 (indexed in World Archives Project); FamilySearch.com, Soundex Index to Naturalization Petitions, Danville, Vermillion, Illinois, 1840–1950, microfilm serial: M1285; microfilm roll: 23. This petition is for Christ Bartges, Danville, certificate no. A-1189, for September 6, 1939. His age is thirty-four, which would make his birth year 1905. See also Christ Bartges, A.c., US, Social Security Death Index, 1935–2014; issue state: Illinois; issue date: 1951–1952. Here Mr. Bartges's birth date is noted as May 1, 1905. He died on February 17, 1994. (All accessed August 12, 2013.)

2. Bayles, "Memories of a Church Bakery," 22.

3. Dean Bartges interview.

4. Phyllis Bartges Bayles interview.

5. Biles, *Illinois*, 226.

6. Langland, *Chicago Daily News Almanac*, 714.

7. Biles, *Illinois*, 226.

8. "Decatur Greeks Talk of War," *DDR*, October 28, 1940, 14. This article, along with an accompanying photo, is about Greek involvement in World War II.

9. "Confectioners," *1899 Decatur City Directory* (Decatur: Review Printing and Stationery, 1899), 616.

10. "John Papadopulos," *1902–1903 Mattoon City Directory* (Mattoon: Mattoon Commercial Print, 1902–3), 286; and *1904–1905 Mattoon City Directory* (Mattoon: Mattoon Commercial Print, 1904), 303.

11. J. A. Papadopulos and Lucretia Papadopulos, A.c., Iowa State Census, 1905; roll: IA_96; card nos.: 808, 809 (accessed September 7, 2013).

12. "John Papadopulos," *1907 Cedar Rapids City Directory* (Rockford, IL: McCoy Directory, 1907–8), 265 (accessed August 10, 2013).

13. "John Papadopulos," *1921 Cedar Rapids City Directory* (Rockford, IL: McCoy Directory, 1921), 455; A.c., Iowa, Wills and Probate Records, 1758–1997; probate case files: 1840–1924; author: Iowa, District Court (Linn County); probate place: Linn, Iowa (accessed January 3, 2019).

14. Louis George Nichols, A.c., 1900 USFC; census place: Decatur Ward 1, Macon, Illinois; roll: 323; p. 10B; line 97; enumeration district: 0047; FHL microfilm: 1240323. In this census Louis's father is Greek and mother German, but this is almost certainly an error as all other records show both parents as Greek. (Accessed October 11, 2013.)

15. "Confectioners," *1901 Decatur City Directory* (Decatur: Review Printing and Stationery, 1901), 381.

16. Louis G. Nichols and Lillian Burrows, A.c., Cook Country, Marriages Index, 1871–1920. Louis was thirty-three and Lillian eighteen (accessed October 12, 2013).

17. Louis G. Nichols, A.c., 1910 USFC; census place: Decatur Ward 7, Macon, Illinois; roll: T624_307; p. 12B; line 55; enumeration district: 0019; FHL microfilm: 1374320. They had three sons, Louis Burrows (1906–77), Robert Francis (1908–58), and John Bennett (1912–2004), and a daughter, Dorothy Jane (1920–88) (accessed October 12, 2013).

18. "Confectioners," *1907 Decatur City Directory* (Decatur: Review Printing and Stationery, 1907), 851.

19. "Princess Confectionery. Successors to L. G. Nichols," *DH*, January 31, 1915, 3; "Confectioners," *1912 Decatur City Directory* (Decatur: Review Printing and Stationery, 1912), 786.

20. Louis G. Nichols, A.c., 1920 USFC; census place: Delaware, Defiance, Ohio; roll: T625_1376; p. 17A; line 33; enumeration district: 10 (accessed October 12, 2013).

21. Lewis [*sic*] G. Nichols, A.c., 1930 USFC; census place: Schoolcraft, Kalamazoo, Michigan; roll: 998; p. 5A; line 39; enumeration district: 0055; FHL microfilm: 2340733 (accessed October 11, 2013).

22. Lewis [sic] G. Nichols, A.c., Michigan, Deaths Records, 1867–1952. Louis Nichols's descendants have placed extensive documentation of his life on Ancestry.com, including photographs of Louis and Lillian. See, for example, http://trees.ancestry.com/tree/322572/person/-2095296079?ssrc= (accessed August 14, 2019).

23. "Sam Malleos Fails to Appear Early [for court date]," *DR*, July 19, 1909, 12.

24. "25 Years Ago Today," *DH*, August 15, 1933, 10.

25. *Find A Grave*, Nick Malleos (4/3/1894–6/15/1952), 64283429; Pete J. Malleos (8/15/1889–4/10/1945), 64242503 (accessed December 12, 2019). But see n. 29 below.

26. "Electric Shock Kills Tom Malleos," *DH*, July 9, 1923, 3; "Sam Malleos Dies Unexpectedly," *DH*, September 27, 1923, 11. Sam's and Thomas's biographical information comes from these two long obituaries.

27. "Sam Malleos Dies Unexpectedly," 11.

28. "Sam's Palace of Sweets," *DH*, September 30, 1923.

29. Malleos, Peter J., A.c., Illinois, Deaths and Stillbirths Index, 1916–1947; birth date: August 18, 1893; death date: April 10, 1945 (accessed September 12, 2013). The birth date and year here conflict with what is on Peter's gravestone (see n. 25 above). The tombstone dates seem more likely.

30. *Find A Grave*, Nick Malleos.

31. "Nicholas J. Malleos, Sam J. Malleos Brothers Co.," and "Malleos, Sam J. Bros. Co. (Nicholas Malleos) confrs 118 Merchant St.," *1948 Decatur City Directory* (Decatur: Huston-Patterson, 1948), 354.

32. See Peter J. Balamos and James D. Kareotes, A.c., 1910 USFC; census place: Decatur Ward 6, Macon, Illinois; roll: T624_308; p. 6A; lines 19, 20; enumeration district: 0117; FHL microfilm: 1374321 (accessed August 21, 2013); and *1910 Decatur City Directory* (Decatur: Review Printing and Stationery, 1910), 926.

33. "P. J. Balamos, Greek Leader, Dies Suddenly," *DDR*, October 28, 1948, 32.

34. "J. G. Kareotes, Ice Cream Maker, Dies," *DDR*, July 28, 1965, 39.

35. "Gus Kareotes Dies at 90," *DDR*, June 13, 1957, 32.

36. "American Confectionery (P. J. Balamos, J.G. Kareotes)," and "Central Park Confectionery (J. G. Kareotes, Gust Pappas, George, Thomas, and Andrew Greanias)," in *1925 Decatur City Directory* (Decatur: McCoy Directory, 1925), 73, 128.

37. "Tom Greanias, Former Owner of Café, Dies," *DH*, December 7, 1959, 13.

38. "A. G. Greanias Dies in Chicago," *DH*, January 18, 1949, 14.

39. "G. C. Greanias Dies at 56," *DH*, November 22, 1952, 2.

40. Peter Bacopulos, Basil Bacopulos, and Basil Geanetos, A.c., 1910 USFC; census place: Jacksonville Ward 2, Morgan, Illinois; roll: T624_313; p. 9B; lines 90–92; enumeration district: 0101 (accessed September 18, 2013).

41. "Princess Confectionery. Successors to L. G. Nichols," 3; "Bacopulos, Basil," "Bacopulos, John," and "Bacopulos, Peter," *1921 Decatur City Directory* (Peoria, IL: Leshnick Directory, 1921), 103–4. It is not clear how John was related to Basil and Peter.

42. "Princess Confectionery Makes Modern Improvement," *DH*, March 10, 1918, 17.

43. "Princess Confectionery Buys $1400 Liberty Bonds," *DH*, May 14, 1918, 3.

44. "Local Man to Be Married in Chicago," *DH*, May 5, 1921, 9; "(Anthe) Bacopulos," obituary, *DHR*, April 3, 1991, 8.

45. "Retired Monticello Café Operator Dies," obituary, *DH*, June 30, 1956, 7; "Peter G. Bacopulos Dies in Monticello," *DH*, June 26, 1954, 2.

46. "Gregory Kept Candle Burning," *DDR*, April 24, 1952, 6.

47. "Bacopulos Sells Princess Café to Acciavatti," *DDR*, July 7, 1946, 3.

48. "Peter Bacopulos, Ex-Candy Store Owner Dies," *DDR*, February 21, 1968, 37.

49. Peter Haikalis phone interview. All the following is from this interview unless

otherwise noted. Sadly, Haikalis, who was a PhD, died in 2017. See *Find A Grave*, Peter Dennis Haikalis (7/23/1934–3/20/2017), 177705148 (accessed June 5, 2019, with obituary).

50. "Mrs. Bessie Geanetos," obituary, *DDR*, June 30, 1957, 20.

51. Basil John Geanetos, A.c., US WW I DRC, 1917–1918; registration state: Illinois; county: Morgan; roll: 1614435 (accessed November 18, 2018). This source gives Basil's birth date as January 1, 1871.

52. By 1920 Basil and Bessie had three children—Jennie (eight years old), George (five), and Catherine (three). Athena, their fourth child, was born on January 8, 1920. Basil Geanetos, A.c., 1920 USFC; census place: Jacksonville Ward 3, Morgan, Illinois; roll: T625–391; p. 6B; lines 36–50; enumeration district: 127 (accessed November 14, 1918). Jennie's age should be nine, as she was born in 1911.

53. "Wedding Announcement. Miss Jennie Geanetos," *DH*, April 19, 1931. Dennis Haikalis died October 17, 1998, at 103 years old. "Haikalis, Dennis P.," *Los Angeles Times*, October 21, 1998, A22. Jennie died December 26, 2002. "Jennie D. Haikalis," *Los Angeles Times*, December 28, 2002, B13.

54. *Find A Grave*, Basil John Geanetos (1871–2/11/1938), 75479662 (accessed February 14, 2019).

55. "James K. Dovekas Revised Edition," *DH*, October 8, 1916, 6, article about his change of name after becoming a naturalized citizen; "Neulah to Be Called 'The Empress,'" *DH*, March 10, 1916, 3.

56. James K. Dovekas, A.c., US WW I DRC, 1917–1918; date: June 5, 1917; registration state: Illinois; registration county: Macon; roll: 1613187; and James K. Dovekas, A.c., US WW II DRC, 1942; National Archives at St. Louis, for the State of Illinois; Record Group title: Records of the Selective Service System, 1926–1975; Record Group number: 147; series number: M2097 (both accessed February 10, 2018).

57. "Constans Sell Confectionery," *DDR*, March 17, 1944, 18.

58. "New Confectionery Beautifully Fitted," *DH*, April 3, 1916, 3.

59. Christ Constantopulos, A.c., US WW I DRC, 1917–1918; date: June 5, 1917; registration state: Illinois; registration county: Macon; roll: 1613187 (accessed July 7, 2018).

60. "Butterfly Shop Name of New Confectionery," *DDR*, January 17, 1921, 3. William Chagoures (Chiagouris) later managed this for him. "Butterfly Confectionery," *1927 Decatur City Directory* (Decatur: McCoy Directory, 1927), 142.

61. There were several Greek-owned theater enterprises in America. See "Theatres," in Koken, Constant, and Canoutas, *History of Greeks*, 103.

62. "15 Years Ago in the Herald. The Purchase of the Avon Theatre," *DH*, July 22, 1949, 8.

63. "[Dovekas] Files Suit to Force Agreement," *DDR*, December 3, 1925, 14. He filed for bankruptcy in 1928. "Auction in the Matter of James K. Dovekas, Bankrupt," *DDR*, November 27, 1928, 25; A.c., US, Social Security Death Index, 1935–2014; number: 338-10-0668; issue state: Illinois (accessed August 8, 2019).

64. "Constantopulos, Gust," *1928 Decatur City Directory* (Decatur: McCoy Directory, 1928), 150.

65. "[Angelos] Constan, Avon Manager, Dies," obituary, *DH*, August 31, 1942. See also *Find A Grave*, Angel Constan (1895–1942), 69211823 (accessed November 12, 2018).

66. Announcement, "Out of Respect," *DH*, February 26, 1965, 9; "Gust Constan, Area Theater Owner, Dies," *DDR*, February 24, 1965, 77.

67. "New Citizens," *DDR*, November 25, 1924, 20; "[Theodore George] Constan," obituary, *DHR*, May 1, 1992, second ed., 6.

68. "Decatur Man Returns with Bride after Being in Greece during Revolt," *DH*, April 7, 1935, 3.

69. "Constans Sell Confectionery," *DDR*, March 17, 1944, 18.

70. "Gust Constant," "Chris Constant," *1959 Decatur City Directory* (Decatur: Huston-Patterson, 1959), 100; Announcement, "Out of Respect," 9; "Gust Constan, Area Theater Owner, Dies," 77. See also *Find A Grave*, Gust Constan (1891–1965), 66966579 (accessed September 28, 2018).

71. "Six Theaters at Mall Are to Open Dec. 1," *DHR*, August 22, 1980, 7.

72. "[Christ George] Constan," obituary, *DH*, May 21, 1978, 32.

73. "Candyland Confectionery," *1922 Decatur City Directory* (Decatur: McCoy Directory, 1922), 555; "Candyland Confectionery," *1927 Decatur City Directory* (Decatur: McCoy Directory, 1927), 145.

74. "Candyland Confectionery," *1938 Decatur City Directory* (Decatur: Huston-Patterson, 1938), 467.

75. "Eureka Confectionery," *1938 Decatur City Directory*, 209.

76. "Eureka Confectionery," *1950 Decatur City Directory* (Decatur: Huston-Patterson, 1950), 12.

77. "Confectioners," *1950 Decatur City Directory*, 549.

78. "Rainbow Confectionery," *1960 Decatur City Directory* (Decatur: Huston-Patterson, 1960), 15.

79. "James Dalmares," obituary, *DH*, September 1, 1974, 25. See also "Ten Years Ago Today, 1944," *DDR*, March 17, 1954, 10.

80. "Kyros Ashemos," obituary, *DH*, March 19, 1979, 21. Kyros's obituary gives his place of birth as Kastanshori, which prior to 1928 was the tiny village of Krampovos, and is now, correctly spelled, Kastanochori.

81. "Gus Ashemos," *1919 Charleston City Directory* (Champaign: Clark Elwell, 1919), 104; obituary, *DH*, July 8, 1963, 3.

82. *Decanois*, Decatur High School yearbook, 1914, 162.

83. *Decanois*, 162.

84. *Decanois*, 192.

85. *Decanois*, 1918, 170.

86. *Decanois*, 1924, 160.

87. *Decanois*, 1923, 116.

88. *Annunciation Greek Orthodox Church*, 2.

89. *Annunciation Greek Orthodox Church*, 17.

90. Peter Coutrakon, A.c., US WW I DRC, 1917–1918; date: September 12, 1918; registration state: Illinois; registration county: Sangamon; roll: 1642740; draft board: 1. In an e-mail, George Coutrakon, grandson of Peter, told me the family came

from Lefkokhoma. In his naturalization papers, Peter Perikle Coutrakon (probably Peter Coutrakon Jr.'s cousin) gives Karaspai (Lefkokhoma) as his hometown. The other Coutrakons usually just give the generic "Sparta" as their birthplace. See Peter Perikle Coutrakon, A.c., Illinois, Federal Naturalization Records, 1856–1991; National Archives at Chicago; Chicago, Illinois; ARC title: Declarations of Intention for Citizenship, 1906–1951; NAI number: 12024215; Record Group title: Records of Districts Courts of the United States, 1685–2009; Record Group number: RG 21 (accessed November 28, 2019).

91. Peter Coutrakon Sr., Peter Coutrakon Jr., John Coutrakon, and Peter [Perikle] Coutrakon, A.c., 1900 USFC; census place: Springfield Ward 5, Sangamon, Illinois; p. 4; lines 49, 50, 51, 52; enumeration district: 0096; FHL microfilm: 1240343 (accessed November 26, 2019). The entry specifically shows Peter Sr. as the head, age fifty-five (his birth date 1845). The next entry is for "Peter, Jr." "son," age twenty-five (birth date 1875) and a "candy maker."

92. "John Coutrakon," *1902–03 City Directory of Lawrence and Douglas Co., Kansas* (St. Louis: Chittenden Directory, 1902), 33, and ad opposite p. 80; "John Coutrakon" and "Pete Coutrakon," *1917 Lawrence City Directory* (Lawrence, KS: R. L. Polk, 1917), 86, 361; "Boston Confectionery," *Lawrence Daily Journal-World,* May 22, 1920, 3.

93. George Coutrakon e-mail; Isabelle Coutrakon, A.c., US, Social Security Death Index, 1935–2014 (accessed November 18, 2019).

94. Peter Coutrakon, Isabelle Coutrakon, George P. Coutrakon, and Basil H. Coutrakon, A.c., 1930 USFC; census place: Springfield, Sangamon, Illinois; p. 3A; lines 18, 19, 20, 21; enumeration district: 0047; FHL microfilm: 2340294 (accessed November 18, 2019). In the 1910 census, Isabelle's birthplace is "Turkey." In the 1920, 1930, and 1940 censuses, Isabelle's birthplace is Syria. This could be the result of the creation of Syria out of the old Ottoman Empire following World War I. Compare 1930 census above with Isabelle Coutrakon, A.c., 1910 USFC; census place: Springfield Ward 5, Sangamon, Illinois; roll: T624_325; p. 3B; line 60; enumeration district: 0047; FHL microfilm: 2340294 (accessed June 22, 2018); and Peter Coutrakon (Contrakon), A.c., US WW I DRC, 1917–1918; date: September 12, 1918; registration state: Illinois; registration county: Sangamon; roll: 1642740; draft board: 1 (accessed November 16, 2019).

95. "Coutrakon, Peter," *1900–1901 Springfield City Directory* (St. Louis: R. L. Polk, 1901), 592; "Kerasotes, Gus" and "Louis Kerasotes," *1902 Springfield City Directory* (St. Louis: R. L. Polk, 1902–3), 154, 696; George Coutrakon e-mail.

96. Gus Kerasotes, A.c., 1920 USFC; census place: Springfield Precinct 13, Sangamon, Illinois; roll: T625_406; p. 6B; line 79; enumeration district: 131. Louis Kerasotes, A.c., 1900 USFC; census place: Springfield Ward 5, Sangamon, Illinois; p. 4; lines 49, 50, 51, 52; enumeration district: 0096; FHL microfilm: 1240343 (both accessed October 21, 2019).

97. "Peter Coutrakon," "Gus Kerasotes," "Louis Kerasotes," and "Coutrakon & Kerasotes," *1902–1903 Springfield City Directory* (Springfield: R. L. Polk, 1902), 154, 349, 696.

98. "Gus Kerasotes Dies at Age 86," *Illinois State Journal* (Springfield), May 20,

1960, 1; "Confectioners," *1908 Springfield City Directory* (St. Louis: R. L. Polk, 1908), 945.

99. "Sam Malleos Opens Store in Springfield," *DH*, April 18, 1914, 9; *1914 Springfield City Directory* (St. Louis: R. L. Polk, 1914), 357, 1097.

100. *Find A Grave,* Angel B. Nases (3/25/1886–4/8/1942), 23594215; Tom B. Nases (7/14/1893–5/20/1962), 124816215; George Basil Nases (4/23/1886–3/15/1928), 57918870, with obituary (accessed November 25, 2019). George's obituary identifies the three as brothers. See also "Nases, Angel" and "Nases, Thomas," *1937 Springfield City Directory* (Springfield: Baldwin and Williamson, 1937), 1091.

101. "Avenue Confectionery Has Record of 20 Years' Service. Store Operated by Charles Coutrakon Will Mark Anniversary Tomorrow," *Illinois State Journal,* April 22, 1937, 8.

102. "Stephen Mastorakas" and "William Mastorakas," *1915 Springfield City Directory* (Springfield: R. L. Polk, 1915), 119; and *1916 Springfield City Directory* (Springfield: R. L. Polk, 1916), 1070.

103. "Boy's Candy Shop," *1919 Springfield City Directory* (Springfield: Jefferson Printing, 1919), 144.

104. *1923 Springfield City Directory* (Springfield: Jefferson Directory, 1923), 1084.

105. *Find A Grave*, Charles Coutrakon (1889–1956), 120741179; Peter P. Coutrakon (1884–1951), 120741241. Peter's World War I draft card says he was born on November 17, 1875. See Peter Coutrakon, A.c., US WW I DRC, 1917–1918; date: September 12, 1918; registration state: Illinois; registration county: Sangamon; roll: 1642740; draft board: 1 (all accessed June 18, 2019).

106. "Sugar Bowl," *1919 Springfield City Directory*, no page number, addition at back of volume, omitted material. See also "Theodore Gray," obituary, *Illinois State Journal-Register* (Springfield), November 16, 1977, 48.

107. Editor, "Sugar Bowl Restaurants."

108. "Gray, J. Theodore," *1914 Springfield City Directory*, 392.

109. Theodore T. Gray and Mary R. Schrock, A.c., Cook County, Marriage Indexes, 1912–1942 (accessed June 15, 2019).

110. Editor, "Sugar Bowl Restaurants"; Editor, "Fast Food in Springfield."

111. *Find A Grave*, Theodore T. Gray (2/9/1892–11/15/1977), 100624675 (accessed June 18, 2019).

112. Laurel Rice (James P. James's granddaughter) e-mail; "James P. James Dies at Hospital," *Illinois State Journal-Register*, May 8, 1960, 8.

113. Antonella H. Konrad, A.c., US, Social Security Applications and Claims Index, 1936–2007; and James P. James, Antonella James, Helen James, and Kathyrn [*sic*] James, A.c., 1930 USFC; census place: Springfield, Sangamon, Illinois; pp. 7A, 7B; lines 50, 51, 52, 53; enumeration district: 0047; FHL microfilm: 2340294 (both accessed June 29, 2019). *1922 Springfield City Directory* (Springfield: Jefferson Directory, 1926), 586, 1084; *1923 Springfield City Directory*, 528, 1084.

114. Dietrich, "Picturing the Past." See also James P. James, A.c., US WW II DRC, 1942, National Archives at St. Louis, for the State of Illinois; Record Group title: Records of the Selective Service System, 1926–1975; Record Group number: 147; series

number: M2097 (accessed June 12, 2018). "James P. James Dies at Hospital," *Illinois State Journal-Register*, May 8, 1960, 8; *1912 Springfield City Directory* (Springfield: R.L. Polk, 1912): 487; *1916 Springfield City Directory*, 1194; *1921 Springfield City Directory* (Springfield: Jefferson Directory, 1921), 564.

115. Laurel Rice e-mail.

116. "James P. James Dies at Hospital," 8.

117. See, for example, *1928 Springfield City Directory* (Springfield: Jefferson Printing, 1928), 1389–90.

118. *Find A Grave*, Charles Poulos (1/14/1887–8/7/1945), 66105894 (accessed July 14, 2013); Charles Poulos, A.c., US WW I DRC, 1917–1918; date: June 5, 1917; registration state: Illinois; registration county: Sangamon; roll: 1642742; draft board: 2 (accessed October 21, 2018).

119. *1908 Springfield City Directory*, 663; *1914 Springfield City Directory*, 767.

120. *1923 Springfield City Directory*, 178. The entry for Poulos is misspelled as "Boulos" and misplaced in the directories for 1923 and 1924. It is corrected in the 1925 directory.

121. *1929 Springfield City Directory* (Springfield: Jefferson Printing, 1929), 438, 1017, 1021.

122. *1930 Springfield City Directory* (Springfield: Jefferson Printing, 1930), 226, 581.

123. *1934 Springfield City Directory* (Springfield: H. L. Williamson, 1934), 688.

124. *1937 Springfield City Directory*, 155, 1121.

125. "Two Die When Automobile Hits Parked Van," *Illinois State Journal-Register*, August 8, 1945, 1, 2.

126. George Xamis, A.c., Illinois, Deaths and Stillbirths Index, 1916–1947; George Xamis, A.c., US WW I DRC, 1917–1918; date: June 5, 1917; registration state: Illinois; registration county: Sangamon; roll: 1642742; draft board: 2 (accessed June 21, 1913).

127. *1919 Springfield City Directory*, 1331.

128. *1919 Springfield City Directory*, 1229; *1923 Springfield City Directory*, 1047, 1085, 1168.

129. There was extensive newspaper coverage of this story. See, for example, "Man Is Slain as Girl Looks On. G. Xamis Is Beaten to Death in His Garage," *Illinois State Journal*, October 17, 1924; "Fill Jury in Murder Case; Pete Xamis Is State Witness," *Illinois State Journal*, April 11, 1925; "Acquits after Seven Hours of Balloting; Defendant Is Elated," *Illinois State Journal*, April 13, 1925, 1, 10.

130. "Man Is Slain as Girl Looks On," 1.

131. *1925 Springfield City Directory* (Springfield: Jefferson Directory, 1925), 1125, 1165; *1930 Springfield City Directory*, 770.

132. See, for example, *1925 Springfield City Directory*, 839–40.

133. Chris Bresvelos (Presvelos), A.c., 1930 USFC; census place: Springfield, Sangamon, Illinois; p. 17B; line 95; enumeration district: 0038; FHL microfilm: 2340294; and Nicolaos [*sic*] Presvelos, A.c., Illinois, Federal Naturalization Records, 1856–1991; National Archives at Chicago; ARC title: Petitions for Naturalization, 1906–1991; NAI number: 6756404; Record Group title: Records of District Courts of the United States, 1685–2009; Record Group number: RG 21 (both accessed June 10, 2018).

134. *1933 Springfield City Directory* (Springfield: Williamson Printing, 1933), 672.

135. *1921 Springfield City Directory*, 1158; *1937 Springfield City Directory*, 1122; *1948 Springfield City Directory* (St. Louis: R. L. Polk, 1948), 526.

136. Alex George Karon, A.c., US WW II DRC, 1942; National Archives at St. Louis, for the State of Illinois; Record Group title: Records of the Selective Service System, 1926–1975; Record Group number: 147; series number: M2097 (accessed June 28, 2019); Editor, "Sugar Bowl Restaurants."

137. Editor, "Sugar Bowl Restaurants."

138. Alex Karon, A.c., 1920 USFC; census place: Vandalia Ward 2, Fayette, Illinois; roll: T625_367; p. 9A; line 32; enumeration district: 94 (accessed June 22, 2018); *1911 Decatur City Directory* (Decatur: Chas. O. Ebel, 1911), 363; *1927 Springfield City Directory* (Springfield: Jefferson Printing, 1927), 157.

139. "Angeline A. Karon," obituary, *Illinois State Journal-Register*, August 5, 1993, 18; Alex Karon and Angeline Karon, A.c., 1930 USFC; census place: Springfield, Sangamon, Illinois; roll: 559; p. 4A; lines 43, 44; enumeration district: 0042; FHL microfilm: 2340294 (accessed June 23, 2018).

140. Editor, "Sugar Bowl Restaurants."

141. Mann, Russo, and Garvert, *Springfield Entertainment*, 106.

142. Editor, "Sugar Bowl Restaurants."

143. Cavanagh, "Gifts of the Greeks."

144. "Polio Ban Forces Kids Off Streets in Springfield," *Freeport (IL) Journal-Standard*, August 3, 1949, 2; Thomas Nelson, "Quarantined Children Hard to Keep Busy," *Harrisburg (IL) Daily Register*, August 3, 1949, 6.

145. *Find A Grave*, Theodore T. Gray (4/22/1922–9/2/1950), 92994246, with obituary (accessed June 14, 2019).

146. "Over 2,000 Attend Benefit Show for Greek War Relief," *Illinois State Journal-Register*, March 23, 1941, 4.

147. "Over 2,000 Attend Benefit Show for Greek War Relief."

148. "Heroism: City Greeks' Relatives Fight," *Illinois State Journal-Register*, March 7, 1941, 3.

149. "Heroism: City Greeks' Relatives Fight."

150. "Heroism: City Greeks' Relatives Fight."

151. Anthony Gus Kerasotes, A.c., WWI, WWII, and Korean War Casualty Listings; *Find A Grave*, Anthony Gus Kerasotes (9/6/1912–12/25/1943), 14814680, with obituary (both accessed June 14, 2019).

152. "Heroism: City Greeks' Relatives Fight," 3.

153. *1953 Springfield City Directory* (St. Louis: R. L. Polk, 1953), 13 (separate paging at end of volume). The Coutrakon Confectionery was now owned by Paul and Angeline Palazzolo (p. 147). Bill Mastorakos and George Sotiropoulos still ran Boy's Candy Shop (p. 69) and Diana's Sweet Shop (p. 177), and Alex Karon still ran the Sugar Bowl II (p. 689). Karon died October 4, 1972. See *Find A Grave*, Alex G. Karon (6/14/1893–10/4/1972), 66102486 (accessed June 18, 2019).

154. "Gus Kerasotes Dies at Age 86," *Illinois State Journal-Register*, May 20, 1960, 1, 2; Editor, "Kerasotes Theatres."

155. Pauline L. Telford, "A Visit to St. Anthony's," *Illinois State Journal-Register*, May 15, 1960, 8.

156. Nick Adam interview.

CHAPTER 8. SMALL-TOWN GREEK CONFECTIONERS

1. "Soup, New Shoes, Sweets, and Greetings at Christmas Time," *Pana (IL) News-Palladium*, December 20, 1984, 9; "New Structure Will Be Built in Downtown Pana. Man Who Came to City 'Without a Dollar' in $35,000 Investment," *DH*, May 16, 1929, 15.

2. "Kehias Candy Shop . . . Celebrating 11th Anniversary," *DH*, November 30, 1925, 2; "Pana Store Owners Close Shop," *DHR*, January 10, 1991, 5; "Pana Soda Fountain Lives On," *DDR*, November 1, 1977, 18.

3. "Gives New Park to City of Pana," *DH*, September 16, 1925, 5.

4. "George A. Kehagias," A.c., US WW I DRC, 1917–1918; date: June 5, 1917; registration state: Illinois; registration county: Christian; roll: 1504088 (accessed April 12, 2013); "Pana Briefs. Private George Kehagias," *DH*, July 23, 1918, 2. George served in the army Quartermaster Department as cook and baker (accessed December 15, 2018). "George A. Kehias," A.c., US, Headstone Applications for Military Veterans, 1925–1963; microfilm publication: M1916, 134 rolls; ARC ID: 596118; Records of the Quartermaster General, Record Group 92 (accessed June 12, 2019). Kehias seems to have changed the spelling from Kehagias to Kehias soon after the draft registration.

5. "Av and Aug, the Candy Men," *Pana News-Palladium*, December 15, 1983, 10–11. Avgary was his Greek grandfather's first name.

6. For their marriage, see "Kehias-Haynes," *MJG*, April 4, 1923, 8; and "Haynes-Kehias," *DH*, April 3, 1923, 2. The entire family is listed in the 1940 census: George Kehias, Katherine (Kathryn in record) Kehias, Avgary Kehias, Stratton C. Kehias, James Kehias, Caroline Kehias, and Georgia Kehias, A.c., 1940 USFC; census place: Pana, Christian, Illinois; roll: m-t0627-00767; p. 17B; lines 48, 49, 50, 51, 52, 53, 54; enumeration district: 11–17 (accessed June 9, 2018).

7. "Av and Aug, the Candy Men," 10–11. For Katherine see the two obituaries "Kehias," *DHR*, March 22, 1998, 10; and "Katherine R. Kehias," *Pantagraph*, March 24, 1998, 9. For their many extensive journeys to Europe and Greece, see "Pana Confectioner to Combine Legion Meet with Homeland Visit," *DH*, September 6, 1927, 2; "Pana Travelers to Return Soon," *DH*, December 3, 1927, 14; "Pana Family Leaves for Native Home in Greece," *DH*, August 15, 1930, 8; and "Pana Family Returns after Trip to Greece," *DH*, December 4, 1930, 11.

8. "Gives New Park to City of Pana," *DH*, September 16, 1925, 5.

9. Georgia Kehias Hamilton phone interview, June 24, 2019.

10. "Spartan Building 'Thing of Beauty and Joy Forever,' Is Erected by George Kehias," *Pana Daily Palladium*, October 30, 1929, 1, 4. See also "George Kehias Dies," *DDR*, October 16, 1953, 5.

11. "Spartan Building 'Thing of Beauty and Joy Forever,' Is Erected by George Kehias," 1, 4. The long quote is also from this article.

12. "New Structure Will Be Built in Downtown Pana," *DH*, May 26, 1929, 15; "Five Pana Stores Change Building," *DH*, May 4, 1940, 9; "Kehias Will Erect Fine New Business Block," *Pana Daily Palladium*, May 21, 1929, 1; "Spartan Building 'Thing of Beauty and Joy Forever,' Is Erected by George Kehias," 1, 4.

13. "George Kehias Dies," *DDR*, October 16, 1953, 5; *Find A Grave*, George A. Kehias (1/1/1894–10/15/1953), 51695833, with obituary (accessed January 8, 2019).

14. Georgia Kehias Hamilton phone interviews, January 29, 2015, and June 24, 2019.

15. Online obituary for Avgary G. "Av" Kehias, February 2012, McCracken-Dean Funeral Home, Pana, pp. 1–5, http://www.mccrackendeanfuneralhome.com/obits/obituaries.php/obitID/235000 (accessed April 22, 2019).

16. Lecas obituary, *DDR*, June 19, 1971, 10; *1925 Pana City Directory* (Chicago: Leshnick Directory, 1925–26), 55, 146; George Lecas, A.c., 1930 USFC; census place: Pana, Christian, Illinois; p. 11B; line 92; enumeration district: 0020; FHL microfilm: 2340146 (accessed November 9, 2018); "Approach of Christmas Season Stirs Activity in Pana Candy Factory," *DH*, November 5, 1957, 9.

17. Entry for "George H. Lecas" in Thompson, *Library of American Lives*, 687.

18. "300,000-Lb. Order of Peanut Brittle Completed in Pana," *DDR*, December 8, 1948, 25.

19. *Find A Grave*, George Lecas (8/10/1899–6/1971), 55848946; Edith B. Lecas (11/19/1902–6/27/2000), 55848951 (accessed November 10, 2019).

20. Thomas Loamis [*sic*], A.c., NYPCL; date of arrival: August 10, 1907; port of arrival: New York, New York; microfilm serial number: T715; microfilm roll: 0962; p. 188; line 25 (accessed November 9, 2018). This says his age is thirty, or birthday 1877. His tombstone says 1880. See *Find A Grave*, Thomas Loomis (1880–1954), 159448119 (accessed November 10, 2019).

21. George came over in 1896 at the age of twenty-nine (birthday c. 1867). His wife, Athanasia (Mouselers) Loomis (age eighteen), came over in 1899 and might have traveled with her father- and mother-in-law, John and Mary, who also came over in that year, but I could not verify this. See Geo J. Loomis, A.c., 1920 USFC; census place: Keokuk Ward 2, Lee, Iowa; roll: T625_498; p. 13A; line 22; enumeration district: 70 (accessed November 8, 2018).

22. *1900–1901 Burlington City Directory* (Burlington, IA: Ora J. Gould, 1901), 212; Jno. Loomis and Peter Loomis, A.c., 1900 USFC; census place: Burlington, Des Moines, Iowa; roll 429; p. 6A; lines 12, 14; enumeration district: 0009; FHL microfilm: 1240429 (accessed November 8, 2018). Jno. Loomis's birthdate is given as July 1842. This census says Peter's father and mother, John and Mary Loomis, came to America in 1899. In the 1902 city directory, G. J. Loomis is "manufacturer and dealer of ice cream & candy." *1902 County and City Directory* (Burlington, IA: Ora J. Gould, 1902–3), 212.

23. In 1900 Peter and Mary's one-year old son, John, died. This may be the reason they left Burlington. See *Find A Grave*, John Loomis (infant, 1900), 103381738 (accessed January 22, 2019).

24. See "George J. Loomis," "Confectioners," *1908 Burlington Business Directory*

(Rockford, IL: McCoy Directory, 1908), 213, 377; George Loomis, A.c., 1910 USFC; census place: Keokuk Ward 1, Lee, Iowa; roll: T624_410; p. 9B; line 80; enumeration district: 0065; FHL microfilm: 1374423 (accessed November 8, 2018).

25. "Grand Opening," *Keokuk (IA) Daily Gate City*, February 4, 1916, 2; Geo. J. Loomis, A.c., 1920 USFC (info given in n. 22 above) (accessed November 9, 2018).

26. "Confectioners," *1905 Decatur City Directory* (Decatur: Review Printing and Stationery, 1905), 403; "Confectioners," *1906 Decatur City Directory* (Decatur: Review Printing and Stationery, 1906), 844; "Confectioners," *1907 Decatur City Directory* (Decatur: Review Printing and Stationery, 1907), 851.

27. P. J. Loomis, A.c., 1910 USFC; census place: Cairo Ward 3, Alexander, Illinois; roll: T624_230; p. 3A; line 18; enumeration district: 0006 (accessed November 9, 2018). Peter is thirty-eight in this census, making his birth year around 1872, but his tombstone has 1870. See n. 30 below.

28. "Peter Loomis," *1915 Cairo City Directory* (Asheville, NC: Piedmont Directory, 1915), 232. His wife, Annie, and daughter, Mary, are also working at the North Pole Candy Kitchen, Mary as a "clerk" (231).

29. Peter Loomis, A.c., 1930 USFC; census place: Cairo, Alexander, Illinois; roll: 406; p. 3A; enumeration district: 0003 (accessed November 9, 2018). See also *1922–1923 Cairo City Directory* (Asheville, NC: Piedmont Directory, 1922–23), 180.

30. *Find A Grave*, Peter John Loomis (1870–1944), 128788958 (accessed February 4, 2017).

31. "Clinton News Notes," *DH*, May 28, 1909, 2. George Loomis of Burlington was visiting brother Thomas, who owned a Clinton confectionery.

32. Goodman, "Greeks—The Candy Kitchen," 75, 79.

33. *The Candy Kitchen: An Original 1920s Soda Fountain Confectionery and Diner*, advertising brochure.

34. *Find A Grave*, Thomas J. Loomis (1880–10/26/1954), 159448119 (accessed February 4, 2017).

35. Goodman, "Greeks—The Candy Kitchen," 74; Swim, "History of the [Greenup] Candy Kitchen."

36. See the ad for the Buffalo Candy Factory, *MJG*, December 1, 1905, 8.

37. See ad, "Fireworks," *MJG*, June 30, 1913, 4.

38. "Buys Fruit Store," *MJG*, July 21, 1909, 1.

39. "Sheopoolos-Montgomery," *MJG*, November 17, 1919, 6.

40. "Sheopoolos Sells Confectionery Store," *MJG*, August 9, 1917.

41. George Sheopoolos, A.c., US WW I DRC, 1917–1918; registration state: Illinois; registration county: Cook; roll: 1493582; draft board: 30 (accessed November 15, 2018).

42. "Uncle of Mattoon Man," *MJG*, February 5, 1915, 6.

43. "Sheopoolos," obituary, *Chicago Tribune*, May 28, 1954.

44. I do not know if Tom Deligianis and his brothers were any relation to the more well-known Deligianis family who ran the Diana Sweet Shoppe in Port Huron, Michigan, for seventy-five years. They came from Aghios Vassilios, north of Tripoli. See Steve Frangos, "Eulogy for the Diana Sweet Shoppe."

45. "Grants Naturalization Papers," *MJG*, October 1, 1914, 1.

46. Thomas Deligianis, A.c., US WW I DRC, 1917–1918; registration state: Illinois; registration county: Marion; roll: 1614346 (accessed November 10, 2018).

47. Thomas Deligianis, A.c., US, Army Transport Service, Passenger Lists, 1910–1939; Record Group title: Records of the Office of the Quartermaster General, 1774–1985; Record Group number: 92; roll or box number: 451 (accessed November 9, 2018).

48. Thomas Deligianis, A.c., 1920 USFC; census place: Centralia Ward 2, Marion, Illinois; roll: T625–391; p. 6B; line 96; enumeration district: 0172 (accessed November 9, 2018).

49. John Deligianis, A.c., US WW I DRC, 1917–1918; registration state: Illinois; registration county: Marion; roll: 1614346 (accessed November 12, 2018).

50. Louis Deligianis, A.c., 1940 USFC; census place: Centralia, Marion, Illinois; roll: m-t0627–00852; pp. 9B, 10A; lines 77–80, 1–3; enumeration district: 61–6 (accessed November 22, 2018).

51. Louis Deley and John Deley, A.c., 1920 USFC; census place: Centralia Ward 3, Marion, Illinois; roll: T625–391; p. 4B; lines 62, 63; enumeration district: 174 (accessed November 20, 2018). Louis also registered for the draft in 1918 with his two brothers and was a Centralia candy maker. See Elias Deligianis, A.c., US WW I DRC, 1917–1918; registration state: Illinois; registration county: Marion; roll: 1614346 (accessed November 12, 2018).

52. Louis Deley, A.c., 1930 USFC; census place: Chicago, Cook, Illinois; p. 9B; lines 66–71; enumeration district: 1125; FHL microfilm: 2340199. Transcribed as "Lomie Dely" on Ancestry.com (accessed November 22, 2018).

53. Louis Deley, A.c., 1940 USFC; census place: Centralia, Marion, Illinois; roll: m-t0627–00852; pp. 9B, 10A; lines 77–80, 1–3; enumeration district: 61–6 (accessed November 22, 2018).

54. "Centralia Is Hail Battered," *MJG*, April 30, 1927, 4.

55. Thomas Deligianis and Stavronla Deligianis, A.c., NYPCL; year: 1927; arrival: New York, New York; microfilm serial: T715, 1897–1957; microfilm roll: 4157; p. 30; lines 20, 21 (accessed November 26, 2018).

56. Thomas Deligianis, A.c., 1930 USFC; census place: Centralia, Marion, Illinois; p. 2A; lines 40–42; enumeration district: 0005; FHL microfilm: 2340278 (accessed November 26, 2018).

57. Thomas Deley, A.c., 1940 USFC; census place: Centralia, Marion, Illinois; roll: m-t0627–00852; pp. 5A, 5B; lines 39, 40, 41; enumeration district: 61–8 (accessed November 25, 2018). The names have been transcribed here as "Dehey," as if the names were not confusing enough.

58. "326th Machine Gun Battalion Meets," *Kinmundy (IL) Express*, November 13, 1947, 3; *Find A Grave*, Tom Deley (Deligianis) (9/17/1890–10/4/1951), 83297192 (accessed January 11, 2019).

59. *Find A Grave*, John Deley (Deligianis) (1895–1942), 83298462; Bertha J. Deley (1912–1982), 83298156. Bertha's birthplace is engraved on the stone as Tripoli (accessed January 15, 2019). Louis Deley, A.c., 1940 USFC; census place: Centralia, Marion, Illinois; roll: m-t0627–00852; pp. 9B, 10A; lines 77–80, 1–3; enumeration district:

61–6 (accessed November 25, 2018). *Find A Grave*, Louis Deley (5/18/1886–2/17/1971), 83295171; Bertha Deley, (8/15/1897–10/4/1990), 83295595 (all accessed January 18, 2019). Bertha's site contains a wedding photo of the couple in 1921.

60. Louis Kehias and Peter Leharis (spelling in census), A.c., 1910 USFC; census place: Chicago Ward 2, Cook, Illinois; roll: T624_242; p. 5B; lines 95, 96; enumeration district: 0177; FHL microfilm: 1374255 (accessed November 26, 2018).

61. See ad/announcement of store's opening, *MJG,* February 17, 1919, 4.

62. "How to Get Cool," advertisement, *MJG,* August 8, 1923, 2.

63. "Kehias Retires; Ran 'Blue Bird' 27 Years," *MJG,* January 1, 1946, 1.

64. "Obituaries: Peter D. Lehares," *MJG,* June 29, 1966, 3.

65. "Tom Rezinas, Lakewood, Dies Sunday," *Shelbyville (IL) Daily Union,* August 18, 1980, 4.

66. *Find A Grave*, Peter Lehares (1879–1966), 62678943 (accessed November 20, 2018). Stella died in 1993. See "Stella Lehares," *MJG,* October 19, 1993, 6.

67. "Obituaries: Louis Kehias," *Coles County (IL) Daily Times-Courier*, April 4, 1972, 3; "It's His Flag," *McAllen (TX) Monitor*, June 16, 1970, 3.

68. "Louis Kehias Here for Centennial," *MJG,* August 29, 1955, 1.

69. "Local Deaths. Louis S. Kehias," *MJG,* April 3, 1972, 5.

70. W. Anderson, *Where Have You Gone, Starlight Café?*, 92–93.

71. Unless otherwise noted, all of the information about Peter Sutter comes from Patsy's account in Charleston and Mattoon Bi-centennial Commission, "Peter Sutter," *History of Coles County, Illinois,* 884–85; and "P. J. Sutter Dies; Rites Thursday," *MJG,* February 14, 1962, 1.

72. "Photo P. Sutter," obituary, *MJG,* December 5, 1977, 5. Peter's wife went by the name Photo, rather than Photula, and that is what is on her gravestone.

73. Peter J. Sutter, A.c., US, Headstone Applications for Military Veterans, 1925–1963 (accessed June 12, 2018).

74. "Louis Kerasotes," *1908–09 Charleston City Directory* (New York: S. H. Moore, 1909), 46; Easter-Shick and Clark, *Round the Square*, 273.

75. "Nicholas G. Alexander," *1916 Charleston City Directory* (Quincy, IL: Hoffman Directories, 1916), 103, 209; "Gust. Ashemus [*sic*], Charleston Confectionery," *1919 Charleston City Directory* (Charleston: Champaign: Clark Elwell, 1919), 104.

76. "Panas, William," *1918 Springfield City Directory* (Springfield: Jefferson Printing, 1918), 841, 1242.

77. "Panas, William" 841, 1242; "William Panas," *1919 Charleston City Directory*, 152.

78. See the following in the *1919 Charleston City Directory*: "Gust. Ashemos," 104, "William Panas," 152, and "Candy Shop," "Charleston Confectionery," 177.

79. "John H. Snyder (Ida), mgr. Candy Shop," *1932 Charleston City Directory* (St. Louis: Schuyler Drury, 1932), 177; "John H. Snyder (Ida), Candy Shop," *1937 Charleston City Directory* (Charleston: Courier Publishing, 1937), 164; *Find A Grave*, John Henry Snyder (10/9/1876–6/21/1941), 178677457 (accessed October 20, 2019).

80. Candy Hoem, "Corner Confectionery: A Charleston Landmark," *Charleston Journal-Gazette*, February 18, 1971, 2.

81. "Business Leader Bill Panas Dies," *Charleston Times-Courier*, May 9, 1977, 1.

82. "Business Leader Bill Panas Dies," 1. Bill Panas was also a member of the Decatur Greek Orthodox Church. See also *Find A Grave*, William A. Panas (3/18/1892–5/7/1977), 196176448 (accessed October 21, 2019).

83. "Stephen J. Papadakos," obituary, *MJG*, May 13, 1947, 9.

84. "Stephen J. Papadakos," *1898 Philadelphia City Directory* (Philadelphia: James Gopsill's Sons, 1898), 1702. Papadakos does not appear in any other year.

85. "Confectioners, Papadakos & Zarafonetis," *1901–1902 Terre Haute City Directory* (Terre Haute: Charles O. Ebel, 1901–2), 544, 761, 921. They lived here as well, perhaps above the store, as was so common.

86. James Zarafonetis and Nicolas Zarafonetis, A.c., 1900 USFC; census place: Philadelphia Ward 10, Philadelphia, Pennsylvania; p. 7; lines 48, 49; enumeration district: 0171; FHL microfilm: 1241455 (accessed March 2, 2018).

87. "Confectioners, Papadakos & Georgopoulos," *1904 Terre Haute City Directory* (Terre Haute: Moore and Langen Printing, 1904), 799. Papadakos also had a second store: on the same page under "Confectioners," and just up the street at 826 Wabash Avenue, was an independent store listed under "Papadakos, Staphe. J."

88. See "Stephen J. Papadakos," obituary, *MJG*, May 13, 1947, 9; T. Day, *History of the Square in Paris, Illinois*, 18; and Steven [*sic*] J. Papadakos, A.c., 1930 USFC; census place: Paris, Edgar, Illinois; roll: 513; p. 4B; line 84; enumeration district: 0017 (accessed April 15, 2018).

89. *Find A Grave*, Stavros John "Steve" Papadakos (9/14/1874–5/10/1947), 193989189 (accessed March 6, 2018).

90. Paul Jacobs interview.

91. James Zarafonetis, A.c., Indiana, Death Certificates, 1899–2011; Indiana Archives and Records Administration, Indianapolis; Death Certificates; year: 1950; roll: 03; and Mary Zarafonetis, A.c., Indiana, Death Certificates, 1899–2011; Indiana Archives and Records Administration, Indianapolis; Death Certificates; year: 1945; roll: 09 (accessed March 9, 2018). The four census records from 1910 to 1940 give four different birth years for James: 1871 (1910), 1872 (1920), about 1875 (1930), and about 1871 (1940), with corresponding differences in his age. To a lesser extent, the same is true for Mary.

92. "A Dish of Ice Cream Free . . . Greek Candy Kitchen," *Brazil (IN) Daily Times*, October 3, 1907, 5; "Louis Zarafonetis, a True Career Man," *Vincennes (IN) Sun-Commercial*, December 11, 1994, 9. Louis was James and Mary's son, and this article recaps the family and store history.

93. "Nicolas Zarafonetis" and "Confectioners," *1908–1909 Vincennes Directory* (Indianapolis: R. L. Polk, 1908), 293, 307.

94. R. Day, *Vincennes*, 148. This town history says the Zarafonetis Brothers Candy Kitchen, owned by James and Nick Zarafonetis, was in business from 1908 to 1959. See also James Zarafonetis, Mary Zarafonetis, and Nicolas Zarafonetis, A.c., 1910 USFC; census place: Vincennes Ward 1, Knox, Indiana; roll: T624–360; p. 5B; lines 85, 86, 92; enumeration district: 0071; FHL microfilm: 1374373. James was thirty-six in 1910, his brother Nick was thirty-four, and Mary (Vlahos) was twenty-one, all born in the Sparta region. Mary and James had five children (all accessed December 1, 2018).

95. Nicolas Zarafonets [*sic*], A.c., 1920 USFC; census place: Clinton Ward 3, Vermillion, Indiana; roll: T625–472; p. 5A; line 40; enumeration district: 99 (accessed December 1, 2018).

96. Nicholas Zarafonetis, A.c., US Passport Applications, 1795–1925; NARA, Washington, DC; roll: 1079; volume: Certificates 174876–175249, February 24, 1920–February 25, 1920 (accessed December 1, 2018).

97. "Vincennes Vignette," *Vincennes Sun-Commercial*, April 1, 1974. A "53 years ago today"–type article from the *Vincennes Sun-Commercial,* reporting that Nick is returning to Greece; "Nicolas Zarafonetis," A.c., Reports of Deaths of American Citizens Abroad, 1835–1974; NARA, Washington, DC; Record Group title: General Records of the Department of State; Record Group: RG59; series number: Publication AI 205; box number: 1850; box description: 1945–1949; Greece H–Z (accessed December 1, 2018).

98. Mary Zarafonetis and James Zarafonetis, A.c., Indiana, Death Certificates, 1899–2011; Indiana Archives and Records Administration, Indianapolis; year: 1950; roll: 03 (accessed December 6, 2018). Mary died on August 21, 1945, James on March 4, 1950.

99. "Louis Zarafonetis, a True Career Man," *Vincennes Sun-Commercial*, December 11, 1994, 9.

100. Dr. Robert Arrol interview.

101. Mike P. Poulos Jr. interview, Tuscola, June 7, 2019. The following history is from this interview unless otherwise noted.

102. Michael P. Poulos, A.c., US WW I DRC, 1917–1918; date: June 5, 1917; registration state: Illinois; registration county: Douglas; roll: 1613181 (accessed September 14, 2018). On this card Mike gives Chios as his birthplace. Elsewhere, including in the obituary cited below, his birthplace is given as Patras, which was of course the immigration port city.

103. *Find A Grave*, Michael P. "Mike" Poulos (8/25/1888–9/8/1965), 112008630 (accessed February 5, 2019, with obituary).

104. "Rites Held Saturday for Mike Poulos, 77, Retired Candy Maker," *Arcola (IL) Record-Herald,* September 16, 1965, 1.

105. Mike P. Poulos Jr. interviews, Decatur, March 20, 2013, and Tuscola, June 7, 2019.

106. Mike P. Poulos Jr. interview, June 7, 2019.

107. See "Better Than Diamonds, Sweet as Honey," an ad for the Original Robinson Candy Kitchen, in the *1911 Robinson Business Directory* (Quincy: W.H. Hoffman, 1911), 153, 157.

108. "Basil, James, confr." and "Souris, John, clr.," *1906 Peoria Directory* (Peoria: John A. White, 1906), 85, 745.

109. Heath with Elliott, *Bittersweet*, 42.

110. John Souris, A.c., 1930 USFC; census place: Alton, Madison, Illinois; roll: 540; p. 5B; line 65; enumeration district: 3; FHL microfilm: 2340275 (accessed December 5, 2018). See also "Souris, John" and "Restaurants, Campus Inn," *1933 Alton City Directory* (Alton: Huber Directory, 1933), 463, 722.

111. See, for example, the entries for "Souris, John (Marie)" and "Paul Souris" in *1928–29 Alton City Directory* (Alton: Huber Directory, 1929), 257. In the 1930 federal census for Alton, John is a merchant working in the confectionery industry. See 1930 USFC info given in n. 110 above (accessed December 3, 2018).

112. "Sweet Dreams: Heath Family's Candy Creation Gains Fame, Popularity Worldwide," *Robinson (IL) Daily News*, supp., *2005 Heath Harvest Festival*, September 28, 2005, 1.

113. Heath with Elliott, *Bittersweet*, 43.

114. Heath with Elliott, 48.

115. This quote is found on p. 2 of a printed brochure for sale in the Heath Company gift shop in Robinson. *Heath*, 2.

116. Maurice Andrew Jonquet, A.c., US WW I DRC, 1917–1918; date: September 12, 1918; registration state: Illinois; registration county: Crawford; roll: 1613185 (accessed December 4, 2018). Interestingly, he gave his occupation as "Mgr. Ice Cream Factory, L. S. Heath, Robinson."

117. Maurice Jonquet, A.c., 1900 USFC; census place: South Bend, St. Joseph, Indiana; roll: 402; p. 20B; line 57; enumeration district: 0128; FHL microfilm: 1240402 (accessed November 30, 2018). Here we learn his father was French and his mother Swiss.

118. "Jonquet, Maurice," *1912 South Bend and Mishawaka City Directory* (South Bend: Hibberd Directory, 1912), 1066.

119. Maurice Jonquet, A.c., 1920 USFC; census place: Decatur, Macon, Illinois; roll: T625_384; p. 5B; lines 51–56; enumeration district: 132 (accessed May 3, 2019). His wife's name was Laura and the children were Eugene (10), Marguerite (8), Gertrude (5), and Robert (under 1).

120. "Jonquet, Maurice," *1922 Decatur City Directory* (Decatur: Review Printing and Stationery, 1922), 291; "Jonquet, Maurice," *1944 Decatur City Directory* (Decatur: Huston-Patterson, 1944), 235. He must have retired shortly after this and died in Litchfield on August 11, 1947. He is buried in Graceland Cemetery, Decatur. See "M. A. Jonquet Dies at 62," *DH*, August 9, 1947, 3.

121. Thomas Kores, A.c., 1910 USFC; census place: Effingham Ward 2, Effingham, Illinois; roll: T624–286; p. 6A; line 10; enumeration district: 0038 (accessed October 21, 2018).

122. Thomas Kores, A.c., 1920 USFC; census place: Effingham Ward 2, Effingham, Illinois; roll; T625_366; p. 6A; lines 13–21; enumeration district 0054 (accessed November 7, 2018).

123. Thomas Kores, A.c., 1910 USFC; census place: Effingham Ward 2, Effingham, Illinois; roll: T624_286; p. 6A; lines 10–15; enumeration district: 0038; FHL microfilm: 1374299 (accessed November 7, 2018). On his World War I draft card, Georgios gives his birthplace as Greece and his occupation as candy and ice cream maker, working for T. Kores. His nearest relative he says is Panagiota (Peter) Louis Kores in Sparta, Greece. See A.c., US WW I DRC, 1917–1918; date: September 12, 1918; registration state: Illinois; registration county: Effingham; roll: 1613398 (both accessed October 14, 2018).

124. *1912 Effingham Standard Directory* (Effingham: LeCrone Press, 1912), 10.

125. Peggy Pulliam, "Bit of Illinois History: History of a Commercial Building," *Effingham Daily News*, November 26, 1973, 6.

126. "Effingham Firemen Play Annual Ball," *DH*, November 14, 1930, 14. A paragraph about Kores returning to Effingham for a visit after several years in Greece is buried in this article. See also "High Grade Candies and Ice Cream," advertisement for the Effingham Candy Kitchen, *1924–1925 City Directory of Effingham and Altamont* (Paris: Paris Directory, 1924–25), 29.

127. "O-Boy-O-Boy Santa's First Choice! Effingham Candy Kitchen, Jim Potakes, Prop.," *Effingham Republican*, December 22, 1938, 8.

128. "Sigel Resident Dies at Hospital," Potakes obituary, *MJG*, August 20, 1958, 3.

129. James Potakes, A.c., US WW I DRC, 1917–1918; date: September 12, 1918; registration state: Illinois; registration county: Fayette County; roll: 1613399 (accessed May 16, 2018).

130. Entries for James Potakes, James and Mary Seolas, and Alex Karon, A.c., 1920 USFC; census place: Vandalia Ward 2, Fayette, Illinois; roll: T 625_367; p. 9A; lines 33, 28, 28, 32; enumeration district: 94 (accessed May 15, 2018).

131. "Potakis, James," *1928 Champaign-Urbana City Directory* (Champaign-Urbana: Flanigan-Pearson, 1928), 275.

132. James Potakes, A.c., 1930 USFC; census place: Champaign, Champaign, Illinois; roll: 409; p. 7B; line 66; enumeration district: 0018; FHL microfilm: 2340144 (accessed May 15, 2018).

133. James J. Potakes, A.c., US, Headstone Applications for Military Veterans, 1925–1963; National Archives microfilm publication: M1916, 134 rolls; ARC ID: 596118; Records of the Office of the Quartermaster General; Record Group Number: 92 (accessed May 17, 2018). James served from September 9, 1942, through September 24, 1943. After he returned, he and Emma resided in Sigel, north of Effingham. He died and was buried in Sigel in 1958. Emma died in 1979. Her obituary says she "owned and operated Em's and Jim's restaurant and tavern . . . for more than 35 years," which suggests they opened the restaurant soon after James left the service. See "Emma A. Potakes," obituary, *MJG*, November 28, 1979, 5.

134. Jim Pappas, Charles Petter, and George Colovos, A.c., 1910 USFC; census place: Vandalia Ward 3, Fayette, Illinois; roll: T624_287; p. 8A; lines 45, 46, 47; enumeration district: 0074; FHL microfilm: 1374300 (accessed May 16, 2018). I could find no other information about these three.

135. James Seolas, A.c., US WW I DRC, 1917–1918; date: June 5, 1917; registration state: Illinois; registration county: Fayette; roll: 1613399. James was self-employed in a confectionery and emigrated from Corinth, Greece. James Seolas, A.c., 1920 USFC; census place: Vandalia Ward 2, Fayette, Illinois; roll: T625_367; p. 9A; line 27; enumeration district: 94 (both accessed May 21, 2018). *Find A Grave*, James G. Seolas (2/4/1889–3/8/1961), 134059334; and Mary A. Talbott Seolas (1897–1981), 134059370 (accessed April 17, 2019).

136. James and Mary moved to Effingham and then to Springfield, where by 1933 James owned a luncheonette there in the Famous Department Store. The Seolas fam-

ily later relocated to Phoenix, Arizona, and there they operated the Capitol Lunch. See "Seolas, James," *1933 City Directory of Springfield* (Springfield: H. L. Williamson, 1933), 745; "Seolas, James," *1937 Phoenix City Directory* (Phoenix: Arizona Directory, 1937), 45; and *Find A Grave*, James G. Seolas (2/4/1889–3/8/1961), 134059334; and Mary A. Talbott Seolas (1897–1981), 134059370 (accessed April 17, 2019).

137. Gust Matalas, A.c., 1940 USFC; census place: Vandalia, Fayette, Illinois; roll: T 627_801; p. 7A; line 12; enumeration district: 26–25 (accessed May 17, 2018). See also marriage of John Matalas to Penelope Kostalas, "Vandalia Greek Weds in Chicago," *DDR*, November 12, 1931, 11. The newspaper article reports that "every individual now in the United States who came from the same town in Greece from whence the Matalas family came, was present Sunday night [in Chicago]."

138. Nicholas Matalas, Constantinos Matalas, and Joannis Matalas, A.c., NYPCL; date of arrival: July 29, 1909; port of arrival: New York, New York; last place of residence: Arachova, Greece; microfilm serial: T715, 1897–1957; microfilm roll: 1308; p. 191; manifest line numbers: 20, 21, 22 (accessed May 15, 2018).

139. This was Nicholas Georgion Matalas, from Arachova, Greece, born December 23, 1885, who had a restaurant and saloon at 223 N. Dearborn St., Chicago. See A.c., US WW I DRC, 1917–1918; registration state: Illinois; registration county: Cook; roll: 1503827; draft board: 46; date: September 12, 1918 (accessed May 17, 2018).

140. Nicholas Matalas and John Matalas, A.c., 1910 USFC; census place: St. Louis Ward 5, St. Louis City, Missouri; roll: T624–813; p. 16B; lines 83, 84; enumeration district: 0077; FHL microfilm: 1374826; "Nicholas Matalas," *1910 City Directory of St. Louis* (St. Louis: Gould's, 1910), 1361.

141. Nicholas Matalas, A.c., Illinois, Deaths and Stillbirths Index, 1916–1947; place: West Frankfort, Franklin, Illinois; death date: July 12, 1917 (accessed May 15, 2018).

142. Penelope Matalas, Gust Matalas, and John Matalas, A.c., 1920 USFC; census place: West Frankfort, Franklin, Illinois; roll: T625_364; p. 6B; lines 92–95; enumeration district: 34 (accessed May 15, 2018).

143. "Matalas, Gust" and "Matalas, John," *1912 Paducah Directory* (Paducah: Caron's Directory, 1912), 328.

144. John Matalas, A.c., US WW I DRC, 1917–1918; date: June 5, 1917; registration state: Illinois; registration county: Franklin; roll: 1613402 (accessed May 15, 2018).

145. "Confectionery Changes Hands," *Mount Carmel Daily Republican-Register*, September 19, 1922, 1.

146. Summerville and Skinner, *Casey*, 163–65.

147. Summerville and Skinner, 109.

148. "Public Sale, Vandalia Confectionery," *DDR*, August 15, 1942, 9. Gust Matalas and John Matalas, A.c., 1930 USFC; census place: Vandalia, Fayette, Illinois; roll: 515; p. 6A; lines 39, 42; enumeration district: 24; FHL microfilm: 2340250. Gust Matalas, A.c., 1940 USFC; census place: Vandalia, Fayette, Illinois; roll: T627_801; p. 7A; lines 12–17; enumeration district: 26–25. "Matalas, Gust" and "Matalas, John," *1944–45 Henderson City Directory* (Henderson, NC: Southern Directory, 1944–45), 215. (All accessed May 16, 2018.) Gus Matalas was working at the Gold Seal Soda Shop and John at the Henderson Candy Kitchen. See also *Find A Grave*, Gus Nicholas Matalas

(1/19/1890–10/18/1981), 71013200; Mary (Komenos) Matalas (9/6/1903–7/7/1981), 71013332; John Nicholas Matalas (7/19/1897–11/19/1958), 65421327; Penelope N. Matalas (5/30/1874–4/19/1950), 59138175; and Penelope (Costalas) Matalas (1/5/1909–3/16/1998), 65421487 (all accessed February 27, 2019). Nearly all other records show John's year of birth as about 1891 or 1892. Only his gravestone says 1897.

149. Zissis Ginos, Apostolos Ginos, and Speros [*sic*] Ginos, A.c., 1910 USFC; census place: Hillsboro, Montgomery, Illinois; roll: T624_313; p. 12B; lines 93, 94, 95; enumeration district: 0092 (accessed October 1, 2018).

150. "Ginos Brothers Will Open Kitchen Tomorrow," *Mt. Carmel (IL) Evening Register*, December 22, 1911, 1.

151. "Ginos Brothers Will Open Kitchen Tomorrow," 1.

152. "Mt. Carmel Candy Kitchen," *Mt. Carmel Evening Register*, December 21, 1914, 5.

153. "Candy Maker Here," *Mt. Carmel Evening Register*, December 13, 1916, 1. Zissis was their brother, not their uncle.

154. "Zissis Ginos," *Mt. Carmel Evening Register*, June 21, 1917, 2.

155. A granddaughter of Spyros, Carol Askin, has an extensive ancestry page on Ancestry.com, with a number of documents and photos relating to Spyros that she has made available on the site, including his Certificate of Naturalization. See Carol Askin (CarolAskin7), "Ancestry Profile," https://www.ancestry.com/connect/Profile/011169c1-0002-0000-0000-000000000000 (accessed August 11, 2019). Future references to these materials will simply cite "Carol Askin, Ancestry Profile," and the type of document. For Zissis Dimitru [*sic*] Ginos, see A.c., US Passport Applications, 1795–1925; NARA; roll: 1498; volume: Certificates 143000–143375, February 17, 1921–February 18, 1921. His birthplace of Kazaclar is also given here.

156. A.c., Cook County, IL, Marriage Indexes, 1912–1942 (accessed January 10, 2019). They were married by Reverend A. Zeller, a "Christian minister." See "Wedding Bells," *The Christian* (Chicago Heights, IL), September 26, 1919, 1; and "Brines-Zinos [*sic*]," *Mt. Carmel Daily Republican-Register*, September 27, 1919, 4. See the family tree for Eunice Lela Brines, constructed by Carol Askin, Ancestry Profile (accessed January 11, 2019). Eunice's brother later went to work for the Ginos brothers at the Hillsboro Candy Kitchen. See "Personal," *Mount Carmel Daily Republican-Register*, July 17, 1919, 6.

157. "Red Cross Benefit. Candy Kitchen to Donate Proceeds to Red Cross Work, Wednesday," *Mt. Carmel Evening Register*, August 6, 1917, 1.

158. "Subscribers of Third Loan," *Mt. Carmel Evening Register*, April 22, 1918, 2.

159. A.c., US WW I DRC, 1917–1918; date: June 5, 1917; registration location: Montgomery County, Illinois; roll: 1614365; draft board: 20; draft cards: G. See cards for Apostolos D. Ginos (birth: 1886), Spiro Athanas Ginos (birth: 1891), and Zissis Demetrios Ginos (birth: 1875) (accessed October 3, 2018).

160. See copies of "Honorable Discharge from the United States Army," "Enlistment Record," "Registration Certificate," "Registration Card," and "Regimental Training School for Cooks, Certificate of Proficiency," at Carol Askin, Ancestry Profile (accessed January 11, 2019). See also "Three Initiated. Masons Lodge, A. F. & A. M.

Admit Three New Members," *Mount Carmel Daily Republican-Register*, May 22, 1918, 1. Spyros and others were all "leaving for training camp within a few days."

161. "Mt. Carmel Candy Kitchen," *Mount Carmel Daily Republican-Register*, December 21, 1918, 9.

162. Hadley came to Mt. Carmel in 1875 and opened a drug store. "Mt. Carmel Business Houses," *Mount Carmel Daily Republican-Register*, December 18, 1918, 2; "Everybody Meets Everybody at Hadley's Confectionery," *Mount Carmel Daily Republican-Register*, July 16, 1923, 34. See also *Mount Carmel Daily Republican-Register*, September 17, 1925, 7, for one example of his ads.

163. See James Govits, A.c., US WWII Draft Cards Young Men, 1940–1947; World War II DRC for Oklahoma, 10/16/1940–03/31/1947; Record Group: Records of the Selective Service System, 147; box: 187. See also *Find A Grave*, Gus B. Govits (2/26/1896–6/10/1981), 85411083 (accessed June 17, 2018).

164. "Ginos Brothers to Leave City," *Mount Carmel Daily Republican-Register*, February 18, 1919, 1. See also "Ginos Brothers Thank the People of Mount Carmel and Vicinity," *Mount Carmel Daily Republican-Register*, February 17, 1919, 1.

165. Advertisements, Mount Carmel Candy Kitchen, *Mount Carmel Daily Republican-Register*, March 27, 1919, 2, and March 28, 1919, 4.

166. "Take New Agency. Govits Brothers Take Agency for Pasco Photograph," and "Mt. Carmel Candy Kitchen," *Mount Carmel Daily Republican-Register*, December 3, 1920, 1, 10.

167. "Govits Brothers Now Own Store," *Mount Carmel Daily Republican-Register*, November 13, 1919, 1.

168. "Gus Govites [*sic*]," A.c., US WW I DRC, 1917–1918; date: June 5, 1917; registration state: Missouri; registration county: St. Louis (Independent City); roll: 1683743; draft board: 6 (accessed October 21, 2018). A note on this card reads "Does not intend to become citizen of USA." Gus must have intended to return to Greece.

169. Gus Govits and James Govits, A.c., 1920 USFC; census place: Mount Carmel Ward 2, Wabash, Illinois; roll: T625_410; p. 3A; lines 7, 8; enumeration district: 221 (accessed October 21, 2018).

170. "Accepts Position. Mick Govits of St. Louis with Mount Carmel Candy Kitchen," *Mount Carmel Daily Republican-Register*, February 2, 1921, 3; *Find A Grave*, Margaritis "Mike" Govitz (8/25/1896–6/14/1987), 155555519 (accessed January 10, 2019). He is buried in St. Matthew Cemetery, St. Louis.

171. "Heavy Loss Caused by Fire," *Mount Carmel Daily Republican-Register*, October 24, 1921, 1.

172. "Gus Govits," *1927 Evansville City Directory* (Evansville, IN: Bennett Directory, 1927), 228; and Gus B. Govits, A.c., 1930 USFC; census place: Evansville, Vanderburgh, Indiana; roll: 632; p. 17B; line: 89; enumeration district: 0006; FHL microfilm: 2340367 (accessed October 21, 2018).

173. "James Govits," *1926 Owensboro [KY] City Directory* (St. Louis: R. L. Polk, 1926), 88, 58.

174. "New Business House Is Open," *Mount Carmel Daily Republican-Register*, April 3, 1922, 1.

175. "Confectionery Changes Hands," *Mount Carmel Daily Republican-Register*, September 19, 1922, 1.

176. "Candies for Christmas," Candyland ad, John Matalas, prop., *Mount Carmel Daily Republican-Register*, December 24, 1923, 10; "Candyland Is Moved to Casey," *Mount Carmel Daily Republican-Register*, January 12, 1925, 5.

177. My husband's father took a teaching position in Casey in 1926, expecting it to become a boomtown.

178. *1915 Mount Vernon City Directory* (Asheville, NC: Piedmont Directory, 1915), 11.

179. *1908 Mount Vernon City Directory* (Quincy: Samson Directory, 1908), 180, 230.

180. *1910 Mount Vernon City Directory* (Mt. Vernon: W. H. Hoffman, 1910), 222.

181. "Nick Chilos," *1912 Mount Vernon City Directory* (Asheville, NC: Piedmont Directory, 1912), 115, 212; *1915 Mount Vernon City Directory*, 116, 223.

182. Tom Notaras, Frank Notaras, and John Notaras, A.c., 1920 USFC; place: Du Quoin, Perry, Illinois; roll: T625_400; p. 2B; lines 86–88; enumeration district: 81 (accessed November 14, 2018).

183. Nick Cholas, John Louis, and Alexandra Louis, A.c., 1920 USFC; place: Mount Vernon Ward 3, Jefferson, Illinois; roll: T625_376; p. 1A; lines 17, 19, 20; enumeration district: 0130 (accessed January 16, 2019); *Find A Grave*, Nick Cheolas (3/9/1860–4/3/1942), 193785680; Katherine Cheolas (6/15/1872–6/28/1940), 193785754 (accessed May 21, 2019).

184. Nick Cholas, John Louis, Alexandra Louis, and Kristefelia Zarkadas, A.c., 1920 USFC; place: Mount Vernon Ward 3, Jefferson, Illinois; roll: T625_376; p. 1A; lines 17, 19, 20; enumeration district: 0130 (accessed January 16, 2019). See also Puckett, *Mt. Vernon, Illinois*, 52; and "John Louis, Candy Kitchen Operator, Dies," *Mt. Vernon (IL) Register-News*, December 1, 1959, 2. I have been unable to determine Louis's Greek name or Nick Cheolas's hometown in Greece. See also *Find A Grave*, Christophil (Kristefelia) (Cheolas) Zarkadas (5/5/1892–3/15/1920), 171216400; and Demetrios Zarkadas (3/29/1888–7/1971), 154740352 (accessed May 23, 2019).

185. Puckett, *Mount Vernon, Illinois*, 101; *1927 Mount Vernon City Directory* (Alton: Huber Directory, 1927), 132.

186. "John Louis, 73, Candy Kitchen Operator, Dies," obituary, *Mt. Vernon Register-News*, December 1, 1959, 2; *Find A Grave*, John Louis (5/1/1881–12/1/1959), 137418922; Alexandria (Cheolas) Louis (11/17/1896–3/28/1947), 137415602 (accessed April 22, 2019).

187. *Find A Grave*, Aristides Zicos (12/7/1877–3/6/1942), 175272661 (accessed January 22, 2019).

188. Jefferson County Historical Society, *Facts and Folks*, 360.

189. "Mrs. Alexandra Zicos, 85, Dies; Funeral Monday," *Mt. Vernon Register-News*, October 31, 1927, 2; *Find A Grave*, Alexandra (Krithariatis) Zicos (9/20/1882–10/20/1967), 175272657 (accessed January 22, 2019). Mama Zicos was born in Constantinople to Greek parents.

190. Jefferson County Historical Society, *Facts and Folks*, 360.

191. "Candy Factory Burns Down at Mount Vernon," *Mount Carmel Daily Republican-Register*, January 13, 1930, 4.

192. Jefferson County Historical Society, *Facts and Folks*, 360; "Mrs. Aris Alexandra Zicos Will Be 85 Tomorrow," *Mt. Vernon Register-News*, September 19, 1967, 5; "Aris Zicos," A.c., 1930 USFC; place: Mount Vernon, Jefferson, Illinois; p. 12B; line 90; enumeration district: 0017; FHL microfilm: 2340256 (accessed January 16, 2019).

193. *Find A Grave*, George Zicos (12/22/1902–1/19/1984), 175272675 (accessed June 22, 2019).

194. Jefferson County Historical Society, *Facts and Folks*, 187; "Nick Hassakis, Mt. V. Café Owner, Dies at Age 88," *Mt. Vernon Register-News*, July 14, 1970, 1–2. He was the last of his seven siblings to die. Nicholas Chassakis [*sic*], A.c., New Orleans, Passenger Lists, 1813–1963; NARA at Washington, DC; Passenger Lists of Vessels Arriving at New Orleans, Louisiana, 1903–1945; NAI number: 4492741; Record Group title: Records of the Immigration and Naturalization Service; Record Group number: 85; arrival date: October 26, 1907 (accessed October 14, 2018).

195. "Spiro D. Hassakis Is Dead at 75," *Mt. Vernon Register-News*, November 10, 1969, 1. See also *Find A Grave*, Nicholas Demetrius Hassakis (8/17/1881–7/14/1970), 161997937; John Demetrius Hassakis (1892–1951), 161997038; Spiro Hassakis (12/13/1895–11/9/1969), 32960822; and Dennis V. Hassakis (12/17/1886–5/6/1974), 161607945 (all accessed May 14, 2019).

196. Jefferson County Historical Society, *Facts and Folks*, 187.

197. "Nick Hassakis, Mt. V. Café Owner, Dies at Age 88," 1–2.

198. "Nick Hassakis, Mt. V. Café Owner, Dies at Age 88," 2.

199. *Mt. Vernon Register-News*, May 13, 1920, 7.

200. "Deaths: Denny Hassakis, Mt. Vernon," *Mt. Vernon Register-News*, May 7, 1974, 2.

201. "John Hassakis, Mt. V. Restaurant Owner, Is Dead," *Mt. Vernon Register-News*, February 22, 1951, 1.

202. "Spiro D. Hassakis Is Dead at 75," 1–2.

203. "Nick Hassakis, Mt. V. Café Owner, Dies at Age 88," 1–2.

204. Athanasias [*sic*] Resinas [*sic*], A.c., NYPCL; year: 1912; arrival: New York, New York; microfilm serial: T715, 1897–1957; microfilm roll: 1904; p. 76; line 14 (accessed November 12, 2018).

205. Athanasios P. Retzinas [*sic*], A.c., US WW I DRC, 1917–1918; date: September 12, 1918; registration state: Illinois; registration county: Clay; roll: 1504090 (accessed March 21, 2014).

206. Shelby County Historical and Genealogical Society, *Shelbyville Past and Present*, 119–21; George Chousouras [*sic*—Tsourunis] and Thomas Reginas [*sic*], A.c., 1920 USFC; census place: Shelbyville, Shelby, Illinois; roll: T625–408; p. 1B; lines 76, 77; enumeration district: 216 (accessed November 12, 2018).

207. William D. Rezinas (Tom's son) phone interview, January 17, 2019, and in person, June 6, 2019.

208. "Tom Rezinas, Lakewood, Dies Sunday," *Shelbyville Daily Union*, August 18, 1980, 4.

209. "Greek Shelbyville Child Is Baptized," *DH*, July 22, 1929, 8.

210. William D. Rezinas interviews.

211. Shelby County Historical and Genealogical Society, *Shelbyville Past and Present*, 120–21.

212. "Twenty-Fourth Annual Shelbyville Chautauqua," *Shelbyville Daily Union*, July 18, 1924, 2. See also "Ku Klux Klan Day," *Shelbyville Daily Union*, August 11, 1924, 1.

213. *Shelbyville Daily Union*, June 5, 1924, 5, and June 21, 1924, 4.

214. William D. Rezinas interviews.

215. "Tom Rezinas, Lakewood, Dies Sunday," 4.

216. Jean Attebery, private correspondence, July 12, 2013.

217. I found very little about Bill Pappas. He was born in Greece in 1894 and died in 1976. His wife was Becky (Beck) Pappas, born in Fairfield in 1901 and died in 1968. Bill had a store in Sullivan for a brief time in the early 1920s before going to Fairfield. In 1930 he was a clerk in a confectionery, so it is not clear when he opened his own store. He closed his confectionery and restaurant with a liquidation sale in June 1950. See William Pappas, A.c., 1920 USFC; census place: Sullivan, Moultrie, Illinois; roll: T625_397; p. 8B; enumeration district: 179; and William Pappas, A.c., 1930 USFC; census place: Fairfield, Wayne, Illinois; roll: 567; p. 3A; enumeration district: 12 (both accessed July 22, 2018). *Find A Grave*, William Pappas (1894–1976), 149589161; and William Pappas, A.c., 1940 USFC; census place: Fairfield, Wayne; Illinois; roll: m-t0627-00903; p. 4A; line 17; enumeration district: 96–7 (both accessed February 5, 2019). Also "Voluntary-Liquidation. Public Auction Sale, Wednesday, June 21," *Mt. Vernon Register-News*, June 16, 1950, 4.

218. See *Find A Grave*, Constantinos George "Gus" Theofanopoulos (1892–8/28/1949), 152416501; and Helen (Chrysovergis) Theofanopoulos (1900–4/3/1973), 152416751 (accessed February 8, 2019). Their hometowns in Greece are on their gravestones.

219. Judith Puckett, "Sweet Memories of the Greek," *Wayne County Press* (Fairfield, IL), June 27, 2013, section 2, p. 1.

220. Puckett, 1.

221. Puckett, 1.

222. Puckett, 1, 4.

223. Puckett, 4.

224. Puckett, 4.

225. Puckett, 4; "Fairfield Man Killed in Effingham Crash," *DDR*, August 29, 1949, 15.

226. Sadly, Jack Frank has passed away since our interview. See *Find A Grave*, Jack E. Frank (3/22/1924–1/9/2018), 186539576; and Eugenia C. *Theofanopoulos* Frank (7/3/1928–2/21/2001), 41564035 (both accessed February 5, 2019).

227. Peter Granupulos and Tom Granupulos, A.c., 1930 USFC; census place: Altamont, Effingham, Illinois; roll: 513; p. 3A; lines 19, 21; enumeration district: 0018; FHL microfilm: 2340248. Peter and Tom Granupulos were in St. Louis before moving to Altamont. See Peter Granupulos and Tom Granupulos, A.c., 1920 USFC; census place: St. Louis Ward 5; St. Louis (Independent City), Missouri; roll: T625_949; p.

1A; lines 44, 46; enumeration district: 98 (all accessed November 24, 2018). Tom was about seven years older than Peter and came to America in 1905. Peter immigrated in 1907, and Tom's wife came over in 1910. Peter's wife, Ina (or Iva), was a non-Greek, born in Illinois. Both were independent businessmen: Peter was a confectioner and Tom had a restaurant. I know nothing more about them or their businesses.

228. Jack Frank phone interview.

229. "Personals. Mrs. Sam Cheorvas," *MJG*, August 2, 1939, 6.

230. Sam W. Cheorvas, A.c., US WW II DRC, 1942, NARA at St. Louis, MO; World War I Draft Registration (Fourth Registration), for the State of Illinois; Record Group title: Records of the Selective Service System, 1926–1975; Record Group number: 147; series number: M2097 (accessed June 17, 2018). The place of birth is clearly written as either Frousena, or the Ancestry.com transcribers have Froiesena, but I cannot find this place under either spelling in Greece today. There is the town of Frousiouna in the regional unit of Argolis in the Peloponnese, so this may be where Sam came from.

231. "Former Altamont Girl Has Greek Ceremony," *DDR*, November 1, 1936, 20; *1941 Richmond City Directory* (Detroit: Polk, 1941), 80; entries for James Chagares (Chagaris), Nick Chagares, Pete Chagares, and William Chagares, A.c., 1940 USFC; census place: Richmond, Wayne, Indiana; roll: m-t0627-01109; p. 6B; lines 42, 43, 44, 46; enumeration district: 89–35 (accessed June 18, 2018).

232. Flora Kiwanis Club and Clay County Regulators, *Prairie Echo*, 147; Sam Cheorvas, A.c., 1930 USFC; census place: Flora, Clay, Illinois; roll: 411; p. 3B; line 71; enumeration district: 06; FHL microfilm: 2340146 (accessed March 21, 1914).

233. "Public Auction of Savoy Café, Flora, ILL.," *Mt. Vernon Register-News,* July 16, 1948, 7.

234. "Central Illinois Deaths: Cheorvas," *DDR*, July 3, 1955, 24; "Central Illinois Deaths: Cheorvas," *DDR*, May 29, 1956, 13.

235. Nokomis Centennial Committee, *1956 Centennial History*, 69.

236. "Married. Miss Mary Viola . . . and Jeno Collebrusco," *DDR*, April 20, 1926, 4.

237. "Candy Kitchen Closes. Teens Lament Loss of Hangout," *DH*, January 18, 1967, 9.

238. George Eliopoulos, A.c., US WW I DRC, 1917–1918; date: June 2, 1917; registration state: Indiana; registration county: Vermillion; roll: 1653180; draft card: E (accessed March 12, 2014). He was born June 24, 1890.

239. George Kouchiveris, A.c., US WW I DRC, 1917–1918; date: June 5, 1917; registration state: Indiana; registration county: Vermillion; roll: 1653180; draft card: K (accessed March 12, 2014). He was born May 25, 1892.

240. "Marriages, George Eliopoulos/Lena Sanders," A.c., Indiana, Marriages, 1810–2001; date: March 14, 1919; place: Vigo County, Indiana, County Clerk's Office; book 50; p. 70; FHL film no: 001378242 (accessed March 12, 2014).

241. Philipos Demitrious Kouchiveris, A.c., US WW I DRC, 1917–1918; date: June 5, 1917; registration state: Illinois; registration county: Cook; roll: 1503988; draft board: 78 (accessed March 12, 2014).

242. "George and Lena Ellis," *1924 Aurora City Directory* (Rockford, IL: McCoy Directory, 1924), 173.

243. "George and Lena Ellis," *1931 Aurora City Directory* (Rockford, IL: McCoy Directory, 1931), 94; "George and Lena Ellis," *1932 Aurora City Directory* (Aurora, IL: Finch and McCullouch, 1932), 89. George Ellis, A.c., 1930 USFC; census place: Aurora, Kane, Illinois; roll: 524: p. 2A; line 29; enumeration district: 23; FHL microfilm: 2340259 (all accessed October 28, 2018).

244. Postcard, 1912, Mary Emerson private collection.

245. Louis Apostle and Peter Apostle, A.c., 1910 USFC; census place: Taylorville Ward 4, Christian, Illinois; roll: T624_235; p. 12B; line 56, 57; enumeration district: 0032; FHL microfilm: 1374248 (accessed October 26, 2018).

246. "Louis Apostel [*sic*]" and "Peter Apostel [*sic*]," *1916–17 Marquette City, MI and County Directory* (Detroit, MI: R. L. Polk, 1916), 52.

247. "Confectioners, Peter and Frank Apostle," *1912 Taylorville Directory* (Bloomington: Charles M. Samson Publishing, 1912), 105.

248. *1912 Taylorville Directory*, Apostle Bros., advertisement at bottom of p. 5.

249. "Decatur Greeks Buy Store in Taylorville," *DH*, August 15, 1914, 6; "Louis Apostle," "Peter Apostle," "James Apostle," and "John Apostle," *1920 Marquette City, MI and County Directory* (Detroit: R. L. Polk, 1920), 55.

250. Gust Moucoulis, A.c., 1910 USFC; census place: Stonington, Christian, Illinois; roll: T624_235; p. 7B; line 100; enumeration district: 0027; FHL microfilm: 1374248 (accessed November 21, 2018).

251. "Moucoulis, Gust," *1910 Decatur City Directory* (Decatur: Review Printing and Publishing, 1910), 532, 682.

252. "Royal Buys New Fountain: Will Have Finest Place in This Part of State," *Taylorville (IL) Daily Breeze*, April 13, 1915, 8.

253. "Royal Buys New Fountain: Will Have Finest Place in This Part of State," 8.

254. "New Royal Fountain Arrives," *Taylorville Daily Breeze*, June 10, 1915, 2.

255. Royal Confectionery advertisement, 1919.

256. "Royal Confectionery," *1926 Taylorville City Directory* (St. Louis: R. L. Polk, 1926), 177. See also "Martin, F. M., Jr.," *1928 Taylorville City Directory* (St. Louis: R. L. Polk, 1928), 245.

257. "Thomas G. Orfanos," *1928 Hammond, Indiana City Directory* (Chicago: R. L. Polk, 1928), 358.

258. "George Moucoulis," "John Moucoulis," and "Gust Moucoulis," *1926 Taylorville City Directory*, 159; *1929 Taylorville City Directory* (St. Louis: R. L. Polk, 1929), 152. In the 1929 directory (p. 130) George and Gust are confectioners along with George Kehias.

259. "Boys Confectionery," *Decatur (IL) Evening Herald*, February 1, 1928, 9; "Taylorville Store Leased by Pana Man," *DH*, January 31, 1928, 13.

260. "Gust Moucoulis" and "George Moucoulis," *1934 Rockford City Directory* (Rockford: McCoy Directory, 1934), 439.

261. See the photo of George's Candy Shop in "Inside George's," Cooper, Lasswell, and Traynor, *Christian County Reunion*, 125; and the ad, "George's Candy Shop Phil Kouchiveris, Prop., Delicious Home Made Candies, Confections, Ice Cream and a

Superb Fountain Service, 100 S. Main," in *1932 Taylorville City Directory* (St. Louis: R. L. Polk, 1932), 87.

262. Taylorville Facebook site, Dan Farrimond, IN, recollections regarding Circa 1965: Square Favorites.

263. Phillip Kouchiveris, A.c., Reports of Deaths of American Citizens Abroad, 1835–1974; NAI number: 613857; Record Group title: General Records of the Department of State; Record Group number: 59, entry 5166; series number: publication A1 5168; box number: 71; box description: 1969 JA-KT. George Kouchiveris, A.c. Reports of Deaths of American Citizens Abroad, 1835–1974; NAI number: 613857; Record Group title: General Records of the Department of State; Record Group number: 59; series number: publication A1 5166; box number: 131; box description: 1974 KL–LZ. (Both accessed November 15, 2018.) Both Philip and George died in Peristeri, an Athens suburb. George became a naturalized US citizen in 1926 but Phil not until 1967. In 1969 the brothers still had a sister living in Chicago and four sisters and a brother in Greece.

264. From census and ship records, Zissis was the first Ginos brother to immigrate, in 1903, and the others followed, Nicholas in 1906, Spyros in 1908, and Paul in 1910. On the 1908 manifest list, Spyros named his brother Zissis as his contact in St. Louis at 2101 Market Street. See Spyros Ginos, A.c., NYPCL; year: 1908; arrival: New York, New York; microfilm serial: 1897–1957; microfilm roll: 1110; p. 197; line 16 (accessed November 12, 2018). Ancestry.com has transcribed the name as "Spefrof Gkinos."

265. Apostolos D. Ginos, A.c., US WW I DRC, 1917–1918; date: June 6, 1917; registration state: Illinois; registration county: Montgomery; roll: 1614365; draft board: 20; A.c., 1920 USFC; census place: Hillsboro, Montgomery, Illinois; roll: T625_394; p. 18A; line 45; enumeration district: 95 (both accessed November 12, 2018). Thomas's birth year comes from "Killed in Haste to Get Jefferson Car," *St. Louis Globe Democrat,* March 3, 1913, 1.

266. Zissos Ginos, Spyros Ginos, and Apostolos Ginos, A.c., 1910 USFC; census place: Hillsboro, Montgomery, Illinois; roll: T624_313; p. 12B; lines 93, 94, 95; enumeration district: 0092; FHL microfilm: 1374326 (accessed November 12, 2018).

267. "Killed in Haste to Get Jefferson Car," 1.

268. *1926 Hillsboro City Directory* (St. Louis: R. L. Polk, 1926), 64.

269. Zissis Dimitru Ginos, A.c., US Passport Applications, 1795–1925; NARA, Washington, DC; roll: 1498; volume: Certificates 143000–143375, February 17, 1921–February 18, 1921; and A.c., NYPCL; date: December 1, 1921; arrival: New York, New York; microfilm serial: T715, 1897–1957; microfilm roll: 3057; p. 27; lines 17, 18. Zissis was forty-five and Nikoletta Ginou [*sic*] twenty. (All accessed November 19, 2018.)

270. Paul Ginos (42), Bessie Ginos (30), George Ginos (5), Thomas Ginos (3), A.c., 1930 USFC; census place: Brooklyn, Kings, New York; roll: 1508; p. 4B; line 71; enumeration district: 1113; FHL microfilm: 2341243. It seems Paul married Bessie Bakoponlos of Manhattan, New York City, in April 1923, came back to Hillsboro, and then returned to New York by 1930. Paul is buried, without Bessie or James, in the Hillsboro Oak Grove cemetery with other Ginos family members. See Paul Ginos and Bessie Bakoponlos, April 9, 1923, A.c., New York, NY, Marriage License Indexes, 1907–2018; New York City Municipal Archives; New York, NY; borough: Manhattan;

volume: 4; and "Ginos, Paul D. (Bessie; Ginos Bros)," *1926 Hillsboro City Directory*, 64; and *Find A Grave*, Paul D. Ginos (1887–1932), 47521997. (All accessed April 22, 2019.)

271. "Zissis Ginos," *1930 Hillsboro City Directory* (St. Louis: R. L. Polk, 1930), 59. Nick and William are still listed as confectioners. For Zissis, his family, and his death, see Zissis Dimitrios Ginos, A.c., Report of Deaths of American Citizens Abroad, 1835—1974; NARA at College Park, MD; NAI number: 302021; Record Group title: General Records of the Department of State; Record Group: 59; series number: publication A1 205; box number: 1745; box description: 1930–1939 Greece D-T (accessed November 18, 2018).

272. Bliss, *Hillsboro*, 71.

273. *Find A Grave*, Spiro Athanas "William" Ginos Sr. (9/25/1891–1/13/1963), 115960210 (accessed April 22, 2019, with a brief obituary for William, his wife Eunice [Brines], and sons William Jr. and George Edwin). I have no information as to when or where Nicholas died.

274. Klaus and the Macoupin County Historical Society, *Story of Macoupin County*, 23.

275. Klaus and the Macoupin County Historical Society, 23.

276. Klaus and the Macoupin County Historical Society, 23.

277. Debra Landis, "Benld's Russian Orthodox Cathedral to Become Monastery," *Illinois State Journal-Register*, January 25, 2010, 3.

278. Landis, 3.

279. Gene Markos interview. Markos died in February 2019.

280. Peter Markos, A.c., US WW I DRC, 1917–1918; date: September 12, 1918; registration state: Illinois; registration county: Macoupin; roll: 1614323; draft board: 1 (accessed November 12, 2018).

281. Peter Markos, A.c., 1920 USFC; census place: Virden Ward 4, Macoupin, Illinois; roll: T625_388; p. 6B; line 52; enumeration district: 80 (accessed November 12, 2018).

282. George Markos, A.c., 1920 USFC; census place: Virden Ward 4, Macoupin, Illinois; roll: T625_388; p. 2A; line 17; enumeration district: 80; and George Markos, A.c., US WW I DRC, 1917–1918; date: June 5, 1918; registration state: Illinois; registration county: Macoupin; roll: 1614323; draft card: M; draft board: 1 (both accessed December 9, 2018).

283. Nick Adam interview.

284. Pete gave his birthplace for the draft registration in 1942, and Nick later confirmed it for me. See Pete N. Adam, A.c., US WW II DRC, 1942; NARA at St. Louis, MO; WW II Draft Registration Cards (Fourth Registration), for the State of Illinois; Record Group title: Records of the Selective Service System, 1926–1975; Record Group number: 147; series number: M2097 (accessed June 21, 2019).

285. Many of the details about Pete Adam's life and the Ariston restaurant were obtained through these sources: Nick Adam interview; Nick Adam and Demi Adam interview; and P. Adam, "My Life." See also Litchfield Sesquicentennial Committee, "Ariston," 144.

286. P. Adam, "My Life."

287. Pete Adam and Tom Bouclamon, A.c., 1920 USFC; census place: Benld, Macoupin, Illinois; roll: T625_388; p. 7A; lines 41, 42; enumeration district: 0042 (accessed December 11, 2018).

288. Nick Adam interview; Nick Adam and Demi Adam interview; P. Adam, "My Life."

289. Chris N. Chrisakis, A.c., US WW II DRC, 1942; NARA at St. Louis, MO; WW II Draft Cards (Fourth Registration), for the State of Illinois; Record Group title: Records of the Selective Service System, 1926–1975; Record Group number: 147; NAI number: 623284; series number: M2097. In 1942 Chris gave his birth date as December 24, 1894. Chris registered for World War I in 1917 at the same time as his brother John, both living in Livingston and working as coal miners. Here he gave his birthdate as February 1894 and birthplace as Andronianous. Chris Chrisagis and John Chrisagis, A.c., US WW I DRC, 1917–1918; date: June 5, 1917; registration state: Illinois; registration county: Madison County, no. 1, Illinois; FHL microfilm: 1614325 (all accessed December 13, 2018). The family name appears differently depending on the record, sometimes Chrisakis, sometimes Chrisagis.

290. Panas Adam, and Chris Chrisakis, A.c., 1930 USFC; census place: Carlinville, Macoupin, Illinois; p. 8B; lines 83, 84; enumeration district: 0021; FHL microfilm: 2340274 (accessed December 13, 2018).

291. Nick Adam interview; Nick Adam and Demi Adam interview; P. Adam, "My Life."

292. Tom Cokinos, A.c., 1930 USFC; census place: Litchfield, Montgomery, Illinois; roll: 545; p. 3B; line 65; enumeration district: 0039; FHL microfilm: 2340280 (accessed December 13, 2018).

293. *Find A Grave*, Emily Adam (10/17/1909–5/8/1995), 83978945; Panos N. "Pete" Adam (10/9/1890–12/27/1976), 83978987 (accessed July 22, 2019).

294. Mary (Galer) Herschelman, "New Owners Take Over Ariston Café," *Litchfield (IL) Journal*-News, July 1, 2018, https://www.thejournal-news.net/stories/new-owners-take-over-ariston-cafe,5868 (accessed July 30, 2018).

295. Tom Cokinos, A.c., 1940 USFC; census place: Litchfield, Montgomery, Illinois; roll: m-t0627-00860; p. 13B; line 66; enumeration district: 68–35 (accessed December 13, 2018). See also "Café Owners Sued," *DH*, January 4, 1941, 8; and "Macoupin Liquor Commission Grants 13 Tavern Permits," *Alton Evening Telegraph*, June 28, 1954, 20.

296. "Cokinos," obituary for Tom's wife, Frieda (Hensley) Cokinos, *DHR*, December 18, 1985, 9.

297. *1907 Litchfield City Directory* (Quincy: Samson Directory, 1907), 121; and *1911 Litchfield City Directory* (Bloomington: Samson Directory, 1911), 120; "New Fountain," *DH*, January 18, 1912, 5.

298. *Find A Grave*, John Cokinos (1877–1941), 8194149; Steve Cokinos (1881–1953), 8194146 (both accessed February 5, 2019).

299. "John Cokinos," *Edwardsville Intelligencer*, February 1, 1941, 2.

300. His gravestone just says 1880, but other records give different dates. On the Illinois record of deaths, for example, his birthdate is given as May 21, 1884. See Gus Skeadas, A.c., Illinois, Deaths and Stillbirths Index, 1916–1947 (accessed December 12, 2018).

301. Gus Skeadas, A.c., 1930 USFC; census place: Litchfield, Montgomery, Illinois; p. 9A; line 75; enumeration district: 0039; FHL microfilm: 2340280 (accessed December 12, 2018).

302. *Find A Grave*, Anna (Vapos) Skeadas (7/4/1892–9/10/1964), 58336912; Konstantinos J. Skeadas (1880–11/6/1939), 58336915 (accessed February 5, 2019).

303. "Gus Skeadas Funeral Set for Thursday," *Litchfield News Herald*, November 1, 1939, 1, 6; *Find A Grave*, Konstantinos J. Skeadas (1880–1939), 46964942 (accessed November 9, 2019).

304. *Find A Grave*, James Skeadas (8/1/1919–12/12/2001), 58336914 (accessed February 5, 2019).

305. "Chris Chrisakis," *1940 Mattoon City Directory* (Parsons, KS: Millin-Kille Publishers, 1940), 132.

306. *Find A Grave*, Chris N. Chrisakis (1894–1966), 175419483 (accessed November 12, 2018).

307. "Gus Chrisagis," *1960 Champaign City Directory* (St. Louis: R. L. Polk, 1960), 87.

308. "Gus Chrisagis," obituary, *MJG*, February 2, 2005, 12.

CONCLUSION

1. Spickard, "Immigration and Race," 2.

2. For a provocative consideration of diasporas as "nonnormative" within a global discourse, see Clifford, "'Diasporas,' Further Inflections."

3. Scourby, "Ethnicity at the Crossroads," 125.

4. Anagnostou, *Contours of White Ethnicity*, 10.

5. Anagnostou, 11.

6. Anagnostou, 14.

7. Scourby, "Ethnicity at the Crossroads," 126.

8. Scourby, 127. See also Scourby, "Three Generations of Greek Americans."

9. Donovan, *Fizz*, 169.

10. Donovan, 169.

11. Orvell, *Death and Life of Main Street*, ix.

12. Jacobs, *Death and Life of Great American Cities*, 45–47.

13. Go to the history page at www.anthony-thomas.com (accessed July 15, 2019). See also The Church, *Ohio Greek Orthodox Church*. See p. 11 for Zanetos.

14. Shupert-Arick, *Lincoln Highway across Indiana*, 55. Their website is www.olympia candykitchen.com (accessed July 1, 2019).

15. See www.canelakescandies.com and www.greatlakescandy.com (accessed July 5, 2019). Pamela Matson e-mail.

16. Jim Froemming e-mail. Visit www.zaharakos.com and www.reginascandies .net (accessed August 15, 2019).

17. Visit www.crowncandykitchen.net (accessed August 15, 2019).

18. Patsovos and Janides, "Interchurch Marriages," 216.

19. Patsovos and Janides, 217.

20. Counelis, "Greek Orthodox Church Statistics," 131–32.

21. Kehayes, "Important Challenge."

BIBLIOGRAPHY

CIVIL RECORDS

Information from the following civil records was researched for the years 1880–1930, and later when warranted. In each case, many individual yearly or daily issues or records were missing.

CENSUS RECORDS (TOWNS)

Alexander, IL
Allegheny, PA
Altamont, IL
Alton, IL
Aurora, IL
Benld, IL
Bloomington, IL
Bloomington, IN
Brooklyn, NY
Burlington, IA
Cahokia, IL
Cairo, IL
Camargo, IL
Carlinville, IL
Casey, IL
Cedar Rapids, IA
Centralia, IL
Champaign, IL
Charleston, IL

Chicago, IL
Clinton, IN
Decatur, IL
Delaware, OH
Du Quoin, IL
East St. Louis, IL
Effingham, IL
Evansville, IN
Fairfield, IL
Flora, IL
Frankfort, IL
Greenville, IL
Hillsboro, IL
Iowa State Census Collection (collected between federal censuses—1905, 1915, 1925)
Jacksonville, IL
Kalamazoo, MI
Keokuk, IA
Litchfield, IL
Marquette, MI
Marshall, IL
Mount Vernon, IL
Mt. Carmel, IL
Nokomis, IL
Pana, IL
Paris, IL
Philadelphia, PA
Pittsburgh, PA
Richmond, IN
Schoolcraft, MI
Shelbyville, IL
South Bend, IN
Springfield, IL
Staunton, IL
St. Louis, MO
Stonington, IL
Sullivan, IL
Taylorville, IL
Terre Haute, IN
Tuscola, IL
Urbana, IL
Vandalia, IL
Vincennes, IN
Virden, IL

CITY DIRECTORIES (TOWNS)

Alton, IL
Atlanta, GA
Aurora, IL
Bloomington, IL
Bloomington, IN
Burlington, IA
Cairo, IL
Cedar Rapids City, IA
Champaign-Urbana, IL
Charleston, IL
Danville, IL
Decatur, IL
East St. Louis, IL
Effingham, IL
Effingham and Altamont, IL
Evansville, IN
Hammond, IN
Henderson, NC
Hillsboro, IL
Lawrence, KS
Lawrence and Douglas County, KS
Litchfield, IL
Marquette City and County, MI
Mattoon, IL
Mount Vernon, IL
Mt. Carmel, IL
New Haven, CT
Owensboro, KY
Paducah, KY
Pana, IL
Peoria, IL
Philadelphia, PA
Phoenix, AZ
Richmond, IN
Robinson, IL
Rockford, IL
South Bend and Mishawaka City, IN
Springfield, IL
Springfield, MO
St. Louis, MO
Taylorville, IL
Terre Haute, IN
Vincennes, IN

HIGH SCHOOL YEARBOOKS (ILLINOIS TOWNS)

Decanois, Decatur High School
The *Echo* and the *Signet*, Effingham High School
Newton Community High School
The *Old Nokomis*, Nokomis Township High School

MISCELLANEOUS ARCHIVAL, INTERNET, AND OTHER RECORDS

Ancestry.com
- Cook County, IL, Marriage Indexes, 1871–1920, Illinois Department of Public Records, Division of Vital Records, Springfield
- Cook County, IL, Marriage Indexes, 1912–1942
- Illinois, Deaths and Stillbirths Index, 1916–1947
- Illinois, Federal Naturalization Records, 1856–1991
- Indiana, Death Certificates, 1899–2011
- Indiana, Marriages, 1810–2001
- Michigan, Death Records, 1867–1952
- New Orleans, Passenger Lists, 1813–1963
- New York, NY, Marriage License Indexes, 1907–2018
- New York, Passenger and Crew Lists (including Castle Garden and Ellis Island), 1820–1957
- Reports of Deaths of American Citizens Abroad, 1835–1974
- United States, Army Transport Service, Passenger Lists, 1910–1939
- United States, Federal Census Records, 1870, 1880, 1900, 1910, 1920, 1930, 1940
- United States, Headstone Applications for Military Veterans, 1925–1963
- United States Naturalization Record Indexes, 1791–1992
- United States Passport Applications, 1795–1925
- United States, Social Security Applications and Claims Index, 1936–2007
- United States, Social Security Death Index, 1935–2014
- United States, World War I Draft Registration Cards, 1917–1918
- United States World War II Draft Cards Young Men, 1940–1947 (National Archives at St. Louis, Missouri)
- United States, World War II Draft Registration Cards, 1942
- WWI, WWII, and Korean War Casualty Listings

Effingham, IL, telephone directories, 1930s
FamilySearch.com
- Soundex Index to Naturalization Petitions for the United States District and Circuit Courts, Northern District of Illinois and Immigration and Naturalization Service

FindAGrave.com
Fold3.com
Hull House Bulletin

Hull House Yearbook
Illinois, County Marriage Records, 1800–1940
Kankakee County, IL, Marriage Index, 1889–1962, Kankakee County Clerk, Kankakee
Michigan, Deaths and Burials Index, 1867–1995
Newspapers.com
New York, NY, Record of Aliens Held for Special Inquiry
Passenger and Crew Lists of Vessels Arriving at New York, NY, 1897–1957
Passenger Lists of Vessels Arriving at New York, NY, 1820–1897
People of the State of Illinois vs. Bensen et al., No. 2792, Douglas County (IL), Circuit Court, p. 48
Samson Raphaelson Transcriptions: Family Tape, 1969–1971, 243, in Samson Raphaelson Papers, RS 26/20/38, University of Illinois Archives, Champaign-Urbana.
Supplemental Manifests of Alien Passengers and Crew Members Who Arrived on Vessels at New York, NY, Who Were Inspected for Admission, and Related Index, compiled 1887–1952
United States, National Archives and Records Administration, General Records of the Department of State
United States, National Archives and Records Administration, Passport Applications

NEWSPAPERS AND MAGAZINES

The Newberry Library in Chicago has an extensive online collection of foreign language newspapers, including the Greek newspapers *Greek News*, *Greek Press*, *Greek Star*, *Loxias*, and the *Saloniki-Greek Press*. All citations for these newspapers, plus the *Illinois Staats-Zeitung*, can be found at Newberry Library, Chicago, Foreign Language Press Survey, https://flps.newberry.org/#filters/group/greek?page=1. Accessed July 10, 2019. All references to these newspapers are noted below with "NLC."

Alton (IL) Evening Telegraph
American Hellenic World
Arcola (IL) Record-Herald
Boston Daily Globe
Brazil (IN) Daily Times
Champaign (IL) Daily News
Champaign-Urbana Courier
Champaign-Urbana News-Gazette
Charleston (IL) Journal-Gazette
Charleston Times-Courier
Chicago Daily Tribune
Chicago Tribune
Chicago Tribune, Daily Southtown
The Christian (Chicago Heights)

Coles County (IL) Daily Times-Courier
Daily Illini (student paper of the University of Illinois, Champaign-Urbana)
Dayton (OH) Journal
Decatur (IL) Daily Review
Decatur Evening Herald
Decatur Herald
Decatur Herald and Review
Des Moines Register
Edwardsville (IL) Intelligencer
Effingham (IL) Daily News
Effingham Republican
Eldorado (IL) Daily Journal
The Fraternalist (St. Joseph, MO) (originally *Missouri Valley Independent*)
Freeport (IL) Journal-Standard
Greek News (NLC)
Greek Press (NLC)
Greek Star (NLC)
Greenup (IL) Jubilee
Harrisburg (IL) Daily Register
Hellenic Heritage
Herrin (IL) Semi-Weekly Herald
Hoopeston (IL) Chronicle
Illinois Staats-Zeitung (NLC)
Illinois State Journal (Springfield)
Illinois State Journal-Register (Springfield)
Kansas City Times
Keokuk (IA) Daily Gate City
Kinmundy (IL) Express
Lawrence (KS) Daily Journal-World
Litchfield (IL) Journal-News
Litchfield News Herald
Los Angeles Times
Loxias (NLC)
Marion (IL) Daily Republican
Mattoon (IL) Daily-Journal-Gazette and Commercial Star
Mattoon Journal Gazette
McAllen (TX) Monitor
Moline (IL) Dispatch
Mount Carmel (IL) Daily Republican-Register
Mt. Carmel Evening Register
Mt. Vernon (IL) Register-News
National Herald
Newton (IL) Press
New York Times

Omaha Mediator
Omaha World-Herald
Pana (IL) Daily Palladium
Pana News-Palladium
The Pantagraph (Bloomington, IL)
Quad-City Times (Davenport, IA)
Rantoul (IL) Press and Chanute Field News
Robinson (IL) Daily News
Saloniki-Greek Press (NLC)
Shelbyville (IL) Daily Union
St. Louis Globe-Democrat
St. Louis Post-Dispatch
St. Louis Star
St. Louis Star and Times
Sullivan (IL) News-Progress
Taylorville (IL) Daily Breeze
Terre Haute (IN) Tribune
Tuscola (IL) Journal
Tuscola Review
Urbana (IL) Daily Courier
Villa Grove (IL) News
Vincennes (IN) Sun-Commercial
Wayne County Press (Fairfield, IL)

INTERVIEWS

All interviews were with me and were conducted in person, via e-mail, in private correspondence, or by telephone.

Nick Adam, Ariston restaurant, Litchfield, IL, August 8, 2013.
Nick Adam and Demi Adam, at home and at the Ariston restaurant, Litchfield, IL, June 25, 2019.
Dr. Robert Arrol, Arcola, IL, March 18, 2013.
Jean Attebery, private correspondence, July 12, 2013.
Dean Bartges, Charleston, IL, August 22, 2013.
Phyllis Bartges Bayles, Charleston, IL, August 5, 2013.
Bree Anne Buckley, e-mail, January 30, 2018.
Laura Catherwood, email, October 28, 30, 2019.
Constance Constant, e-mail, June 17, 2019.
George Coutrakon, e-mail, July 3, 2019.
Margaret Leonard Flesor, 2002. A copy of this interview with my mother about her experiences at Hull House as a young girl can be found in Special Collections, box 3, folder 30, "Margaret Leonard Flesor," Hull House Oral History Collection, 1974–2002, University of Illinois, Chicago.
Paul G. Flesor, July 17, 1978. Family copy of this interview. Original conducted as part of Danville Junior College Oral History Project.

Jim Flessor, e-mail, September 23, 2019.
Lee Flessor, Lansing, IL, August 3, 2010.
Jack Frank, phone interview, February 27, 2013.
Jim Froemming, e-mail, December 30, 2018.
Peter Haikalis, phone interview, June 10, 2013.
Georgia Kehias Hamilton, e-mail, July 5, 2019, and phone interviews, January 29, 2015, and June 24, 2019.

Paul Jacobs, Flesor's Candy Kitchen, Tuscola, IL, December 4, 2013.
Christine Katris Kockler, Lansing, IL, August 3, 2010.
Diana Vriner Krandel, Champaign, IL, November 4, 2013, and June 5, 2019.
Peter Lessaris, Champaign, IL, June 23, 2011.
Gene Markos, Hillsboro, IL, August 30, 2013.
Pamela Matson, e-mail, July 5, 2019.
Jeni Pelafos Mechalas, phone interviews, August 25, 2013, and September 18, 2013, and in person, Danville, IL, June 3, 2019.
Mark Pelafos, Champaign, IL, June 24, 2011.
Mike P. Poulos Jr., Decatur, IL, March 20, 2013, and at Flesor's Candy Kitchen, Tuscola, IL, June 7, 2019.
William D. Rezinas phone interview, January 17, 2019, and in person, Shelbyville, IL, June 6, 2019.
Laurel Rice, e-mail, July 3, 2019.
Fred Ross, private correspondence, April 17, 2010.
Alexander "Lex" Samaras, Tuscola, IL, June 15, 2011.
Peter Tomaras, Champaign, IL, June 23, 2011.
James Vaky, Champaign, IL, June 11, 2011.

THESES, MISCELLANEOUS PRIVATE CORRESPONDENCE, PRIVATE PAPERS, AND EPHEMERA

Adam, Pete. "My Life." Unpublished, brief autobiography written in 1975. The original is in the possession of Nick Adam, who kindly gave me a copy.

Askin, Carol, Ancestry.com. Carol is the granddaughter of Spyros Ginos and has a large collection of documents and photos on this site. See CarolAskin7, "Ancestry Profile," https://www.ancestry.com/connect/Profile/011169c1-0002-0000-0000-000000000000. Accessed January 11, 2019.

Beck, Ann Flesor. "Greek Immigration to, and Settlement in, Central Illinois, 1880–1930." Ph.D. diss., University of Illinois, Champaign/Urbana, Illinois, 2014.

Booth, Stephane Elise. "The Relationship between Radicalism and Ethnicity in Southern Illinois Coal Fields, 1870–1940." D.A. diss., Illinois State University, Bloomington, 1983.

The Candy Kitchen: An Original 1920s Soda Fountain Confectionery and Diner. Advertising brochure for Greenup, IL, Candy Kitchen, in the private collection of Ann Beck.

Heath. Robinson, IL: L. S. Heath and Sons, n.d. Printed brochure for sale in the Heath Company gift shop in Robinson, IL.

Lincoln, Frank. "History of the Tuscola, Illinois Masonic Lodge, Lodge No. 32." This brief, typed history was written by a Tuscola citizen and lodge member. I am grateful to Mr. Lincoln for giving me a copy, along with copies of some records of my grandfather's membership in the lodge.

McLean, Francis H. "Summary of Important Finds and Recommendations, August 31, 1916." In "Survey of Charities of St. Louis," Western Historical Manuscript Collection, Health and Welfare Council Social Research, 1916, collection no. SO434, box 11, folder 293. Collection housed at the University of Missouri, St. Louis, campus.

Postcard, 1912. Mary Emerson private collection, Christian County Historical Society Collection, Taylorville, IL.

Royal Confectionery advertisement, 1919. Courtesy of Christian County Historical Society Collection, Taylorville, IL.

Swim, Tina. "The History of the [Greenup] Candy Kitchen." Unpublished personal history, 2002. Copy in my possession.

Taylor, Ruth Koutsoumpas. "Brief Biography of the Koutsoumpas Family." Unpublished manuscript. Copy in my possession.

Taylorville Facebook site. Dan Farrimond, IN, recollections regarding Circa 1965: Square Favorites, sent to me July 28, 2013, via Chris Martin.

Three Hierarchs Greek Orthodox Church, Champaign-Urbana, IL, History. www.threehierarchs.org/history, pp. 1–3. Accessed October 21, 2012.

Tomaras, Peter. "Recollections." Copy of unpublished manuscript sent via email to me, June 5, 2011.

Vaky, James. University of Illinois Student Life, 1928–38 Oral History Project, James Russell Vaky, Class of 1933, Champaign, May 22, 2001.

Vriner, John. Private family history. Copy in my possession.

PUBLISHED SECONDARY SOURCES

Abbott, Grace. "A Study of the Greeks in Chicago." *American Journal of Sociology* 15, no. 3 (November 1909): 379–93.

Acel, Ervin S. "The Foreign Language Press as a Dealer's Medium." *Advertising and Selling*, July 5, 1919.

Addams, Jane. "Americanization." *American Sociological Society Publications* 14 (March 1920): 206–15. This issue contained the papers and proceedings of the 14th Annual Meeting of the Society in Chicago, December 29–31, 1919. Addams and Grace Abbott originally presented the paper on December 31.

———. *Jane Addams on Education.* Edited by Ellen Condliffe Lagemann. New York: Teachers College Press, 1985.

———. *The Second Twenty Years at Hull-House, September 1909 to September 1929, with a Record of a Growing World Consciousness.* New York: Macmillan, 1930.

———. *Twenty Years at Hull-House: With Autobiographical Notes.* Edited with an introduction by Victoria Bissell Brown. 1910. Repr., Boston: Bedford/St. Martin's, 1999.

———. "What the Theater at Hull House Has Done for the Neighborhood People." *Charities: A Weekly Review of Local and General Philanthropy*, March 29, 1902, 284–86.

Aldrich, Howard E., and Roger Waldinger. "Ethnicity and Entrepreneurship." *Annual Review of Sociology* 16 (1990): 111–35.

Alexander, June. *Ethnic Pride, American Patriotism: Slovaks and Other New Immigrants*. Philadelphia: Temple University Press, 2008.

Almaguer, Tomás. *Racial Fault Lines: The Historical Origins of White Supremacy in California*. Berkeley: University of California Press, 1994.

American Legion. *Americanism Manual*. Indianapolis: American Legion, National Americanism Commission, 2001.

American Unity League. *Is Your Neighbor a Kluxer?* Chicago: Tolerance Publishing, 1923.

Anagnostou, Yiorgos. *Contours of White Ethnicity: Popular Ethnography and the Making of Usable Pasts in Greek America*. Athens: Ohio University Press, 2009.

———. "Forget the Past, Remember the Ancestors! Modernity, 'Whiteness,' American Hellenism, and the Politics of Memory in Early Greek America." *Journal of Modern Greek Studies* 22, no. 1 (2004): 25–71.

———. "'That Imagination Called Hellenism': Connecting Greek Worlds, Past and Present, in Greek America." *Classical Bulletin* 80, no. 2 (December 2004): 247–81.

Anderson, Benedict. *Imagined Communities: Reflections on the Origin and Spread of Nationalism*. Rev. ed. New York: Verso, 1983.

Anderson, Will. *Where Have You Gone, Starlight Café? America's Golden Era Roadside Restaurants*. Portland, ME: Anderson and Sons, 1998.

Andrews, Thomas G. *Killing for Coal: America's Deadliest Labor War*. Cambridge, MA: Harvard University Press, 2008.

Angle, Paul M. *Bloody Williamson: A Chapter in American Lawlessness*. Urbana: University of Illinois Press, 1952.

Annunciation Greek Orthodox Church, 70th Anniversary, 1927–1997. Decatur, IL: Annunciation Greek Orthodox Church, 1997.

Anonymous. "Communicable Diseases during May." *Illinois Medical Journal* 29 (June 1916): 461.

———. "Medical News, Typhoid Dangers." *Journal of the American Medical Association* 66, no. 2 (June 1916): 1862.

Arafat, Karim, and Catherine Morgan. "Architecture and Other Visual Arts." In *The Cambridge Illustrated History of Ancient Greece*, edited by Paul Cartledge, 250–87. Cambridge: Cambridge University Press, 2007.

Ayabe, Masatomo. "Ku Kluxers in a Coal Mining Community: A Study of the Ku Klux Klan Movement in Williamson, Illinois 1923–1926." *Journal of the Illinois State Historical Society* 102, no. 1 (Spring 2009): 73–100.

Baiamonte, John V. *Immigrants in Rural America: A Study of the Italians of Tangipahos Parish, Louisiana*. New York: Garland, 1990.

Balk, Helen H. "Economic Contributions of the Greeks to the United States." *Economic Geography* 19, no. 3 (July 1943): 270–75.

Balodimas-Bartolomei, Angelyn. "Greek American Identities in the 21st Century: A Generational Approach." *Journal of the Hellenic Diaspora* 38, nos. 1–2 (2012): 71–98.

Barrett, James R. "Americanization from the Bottom Up: Immigration and the Remaking of the Working Class in the United States, 1880–1930." *Journal of American History* 79, no. 3 (December 1992): 996–1020.

———. *The Irish Way: Becoming American in the Multiethnic City*. New York: Penguin Press, 2012.

Barrett, James R., and David R. Roediger. "In between Peoples: Race, Nationality, and the 'New Immigrant' Working Class." *Journal of American Ethnic History* 16, no. 3 (Spring 1997): 3–44.

Bayles, Phyllis Bartges. "Memories of a Church Bakery." In *Occasional Writers: Bringing the Past Forward*, edited by Daiva Markelis, 1–27. Charleston, IL: Cantraip Press, 2011.

Beier, Lucinda McCray. *Health Culture in the Heartland, 1880–1980: An Oral History*. Urbana: University of Illinois Press, 2009.

Bennett, David H. *The Party of Fear: From Nativist Movements to the New Right in American History*. Chapel Hill: University of North Carolina Press, 1988.

Berg, A. Scott. *Wilson*. New York: G. P. Putnam's Sons, 2013.

Berkin, Carol Ruth, and Mary Beth Norton, eds. *Women of America: A History*. Boston: Houghton Mifflin, 1979.

Bernard, William S. "Immigration: History of U.S. Policy." In *Harvard Encyclopedia of American Ethnic Groups*, edited by Stephan Thernstrom, 486–95. Cambridge, MA: Belknap Press of Harvard University Press, 1980.

Berrol, Selma Cantor. *Growing Up American: Immigrant Children in America Then and Now*. Twayne's History of American Childhood. New York: Twayne, 1995.

Berry, Kate A., and Martha L. Henderson, eds. *Geographical Identities of Ethnic America: Race, Space, and Place*. Reno: University of Nevada Press, 2002.

Betts, Carol Bolton, preparer. "Vriner's Confectionery, National Register of Historic Places Inventory—Nomination Form, January 11, 1983." United States Department of the Interior, National Park Service, National Register of Historic Places. http://gis.hpa.state.il.us/pdfs/201345.pdf. Accessed March 24, 2013.

Bhabha, Homi K., ed. *Nation and Narration*. New York: Routledge, 1990.

Bial, Raymond. *Images of America: Champaign*. Charleston, SC: Arcadia, 2008.

Biles, Roger. *Illinois: A History of the Lands and Its People*. DeKalb: Northern Illinois University Press, 2005.

Bitzes, John G. "The Anti-Greek Riot of 1909—South Omaha." *Nebraska History* 51, no. 2 (1970): 199–224.

Blee, Kathleen M. "Becoming a Racist: Women in Contemporary Ku Klux Klan and Neo-Nazi Groups." *Gender and Society* 10, no. 6 (December 1996): 680–702.

———. *Women of the Klan: Racism and Gender in the 1920s*. New ed. Berkeley, CA: University of California Press, 2009.

Bliss, Dorothy. *Hillsboro: A History*. Based on writings by the late Tom Bliss. Hillsboro, IL: Montgomery County News, 1989.

Bodnar, John E. *The Transplanted: A History of Immigrants in Urban America*. Bloomington: Indiana University Press, 1985.

Borosini, Victor von. "Our Recreation Facilities and the Immigrant." *Annals of the American Academy of Political and Social Science* 35, no. 2 (March 1910): 141–51.

Brettell, Caroline B., and James Frank Hollifield. *Migration Theory: Talking across Disciplines*. 2nd ed. New York: Routledge, 2008.

Brown, L. Carl. *International Politics and the Middle East: Old Rules, Dangerous Game*. London: I. B. Tauris, 1984.

Budin, Stephanie Lynn. *The Ancient Greeks: New Perspectives*. Santa Barbara, CA: ABC-CLIO, 2004.

Buhle, Paul, and Dan Georgakas, eds. *The Immigrant Left in the United States*. Albany: State University of New York Press, 1996.

Burgess, Thomas. *Greeks in America*. New York: Arno Press, 1970.

Burkholder, Zoë. *Color in the Classroom: How American Schools Taught Race, 1900–1954*. New York: Oxford University Press, 2011.

Burnett, Robyn, and Ken Luebbering. *Immigrant Women in the Settlement of Missouri*. Missouri Heritage Readers. Columbia: University of Missouri Press, 2005.

Callinicos, Constance. *American Aphrodite: Becoming Female in Greek America*. New York: Pella, 1990.

Campbell, Ballard C., ed. *The Human Tradition in the Gilded Age and Progressive Era*. The Human Tradition in America 3. Wilmington, DE: Scholarly Resources, 2000.

Campbell, John Kennedy. *Honour, Family, and Patronage: A Study of Institutions and Moral Values in a Greek Mountain Community*. Oxford: Clarendon Press, 1967.

Candeloro, Dominic. "Chicago's Italians: A Survey of the Ethnic Factor, 1850–1999." In *Ethnic Chicago: A Multicultural Portrait*, edited by Melvin G. Holli and Peter d'Alroy Jones, 229–59. 4th ed. Grand Rapids, MI: Wm. B. Eerdmans, 1995.

Cannato, Vincent J. *American Passage: The History of Ellis Island*. New York: Harper, 2009.

Carlson, Allan C. *The "American Way": Family and Community in the Shaping of the American Identity*. Wilmington, DE: ISI Books, 2003.

Carlson, Robert A. *The Americanization Syndrome: A Quest for Conformity*. New York: St. Martin's Press, 1987.

Carson, Mina Julia. *Settlement Folk: Social Thought and the American Settlement Movement, 1885–1930*. Chicago: University of Chicago Press, 1990.

Cartledge, Paul, ed. *The Cambridge Illustrated History of Ancient Greece*. Cambridge: Cambridge University Press, 2007.

———. "Peoples: Who Were the Greeks?" In *The Cambridge Illustrated History of Ancient Greece*, edited by Paul Cartledge, 35–53. Cambridge: Cambridge University Press, 2007.

———. "War and Peace." In *The Cambridge Illustrated History of Ancient Greece*, edited by Paul Cartledge, 166–92. Cambridge: Cambridge University Press, 2007.

Cassimatis, Louis P. *American Influence in Greece, 1917–1929*. Kent, OH: Kent State University Press, 1988.

Castleden, Rodney. *Minoans: Life in Bronze Age Crete*. London: Routledge, 1993.

———. *The Mycenaeans*. London: Routledge, 2005.

Cavanagh, Bob. "The Gifts of the Greeks." *Illinois Times*, April 14, 2005. http://illinoistimes.com/article-1984-the-gifts-of-the-greeks.html. Accessed June 3, 2019.

Chalmers, David Mark. *Hooded Americanism: The History of the Ku Klux Klan*. 3rd ed. Durham: Duke University Press, 2003.

Chan, Sucheng. "European and Asian Immigration into the United States in Comparative Perspective, 1820s to 1920s." In *Immigration Reconsidered: History, Sociology, and Politics*, edited by Virginia Yans-McLaughlin, 37–75. New York: Oxford University Press, 1990.

Charleston and Mattoon Bi-centennial Commission. "Peter Sutter." In *History of Coles County, Illinois, 1876–1976*, 884–85. Charleston and Mattoon, IL: Charleston and Mattoon Bi-centennial Commission, 1976.

Chock, Phyllis Pease. "The Greek-American Small Businessman: A Cultural Analysis." *Journal of Anthropological Research* 37, no. 1 (April 1981): 46–60.

———. "'The Self-Made Woman': Gender and the Success Story in Greek-American Family Histories." In *Naturalizing Power: Essays in Feminist Cultural Analysis*, edited by Sylvia Yanagisako and Carol Delaney, 239–55. New York: Routledge, 1995.

The Church. *Ohio Greek Orthodox Church, 1912–1987, "The Annunciation," 75th Anniversary, Diamond Jubilee*. Columbus, OH: The Church, 1988.

Clark County Democrat, comp. "Koutsoumpas." In *History of Marshall, Illinois and Eastern Clark County.* Marshall, IL: Clark County Democrat, 1978.

Clifford, James. "'Diasporas,' Further Inflections: Toward Ethnographies of the Future." *Cultural Anthropology* 9, no. 3 (August 1994): 302–38.

Clogg, Richard. *A Concise History of Greece*. 2nd ed. Cambridge: Cambridge University Press, 2002.

Cohen, Robin, ed. *The Cambridge Survey of World Migration*. Cambridge: Cambridge University Press, 1995.

Commons, John Rogers. *Races and Immigrants in America*. New York: Macmillan, 1920.

Constant, Constance M. *Austin Lunch: Greek-American Recollections*. River Vale, NJ: Cosmos Publishing, 2005.

Constantakos, Chrysie M. "Ethnic Language as a Variable in Subcultural Continuity." In *The Greek American Community in Transition*, edited by Harry J. Psomiades and Alice Scourby, 137–70. Modern Greek Research Series 4. New York: Pella, 1982.

Constantinou, Stavros T. "Profiles of Greek Americans." In *Geographical Identities of Ethnic America: Race, Space, and Place*, edited by Kate A. Berry and Martha L. Henderson, 92–115. Reno: University of Nevada Press, 2002.

Constantinou, Stavros T., and Nicholas D. Diamantides. "Modeling International Migration: Determinants of Emigration from Greece to the United States, 1820–1980." *Annals of the Association of American Geographers* 75, no. 3 (September 1985): 352–69.

Constantinou, Stavros T., and M. E. Harvey. "Dimensional Structure and Intergenerational Differences in Ethnicity: The Greek Americans." *Sociology and Social Research* 69 (1985): 234–54.

Cooper, Wilda Q., Maryless C. Lasswell, and Sallie C. C. Traynor, eds. *Christian County Reunion: A Pictorial History of Christian County*. Taylorville, IL: Taylorville Breeze-Courier and the Christian County Genealogical Society, 1994.

Coumantaros, Stella. "The Greek Orthodox Ladies Philoptochos Society and the Greek American Community." In *The Greek American Community in Transition*, edited by Harry J. Psomiades and Alice Scourby, 191–96. New York: Pella, 1992.

Counelis, James Steve. "Greek Orthodox Church Statistics of the United States, 1949–1989: Some Ecclesial and Social Patterns." *Journal of the Hellenic Diaspora* 16, nos. 1–4 (1989): 129–59.

Cranshaw, Whitney, and Richard Redak. *Bugs Rule! An Introduction to the World of Insects.* Princeton, NJ: Princeton University Press, 2013.

Crawford, Ruth Elizabeth. *The Immigrant in St. Louis: A Survey*. Studies in Social Economics. St. Louis: St. Louis School of Social Economy, 1916.

Crouthamel, James L. "The Springfield Race Riot in 1908." *Journal of Negro History* 45, no. 3 (July 1960): 164–81.

Curry, Lynne. *Modern Mothers in the Heartland: Gender, Health, and Progress in Illinois, 1900–1930*. Columbus: Ohio State University Press, 1999.

Cutler, Irving. "The Jews of Chicago. A Multicultural Portrait." In *Ethnic Chicago: A Multicultural Portrait*, edited by Melvin G. Holli and Peter d'Alroy Jones, 122–72. Grand Rapids, MI: Wm. B. Eerdmans, 1995.

Dakin, Douglas. *The Greek Struggle for Independence, 1821–1833*. Berkeley: University of California Press, 1973.

———. *The Unification of Greece, 1770–1923*. New York: St. Martin's Press, 1972.

Dalby, Andrew. "Greece, Ancient." In *Food Production to Nuts*, vol. 2 of *Encyclopedia of Food and Culture*, edited by Solomon H. Katz and William Woys Weaver, 149–51. New York: Thomson Gale, 2003.

Dalby, Andrew, and Rachel Dalby. *Gifts of the Gods: A History of Food in Greece*. London: Reaktion Books, 2018.

Dana, Léo-Paul, ed. *Entrepreneurship and Religion*. Northampton, MA: Edward Elgar, 2010.

Daniels, Roger. "Chinese and Japanese as Urban Americans, 1850–1940." *History Teacher* 25, no. 4 (August 1992): 427–41.

———. *Coming to America: A History of Immigration and Ethnicity in American Life*. 2nd ed. New York: Perennial, 2002.

———. *Guarding the Golden Door: American Immigration Policy and Immigrants since 1882*. New York: Hill and Wang, 2004.

———. *Not Like Us: Immigrants and Minorities in America, 1890–1924*. Chicago: Ivan R. Dee, 1997.

Daniels, Roger, and Otis L. Graham. *Debating American Immigration, 1882–Present*. New York: Rowman and Littlefield, 2001.

Davis, Angela. "Racism, Birth Control, and Reproductive Rights." In *From Abortion to Reproductive Freedom: Transforming a Movement*, edited by Marlene Gerber Fried, 15–26. Boston: South End Press, 1990.

Davis, Philip, and Bertha Schwartz, eds. *Immigration and Americanization: Selected Readings*. Boston: Ginn, 1920.

Davros, Michael George, ed. *Images of America: Greeks in Chicago*. Charleston, SC: Arcadia, 2009.

Day, Richard. *Vincennes: A Pictorial History.* Vincennes, IN: G. Bradley, 1988.

Day, Teddy. *A History of the Square in Paris, Illinois, Edgar County*. Paris, IL: self-published, 2002.

Dean-Jones, Lesley. "Philosophy and Science." In *The Cambridge Illustrated History of Ancient Greece*, edited by Paul Cartledge, 288–319. Cambridge: Cambridge University Press, 2007.

Dechenne, David. "Recipe for Violence: War Attitudes, the Black Hundred Riot, and Superpatriotism in an Illinois Coalfield, 1917–1918." *Illinois Historical Journal* 85, no. 4 (Winter 1992): 221–38.

De Léon, Arnoldo. *Racial Frontiers: Africans, Chinese, and Mexicans in Western America, 1848–1890*. Albuquerque: University of New Mexico Press, 2002.

Demos, Vasilike. "Maintenance and Loss of Traditional Gender: Boundaries in Two Greek Orthodox Communities." *Journal of the Hellenic Diaspora* 16, nos. 1–4 (1989): 77–93.

Dickson, Peter W. "The Greek Pilgrims: Tsakonas and Tsintzinians." In *New Directions in Greek American Studies*, edited by Dan Georgakas and Charles C. Moskos, 35–54. New York: Pella, 1991.

Dietrich, Matthew. "Picturing the Past: James Confectionery on South Grand." SangamonLink, November 14, 2013. http://www.sangamoncountyhistory/wp/?p=2928. Accessed August 22, 2019.

Diner, Hasia. "History and the Study of Immigration: Narratives of the Particular." In *Migration Theory: Talking across Disciplines*, edited by Caroline B. Brettell and James F. Hollifield, 31–49. New York: Routledge, 2000.

Diner, Steven J. *A Very Different Age: Americans of the Progressive Era*. New York: Hill and Wang, 1998.

Donovan, Tristan. *Fizz: How Soda Shook Up the World.* Chicago: Chicago Review Press, 2014.

Doukas, Kimon A. "The Story of Ahepa." *Athene* 11, no. 2 (Summer 1950): 39–43.

Doulis, Thomas. *A Surge to the Sea: The Greeks in Oregon; A Photographic History of the Holy Trinity Greek Orthodox Community of Oregon and Southern Washington*. N.p.: J. Lockie, 1977.

Drachsler, Julius. *Intermarriage in New York City: A Statistical Study of the Amalgamation of European Peoples*. New York: Columbia University Press, 1921.

Dublin, Thomas. *Immigrant Voices: New Lives in America, 1773–1986*. Urbana: University of Illinois Press, 1993.

Dusselier, Jane. "Bonbons, Lemon Drops, and Oh Henry! Bars: Candy, Consumer Culture and the Construction of Gender, 1895–1920." In *Kitchen Culture in America: Popular Representations of Food, Gender and Race*, edited by Sherrie A. Inness, 13–49. Philadelphia: University of Pennsylvania Press, 2001.

Easter-Shick, Nancy, and Bonnie Brooks Clark. *Round the Square: Life in Downtown Charleston, Illinois, 1830–1998.* Charleston: Easter-Shick Publishing, 1999.

Ebert, Roger. "Roger Ebert's Journal: I Was a Teenage Newshound." RogerEbert.com, May 1, 2008. https://www.rogerebert.com/rogers-journal/i-was-a-teenage-newshound. Accessed September 21, 2019.

Edgar Cemetery Burial Records. Paris, IL: Acorn Press, 1981.

Ekonomidou, Maria Sarantopoulou. "The Greeks in America as I Saw Them." *Journal of the Hellenic Diaspora* 20, no. 1 (1994): 35–42.

Ellis, Ann W. "The Greek Community in Atlanta, 1900–1923." *Georgia Historical Quarterly* 58, no. 4 (December 1974): 400–408.

Ellis, Bill. "Whispers in the Ice Cream Parlor: Culinary Tourism, Contemporary Legends, and the Urban Interzone." *Journal of American Folklore* 122, no. 483 (Winter 2009): 53–74.

Engelman, Peter C. *A History of the Birth Control Movement in America.* Westport, CT: Praeger, 2011.

Erickson, John H. *Orthodox Christians in America: A Short History.* New York: Oxford University Press, 2008.

Fairchild, Henry Pratt. *Greek Immigration to the United States.* New Haven, CT: Yale University Press, 1911.

———. *Immigration: A World Movement and Its American Significance.* New York: Macmillan, 1920.

———. "The Literacy Test and Its Making." *Quarterly Journal of Economics* 31, no. 3 (May 1917): 447–60.

———. *The Melting-Pot Mistake.* Boston: Little, Brown, 1926.

Fein, Seth. "Vriner's Confectionary: Age Old Sweet Makers without a Home." Smile Politely, December 14, 2007. http://www.smilepolitely.com/culture/vriners_confectionary_age_old_sweet_makers_without_a_home/. Accessed March 24, 2013.

Findling, John E., and Kimberly D. Pelle, eds. *Encyclopedia of the Modern Olympic Movement.* Westport, CT: Greenwood Press, 2004.

Firkins, Oscar W. "To a Greek Bootblack." *Atlantic Monthly*, April 1908, 537–38.

Fisher, Nick. "Rich and Poor." In *The Cambridge Illustrated History of Ancient Greece*, edited by Paul Cartledge, 82–99. Cambridge: Cambridge University Press, 2007.

Fitzgerald, Craig. "The American Soda Fountain Company." Originally in *By the Way Online Magazine,* Fall 2002. http://americansodafountain.com/id5.html. Accessed January 15, 2019.

Flora Kiwanis Club and Clay County Regulators. *The Prairie Echo.* Flora, IL: Flora Kiwanis Club and Clay County Regulators, 1976.

Foner, Nancy. *In a New Land: A Comparative View of Immigration.* New York: New York University Press, 2005.

Foner, Nancy, Ruben G. Rumbaut, and Steven J. Gold, eds. *Immigration Research for a New Century: Multidisciplinary Perspectives.* New York: Russell Sage Foundation, 2000.

Force, Pierre. "The House on Bayou Road: Atlantic Creole Networks in the Eighteenth and Nineteenth Centuries." *Journal of American History* 100, no. 1 (June 2013): 21–45.

Fox, Robin Lane. *Pagans and Christians*. New York: Knopf, 1987.

Frangos, Stavros K. *Greeks in Michigan*. Discovering the Peoples of Michigan. East Lansing: Michigan State University Press, 2004.

Frangos, Steve. "1821: 'Grecian Fever' Spreads to America." In *The Greeks: The Triumphant Journey from the Ancient Greeks and the Greek Revolution of 1821, to Greek Americans*, edited by Steve Frangos, 122–29. New York: National Herald, 2001.

———. "Eulogy for the Diana Sweet Shoppe." *National Herald*, March 1–2, 2003, 1, 6–7.

———, ed. *The Greeks: The Triumphant Journey from the Ancient Greeks and the Greek Revolution of 1821, to Greek Americans*. New York: National Herald, 2001.

———. "How the Tsintzinians Conquered America." *National Herald*, August 1–7, 2015, 1, 7.

———. "Oh, Those Sweet Greek Americans!" *National Herald*, April 30, 2005, 1, 10, 18.

———. "The Origins of AHEPA." *Hellenic Heritage* 50, no. 10 (October 1997): 13–16.

———. "The Picture Bride Era." *National Herald*, special issue, *Greek Weddings*, March 12, 2005, 4, 5, 8.

———. "The Pioneers of Confection in America." *National Herald*, February 21, 2004, 1, 5.

———. "Sweet Memories." *Greek American*, December 27, 1997, 12.

———. "The Sweet Smell of Success." *National Herald*, January 2–3, 2004, 1, 5.

———. "Vriner's Confectionery: Another Sweet Greek-American Historical Tradition." *National Herald*, March 14, 2017. https://www.thenationalherald.com/154284/vriners-confectionery-another-sweet-greek-american-historical-tradition/. Accessed August 22, 2019.

Frank, André Gunder. *World Accumulation, 1492–1789*. New York: Monthly Review Press, 2009.

Franklin, Benjamin. "Information to Those Who Would Remove to America." Essay dated March 9, 1784. See FranklinPapers.org, https://franklinpapers.org/framedVolumes.jsp, with this title and date.

———. "Observations Concerning the Increase of Mankind." Essay published in 1751. See FranklinPapers.org, https://franklinpapers.org/framedVolumes.jsp, with this title and date.

Fredrickson, George M., and Dale T. Knobel. "History of Prejudice and Discrimination." In *Harvard Encyclopedia of American Ethnic Groups*, edited by Stephan Thernstrom, 829–47. Cambridge, MA: Belknap Press of Harvard University Press, 1980.

Freeman, Charles. *The Greek Achievement: The Foundation of the Western World*. New York: Penguin, 2000.

Friedman, Jacob. *Friedman's Common-Sense Candy Teacher: A Most Complete Line of Up-to-Date Formulas, with All Instructions in the Art of Making Candies, Both Steam and Open Fire Work, for the Large Manufacturer or the Beginner* . . . 4th ed., with an enlarged supplement. Chicago: Jonas M. Bell, 1915.

Friedman, Max Paul. *Rethinking Anti-Americanism: The History of an Exceptional Concept in American Foreign Relations*. Cambridge: Cambridge University Press, 2012.

Funderburg, Anne Cooper. *Sundae Best: A History of Soda Fountains.* Bowling Green, OH: Bowling Green State University Popular Press, 2002.

Gabaccia, Donna R. "Female Migration and Immigrant Sex Ratios, 1820–1928." Washington, DC: Unpublished paper, 1989.

———. *We Are What We Eat: Ethnic Food and the Making of Americans.* Cambridge, MA: Harvard University Press, 1998.

———. "Women of the Mass Migrations: From Minority to Majority, 1820–1930." In *European Migrants: Global and Local Perspectives*, edited by Dirk Hoerder and Leslie Page Moch, 90–114. Boston: Northeastern University Press, 1996.

Gabaccia, Donna R., and Colin Wayne Leach. *Immigrant Life in the US: Multi-disciplinary Perspectives.* New York: Routledge, 2004.

Gallant, Thomas W. *Modern Greece.* London: Arnold, 2001.

Gans, Herbert. "Filling in Some Holes: Six Areas of Needed Immigration Research." In *Immigration Research for a New Century: Multidisciplinary Perspectives*, edited by Nancy Foner, Ruben G. Rumbaut, and Steven J. Gold, 76–89. New York: Russell Sage Foundation, 2000.

Garland, Robert. *Daily Life of the Ancient Greeks.* Westport, CT: Greenwood Press, 1998.

Gavin, Eileen A., Aphrodite Clamar, and Mary Ann Siderits, eds. *Women of Vision: Their Psychology, Circumstances, and Success.* Focus on Women. New York: Springer, 2007.

Georgakas, Dan. "Greek-American Radicalism: The Twentieth Century." In *The Immigrant Left in the United States*, edited by Paul Buhle and Dan Georgakas, 207–32. Albany: State University of New York Press, 1996.

———. "The Greeks in America." *Journal of the Hellenic Diaspora* 14, nos. 1–2 (1987): 5–53.

Georges, Robert A. "The Many Ways of Being Greek." *Journal of Folklore Research* 21, nos. 2–3 (December 1984): 211–19.

Gildemeister, Theda. *Minnesota Course of Study for Elementary Schools and Manual for Teachers.* Winona, MN: Jones and Kroeger, 1918.

Glazer, Nathan, Ueda Reed, and Stephan Thernstrom. "Policy against Prejudice and Discrimination." In *Harvard Encyclopedia of American Ethnic Groups*, edited by Stephan Thernstrom, 847–58. Cambridge, MA: Belknap Press of Harvard University Press, 1980.

Gleason, Philip. "American Identity and Americanization." In *Harvard Encyclopedia of American Ethnic Groups*, edited by Stephan Thernstrom, 31–58. Cambridge, MA: Belknap Press of Harvard University Press, 1980.

———. *Speaking of Diversity: Language and Ethnicity in Twentieth-Century America.* Baltimore: Johns Hopkins University Press, 1992.

Glowacki, Peggy, and Julia Hendry. *Images of America: Hull-House.* Charleston, SC: Arcadia, 2004.

Goddard, Leslie. *Images of America: Chicago's Sweet Candy History.* Charleston, SC: Arcadia, 2012.

Goings, Kenneth W., and Raymond A. Mohl, eds. *The New African American Urban History.* Thousand Oaks, CA: SAGE, 1996.

Goldberg, David Joseph. *Discontented America: The United States in the 1920s*. Baltimore: Johns Hopkins University Press, 1999.

———. "Unmasking the Ku Klux Klan: The Northern Movement against the KKK, 1920–1925." *Journal of American Ethnic History* 15, no. 4 (Summer 1996): 32–48.

Goodman, Bobbie Claire. "The Greeks—The Candy Kitchen." In *Greenup (IL) Jubilee 150, 1834–1984*, 73–74. Dixon, IL: Print Shop, compiled and published by Cumberland County Historical Society, 1984.

Goodwin, Doris Kearns. *The Bully Pulpit: Theodore Roosevelt, William Howard Taft, and the Golden Age of Journalism*. New York: Simon and Schuster, 2013.

Gossett, Thomas F. *Race: The History of an Idea in America*. 2nd ed. New York: Oxford University Press, 1997.

Guglielmo, Thomas A. "Encountering the Color Line in the Everyday: Italians in Interwar Chicago." In *Race and Immigration in the United States: New Histories*, edited by Paul R. Spickard, 148–77. New York: Routledge, 2012.

———. *White on Arrival: Italians, Race, Color, and Power in Chicago, 1890–1945*. Oxford: Oxford University Press, 2003.

Gyory, Andrew. *Closing the Gate: Race, Politics, and the Chinese Exclusion Act*. Chapel Hill: University of North Carolina Press, 1998.

Hale, Stan J., ed. *Williamson County Illinois Sesquicentennial History*. Paducah, KY: Turner Publishing, 1993.

Hall, Edith. "Literature and Performance." In *The Cambridge Illustrated History of Ancient Greece*, edited by Paul Cartledge, 219–49. Cambridge: Cambridge University Press, 2007.

Hall, Prescott F. *Immigration and Its Effects upon the United States*. New York: Henry Holt, 1906.

Hamilton, Samuel. *Complete Arithmetic*. New York: American Book, 1909.

Handlin, Oscar. "Education and the European Immigrant, 1820–1920." In *American Education and the European Immigrant, 1840–1940*, edited by Bernard J. Weiss, 3–16. Urbana: University of Illinois Press, 1982.

———. *The Uprooted*. 2nd ed. Philadelphia: University of Pennsylvania Press, 2002.

Hansen, Marcus Lee. *The Atlantic Migration, 1607–1860: A History of the Continuing Settlement of the United States*. Cambridge, MA: Harvard University Press, 1940.

———. "The History of American Immigration as a Field of Research." *American Historical Review* 32, no. 3 (April 1927): 500–518.

———. *Immigration: A Field for Research*. New York: Common Council for American Unity, 1941.

———. *The Problem of the Third Generation Immigrant*. Rock Island, IL: Augustana Historical Society, 1938.

Harper, Richard Conant. *The Course of the Melting Pot Idea to 1910*. New York: Arno Press, 1980.

Harzig, Christiane, Dirk Hoerder, and Donna Gabaccia. *What Is Migration History?* Cambridge: Polity, 2009.

Hatzidimitriou, Constantine G. "The American Response to the Greek War of Independence." In *The Greeks: The Triumphant Journey from the Ancient Greeks and the Greek Revolution of 1821, to Greek Americans*, edited by Steve Frangos, 117–21. New York: National Herald, 2001.

Heath, Richard J., with Ray Elliott. *Bittersweet: The Story of Heath Candy Co.* Urbana, IL: Tales, 1994.

Hecht, Stuart J. "Social and Artistic Integration: The Emergence of Hull-House Theatre." *Theatre Journal* 34, no. 2 (May 1982): 172–82.

Hecker, Melvin, and Heike Fenton, eds. *The Greeks in America, 1528–1977: A Chronology and Fact Book*. Dobbs Ferry, NY: Oceana Publications, 1978.

Herodotus. *The Landmark Herodotus: The Histories*. Edited by Richard B. Strassler. Translated by Andrea L. Purvis. New York: Anchor Books, 2009.

Herrin, Judith. *Byzantium: The Surprising Life of a Medieval Empire*. Princeton, NJ: Princeton University Press, 2008.

Hicken, Victor. "The Virden and Pana Mine Wars of 1898." *Journal of Illinois State History* 52, no. 2 (Summer 1959): 263–78.

Higgins, Michael Denis, and Reynold Alleyne Higgins. *A Geological Companion to Greece and the Aegean*. Ithaca, NY: Cornell University Press, 1996.

Higham, John. *Send These to Me: Immigrants in Urban America*. Baltimore: Johns Hopkins University Press, 1984.

———. *Strangers in the Land: Patterns of American Nativism, 1860–1925*. New York: Atheneum, 1973.

Hirata, Lucie Cheng. "Chinese Immigrant Women in Nineteenth-Century California." In *Women of America: A History*, edited by Carol Ruth Berkin and Mary Beth Norton, 223–44. Boston: Houghton Mifflin, 1979.

Hirota, Hidetaka. "The Moment of Transition: State Officials, the Federal Government, and the Formation of American Immigration Policy." *Journal of American History* 99, no. 4 (March 2013): 1092–108.

Hirschman, Charles. "America's Melting Pot Reconsidered." *Annual Review of Sociology* 9 (1983): 397–423.

Hoerder, Dirk. *To Know Our Many Selves: From the Study of Canada to Canadian Studies*. Edmonton, AB, Canada: Athabasca University Press, 2010.

Hofstadter, Richard. *The Age of Reform: From Bryan to F.D.R.* New York: Vintage Books, 1955.

Hoganson, Kristin. "Meat in the Middle: Converging Borderlands in the U.S. Midwest, 1865–1900." *Journal of American History* 98, no. 4 (March 2012): 1025–51.

Holli, Melvin G., and Peter d'Alroy Jones. *Ethnic Chicago: A Multicultural Portrait*. 4th ed. Grand Rapids, MI: Wm. B. Eerdmans, 1995.

Horowitz, David A. "The Normality of Extremism: The Ku Klux Klan Revisited." *Society* 35, no. 6 (1998): 71–77.

Hourwich, Isaac Aaronovich. *Immigration and Labor: The Economic Aspects of European Immigration to the United States*. New York: G. P. Putnam's Sons, 1912.

Howarth, David Armine. *The Greek Adventure: Lord Byron and Other Eccentrics in the War of Independence*. 1st American ed. New York: Atheneum, 1976.

Hughes, J. Donald, and J. V. Thirgood. "Deforestation, Erosion, and Forest Management in Ancient Greece and Rome." *Journal of Forest History* 26, no. 2 (April 1982): 60–75.

Huling, Charles C. *American Candy Maker*. Philadelphia: Published by author, 1902.

Ingram, W. Scott. *Greek Immigrants*. Immigration to the United States. New York: Facts on File, 2005.

Illinois State Board of Health. "Typhoid Fever at Tuscola." *Illinois Health News* 2, no. 7 (July 1916): 143–44.

Innis-Jiménez, Michael. *Steel Barrio: The Great Mexican Migration to South Chicago, 1915–1940*. New York: New York University Press, 2013.

Jackson, Kenneth T. *The Ku Klux Klan in the City, 1915–1930*. New York: I. R. Dee, 1967.

Jackson, Shannon. *Lines of Activity: Performance, Historiography, Hull-House Domesticity*. Ann Arbor: University of Michigan Press, 2001.

Jacobs, Jane. *The Death and Life of Great American Cities*. New York: Modern Library, Random House, 1993.

Jacobson, Matthew Frye. *Whiteness of a Different Color: European Immigrants and the Alchemy of Race*. Cambridge, MA: Harvard University Press, 1998.

James, William. *Pragmatism, a New Name for Some Old Ways of Thinking: Popular Lectures on Philosophy*. London: Longmans, Green, 1908.

Jaret, Charles. "The Greek, Italian, and Jewish American Ethnic Press: A Comparative Analysis." *Journal of Ethnic Studies* 7, no. 2 (Summer 1979): 47–70.

Jarvis, Charles E. *The Tyrants*. Lowell, MA: Ithaca Press, 1977.

Jefferson County Historical Society. *Facts and Folks: A History of Jefferson County, Illinois*. Mount Vernon, IL: Jefferson County Historical Society, 1978.

Jenks, Jeremiah Whipple, William Jett Lauck, and Rufus Daniel Smith. *The Immigration Problem: A Study of American Immigration Conditions and Needs*. 6th ed. New York: Funk and Wagnalls, 1926.

Jusdanis, Gregory. *The Necessary Nation*. Princeton, NJ: Princeton University Press, 2001.

Kalogeras, Yiorgos D. "Narrating an Ethnic Group." *Journal of the Hellenic Diaspora* 18, no. 2 (1992): 13–34.

Karampetsos, E. D. "Nativism in Nevada: Greek Immigrants in White Pine County." *Journal of the Hellenic Diaspora* 24, no. 1 (1998): 61–95.

Kaufman, Ned. *Place, Race, and Story: Essays on the Past and Future of Historic Preservation*. New York: Routledge, 2009.

Kehayes, Peter. "An Important Challenge for Greek Orthodox Christianity." Orthodox Christian Laity, November 21, 2012. https://ocl.org/an-important-challenge-for-greek-orthodox-christianity. Accessed July 21, 2019.

Kienzler, Mike. "Fast Food in Springfield." SangamonLink, October 28, 2013. http://sangamoncountyhistory.org/wp/?p=2275. Accessed June 3, 2019.

Kienzler, Mike. "Kerasotes Theatres." SangamonLink, October 21, 2013. http://sangamoncountyhistory/wp/?p=1889. Accessed May 1, 2019.

Kienzler, Mike. "The Sugar Bowl Restaurants." SangamonLink, November 14, 2013. http://sangamoncountyhistory.org/wp/?p=2928. Accessed June 3, 2019.

King, Desmond. *Making Americans: Immigration, Race, and the Origins of the Diverse Democracy*. Cambridge, MA: Harvard University Press, 2009.

King, John W., ed. *History of Douglas County, Illinois*. Chicago: Munsell Publishing, 1910.

Kiriakopoulos, G. C. "The First Greeks in America and the St. Photios National Shrine." *Greek-American Review* 50, no. 2 (February 1997): 11–13.

Klaus, Lucy Purdom, and the Macoupin County Historical Society, comps. *The Story of Macoupin County, 1829–1979*. Carlinville, IL: Carlinville and Macoupin County Sesquicentennial, Inc., 1979.

Knight, Louise W. *Citizen: Jane Addams and the Struggle for Democracy*. Chicago: University of Chicago Press, 2008.

Kochilas, Diane. *The Glorious Foods of Greece: Traditional Recipes from the Islands, Cities, and Villages*. New York: Harper Collins, 2001.

Koken, Paul, Theodore N. Constant, and Seraphim George Canoutas. *A History of the Greeks in the Americas, 1453–1938*. Ann Arbor, MI: Proctor Publications, 1995.

Koliopoulos, Giannēs. *Brigands with a Cause: Brigandage and Irredentism in Modern Greece, 1821–1912*. Oxford: Clarendon, 1987.

Kolokotronis, Theodoros. "Social Banditry: The Memoirs of Theodoros Kolokotronis." In *The Greeks: The Triumphant Journey from the Ancient Greeks and the Greek Revolution of 1821, to Greek Americans*, edited by Steve Frangos, 106–11. New York: National Herald, 2001.

Kopan, Andrew T. *Education and Greek Immigrants in Chicago, 1892–1973: A Study in Ethnic Survival*. New York: Garland, 1990.

Kopan, Andrew T., and Alice Orphanos Kopan. "Georgia Bitzis Pooley (1849–1945)." In *Greek-American Pioneer Women of Illinois: The Stories of Georgia Bitzis Pooley, Presbytera Stella Christoulakis Petrakis, Theano Papazoglou Margaris, Venette Askounes Ashford, and Senator Adeline J. Geo-Karis*, edited by Elaine Cotsirilos Thomopoulos and Greek Women's University Club, 9–18. Charleston, SC: Arcadia, 2000.

———. "Pooley, Georgia Bitzis." In *Women Building Chicago, 1790–1990: A Biographical Dictionary*, edited by Rima Lunin Schultz and Adele Hast, 707–9. Bloomington: Indiana University Press, 2001.

Kourvetaris, George A. *First and Second Generation Greeks in Chicago: An Inquiry into Their Stratification and Mobility Patterns*. Athens, Greece: National Centre of Social Research, 1971.

———. "Greek American Professionals and Entrepreneurs." *Journal of the Hellenic Diaspora* 16, no. 4 (1989): 105–28.

———. "Greek-American Professionals: 1820's-1970's." *Balkan Studies* 18, no. 2 (1977): 285–317.

———. *Studies on Greek Americans*. New York: East European Monographs; Columbia University Press, 1997.

Kraut, Alan M. *Silent Travelers: Germs, Genes, and the Immigrant Menace*. Baltimore: Johns Hopkins University Press, 1994.

Kremezi, Aglaia. *The Foods of Greece*. New York: Stewart, Tabori, and Chang, 1993.

———. "Greece and Crete." In *Food Production to Nuts*, vol. 2 of *Encyclopedia of Food and Culture*, edited by Solomon H. Katz and William Woys Weaver, 151–55. New York: Thomson Gale, 2003.

Kunkelman, Gary. *The Religion of Ethnicity: Belief and Belonging in a Greek-American Community*. New York: Garland, 1990.

Lamprini, Thoma, "Between Black and White: Greek-Americans in the 20th Century" (© 2020 Barricade M.I.K.E.), https://www.youtube.com/watch?v=DziGTSRMQic.

Langland, James, ed. *Chicago Daily News Almanac and Year-Book for 1924*. Chicago: Chicago Daily News, 1923.

Lasch-Quinn, Elisabeth. *Black Neighbors: Race and the Limits of Reform in the American Settlement Movement, 1890–1945*. Chapel Hill: University of North Carolina Press, 1993.

Lawson, Michael L. "Omaha, a City in Ferment: Summer of 1919." *Nebraska History* 58, no. 3 (Fall 1977): 395–417.

Lay, Shawn, ed. *The Invisible Empire in the West: Toward a New Historical Appraisal of the Ku Klux Klan of the 1920s*. Urbana: University of Illinois Press, 2004.

Leber, George J. *The History of the Order of Ahepa (The American Hellenic Educational Progressive Association), 1922–1972: Including the Greeks in the New World, and Immigration to the United States*. Washington, DC: Order of Ahepa, 1972.

Lee, Erika. *America for Americans: A History of Xenophobia in the United States*. New York: Basic Books, 2019.

———. "The Chinese Exclusion Example: Race, Immigration, and American Gatekeeping, 1882–1924." *Journal of American Ethnic History* 21, no. 3 (Spring 2002): 36–62.

LeMay, Michael C. *From Open Door to Dutch Door: An Analysis of U.S. Immigration Policy since 1820*. New York: Praeger, 1987.

———. *The Struggle for Influence: The Impact of Minority Groups on Politics and Public Policy in the United States*. Lanham, MD: University Press of America, 1985.

Lennartz, Karl, and Stephen Wassong. "Athens 1896." In *Encyclopedia of the Modern Olympic Movement*, edited by John E. Findling and Kimberly D. Pelle, 17–25. Westport, CT: Greenwood Press, 2004.

Leontis, Artemis. *Topographies of Hellenism: Mapping the Homeland*. Ithaca: Cornell University Press, 1995.

Lewis, Earl. "Connecting Memory, Self, and the Power of Place in African American Urban History." In *The New African American Urban History*, edited by Kenneth W. Goings and Raymond A. Mohl, 116–41. Thousand Oaks, CA: SAGE, 1996.

Lewis, Sinclair. *Main Street*. New York: P. F. Collier and Son, 1920.

Litchfield Sesquicentennial Committee. "The Ariston." In *A Pictorial Narrative: 150 Year History of Our City and Families, 1853–2003, Litchfield, Illinois*. Paducah, KY: Turner Publishing, 2002.

Lloyd George, David. *The Truth about the Peace Treaties*. London: V. Gollancz, 1938.

Loewen, James W. *Sundown Towns: A Hidden Dimension of American Racism*. New York: New Press, 2005.

Lovell-Troy, Lawrence Allen. *The Social Basis of Ethnic Enterprise: Greeks in the Pizza Business*. New York: Garland, 1990.

Lucassen, Jan, Leo Lucassen, and Patrick Manning, eds. *Migration History in World History: Multidisciplinary Approaches*. Leiden, Netherlands: Brill, 2010.

Luebke, Frederick C. *Bonds of Loyalty: German-Americans and World War I*. DeKalb: Northern Illinois University Press, 1974.

MacDonald, John S., and Leatrice D. MacDonald. "Chain Migration, Ethnic Neighborhood Formation, and Social Networks." *Milbank Memorial Fund Quarterly* 42, no. 1 (January 1964): 82–97.

Mackridge, Peter. *Language and National Identity in Greece, 1766–1976*. Oxford: Oxford University Press, 2010.

MacLean, Nancy K. *Behind the Mask of Chivalry: The Making of the Second Ku Klux Klan*. New York: Oxford University Press, 1994.

MacMillan, Margaret. *Paris 1919: Six Months That Changed the World*. 1st US ed. New York: Random House, 2002.

Malafouris, Babis. "The Struggle for a Living." *Journal of the Hellenic Diaspora* 14, nos. 1–2 (1987): 79–104.

Malafouris, Charalambos. *Hellenes Tes Amerikes, 1528–1948* [Greeks in America, 1528–1948]. New York: Isaac Goldman, 1948.

Mann, Curtis, Edward Russo, and Melinda Garvert. *Springfield Entertainment: A Pictorial History*. St. Louis: G. Bradley, 1996.

Manning, Patrick. *Migration in World History*. 2nd ed. Themes in World History. New York: Routledge, 2013.

Maragni, Bob. "Riot of 1920." City of West Frankfort (IL) website, http://www.westfrankfort-il.com/default.asp?id=267. Accessed June 10, 2019.

Martelle, Scott. *Blood Passion: The Ludlow Massacre and Class War in the American West*. New Brunswick, NJ: Rutgers University Press, 2008.

McClymer, John F. "The Americanization Movement and the Education of the Foreign-Born Adult, 1914–1925." In *American Education and the European Immigrant, 1840–1940*, edited by Bernard J. Weiss, 96–116. Urbana: University of Illinois Press, 1982.

McGrew, William W. *Land and Revolution in Modern Greece, 1800–1881: The Transition in the Tenure and Exploitation of Land from Ottoman Rule to Independence*. Kent, OH: Kent State University Press, 1985.

McNall, Scott G. *The Greek Peasant*. Washington, DC: American Sociological Association, 1974.

McVeigh, Rory. "Structural Incentives for Conservative Mobilization: Power Devaluation and the Rise of the Ku Klux Klan, 1915–1925." *Social Forces* 77, no. 4 (June 1999): 1461–96.

Michalaros, Demetrios A. *Sonnets of an Immigrant*. Chicago: American Hellenic Book Publishing, 1930.

Mink, Gwendolyn, and Alice O'Connor, eds. *Poverty in the United States*. 2 vols. Santa Barbara, CA: ABC-CLIO, 2004.

Minoglou, Ioanna Pepelasis. "Toward a Typology of Greek-Diaspora Entrepreneurship." In *Diaspora Entrepreneurial Networks: Four Centuries of History*, edited by Ina Baghdiantz McCabe, Gelina Harlaftis, and Ioanna Pepelasis Minoglou, 173–89. New York: Berg, 2005.

Moch, Leslie Page. *Moving Europeans: Migration in Western Europe since 1650*. Bloomington: Indiana University Press, 1992.

Model, Suzanne W. "Work and Family: Blacks and Immigrants from South and East Europe." In *Immigration Reconsidered: History, Sociology, and Politics*, edited by Virginia Yans-McLaughlin, 130–59. New York: Oxford University Press, 1990.

Moffett, William Henry. "Notes." In *Garden and Forest* 2 (December 18, 1889): 612.

Mooney, Peter J. *The Impact of Immigration on the Growth and Development of the U.S. Economy, 1890–1920*. New York: Garland, 1990.

Moore, Leonard J. "Historical Interpretations of the 1920's Klan: The Traditional View and the Populist Revision." *Journal of Social History* 24, no. 2 (Winter 1990): 341–57.

Morawska, Ewa T. *For Bread with Butter: The Life-Worlds of East Central Europeans in Johnstown, Pennsylvania, 1890–1940*. Cambridge: Cambridge University Press, 1985.

———. *Insecure Prosperity: Small-Town Jews in Industrial America, 1890–1940*. Princeton, NJ: Princeton University Press, 1996.

Mormino, Gary Ross. *Immigrants on the Hill: Italian-Americans in St. Louis, 1882–1982*. Columbia: University of Missouri Press, 2002.

Moskos, Charles C., Jr. "Growing Up Greek American." *Society* 14, no. 2 (February 1977): 64–71.

Moskos, Charles C., Jr., and Peter C. Moskos. *Greek Americans: Struggle and Success*. 3rd ed. New York: Routledge, 2017.

Mowry, George Edwin. *The Era of Theodore Roosevelt and the Birth of Modern America, 1900–1912*. New American Nation Series. New York: Harper Torchbooks, 1958.

Myres, John Linton. *Who Were the Greeks?* Berkeley: University of California Press, 1930.

Ngai, Mae M. "The Architecture of Race in American Immigration Law: A Reexamination of the Immigration Act of 1924." *Journal of American History* 86, no. 1 (June 1999): 67–92.

———. "Nationalism, Immigration Control, and the Ethnoracial Remapping of America in the 1920s." *OAH Magazine of History* 21, no. 3 (July 2007): 11–15.

Nokomis Centennial Committee. *1956 Centennial History of Nokomis, 1856–1956*. Nokomis, IL: Centennial Committee, 1956.

Norwich, John Julius. *A Short History of Byzantium*. 1st American ed. New York: Knopf, 1997.

Nugent, Walter T. K. *Crossings: The Great Transatlantic Migrations, 1870–1914*. Bloomington: Indiana University Press, 1992.

Oldani, John L. *Sweetness Preserved: The Story of the Crown Candy Kitchen*. St. Louis: Virginia Publishing, 2005.

"The Old Stock and the New." *The Outlook*, June 13, 1914.

Olneck, Michael R. "Americanization and the Education of Immigrants, 1900–1925: An Analysis of Symbolic Action." *American Journal of Education* 97, no. 4 (August 1989): 398–423.

Olneck, Michael R., and Marvin Lazerson. "Education." In *Harvard Encyclopedia of*

American Ethnic Groups, edited by Stephan Thernstrom, 303–19. Cambridge, MA: Belknap Press of Harvard University Press, 1980.

Orfanos, Spyros D., ed. *Reading Greek America: Studies in the Experience of Greeks in the United States*. New York: Pella, 2002.

Orfanos, Spyros D., Harry J. Psomiades, and John Spiridakis, eds. *Education and Greek Americans: Process and Prospects*. New York: Pella, 1987.

Orvell, Miles. *The Death and Life of Main Street: Small Towns in American Memory, Space, and Community*. Chapel Hill: University of North Carolina Press, 2012.

Papadopoulos, Yiota. "Prejudice and Its Relationship to Acculturation for the Greek Immigrant in the United States." In *Reading Greek America: Studies in the Experience of Greeks in the United States*, edited by Spyros D. Orfanos, 345–60. New York: Pella, 2002.

Papanikolas, Helen Zeese. *An Amulet of Greek Earth: Generations of Immigrant Folk Culture*. Athens: Swallow Press/Ohio University Press, 2002.

———. "Greek Immigrant Women in the Intermountain West." *Journal of the Hellenic Diaspora* 16, nos. 1–4 (1989): 17–35.

———. *Small Bird, Tell Me: Stories of Greek Immigrants in Utah*. Athens: Swallow Press/Ohio University Press, 1993.

———. "Travels in the Land of Greekness." *Greek Orthodox Theological Review* 45, no. 1 (2000): 413–25.

Papanikolas, Zeese. *Buried Unsung: Louis Tikas and the Ludlow Massacre*. Salt Lake City: University of Utah Press, 1982.

———. "To a Greek Bootblack." *Journal of the Hellenic Diaspora* 20, no. 1 (1994): 64–85.

Park, Robert Ezra. "Human Migration and the Marginal Man." *American Journal of Sociology* 33, no. 6 (May 1928): 881–93.

———. *Race and Culture*. Glencoe, IL: Free Press, 1950.

Park, Robert Ezra, and Ernest Watson Burgess. *Introduction to the Science of Sociology*. Chicago: University of Chicago Press, 1921.

Park, Robert Ezra, Herbert Adolphus Miller, and Kenneth Thompson. *Old World Traits Transplanted: The Early Sociology of Culture*. New York: Harper, 1921.

Patsovos, Lewis J., and Charles J. Janides. "Interchurch Marriages: An Orthodox Perspective." *International Academy for Marital Spirituality Review* 6 (2000): 215–23.

Peck, Gunther. "Reinventing Free Labor: Immigrant Padrones and Contract Laborers in North America, 1885–1925." *Journal of American History* 83, no. 3 (December 1996): 848–71.

Pegram, Thomas R. *One Hundred Percent American: The Rebirth and Decline of the Ku Klux Klan in the 1920s*. Chicago: Ivan R. Dee, 2011.

Perlman, Joel, and Roger Waldinger. "Second Generation Decline? Children of Immigrants, Past and Present—A Reconsideration." *International Migration Review* 31, no. 4 (Winter 1997): 893–922.

Petit, Jeanne D. *The Men and Women We Want: Gender, Race, and the Progressive Era Literacy Test Debate*. Rochester, NY: University of Rochester Press, 2013.

Petrakis, Harry Mark. *The Odyssey of Kostas Volakis*. Lincoln, NE: iUniverse, 2000.
Pettigrew, Thomas F. "Prejudice." In *Harvard Encyclopedia of American Ethnic Groups*, edited by Stephan Thernstrom, 820–29. Cambridge, MA: Belknap Press of Harvard University Press, 1980.
Pickus, Noah. *True Faith and Allegiance: Immigration and American Civic Nationalism*. Princeton, NJ: Princeton University Press, 2009.
Portes, Alejandro. "Immigration Theory for a New Century: Some Problems and Opportunities." *International Migration Review* 31, no. 4 (December 1997): 799–825.
Psomiades, Harry J., and Alice Scourby, eds. *The Greek American Community in Transition*. Modern Greek Research Series 4. New York: Pella, 1982.
Puckett, Thomas A. *Mt. Vernon, Illinois: A Pictorial History*. St. Louis: G. Bradley Publishing, 1991.
Rassogianis, Alexander. *The Entrepreneurial Spirit of the Greek Immigrant in Chicago, Illinois: 1900–1930*. Bloomington, IN: iUniverse, 2015.
Repouli, Emmanuel. *A Study of Immigration, with Suggested Legislation* (in Greek). Athens, Greece: n.p., 1912.
Richardson, Tim. *Sweets: A History of Candy*. New York: Bloomsbury, 2002.
Rigby, Will O., and Fred Rigby. *Rigby's Reliable Candy Teacher: With Complete and Modern Soda, Ice Cream and Sherbet Sections* . . . 13th ed. Topeka: Rigby, 1920.
Rippley, La Vern J. "The Ethnic Frontier: Rural Germans and the Settlement of America." In *Immigrant America: European Ethnicity in the United States*, edited by Timothy Walch, 197–214. New York: Garland, 1994.
Roberts, Peter. *Immigrant Races in North America*. New York: Young Men's Christian Association Press, 1910.
Roediger, David R. *Colored White: Transcending the Racial Past*. Berkeley: University of California Press, 2002.
———. *How Race Survived U.S. History: From Settlement and Slavery to the Obama Phenomenon*. New York: Verso, 2008.
———. *Working toward Whiteness: How America's Immigrants Became White; The Strange Journey from Ellis Island to the Suburbs*. New York: Basic Books, 2005.
Rogg, Eleanor Meyer. "American Immigration and Ethnicity-Filling Gaps in the Literature and Reconceptualizing Critical Issues." *International Migration Review* 27, no. 4 (Winter 1993): 886–92.
Roosevelt, Theodore. *Fear God and Take Your Own Part*. New York: George H. Doran, 1916.
———. *Newer Roosevelt Messages: Speeches, Letters and Magazine Articles Dealing with the War, before and after, and Other Vital Topics*. Edited by William Griffith. Vol. 3. New York: Current Literature Publishing, 1919.
Root, Rebecca K. "Dillingham Commission." In *Poverty in the United States*, edited by Gwendolyn Mink and Alice O'Connor, 1:230–31. Santa Barbara, CA: ABC-CLIO, 2004.
Rouvelas, Marilyn. *A Guide to Greek Traditions and Customs in America*. Bethesda, MD: Attica Press, 1993.

Rumbold, Charlotte. *Housing Conditions in St. Louis: Civic League of Saint Louis, Housing Committee.* St. Louis: Civic League of St. Louis, 1908.

Saloutos, Theodore. "Cultural Persistence and Change: Greeks in the Great Plains and Rocky Mountain West, 1890–1970." *Pacific Historical Review* 49, no. 1 (February 1980): 77–103.

———. "Exodus U.S.A." In *In the Trek of the Immigrants: Essays Presented to Carl Wittke*, edited by O. Fritiof Ander, 197–215. Rock Island, IL: Augustana College Library, 1964.

———. "The Greek Orthodox Church in the United States and Assimilation." *International Migration Review* 7, no. 4 (December 1973): 395–407.

———. "Greeks." In *Harvard Encyclopedia of American Ethnic Groups*, edited by Stephan Thernstrom, 430–40. Cambridge, MA: Belknap Press of Harvard University Press, 1980.

———. *The Greeks in the United States*. Cambridge, MA: Harvard University Press, 1964.

———. *They Remember America: The Story of the Repatriated Greek-Americans*. Berkeley: University of California Press, 1956.

Salyer, Lucy E. *Laws Harsh as Tigers: Chinese Immigrants and the Shaping of Modern Immigration Law*. Chapel Hill: University of North Carolina Press, 1995.

Sanchez, George J. *Becoming Mexican American: Ethnicity, Culture, and Identity in Chicano Los Angeles, 1900–1945*. New York: Oxford University Press, 1995.

Sandis, Eva E. "The Greek Population of New York City." In *The Greek American Community in Transition*, edited by Harry J. Psomiades and Alice Scourby, 65–92. Modern Greek Research Series 4. New York: Pella, 1982.

Schultz, Rima Lunin, and Adele Hast, eds. *Women Building Chicago, 1790–1990: A Biographical Dictionary*. Bloomington: Indiana University Press, 2001.

Schultz, Sandra L. "Adjusting Marriage Tradition: Greeks to Greek-Americans." *Journal of Comparative Family Studies* 12, no. 2 (April 1981): 205–18.

Scofield, James S. "AHEPA and the Ku Klux Klan: The Final Triumph of Hellenism in America over the Evil Klan, Part 2." *Hellenic Heritage* 50, no. 9 (September 1997): 15–17.

———. "AHEPA and the Ku Klux Klan: Winning the Battle against Bigotry, Part I." *Hellenic Heritage* 50, no. 7 (August 1997): 5–8.

Scourby, Alice. "Ethnicity at the Crossroads: The Case of Greek America." *Journal of the Hellenic Diaspora* 20, no. 1 (1994): 123–33.

———. *The Greek Americans*. Boston: Twayne, 1984.

———. *Third Generation Greek Americans: A Study of Religious Attitudes*. New York: Arno Press, 1980.

———. "Three Generations of Greek Americans: A Study in Ethnicity." *International Migration Review* 14, no. 1 (April 1980): 43–52.

Seligman, Vincent Julian. *The Victory of Venizelos: A Study of Greek Politics, 1910–1918*. London: G. Allen and Unwin, 1920.

Seller, Maxine S. "Success and Failure in Adult Education: The Immigrant Experience, 1914–1924." *Adult Education Quarterly* 28, no. 2 (January 1978): 83–99.

Seonnichsen, John. *The Chinese Exclusion Act of 1882*. Santa Barbara, CA: ABC-CLIO, 2011.

Shelby County Historical and Genealogical Society. *Shelbyville Past and Present*. Shelbyville, IL: Shelby County Historical and Genealogical Society, 1999.

Shelmerdine, Cynthia W. *The Cambridge Companion to the Aegean Bronze Age*. Cambridge: Cambridge University Press, 2008.

Shinn, Rinn S., and Eugene K. Keefe. *Greece: A Country Study*. 3rd ed. Washington, DC: United States Government Printing Office, 1986.

Shupert-Arick, Jan. *The Lincoln Highway across Indiana*. Charleston, SC: Arcadia, 2009.

Smith, Andrew F. "Chocolate Confections." In *Fast Food and Junk Food: An Encyclopedia of What We Love to Eat*, 1:129–31. Santa Barbara, CA: Greenwood, 2012.

Sodowsky, G. R., and B. S. Plake. "Psychometric Properties of the American-International Relations Scale." *Educational and Psychological Measurement* 51 (1991): 207–16.

Solberg, Winton U. "The Early Years of the Jewish Presence at the University of Illinois." *Religion and American Culture: A Journal of Interpretation* 2, no. 2 (Summer 1992): 215–45.

Solomon, Barbara Miller. *Ancestors and Immigrants: A Changing New England Tradition*. Cambridge, MA: Harvard University Press, 1956.

Spear, Allan H. "Marcus Lee Hansen and the Historiography of Immigration." *Wisconsin Magazine of History* 44, no. 4 (Summer 1961): 258–68.

Spickard, Paul R. "Immigration and Race in United States History." In *Race and Immigration in the United States: New Histories*, edited by Paul R. Spickard, 1–12. New York: Routledge, 2012.

Stanley, Amy Dru. *From Bondage to Contract: Wage Labor, Marriage, and the Market in the Age of Slave Emancipation*. Cambridge: Cambridge University Press, 1998.

Steinberg, Stephen. *The Ethnic Myth: Race, Ethnicity, and Class in America*. Boston: Beacon Press, 1989.

Stephanopoulos, Robert G. "'Being Greek' in America: A Guide to Greek Traditions and Customs in America." *Hellenic Heritage* 46, no. 12 (December 1993): 43.

Stevenson, D. *Cataclysm: The First World War as Political Tragedy*. New York: Basic Books, 2004.

Sullivan, Margaret Lo Piccolo. *Hyphenism in St. Louis, 1900–1921: The View from the Outside*. New York: Garland, 1990.

Sullivan, Patricia. *Lift Every Voice: The NAACP and the Making of the Civil Rights Movement*. New York: New Press, 2009.

Summerville, Loistel, ed. and indexer, and Joyce Van Dyke Skinner, comp. *Casey: The Early Years, from the 1830's to 2003*. Casey, IL: self-published, 2003.

Talbot, Winthrop, comp. and ed. *Americanization: Principles of Americanism, Essentials of Americanization, Technic of Race-Assimilation, Annotated Bibliography*. New York: H. W. Wilson, 1917.

Tassiopoulos, Dimitri. "Greek Christian Orthodoxy and Entrepreneurship." In *Entrepreneurship and Religion*, edited by Léo-Paul Dana, 113–35. Northampton, MA: Edward Elgar, 2010.

Thelen, David. "Memory and American History." *Journal of American History* 75, no. 4 (March 1989): 1117–29.

Theobald, Paul. *Call School: Rural Education in the Midwest to 1918*. Carbondale: Southern Illinois University Press, 1995.

Thomopoulos, Elaine Cotsirilos. "Presbytera Stella Christoulakis Petrakis." In *Greek-American Pioneer Women of Illinois: The Stories of Georgia Bitzis Pooley, Presbytera Stella Christoulakis Petrakis, Theano Papazoglou Margaris, Venette Askounes Ashford, and Senator Adeline J. Geo-Karis*, edited by Elaine Cotsirilos Thomopoulos and Greek Women's University Club, 19–57. Charleston, SC: Arcadia, 2000.

Thompson, Charles. *Library of American Lives, Illinois Edition, 1950*. Vol. 1. Champaign, IL: Historical Record Association, 1950.

Thucydides. *The Landmark Thucydides: A Comprehensive Guide to the Peloponnesian War*. Edited by Richard B. Strassler. Translated by Richard Crawley. New York: Free Press, 2008.

Tichenor, Daniel J. *Dividing Lines: The Politics of Immigration Control in America*. Princeton, NJ: Princeton University Press, 2009.

Treudley, Mary Bosworth. "Formal Organization and the Americanization Process. With Special Reference to the Greeks of Boston." *American Sociological Review* 14, no. 1 (February 1949): 44–53.

Tsemberis, Sam J., Harry J. Psomiades, and Anna Karpathakis, eds. *Greek American Families: Traditions and Transformations*. New York: Pella, 1999.

Tucker, Spencer. *The Great War, 1914–18*. Bloomington: Indiana University Press, 1998.

Turner, Frederick Jackson. *The Frontier in American History*. New York: H. Holt, 1920.

Turner, Frederick Jackson, and John Mack Faragher. *Rereading Frederick Jackson Turner: "The Significance of the Frontier in American History" and Other Essays*. New York: H. Holt, 1994.

Turner, Katherine Leonard. *How the Other Half Ate: A History of Working-Cass Meals at the Turn of the Century*. Berkeley: University of California Press, 2014.

United States, Department of the Interior, Bureau of Education, and Commissioner James Eaton. *Education in Italy and Greece*. Washington, DC: United States Government Printing Office, 1883.

United States Immigration Commission and William Paul Dillingham. *Immigrants in Cities: A Study of Selected Districts in New York, Chicago, Philadelphia, Boston, Cleveland, Buffalo, and Milwaukee*. 2 vols. Reports of the Immigration Commission. Washington, DC: United States Government Printing Office, 1911.

"United States Immigration Commission. 'Report of the Immigration Commission.' Senate Documents of the 61st Congress, Second and Third Sessions." Vol. 41. Washington, DC: United States Government Printing Office, 1911.

University of Illinois. *The Illio*. Champaign: Twin City Printing, 1918.

Vaky, Russell. *Vaky's Confectionery: A Transcription of a Speech by Russell Vaky*. Urbana, IL: Champaign County Historical Society, Urbana Free Library, 2000.

Vardoulakis, Mary. *Gold in the Streets*. New York: Dodd, Mead, 1945.

Veblen, Thorstein. *The Theory of the Leisure Class*. Mineola, NY: Courier Dover, 1994.

Villa Grove News. Villa Grove and Surrounding Areas: A Pictorial History. Villa Grove, IL: Villa Grove News, 1985.

Vlachos, Evan. *The Assimilation of Greeks in the United States, with Special Reference to the Greek Community of Anderson, Indiana.* Athens, Greece: National Centre of Social Research, 1968.

Wade, Wyn Craig. *The Fiery Cross: The Ku Klux Klan in America.* New York: Simon and Schuster, 1987.

Walch, Timothy, ed. *Immigrant America: European Ethnicity in the United States.* New York: Garland, 1994.

Walch, Timothy, and Edward R. Kantowicz. *European Immigrants and American Society.* New York: Garland, 1990.

Walker, Natalie. "Chicago Housing Conditions. X. Greeks and Italians in the Neighborhood of Hull House." *American Journal of Sociology* 21, no. 3 (November 1915): 285–316.

Wallerstein, Immanuel Maurice. *World-Systems Analysis: An Introduction.* Durham, NC: Duke University Press, 2004.

Watson, Charles H. "Need of Federal Legislation in Respect to Mob Violence in Cases of Lynching of Aliens." *Yale Law Journal* 25, no. 7 (May 1916): 561–81.

Weiss, Bernard J., ed. *American Education and the European Immigrant, 1840–1940.* Urbana: University of Illinois Press, 1982.

Welskopp, Thomas. "Prohibition in the United States: The German-American Experience, 1919–1933." *Bulletin of the German Historical Institute* 53 (Fall 2013): 31–53.

White, Paul. *100 Years of Masonry in Tuscola, Illinois: 1860–1960.* Tuscola: Publication of the Tuscola Lodge No. 332, Ancient Free and Accepted Masons, April 3, 1960.

White, Richard. *Remembering Ahanagran: A History of Stories.* Seattle: University of Washington Press, 1998.

Wilson, Woodrow. "Address to the Citizenship Convention, Washington, DC, July 13, 1916." In *Americanization: Principles of Americanism, Essentials of Americanization, Technic of Race-Assimilation, Annotated Bibliography*, compiled and edited by Winthrop Talbot, 28–31. New York: H. W. Wilson, 1917.

———. *Reunion and Nationalism.* Vol. 10 of *A History of the American People.* Documentary ed. New York: Harper and Brothers, 1918.

Winthrop, John. *The Journal of John Winthrop, 1630–1649.* Edited by Richard S. Dunn and Laetitia Yeandle. Cambridge, MA: Harvard University Press, 1996.

———. "A Model of Christian Charity." In *The Journal of John Winthrop, 1630–1649*, edited by Richard S. Dunn and Laetitia Yeandle, 1–11. Cambridge, MA: Harvard University Press, 1996.

Wood, Gordon S. *The Americanization of Benjamin Franklin.* New York: Penguin Books, 2004.

Woodhouse, C. M. *Capodistria: The Founder of Greek Independence.* London: Oxford University Press, 1973.

———. *Modern Greece: A Short History.* 5th ed., rev. London: Faber and Faber, 1991.

WPA Writers' Program in New York State. *New York: A Guide to the Empire State.* New York: Oxford University Press, 1940.

Wyman, Mark. *Round-Trip to America: The Immigrants Return to Europe, 1880–1930.* Ithica: Cornell University Press, 1993.

Xenides, J. P. *The Greeks in America*. New York: George H. Doran, 1922.

Yans-McLaughlin, Virginia, ed. *Immigration Reconsidered: History, Sociology, and Politics*. New York: Oxford University Press, 1990.

Zaffer, Theodore J. *We Make Our Own Candy*. New York: Vantage Press, 1976.

Ziegelman, Jane. *97 Orchard: An Edible History of Five Immigrant Families in One New York Tenement*. New York: Harper, 2010.

Zinn, Howard. *The Politics of History*. Urbana: University of Illinois Press, 1990.

Zolberg, Aristide R. *A Nation by Design: Immigration Policy in the Fashioning of America*. Cambridge, MA: Harvard University Press, 2006.

INDEX

Page numbers in italics refer to illustrations.

ANN FLESOR BECK is a third-generation Greek confectioner and independent scholar. With her sister, she co-owns and operates Flesor's Candy Kitchen in Tuscola, Illinois.

HEARTLAND FOODWAYS

From the Jewish Heartland: Two Centuries of Midwest Foodways
Ellen F. Steinberg and Jack H. Prost
Farmers' Markets of the Heartland *Janine MacLachlan*
A Perfect Pint's Beer Guide to the Heartland *Michael Agnew*
Midwest Maize: How Corn Shaped the U.S. Heartland *Cynthia Clampitt*
Local Vino: The Winery Boom in the Heartland *James R. Pennell*
Baking Powder Wars: The Cutthroat Food Fight That Revolutionized Cooking
Linda Civitello
The Chicago Food Encyclopedia *Edited by Carol Mighton Haddix, Bruce Kraig, and Colleen Taylor Sen*
Sweet Greeks: First-Generation Immigrant Confectioners in the Heartland
Ann Flesor Beck

The University of Illinois Press
is a founding member of the
Association of University Presses.

University of Illinois Press
1325 South Oak Street
Champaign, IL 61820-6903
www.press.uillinois.edu